D0944888

# The Sociolinguistics of the Deaf Community

# The Sociolinguistics of the Deaf Community

Edited by

## Ceil Lucas

Department of Linguistics and Interpreting
Gallaudet University
Washington, D.C.

ACADEMIC PRESS, INC.
**Harcourt Brace Jovanovich, Publishers**
San Diego   New York   Boston
London   Sydney   Tokyo   Toronto

Lines from Robert Frost, "Two Tramps in Mud Time," reprinted by permission of Henry Holt and Company, Inc. from *The Poetry of Robert Frost,* edited by Edward Connery Lathem.

COPYRIGHT © 1989 BY ACADEMIC PRESS, INC.
ALL RIGHTS RESERVED.
NO PART OF THIS PUBLICATION MAY BE REPRODUCED OR
TRANSMITTED IN ANY FORM OR BY ANY MEANS, ELECTRONIC
OR MECHANICAL, INCLUDING PHOTOCOPY, RECORDING, OR
ANY INFORMATION STORAGE AND RETRIEVAL SYSTEM, WITHOUT
PERMISSION IN WRITING FROM THE PUBLISHER.

ACADEMIC PRESS, INC.
San Diego, California 92101

*United Kingdom Edition published by*
ACADEMIC PRESS LIMITED
24-28 Oval Road, London NW1 7DX

**Library of Congress Cataloging-in-Publication Data**

The Sociolinguistics of the deaf community.

Includes index.
1. Deaf—Means of communication.
2. Sociolinguistics.  I. Lucas, Ceil.
HV2471.S57   1989   419                       88-8065
ISBN   0-12-458045-9   (alk. paper)

PRINTED IN THE UNITED STATES OF AMERICA
90  91  92      9  8  7  6  5  4  3  2

His fellow contributors present this volume to Dr. Robert E. Johnson, Chairman of the Department of Linguistics and Interpreting at Gallaudet University since 1981, in overdue recognition of his excellent work in developing and maintaining the Master's Program in Linguistics, and in establishing the Master's Program in Sign Language Interpreting. We wish to recognize his seemingly boundless energy and enthusiasm for both teaching and research, and his generosity, wisdom, honesty, insight, and humor in his interaction with his colleagues and his students.

But yield who will to their separation,
My object in living is to unite
My avocation and my vocation
As my two eyes make one in sight.
Only where love and need are one,
And the work is play for mortal stakes,
Is the deed ever really done . . .

Robert Frost
*Two Tramps in Mud Time*

# Contents

Transcription Conventions    ix
Contributors    xi
Preface    xiii

1. *Introduction*    1
   Ceil Lucas


## *I. VARIATION AND LANGUAGE CONTACT*

2. *Language Contact in the American Deaf Community*    11
   Ceil Lucas and Clayton Valli

3. *Ethnicity and Socialization in a Classroom for Deaf Children*    41
   Robert E. Johnson and Carol Erting

4. *Distinguishing Language Contact Phenomena in ASL Interpretation*    85
   Jeffrey Davis

5. *Sociolinguistic Aspects of the Black Deaf Community*    103
   Anthony J. Aramburo


## *II. LANGUAGE POLICY*

6. *Language Planning in Deaf Education*    123
   Claire L. Ramsey

7. *Transliteration: What's the Message?*    147
   Elizabeth A. Winston

8. *Visually Oriented Teaching Strategies with Deaf Preschool Children*    165
   Susan A. Mather

## III. LANGUAGE ATTITUDES

9. *An Examination of Deaf College Students' Attitudes toward ASL and English*    191
   Barbara Kannapell

10. *An Examination of Language Attitudes of Teachers of the Deaf*    211
    Julie Ward Trotter

## IV. DISCOURSE ANALYSIS

11. *Features of Discourse in an American Sign Language Lecture*    231
    Cynthia B. Roy

12. *Toward a Description of Register Variation in American Sign Language*    253
    June Zimmer

13. *Conversational Features and Gender in ASL*    273
    Elizabeth Nowell

Bibliography    289
Index    305

# *Transcription Conventions*

Since many of the chapters in this volume include examples from American Sign Language (ASL), a word is in order about the transcription conventions. ASL signs are represented by English glosses in upper case. These glosses are not translations but labels for signs. Glosses are used both for single examples and in more lengthy transcriptions. In the latter case, an English translation is provided in regular type and set off by single quotation marks. Uppercase letters separated by hyphens indicate fingerspelling. Special conventions for individual chapters are explained where appropriate.

# Contributors

**Anthony J. Aramburo** Rehabilitation Specialist, 1016 North Johnson, New Orleans, Louisiana 70116-2107

**Jeffrey Davis** Department of Linguistics and Interpreting, Gallaudet University, Washington, D.C. 20002

**Carol Erting** Culture and Communication Studies Program, Gallaudet University, Washington, D.C. 20002

**Robert E. Johnson** Department of Linguistics and Interpreting, Gallaudet University, Washington, D.C. 20002

**Barbara Kannapell** Consultant, 4527 South Dakota Avenue N.E., Washington, D.C. 20017

**Ceil Lucas** Department of Linguistics and Interpreting, Gallaudet University, Washington, D.C. 20002

**Susan A. Mather** Gallaudet Research Institute, Gallaudet University, Washington, D.C. 20002

**Elizabeth Nowell** English Language Institute, Gallaudet University (N.W. Campus), Washington, D.C. 20012

**Claire L. Ramsey** Graduate School of Education, University of California, Berkeley, Berkeley, California 94720

**Cynthia B. Roy** Department of Linguistics and Interpreting, Gallaudet University, Washington, D.C. 20002

**Julie Ward Trotter** Arizona State School for the Deaf and Blind, Tucson, Arizona 85703

**Clayton Valli** Department of Linguistics and Interpreting, Gallaudet University, Washington, D.C. 20002

**Elizabeth A. Winston** Interpreting Consultant, 902 7th Street N.E., Washington, D.C. 20002

**June Zimmer** Department of Linguistics, Georgetown University, Washington, D.C. 20057

# Preface

The idea for this volume grew directly out of the frustration that I experienced in January of 1987 as I tried to put together a reading list for a graduate seminar on the sociolinguistics of the deaf community. The frustration was caused by the fact that, although a number of articles, dissertations, and working papers had been completed since the late 1960s on various sociolinguistic aspects of the deaf community, there did not exist a volume that raised and discussed the issues in a unified and focused way. My frustration suggested the need for a volume that defined the sociolinguistic issues central to the deaf community, one that examined and illustrated these issues through empirical studies. A basic goal of this volume is to fill that need.

A guiding premise in this work is that the deaf community is not simply "another sociolinguistic community" but rather offers a unique situation that can bring new theoretical perspectives to the study of sociolinguistics, be it in spoken-language or sign-language communities. For this reason, the following chapters will be of interest to researchers and students in all areas of sociolinguistics. But their value is not only theoretical. The studies presented here are empirical in nature; they reflect the sociolinguistic reality of everyday human lives. As such, they will be of interest to a wide professional audience, especially educators, teacher trainers, and administrators in deaf education, sign language interpreters and interpreter trainers, sign language teachers, counselors, and legislators and policy makers. An important goal of this volume is to serve the different members of this wide audience.

A number of many people deserve recognition and thanks for their help in the preparation of this volume. I would like to thank Scott Liddell, Walt Wolfram, and Bob Johnson for valuable and painstaking comments on several portions of the manuscript; William Woodcock, my editor, for his patience, encouragement, and Montana humor; Barbara Heiman and John Thomas of Academic Press, for their patience and perspective; my students and co-contributors for their support; Paul Setzer for the preparation of the drawings; Cynthia Vaughn and Su Cook for their word-processing skills; and Kathleen, Jane, Jim, and Doni, for their cheerful refrain, "How's your book?"

# 1

# *Introduction*

Ceil Lucas

Sunday evening, March 6, 1988. Word was out that the Board of Trustees of Gallaudet University would announce its selection for the seventh president of the 124-year-old institution. It is well-known that Gallaudet has never had a deaf president. Indeed, Arden Neisser (1983) has remarked that the only president of Gallaudet skilled as a native signer was the first, Edward Miner Gallaudet, whose mother was deaf. He retired in 1911. At any rate, the word was that a formal announcement would be made at seven o'clock that evening in the gymnasium on the main campus. People started gathering outside the fieldhouse between five-thirty and six. There was anticipation and restlessness. Suddenly, well before seven, someone appeared with a large stack of press releases. The reality struck: there wasn't going to be a formal announcement; there wasn't going to be an announcement at all. A hearing person who was both unable to sign and unfamiliar with the deaf world had been selected as president over two deaf finalists.

What followed is world history: The campus erupted into a week of protests. The week culminated with the resignation of the newly appointed president and of the chairman of the Board of Trustees, the reconstitution of the board to contain a majority of deaf people, the selection of a deaf president, and the promise of no reprisals against the protesters. With these four demands, one rallying cry had been the American Sign Language sign, "4." With the appointment of a deaf person as chairman of the Board of Trustees, one new symbol of victory became the sign "5," four demands, five results.

THE SOCIOLINGUISTICS OF THE DEAF COMMUNITY                                    1
Copyright © 1989 by Academic Press Inc.
All rights of reproduction in any form reserved.

The events at Gallaudet provide a very clear example of the actuality and immediacy of sociolinguistic issues in the deaf community. The protest is perhaps a fairly dramatic example, made more so by the worldwide attention that it commanded. Nevertheless, it is only one example of numerous sociolinguistic issues that range from variation, language contact, and bilingualism to language planning and policy, interpreting, language attitudes, and discourse analysis. This volume brings together studies on these issues, treated not as abstract or purely theoretical concerns but as matters whose debate and resolution have very direct and tangible effects on the everyday lives of real people.

The protest provides a case in point, and a point of departure for the volume. The major demand was for a deaf president. The issues underlying that demand are fundamentally sociolinguistic in nature. In his volume, *The Sociolinguistics of Society,* Fasold (1984, p. ix) observes that the essence of sociolinguistics depends on two facts about language: first, that language varies, which is to say that "speakers have more than one way to say more or less the same thing"; and second, that language serves a broadly encompassing purpose just as critical as the obvious one of transmitting information and thoughts from one person to another. Namely, speakers use language to make statements about who they are, what their group loyalties are, how they perceive their relationship to interlocutors, and what kind of speech event they consider themselves to be involved in. Fasold (1984, pp. ix–x) elaborates on these two major functions of language as follows:

> The two tasks (communicating information and defining the social situation) can be carried out simultaneously precisely because language varies— speakers can choose among alternative linguistic means, any of which would satisfactorily communicate the propositional information. It is the selection among these alternatives that defines the social situation. The study of the interplay between these two facts about language is exactly sociolinguistics.

Crucial to an understanding of the events at Gallaudet is the critical purpose that language serves in defining one's identity, group loyalty, relationship to interlocutors, and understanding of the speech event. On the one hand, it was repeatedly declared with disdain during the protest that Dr. Zinser, the newly selected president, could not sign and had only just begun learning sign language. On the other hand, in remarks following her resignation, Dr. Zinser (*Washington Post,* March 12, 1988) stated:

> I would like to acknowledge that because signing is important symbolically within the deaf community, it would be enormously wise for the board members to learn a little sign. I know it is not easy because I'm learning it. But to just say a few basic phrases, some warm sentences when they meet people around the school.

For deaf people and their supporters, Dr. Zinser's lack of knowledge about the deaf community was directly linked to and, indeed, symbolized by her lack of knowledge of sign language. The reality of her linguistic repertoire and the language choices at her disposal made clear and inevitable statements about who she was, her group loyalty, and how she perceived her relationship to her interlocutors. And those statements could not be reconciled with the qualifications that the deaf community required of the next president. That individual clearly had to be deaf and knowledgeable about the deaf world and its language. Indeed, there appears to be a delicate balance between sociolinguistic and cultural factors and audiological realities. For example, the individual who was eventually chosen, Dr. I. King Jordan, was not born deaf but became deaf at age twenty-one. He is, like Dr. Zinser, a native English user and hence not "culturally deaf." Audiologically, however, he is deaf, a crucial factor in his selection. In considering the relative valence of all the factors involved, a question arises: would there have been a protest had the choice been between Dr. Jordan and, say, the hearing child of deaf parents, that is, an ASL-English bilingual, culturally deaf but audiologically hearing?

With her observation that signing is important symbolically within the deaf community and that board members should "learn a little sign," Dr. Zinser focused on the symbolic role of signing while ignoring the fact that signing is, first of all, a communication system. The high symbolic value of sign language derives in part from the fact that signing allows people to communicate unhindered, with a focus not on the medium but on the message. To patronizingly suggest that board members "learn a little sign . . . some warm sentences" is to patently misunderstand the sociolinguistic reality of the deaf community and to misperceive the particular form of the interplay between communicating information and defining the social situation in the deaf community.

This volume brings together studies on different facets of the sociolinguistic reality of deaf people. The studies share two major themes. First, there is a recognition that the deaf community is a sociolinguistic community as intricate and complex as any other sociolinguistic community. Second, there is a recognition that the deaf community is not simply "just another sociolinguistic community" in which known principles of sociolinguistics can be illustrated; instead, it is a unique situation that can bring fresh insights to the study of sociolinguistic phenomena, whether in spoken language or sign language communities. The question can thus be raised of how the complex sociolinguistic issues in the deaf community now serve to challenge the fundamental tenets of sociolinguistics, as formulated during the sixties.

There are at least two lines of response to this question. One concerns the linguistic status of American Sign Language (ASL). Certainly until

William Stokoe's pioneering work in the early sixties, the status of ASL as an autonomous and viable linguistic system was widely in dispute. There is ample evidence that even now this status is a matter of doubt and confusion among both professionals and laymen. Every sign language linguist has had to contend with amazingly naive questions and opinions of linguists trained and knowledgeable in the workings of spoken languages. Frequently, the parallels in structure between spoken languages and sign languages simply become camouflaged, and the study of sign language structure is derided, belittled, and not deemed worthy of effort. One is reminded here of the earliest days of pidgin and creole studies, and of Mühlhäusler's (1986, p. 24) remarks that "In spite of some pioneering attempts by scholars such as Schuchardt and Hall in the field of pidgin and creole studies, the view that these are parasitic rather than independent language systems is still widely found." This view notwithstanding, studies of pidgins and creoles have proved to be invaluable both for an understanding of those systems and for the light that is shed on the nature of language structure in general, language acquisition, language contact, and language change. In a similar vein, in the preface to a volume on sign language structure, Charles Fillmore (1977, pp. viii–ix) remarked that

> learning about language in a gestural/visual modality can give us new ways of thinking about language in the oral/auditory modality. . . . There will doubtless be readers who look to this book for an answer to the question of whether ASL "is a language". . . . Clearly, either the scope of linguistics must reach beyond "language" strictly defined, or the concept of language must be extended to include the rich and powerful symbolic systems of the kind we see described here.

It is striking and perhaps discouraging that, more than a decade later, these remarks need to be reiterated.

The linguistic status of ASL is also repeatedly questioned by laymen, both hearing and deaf individuals who may have personal or professional stakes in sign language. This includes professional educators and the parents of deaf children. A recent example is seen in the recommendations put forth by the Commission on the Education of the Deaf (1988). The Commission was established by the Education of the Deaf Act of 1986 to study the quality of education of deaf people and was composed of both deaf and hearing professionals, all of whom had personal or professional knowledge of deafness. The second Notice of Draft Recommendations was published in the Federal Register on October 14, 1987, and included the following recommendations along with a significant qualification:

- The Commission on Education of the Deaf recognizes American Sign Language as a legitimate language.

# Part I

## VARIATION AND LANGUAGE CONTACT

# 2

# Language Contact in the American Deaf Community

Ceil Lucas and Clayton Valli

## INTRODUCTION

One of the major sociolinguistic issues in the deaf community concerns the outcome of language contact. Specifically, there exists a kind of signing that results from the contact between American Sign Language (henceforth, ASL) and English and exhibits features of both languages.[1] It has been claimed (Woodward, 1973b; Woodward and Markowicz, 1975) that this kind of signing is a pidgin and that it is the result of deaf-hearing interaction. The goal of this study is to reexamine this claim, based on a preliminary structural description of contact signing resulting from naturalistic interaction. The objectives of the study are (1) to describe the data-collection methodology used to induce switching between ASL and this contact signing;[2] (2) to describe the sociolinguistic factors that sometimes correlate with the production of signing other than ASL; and (3) to describe

[1]American Sign Language (ASL) is the visual-gestural language used by members of the deaf community in the United States. It is a natural language with an autonomous grammar that is quite distinct from the grammar of English. ASL is also quite distinct from artificially developed systems that attempt to encode English and can include the use of speech, ASL signs, and invented signs used to represent English morphemes. There are a number of such systems, which are often referred to by the generic term Signed English.

[2]Based on a preliminary examination of the linguistic and sociolinguistic data, we are reluctant at this point to call the contact signing that we have observed a *variety* or a *dialect,* and the absence of such labels in the present study is conscious. Further study may reveal the need for such a label.

THE SOCIOLINGUISTICS OF THE DEAF COMMUNITY
Copyright © 1989 by Academic Press Inc.
All rights of reproduction in any form reserved.

some aspects of the morphological, syntactic, and lexical structure of the contact signing. The preliminary evidence suggests that the outcome of language contact in the American deaf community is unique, and quite different than anything that has been described to date in spoken language communities. The overall goal, then, is reexamination as a way of getting at an accurate characterization of this unique and complex phenomenon.

The first step toward understanding language contact in the deaf community involves recognizing the complexity of the contact situation with respect to not only the characteristics of participants but also the varieties of language available to those participants. For example, with participant characteristics, it is clearly not enough to simply distinguish deaf individuals from hearing individuals. Participants in a contact situation can be deaf ASL-English bilinguals who attended a residential school at an early age (entering, say, at age three or four), learned ASL as a first language from other children, and were taught some form of English, usually by hearing teachers who did not sign natively.[3] Alternatively, the participants can be deaf individuals who were mainstreamed at an early age and learned to sign relatively late, whether with ASL, Signed English, or both. Or, they can be the hearing children of deaf parents, again ASL-English bilinguals who learned ASL at home natively. They can even be hearing individuals who learned ASL or some variety of Signed English relatively late in life. Participants in a language contact situation can also include hearing individuals who are English monolinguals and do not sign, as well as deaf ASL monolinguals with a minimal command of English in any form. Similarly, the varieties of language available to participants in a contact situation range from ASL to spoken English or Signed English, and to a variety of codes for English that have been implemented in educational settings. (See Ramsey, this volume.) The participants in any given language

---

[3]At this point, evidence for the occurrence of signed or spoken English in the home, along with ASL, is largely anecdotal. For example, a Gallaudet undergraduate whose parents are deaf and who signs ASL as a first language remarked, in a class journal, "At first when I was born, my parents thought I was hearing due to a *VERY* little hearing loss. Afraid that I may have poor speech and English skills, they decided to use straight English and their voices whenever talking to me." She later remarks that her parents went back to using ASL. And another student states, "I was introduced to ASL since I'm the daughter of deaf parents and the fifth deaf generation. When SEE [Signing Exact English, a manual code for English] was emphasized in the 70s—my mama decided to learn SEE and placed me in a mainstream program where SEE was strongly used." Both of these comments imply the use of some form of English signing by native ASL signers in the home with their children. Furthermore, Woodward (1973c, p. 44) observes that, "It has been estimated that 10–20 percent of the deaf population has deaf parents. A tiny proportion of these parents are highly educated and have native English competence. In this tiny minority of the deaf, PSE [Pidgin Sign English, Woodward's term for the outcome of language contact in the deaf community—editor's note] may be learned with ASL from infancy." However, sociolinguistic and ethnographic data to support comments and observations such as these are nonexistent.

contact situation may have been exposed to some or all of the above and may display a wide range of linguistic skills. Finally, it is crucial to understand that the participants in a language contact situation have both the vocal channel and the visual channel available, the latter including both manual and nonmanual grammatical signals. That is, the participants in a language contact situation have hands, mouth, and face available for the encoding of linguistic messages.

With spoken languages, two language communities can be in contact but there may not actually be many bilingual individuals in those communities. The linguistic outcome of language contact in that situation is different from the linguistic outcome of the interaction of bilingual individuals. In turn, the interaction of bilingual individuals who share the same native language is apt to be different from the interaction of bilinguals who have different native languages. Compare, say, two French-English Canadian bilinguals who both speak French as a first language, as opposed to two French-English Canadian bilinguals, one of whom claims French as a first language and the other of whom claims English as a first language. Code-switching can occur in both of these situations, for example, but the reasons for it and the linguistic form it takes can be quite different. And this is all in contrast, finally, with the interaction of a bilingual speaker with a monolingual speaker, whether that interaction is conducted in the second language of the bilingual (and the native language of the monolingual), or vice versa. The case of a Spanish-English bilingual interacting with a monolingual English speaker is but one example. If the bilingual's first language is Spanish and the interaction is in English, the linguistic outcome of the interaction will probably be different from any interaction in Spanish with the monolingual who is in the earliest stages of learning Spanish.

Parallels exist for all of these situations in the deaf community, and, as explained earlier, participant characteristics can vary widely between language contact situations. The following is a partial outline of possible language contact situations in the American deaf community, according to participant characteristics:

- Deaf bilinguals with hearing bilinguals
- Deaf bilinguals with deaf bilinguals
- Deaf bilinguals with hearing spoken English monolinguals
- Hearing bilinguals with deaf English signers
- Deaf bilinguals with deaf English signers
- Deaf English signers with hearing spoken English monolinguals
- Deaf English signers with hearing bilinguals
- Deaf English signers with deaf ASL monolinguals
- Deaf bilinguals with deaf ASL monolinguals
- Deaf ASL monolinguals with hearing bilinguals

## ISSUES OF DEFINITION

Several issues arise from this outline. One concerns the problematic and relative concept of bilingualism. As in spoken language situations, participants in language contact situations in the deaf community display a range of competence both in ASL and in English, and in the latter, both in forms of English-like signing and in written English. For the purposes of the present study, bilingualism is defined in demographic terms: Deaf bilinguals are individuals who not only learned ASL natively, either from their parents or at an early age from their peers in residential school settings, but also have been exposed to spoken and written English all their lives, beginning with the school system and continuing into adulthood through interaction with native English speakers. In contrast, hearing bilinguals are native English speakers who learned to sign as adults, both through formal instruction and through interaction with deaf people. Although not native ASL signers, hearing bilinguals do not use manual codes for English, either. Specific sign use in the present study will be discussed later. Again, it is crucial to recognize a range of competence in hearing bilinguals. For example, the linguistic outcome of an interaction between a hearing child of deaf parents (hence, possibly, a native user of ASL) and a deaf bilingual can be quite different from that of a deaf bilingual and a hearing bilingual who, while competent, learned ASL as an adult.

Another issue that arises concerns the distinction between deaf people and hearing people. Informal observation and anecdotal evidence suggest that this distinction is an important variable in the outcome of language contact in the American deaf community. Deaf individuals not only can sign quite differently with other deaf individuals than with hearing individuals but also can initiate an interaction in one language and radically switch when the interlocutor's ability to hear is revealed. For example, a deaf native ASL user may initiate an interaction with another individual whom he believes to be deaf or whose audiological status has not been clarified. The latter participant may well be a near-native user of ASL. Once the latter's hearing ability becomes apparent, however, it is not unusual for the deaf participant to automatically switch "away from ASL" to a more English-based form of signing. Code choice is thus sensitive to the ability versus inability of participants to hear and this distinction is carefully attended to in the present study of contact phenomena in the deaf community.

One might predict that the different contact situations outlined earlier here yield different linguistic outcomes, all of them of interest. For example, there is substantial informal observational evidence that when speaking English away from deaf individuals, hearing bilinguals occasionally code-switch into ASL and code-mix English and ASL features. Another outcome is seen, when, in interaction with hearing individuals who do not sign at all, a deaf bilingual who does not otherwise use his voice (in interaction with other deaf people or with hearing people who sign) opts to use spoken English in combination with gestures. Similarly, there is informal observational evidence that in interacting with hearing individuals who are in the early stages of learning to sign, deaf native ASL users use a form of "foreigner talk." Finally, the outcome of language contact between native signers of different sign languages (for example, ASL and Italian Sign Language) can have unique characteristics. There is anecdotal and casual observational evidence for the existence of all of the language contact situations outlined. What is clearly required at this point is carefully collected ethnographic data on videotape and descriptive analyses of these interactions.

The present study focuses on the outcome of language contact in the first situation in the outline: deaf bilinguals with hearing bilinguals. The reason for choosing this focus is that characterizations of language contact in the American deaf community have thus far been limited to the interaction between deaf people and hearing people, and this interaction contact has been characterized as producing a kind of pidgin. As stated earlier, one of the objectives of this study is to reexamine this characterization, in part by way of a preliminary description of the lexical, morphological and syntactic features of language production that result from the interaction of deaf and hearing people. There are suggestions in the literature that the outcome of the interaction of deaf bilinguals with other deaf bilinguals is sometimes a language variety other than ASL. In the present study, we collected considerable data on such interactions, a very general description of which is provided here. A detailed linguistic analysis of the deaf-deaf variety of interaction, as well as a comparison of that variety with the hearing-deaf variety, are reserved for future study.

## THE OUTCOME OF LANGUAGE CONTACT

Given the variety in both participant characteristics and languages available, it is not surprising that the linguistic outcome of language contact is something that cannot be strictly described as ASL or as a signed representation of English. The issue is not that contact signing occurs, nor what label to attach to the system of signs, but rather how to characterize the system. Contact signing is characterized as "an interface between deaf signers and hearing speakers" by Fischer (1978, p. 314) and is labeled Pidgin Sign English (PSE) by Woodward (1972, 1973b). The linguistic characteristics of this so-called PSE are examined in three studies: Woodward (1973b), Woodward and Markowicz (1975), and Reilly and McIntire (1980).

Woodward (1973b, p. 17) states that "Sometimes people sign something that seems to be a pidginized version of English. The syntactic order is primarily English, but inflections have been reduced in redundancy, and there is a mixture of American Sign Language and English structure." Further details are provided (Woodward, 1973b, p. 42):

> These characteristics point up some close similarities between PSE and other pidgins. In most pidgins, articles are deleted; the copula is usually uninflected; inflections such as English plural are lost and most derivations are lost, just as they are in PSE. Perfective aspect in pidgins is often expressed through *finish* or a similar verb like *done.*

Woodward (1973b) and Woodward and Markowicz (1975) provide a description of some of the linguistic characteristics of PSE, which are summarized in Table I. Their inventory of features includes agent-beneficiary directionality, negative incorporation, and number incorporation. They also discuss PSE phonology, specifically, handshapes, location, and movement.

Reilly and McIntire (1980, p. 151) define PSE as "a form of signing used by many hearing people for interacting with deaf people and thus is a commonly encountered dialect of ASL." They (1980, p. 152) point out that

> although PSE has been classified as a pidgin language, it differs from most pidgins in important ways. . . . Syntactically, PSE does not appear as many other pidgins. Because it does make use of a number of English grammatical devices for creating complex sentences, it has access to a wider range of grammatical constructions than do most pidgins.

**Table I**
Linguistic Characteristics of Pidgin Sign English (PSE)

| Feature | ASL | Sign English | PSE |
|---|---|---|---|
| Articles | No | Yes | Variable: *a, t-h-e* (fingerspelled) |
| Plurality | Noun pluralization by reduplication | *-s,* etc. | Some reduplication, generally does not use marker to represent English *s* plural |
| Copula | No | Yes | With older signers, represented by the sign TRUE |
| Progressive | Verb reduplication | *-ing* | "PSE retains verb reduplication in a few heavily weighted environments, e.g., 'run', 'drive'. PSE uninflected copula or inflected forms plus a verb for Standard English be + ing. PSE, however, drops the redundant + ing" (Woodward, 1973b; p. 41). |
| Perfective | FINISH | | $FINISH_2$, an allomorph of ASL FINISH |

The PSE label is very widely used and the analogy with spoken language pidgin situations and language contact in general is extended to include the idea of diglossic variation along a continuum. The suggestion that Ferguson's (1959) concept of diglossia might be applicable to the deaf community was first made by Stokoe (1969). By the low (L) variety, Stokoe is referring to ASL. As he (Stokoe, 1969, p. 23) states, "The H ('superposed' or 'high') variety is English. However, this English is a form most unfamiliar to usual linguistic scrutiny. It is not spoken but uttered in 'words' which are fingerspelled or signed." As Lee (1982, p. 131) points out, "The concept of a sign language 'continuum' linking the H and L varieties . . . has become quite popular. This continuum represents a scale of all the varieties of ASL and English produced by both deaf and hearing signers. These varieties imperceptibly grade into ASL on one extreme and English on the other." It is claimed that a number of varieties exist along the continuum, and it is some complex of these varieties that the label Pidgin Sign English (PSE) is said to identify.

A notable problem with earlier descriptions concerns lack of data or problems with the data used to back up claims about the linguistic nature of the signing being described. Neither in Woodward (1973b) nor in Woodward and Markowicz (1975) is there any description of the sample that serves as the source for the list of features proposed for PSE. J. C. Woodward (personal communication, 1988) has indicated that the description of PSE was based in part on a sample from his dissertation: 140 individuals, ranging in age from thirteen to fifty-five, with 9 black signers and 131 white signers. But these data are still problematic as the basis for a description of language contact because (1) the data were elicited by a hearing researcher on a one-on-one basis with the use of a questionnaire, and were not interactional; and (2) the signers providing these data range from deaf native ASL signers to hearing nonnative signers, making it virtually impossible to separate out features of the language produced that are a function of language contact from features that are a function of second-language acquisition. For example, Woodward and Markowicz (1975, p. 18) claim that the ASL rule of negative incorporation can occur in PSE, but that "deaf signers use more negative incorporation than hearing signers." This may indeed be true, but it might also reflect a difference in language competence (i.e., native signers knowing and competently using a rule that nonnative signers may be in the process of learning), rather than a reflection of language contact between hearing and deaf signers.

It seems that deaf language production and hearing language production in a language contact situation are necessarily different by virtue of differences in language acquisition backgrounds. Also, the features of contact signing (PSE) cannot be described based on data that not only combine native and nonnative signers' productions but also are not interactional.

Researchers are certainly aware of the need to distinguish between native and nonnative production. In fact, Lee (1982, p. 131) reports that

> Stokoe (personal communication) suggests that there may in fact be two PSE continua: a $PSE_d$ produced by deaf signers and a $PSE_h$ produced by hearing signers. $PSE_d$ is likely to have more ASL grammatical structures and to omit English inflections. $PSE_h$ tends to have greater English influence and rarely approaches the ASL extreme of the continuum.

The need for separation of data sources is thus recognized, but this need is not reflected in the actual descriptions of PSE that are produced. Thus, Reilly and McIntire (1980) base their description of the differences between PSE and ASL on videotapes of a children's story that was signed by four informants. Three of these informants are hearing. Three have deaf parents and two of the three hearing informants did not use sign in childhood. The instructions for different versions of the story were given either in ASL or, as Reilly and McIntire (1980, p. 155) describe, "in PSE and spoken English simultaneously . . . or interpreted, i.e., signed as they were being read aloud by the investigator."

Although there is an awareness of the need to control for the variable of signer skill, and even though the description of PSE is based on videotaped data, the problem of separating the consequences of language contact from the consequences of second language learning arises in Reilly and McIntire's (1980) study. In their conclusions, they (1980, p. 183) observe:

> It seems that there is a gradation from structures that are more obvious to the language learner (classifiers and directional verbs) to those that are more and more subtle (sustained signs and facial and other non-manual behaviors). This gradation is reflected in differential usage by different signers.

Once again, we encounter the "apples and oranges" dilemma resulting from descriptions of PSE based on the sign production of signers with different levels of competence and ages of acquisition. Furthermore, data collection in analogous spoken language situations does not typically yield naturalistic data, and, accordingly, it is not clear that the data upon which Reilly and McIntire's description of PSE is based bear any resemblance to language production in a natural language contact situation.

Clearly, any study that proposes to describe the linguistic outcome of language contact in the American deaf community should at the very least take its departure from data collected in naturalistic interactional settings that reflect actual language contact situations as closely as possible. It is fair to say that studies claiming to describe the linguistic outcome of language contact in the American deaf community to date may not reflect the actual situation, owing to either a lack of data or problematic data. In light of the problems presented by the data in research to date, the characterizations of language contact in the American deaf community—pidginization, foreigner talk, learner's grammars, diglossic continuum—warrant reexamination.

## THE PRESENT STUDY

Given the enormous complexity of language contact in the American deaf community, and the problems inherent in earlier studies attempting to describe the situation, we focused on only one particular type of interaction. The major goals of the present study are (1) to provide a preliminary description of the signing of deaf bilinguals when signing with hearing bilinguals, and (2) to base that description on carefully collected data that reflect natural interaction as closely as possible. Toward this end, six dyads of informants were formed. Eleven of the twelve informants rated themselves as very skilled in ASL, and all twelve rated themselves as skilled in English. Of the twelve informants, nine were born deaf, one was born hard of hearing and is now deaf, and two were born hearing and became deaf at fifteen months of age and three years of age, respectively. Five of the twelve came from deaf families, and of the remaining seven, five attended residential schools for the deaf and learned ASL at an early age. One informant learned ASL from other deaf students in a mainstream program. Considering the family and educational background of all but one of the informants, their self-evaluations of personal language skills are accurate: They are bilinguals who learned ASL either natively from their parents or at a very early age from peers (all but one in a residential school setting). They have had exposure to and contact with English all of their lives. The data from one informant who did not learn ASL until age 21 (born deaf, hearing family) is excluded from the analysis, and, in fact, the videotapes for this informant reveal minimal use of ASL.

The composition of each of the six dyads is shown in Table II. The participants in dyads 1 and 2 share similar backgrounds, as do the participants in dyads 4, and 5 and 6. Dyad 3 was deliberately "mixed," consisting of one individual born deaf in a deaf family and one individual born deaf in a hearing family, but both having attended residential school. In dyads 1, 3, and 6, the participants did not know each other; in dyads 2, 4, and 5, they did.

In the first part of the data collection, the videocameras were present, but at no point were the technicians visible. The sign production of the six dyads was videotaped during interaction with, first, a deaf interviewer who

**Table II**
Composition of Dyads

| Dyad | Participant A | Participant B |
|------|---------------|---------------|
| 1 | Deaf family, born deaf, residential school | Deaf family, deaf at 15 mos., public school |
| 2 | Deaf family, born deaf, deaf day school | Deaf family, born hard of hearing, now profoundly deaf, deaf day school |
| 3 | Deaf family, born deaf, residential school | Hearing family, born deaf, residential school |
| 4 | Hearing family, born deaf, residential school | Hearing family, deaf at age 3, residential school |
| 5 | Hearing family, born deaf, residential school | Hearing family, born deaf, mainstream program |
| 6 | Hearing family, deaf at age 3, residential school | Hearing family, born deaf, learned ASL at age 21, public school |

signed ASL, then the dyad alone; next with a hearing interviewer who produced English-like signing and used her voice while she signed, then the dyad alone again; finally, with the deaf interviewer again. The whole interview experience began with exclusive contact with the deaf interviewer.

Each interview consisted of a discussion of several broad topics of interest to members of the deaf community. Four statements were presented and participants were asked if they agreed or disagreed, and why.[4] It was predicted that (1) the situation with the deaf researcher will induce ASL, but the relative formality of the situation and the presence of a stranger can preclude it; (2) the situation with the hearing researcher will induce a shift away from ASL to contact signing; and (3) the informants alone with each other will elicit ASL. The structure of the interviews in terms of relative formality and informality is summarized in Table III.

This interview structure has strong parallels with V. Edwards' (1986) research design for a study of British Black English. V. Edwards's (1986, p. 9) major concern in that study was the improvement of methodology "so as to ensure that this corpus authentically reflects the range of individual

---

[4]The four statements introduced for discussion are as follows:

1. Someone in a public place (airport, restaurant) discovers that you're deaf and wants to help you. That is acceptable. Agree or disagree?
2. The hearing children of deaf people are members of deaf culture. Agree or disagree?
3. Gallaudet University should have a deaf president. Agree or disagree?
4. Mainstreaming is better than residential schools. Agree or disagree?

**Table III**
Interview Structure

| Situation Type | Formal | Informal |
|---|---|---|
| With deaf interviewer | + | |
| Dyad alone | | + |
| With hearing interviewer | + | |
| Dyad alone | | + |
| With deaf interviewer | + | |

and situational variation which exists within the black community." Edwards recognized the obvious need for the black interviewers in gaining access to vernacular speech. V. Edwards (1986, p. 17) was assured that the presence of a sympathetic, young Black interviewer, that is, a peer, would guarantee the use of the vernacular by the informants. But

> Our observation made it clear that many young black people use Patois only in in-group conversation, so that the presence of any other person, even the young black fieldworker, would be enough to inhibit Patois usage. The obvious solution was to create a situation in which the young people were left alone.

As in the Edwards study, participants in the present study were left alone twice and asked to continue discussing the topics introduced by the interviewers. In the first instance, the deaf interviewer was called away for "an emergency phone call." After an eight to ten minute period, the hearing interviewer arrived and explained that she would be taking the deaf interviewer's place. The interview continued and the hearing interviewer then left to check on the deaf interviewer. The dyad was again left alone until the return of the deaf interviewer for the remainder of the interview session. Following the completion of the interview, the participants were told that there had in fact been no emergency, and the reason for the deaf interviewer's departure was explained. The participants viewed portions of the tapes and discussed the purpose of the study with the researchers. All the participants were glad to be told that the "emergency" was false, but accepted it as part of the data collection procedure.

Based on a preliminary examination of the data, some important observations can be made. These observations fall into two broad categories: (1) the overall pattern of language use during the interviews, and (2) the linguistic properties of the contact signing produced by deaf native ASL signers during deaf-hearing interaction. As assessed by a deaf native ASL user, the distributional pattern of language choice during the interviews is summarized in Table IV.[5] The information in this table should be read as follows: In the first dyad, participant *A* uses ASL across all of the situations of interaction; *A*'s language use here contrasts with *B*'s, who uses contact signing and Signed English with the deaf interviewer, contact signing with *A*, and Signed English with the hearing interviewer, and so on, for all six dyads. As the distributional contrasts in Table IV reveal, some participants start out with one kind of signing in a particular condition and then change to another kind of signing, within the same condition. Participant *B* in dyad 5, for example, produces contact signing with the deaf interviewer. When alone with *A*, *B* produces ASL and then produces contact signing again when the hearing interviewer appears. When the hearing interviewer leaves, and *A* and *B* are again alone, *B* continues to produce contact signing for a while and then produces ASL. *B* continues to produce ASL upon the return of the deaf interviewer and does so until the end of the interview.

In keeping with our prediction, ten of the twelve informants produce a form of signing that is other-than-ASL with the hearing interviewer—either contact signing or Signed English with voice. In some cases, the informants produce ASL with the deaf interviewer and while alone with each other, as was expected. However, some unexpected results emerged. For example, three informants use ASL with the hearing interviewer, contrary to a widely held belief that deaf native signers automatically switch away from ASL in the presence of a nonnative signer. Furthermore, two of the informants (*1A* and *4A*) use ASL consistently across all of the situations. One might predict that both of these informants come from deaf families; however, *4A* is from a hearing family. Another unexpected result is the production of contact signing both with the deaf interviewer and when the informants are left alone. The deaf interviewer consistently signs ASL, and it was predicted that the informants would produce ASL in this situation and when left alone. But this is not the actual outcome. Indeed, in one case, an informant

---

[5]At this stage of the study, assessment of the signing on the tapes (i.e., ASL vs. other-than-ASL vs. Signed English) is based on the judgment of the researchers. ASL and other-than-ASL were judged by a deaf native signer; Signed English consistently included the use of voice and hence included input from the hearing researcher. The final analysis, however, will not be limited to the judgment of the researchers. The second part of the data collection will consist of having native signers view each tape at least twice and indicate by pushing a button when switches away from ASL or back to ASL take place. These native-signer judges will be asked to characterize the language production between the switch points, and it is this production that will form the data base for the eventual description of contact signing. The entire methodology was first designed and employed by Robert E. Johnson, Scott Liddell, Carol Erting, and Dave Knight in a pilot project entitled "Sign Language and Variation in Context," sponsored by the Gallaudet Research Institute. The data base will eventually include the signing production of twenty individuals: twelve white and eight black. The sign production of the black informants reflects their interaction with both black and white, and hearing and deaf, interviewers.

**Table IV**

Distribution of Language Choice, by Interview Situation and Participant

| Situation | Dyad 1 Participants | | Dyad 2 Participants | | Dyad 3 Participants | | Dyad 4 Participants | | Dyad 5 Participants | | Dyad 6 Participants | |
|---|---|---|---|---|---|---|---|---|---|---|---|---|
| | A | B | A | B | A | B | A | B | A | B | A | B |
| With deaf interviewer | ASL | CS/SE[a] | ASL | ASL/CS | ASL/CS | CS | ASL | SE | ASL | CS | ASL | CS |
| Dyad alone | ASL | CS | ASL/CS | ASL | ASL/CS | ASL/CS | ASL | CS | ASL | ASL | CS | CS |
| With hearing interviewer | ASL | SE | ASL/CS | CS | CS | SE | ASL | CS | CS | CS | CS | CS |
| Dyad alone | ASL | CS | ASL | ASL | ASL/CS | ASL/CS | ASL | CS | CS/ASL | CS/ASL | CS/ASL | CS/ASL |
| With deaf interviewer | ASL | CS | ASL | ASL/CS | ASL/CS | ASL/CS | ASL | CS | ASL | ASL | ASL | CS |

[a]CS, Contact Signing; SE, Signed English, with voice.

produces Signed English with the deaf interviewer. These results are particularly noteworthy given another widely held belief that deaf native signers will consistently sign ASL with each other if no hearing people are present. The observations on the overall pattern of language use during the interviews can be summarized as follows:

- Some informants use contact signing or Signed English with the hearing interviewer, as expected; others use ASL throughout.
- ASL is used with the hearing interviewer by some informants but not others.
- Contact signing is produced with the deaf interviewer and when the informants are alone.
- ASL is used not only by deaf informants from deaf families but also by deaf informants from hearing families.

These observations appear to challenge the traditional perspective on language contact in the American deaf community. For example, it is traditionally assumed that contact signing (known as PSE) appears in deaf-hearing interaction, mainly for the obvious reason that the hearing person might not understand ASL. On the extreme is the position that the very purpose of contact signing is to prevent hearing people from learning ASL (Woodward and Markowicz, 1975, p. 12). More measured approaches simply describe contact signing as the product of deaf-hearing interaction. Little is said, however, about the use of contact signing in exclusively deaf settings. Although the need for comprehension might explain the occurrence of contact signing in deaf-hearing interaction, it is clearly not an issue in portions of the interviews described here, as all of the participants are native or near-native signers and, in some instances, sign ASL with each other. The choice to use contact signing with other deaf ASL natives, then, appears to be motivated by sociolinguistic factors. Two of three factors identified in the present study are the formality of the interview situation (including the presence of videotape equipment) and the participant's lack of familiarity in some cases with both the interviewer and the other informant. The videotaped data also clearly present counterevidence to the claim that deaf people never or rarely sign ASL in the presence of hearing people, as two of the informants chose to sign ASL throughout their respective interviews. This choice may be motivated by other sociolinguistic factors, such as the desire to establish one's social identity as a bona fide member of the deaf community or cultural group, a desire that may supersede considerations of formality and lack of familiarity with one's cointerlocutor(s). Different sociolinguistic factors motivate the language choices of different individuals. This is further illustrated by the differences among informants in language choice within a given interview situation.

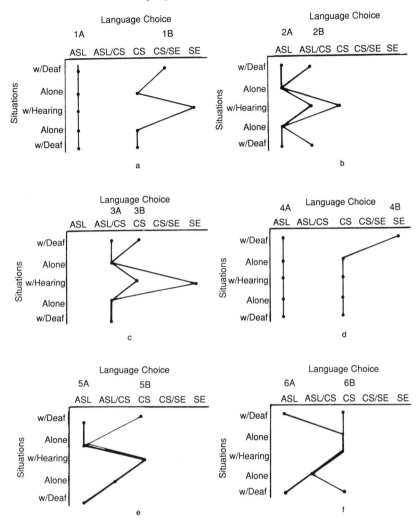

**Fig. 1**  Patterns of language choice: (a) dyad 1; (b) dyad 2; (c) dyad 3; (d) dyad 4; (e) dyad 5; (f) dyad 6.

Figure 1 provides a more graphic summary of informant language use within the interviews. Three distinct patterns are discernible here. One pattern, as seen with dyads 1 and 4, consists of the two informants using distinctly different kinds of signing and never overlapping with each other. For example, in dyad 1, informant *1A* consistently uses ASL throughout the interview, even though *1B* starts out with contact signing and Signed English, then moves first to contact signing, then to Signed English, and then back to contact signing. Similarly, in dyad 4, informant *4A* consistently uses ASL, while *4B* starts out with signed English and then consistently uses contact signing. Neither *1B* nor *4B* ever approaches the use of ASL during the interview. The first pattern, then, is that one participant's choice of signing during the interview is consistently distinct from the coparticipant's choice or choices.

In dyads 2 and 6, we see a second pattern, where the informants use different kinds of signing during the first part of the interview with the deaf interviewer but, when left alone with each other, use the same kind of signing. In dyad 2, informant *2A* continues with ASL, and *2B* switches to ASL; in dyad 6, informant *6B* continues with contact signing, and *6A* switches to contact signing. In dyad 6, the informants use the same kind of signing and switch in the same way towards ASL when left alone and then sign quite differently with the deaf interviewer. In dyad 2, the informants do not sign in exactly the same way, but they do shift in the same direction. Also noteworthy in both dyads is the fact that despite shifting during the interview, each informant signs the same way with the deaf interviewer at the end of the interview as at the beginning.

The third pattern is seen in dyads 3 and 5, where the informants begin the interview with different kinds of signing. One informant then shifts toward the other, and then both informants either together use the same kind of signing for the remainder of the interview (dyad 5) or use the same kind of signing, then shift in the same direction, and then together use the same kind of signing again (dyad 3).

One central question is what accounts for the use of different kinds of signing by individual informants within the interviews. Switching that seems to be motivated by the presence of a hearing person can be seen in these data: seven of the twelve informants switch from ASL signing or ASL signing with some contact signing features to contact signing or Signed English with voice in the presence of the hearing interviewer. Of the remaining five informants, two consistently sign ASL in all situations; the other three produce contact signing when the hearing interviewer arrives and maintain this choice for the duration of her presence. Five of the twelve informants are from deaf families, and it is important to note that four of those five are among those who switched in the presence of the hearing interviewer. Of the five informants who did not switch with the hearing interviewer, only one is from a deaf family.

Signing behavior produced in the presence of a hearing person does not explain the occurrence of contact signing with the deaf interviewer or when the informants are alone. The use of contact signing in the latter situations can be accounted for by several factors, such as the formality of the interview situation and the lack of familiarity of the informants with the deaf interviewer. Attitudes concerning the kind of signing that is appropriate in different situations have long been noticed and described. Indeed, it is this interrelationship between language attitudes and language choices that prompted Stokoe (1969) to describe the language situation in the deaf community as diglossic—that is, ASL strictly in some contexts and a more English-like signing strictly for other contexts, with no overlap. In reexamining this characterization of the language situation in the deaf community as diglossic, Lee (1982, p. 127) states that although "there is indeed variation [in the deaf community] . . . code-switching and style shifting rather than diglossia appear to be the norm." Three of Ferguson's (1959) nine criteria for diglossia are linguistic (lexicon, phonology, and grammar), while six are described by Lee as sociolinguistic (literary heritage, standardization, prestige, stability, acquisition, and function). As she (Lee, 1982, p. 147) observes, "I have found none of the nine characteristics actually consistent with diglossia, at least in some parts of the linguistic community."

Even though it is not clear at this point what the roles of code-switching and style shifting are in the deaf community, it is clear from Lee's reexamination of Stokoe's (1969) work and from the present data that the language situation in the deaf community is not strictly diglossic. Clearly, some of the informants in our study see ASL as inappropriate for any part of the interview. Specifically, informants *1B* and *4B* never use ASL. Other informants see ASL as appropriate only when no interviewer is present. In each one of the six dyads, a shift occurs when the deaf interviewer departs and the informants are alone, and it is striking that whenever the signing of one informant shifts toward the signing of another, it is, with one exception, a shift from contact signing or Signed English to or toward ASL. That is, informants *1A, 2A, 3A, 4A,* and *5A* use ASL with the deaf interviewer at the beginning of the interview, and informants *1B, 2B, 3B, 4B,* and *5B* use contact signing or Signed English. When the deaf interviewer departs, the latter informants switch to or toward ASL. The one exception is informant *6A,* who uses ASL with the deaf interviewer and then switches to contact signing when left alone with *6B,* who continues to use contact signing. This may have occurred because, of the twelve informants, *6B* is the only one who learned ASL relatively late. *6A* may have switched to contact signing in an attempt to accommodate *6B.* The claim that ASL is regarded as appropriate only when the interviewers are absent is further supported by the two informants (*2B* and *6B*) who switch away from ASL to contact signing when the deaf interviewer reappears at the end of the interview. Any attempt, however, to claim that this is evidence of diglossia is quickly thwarted by the informants who use ASL in all of the interview situations, with no apparent regard for formality, familiarity, or audiological status of the cointerlocutor(s).

The patterns seen in Figure 1 provide an illustration of Giles's (1977) theory of accommodation in linguistic behavior (also, see Valli, 1988). That accommodation can take the form of convergence, nonconvergence, or divergence. With convergence, a speaker chooses a language variety that seems to fit the needs of the cointerlocutor(s). Under some conditions, however, a speaker can diverge in order to dissociate from the cointerlocutor(s), perhaps to emphasize loyalty to his group. Nonconvergence occurs when one speaker does not move away from another but simply continues using a variety that differs from other speakers. Figure 1 provides examples of all three types of accommodation. In dyad 1, for example, participant *1B* converges with or shifts toward *1A* when the dyad is alone. *1B* then converges with the hearing interviewer by shifting to Signed English, while *1A* provides an example of nonconvergence with the hearing interviewer by continuing to use ASL. In all of the dyads except 6, the *B* participants converge toward the *A* participants, which is to say, toward ASL. As mentioned earlier about dyad 6, participant *A* may converge toward *B* because *B* learned sign language relatively late and may not be comfortable using ASL.

A major goal of this chapter is to describe the sociolinguistic conditions that accompany the production of signing other than ASL, signing that has been labeled PSE. Contrary to claims that this kind of signing occurs in the presence of hearing people, either to aid their comprehension or to deny them access to ASL, the videotaped data in this study clearly demonstrate that contact signing is produced among deaf native ASL signers in the absence of hearing people. The sociolinguistic factors that motivate this language choice appear to include the relative formality of the interview situation and the lack of familiarity with cointerlocutors. There is clear evidence that contact signing is considered more appropriate than ASL in some situations. Furthermore, an examination of the conditions of language contact situations in the deaf community reveals that, from a sociolinguistic standpoint, these situations are not at all analogous to the sociolinguistic conditions that give rise to spoken language pidgins.

## *LINGUISTIC FEATURES OF CONTACT SIGNING*

Another goal of this chapter is to describe some of the morphological, lexical, and syntactic features of contact signing. As explained earlier, a complete linguistic description of contact signing is planned and will be based on a corpus formed from native signer judgments of the language production on the videotapes. This linguistic description will encompass each informant's signing in all of the interview situations, that is, with the deaf interviewer, with the hearing interviewer, and alone with the other informant. The present preliminary description focuses on each informant's interaction with the hearing interviewer and is based on thirty seconds of transcription per informant.[6] From this sample, Table V summarizes various features of contact signing.

The lexical forms found in contact signing are ASL signs. It is important to observe that these lexical forms are consistently accompanied by the mouthing of corresponding English lexical items. This mouthing is produced without voicing. Although most of the lexical forms are ASL signs with ASL meaning and function, sometimes the lexical forms have English meanings and functions. For example, the ASL sign GROW (the sign used when discussing the growth of plants, for example) is produced with the lexicalized fingerspelled sign #UP, in a discussion of the hearing children of deaf parents. Even though the sign GROW used by our informant is an ASL sign, it is not the sign typically used in ASL for talking about the growth of children. The result, then, is the use of an ASL form with a meaning not usually associated with that sign. This example is analogous to examples in the various manual codes for English, where one ASL sign is used for a wide variety of English meanings, even though separate ASL signs exist for those meanings. For example, the ASL sign RUN (as in 'run down the street') is cited in these systems for the meanings of 'run for president', 'run a business', or 'run in a stocking'. The occurrence of the sign GROW with the fingerspelled #UP may be a reflection of the signer's exposure to manually coded systems for English in the educational system. And in a situation deemed appropriate for more English-like signing, evidence of those systems emerges. GROW, then, is a case of an ASL sign that is not being used with its ASL meaning. In that usage it has an English meaning. Another example in the data of ASL lexical forms with English meaning and function is the sign MEAN, which in ASL is generally used as a verb, as in

WH
‾‾‾‾‾‾‾‾‾‾
WORD MEAN

'what does the word mean?' In the data, however, this sign occurs with the meaning and function of the English noun meaning, as in the sequence WHAT MEAN OF QUOTE DEAF CULTURE 'what is the meaning of "deaf culture"?'

Both morphologically and syntactically, the contact signing examined here shows drastic reduction of both the ASL and English systems. Word order follows English patterns, as does the use of prepositional phrases, conjunctions, embedded constructions with *that*, personal pronouns, and

---

[6]These thirty seconds of data per informant were transcribed by a deaf native signer. The transcription process was as follows: after a shift to contact signing was perceived by the transcriber, thirty seconds were allowed to elapse and then the next thirty seconds were transcribed. This transcription procedure was followed for all twelve informants.

**Table V**
Linguistic Features of Contact Signing

| Lexical Form | Lexical Meaning and Function | Morphological Structure | Syntactic Structure |
|---|---|---|---|
| ASL and ASL-like lexical items, English mouthing | ASL, idiosyncratic, English | Reduced ASL and English, reduction and/or absence of nonmanual signals | Reduced English, idiosyncratic constructions |

collocations. English inflectional and derivational morphology is nonexistent, yielding a very analytic (as opposed to synthetic) picture. This extends to the mouthing of English lexical items that is a feature of contact signing. The mouthing does not include any bound English morphemes such as plural -*s*, third-person possessive -*s*, past tense -*ed*, and so forth.

Davis (this volume) draws a distinction between clear English mouthing and reduced English mouthing. The former consists of the completely silent pronunciation of a word. The latter consists of the partially silent pronunciation of a word. For example, one signer fingerspells #ED 'education' and mouths "educa-." These data contain examples of both complete and partial mouthing. Furthermore, ASL inflectional and derivational morphology are virtually absent. There is also considerable use of deictic signs, such as pronouns. Finally, the contact signing yields some examples of what can only be called idiosyncratic syntactic constructions, constructions that fit neither the ASL nor the English grammatical system. Examples include sequences such as

+ mouthing ⟶

GROW#UP   OF   BE   DEAF,

and

+ mouthing ⟶

COOPERATIVE   TEAMWORK   #IS   REAL   MOST   KEY   THEIR   #GOALS.

Figure 2 provides an example of the contact signing produced by one informant in discussing whether mainstreaming is preferable to residential schools. This particular informant favors residential schools. Examples of the features of contact signing here include English word order, use of conjunctions, prepositional phrases, consistent mouthing without voice of English lexical items, idiosyncratic constructions, and the absence of determiners. Inflectional morphemes are absent except for the invented sign for English -*ing* and the fingerspelled copula, #IS. There are also examples of deictic ASL signs (e.g., pronouns), lexicalized fingerspelling (#OF, #ED), and an ASL discourse marker ('WELL'). Finally, there is the occurrence of a single spoken English word, "*so.*" Recall that Woodward (1973b) and

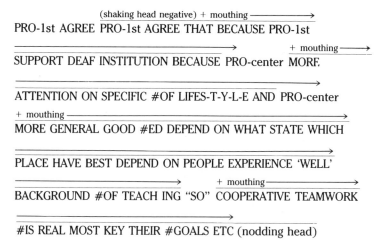

(shaking head negative) + mouthing ————————→
PRO-1st AGREE PRO-1st AGREE THAT BECAUSE PRO-1st

————————————————————→    + mouthing ————→
SUPPORT DEAF INSTITUTION BECAUSE PRO-center MORE

————————————————————————→
ATTENTION ON SPECIFIC #OF LIFES-T-Y-L-E AND PRO-center

+ mouthing ————————————————————→
MORE GENERAL GOOD #ED DEPEND ON WHAT STATE WHICH

————————————————————————→
PLACE HAVE BEST DEPEND ON PEOPLE EXPERIENCE 'WELL'

————————————→    + mouthing ————————→
BACKGROUND #OF TEACH ING "SO" COOPERATIVE TEAMWORK

————————————————→
#IS REAL MOST KEY THEIR #GOALS ETC (nodding head)

'I don't agree with that because I support deaf residential schools because they place more attention on the specifics of lifestyle and the education, in general, is better—depending on what state, which place has the best—that depends on the people's experience, on their teaching background—so, cooperative teamwork is really the key to their goals.'

**Fig. 2**  Contact signing. The transcription is relatively broad. The notation +mouthing indicates the mouthing without voice of English phrases or sentences that parallels the signed message. The term PRO is used for what appear to be pronominal forms. The gloss 'WELL' indicates the placement of a discourse marker.

Woodward and Markowicz (1975), in their inventory of PSE features, include English word order and the absence of determiners, two of the features of the present data. However, there are many other features in these data that are not found in their inventory.

The *linguistic* outcome of contact between ASL and English is not most aptly described as a pidgin. This observation is in accord with that of Cokely (1983). In reviewing the preconditions defined by other researchers for the emergence of a pidgin (e.g., Ferguson and DeBose, 1977), Cokely (1983, pp. 11, 20) finds that the ASL-English contact situation

> can be described as one in which members of the Deaf community communicate with hearing people in a foreigner talk register of ASL, and members of the hearing community communicate with Deaf people in a foreigner talk register of English. . . . The ASL-English contact situation does not, in fact, result in the emergence of a pidgin. Although the process of pidginization may be detected in the ASL-English situation, the preconditions for the development of a pidgin language are not adequately met. Instead the variation along the ASL-English continuum of varieties or registers can be accounted for by the dynamic interplay of foreigner talk, judgments of proficiency, and learners' attempts to master the target language—whether this is ASL for hearing users or English for Deaf users.

There is one apparent difficulty with Cokely's characterization of language contact in the deaf community. Consider an analogy from spoken language contact situations. In the contact between a native speaker of Italian, for example, and a nonnative speaker, it would be quite strange to expect that the "foreigner talk" variety of Italian used by the native speaker would include any elements of the nonnative speaker's first language. More likely, the "foreigner talk" variety would simply be a modified version of Italian. The variety of signing that the deaf native ASL signer typically uses with hearing people, however, seems to include at least some features of English and thus does not qualify strictly as "foreigner talk." This is also the case for the variety of signing that hearing people use with deaf people.

Woodward (1985, p. 19) describes Cokely's observations as "challenging to Woodward's (1973b) analysis of the varieties between ASL and English as a pidgin language" and contends that "by 1980, however, the notion that varieties referred to by 'PSE' as a discrete pidgin had already been abandoned." He (1985, p. 19) cites his own 1980 work to support this contention: "While it is true that PSE is different from pure ASL and from pure English, it is not a separate language. There is no way in the world to define where PSE begins and ends." Bochner and Albertini (1988) address the issue of PSE within the context of language acquisition and correctly observe that it is difficult to draw a clear parallel between spoken language pidgins and PSE. Although their claims are not data based, they (Bochner and Albertini, 1988, pp. 13–14) note that "a pidgin may be developing in North American schools and workplaces among users of mutually unintelligible sign systems . . . Objective and detailed descriptions of the structure and function of signing being used in these situations would clarify the picture."

To fully understand the preliminary inventory of contact signing features in these data, and to get a clearer understanding of what kind of linguistic phenomenon contact signing is, it is useful to compare it to (1) inventories of the features of English-based spoken language pidgins and (2) features of other kinds of signing such as Signed English, which by its nature is English-based. From the comparison in Table VI, we can see that the contact signing examined thus far is distinct from both English-based spoken language pidgins and from Signed English. Specifically, virtually the only way in which an analogy of contact signing with spoken language pidgins may hold is with the reduction in morphology. In all other ways, contact signing and spoken language pidgins are quite different in their inventory of features. Compared to English-based pidgins, which consist of mainly English lexical items with English meanings and functions in a reduced English morphological and syntactic system, contact signing uniquely combines ASL and ASL-like lexical items in a reduced English syntactic system.

The outcome of this language contact situation appears to be a kind of code-mixing that is quite different from those described thus far for spoken

**Table VI**

Comparison of Linguistic Features among Various Systems

| Features | Spoken English | ASL | Signed English | Contact Signing | English-based Spoken Language Pidgins[a] |
|---|---|---|---|---|---|
| Lexical form | English | ASL | ASL, ASL-like signs, non-ASL-like signs, spoken English | ASL and ASL-like signs, English mouthing | English, some substrate, some idiosyncratic |
| Lexical function and meaning | English | ASL | English | ASL, idiosyncratic, English | Usually English, some idiosyncratic |
| Morphology | English | ASL | Reduced English and ASL, signed representation of bound morphemes | Reduced ASL and English, reduction and/or absence of nonmanual signals | Reduced English |
| Syntax | English | ASL | Reduced English | Reduced English, some idiosyncratic constructions, code-switching to ASL | Basically SVO, reduced use of pronouns and prepositions, embedding rare |

[a]From Mühlhäusler (1986).

languages. For example, Bokamba (1985, p. 4) defines code-switching as an *inter*sentential event, the embedding or mixing of words, phrases, and sentences from two codes within the same speech event and across sentence boundaries. And code-mixing is an *intra*sentential event, the embedding or mixing of various linguistic units, that is, affixes, words, phrases, and clauses from two distinct grammatical systems or subsystems within the same sentence and the same speech situation. Kachru (1978b) and Sridhar and Sridhar (1980) offer similar definitions. Central to understanding both code-switching and code-mixing in spoken languages is that even though the parts of two different codes can be switched intersententially or mixed intrasententially, the switching or mixing is sequential in nature, as opposed to being simultaneous. That is, units in spoken languages, whether phonological, morphological, or syntactic, are necessarily produced one after the other. If, in a code-mixing situation, the verb of one language is marked with an inflection from another language, this event is also sequential, that is, first the verb is produced, followed by the inflection. It is safe to say that code-mixing, for spoken languages, does not mean the consistent use of the lexical items of one language in the syntactic system of another.

There may be some parallels to code-mixing in Whinnom's (1971) description of cocoliche, the Spanish spoken by Italian immigrants in Argentina (but not spoken by Argentines). After introducing the notion of linguistic hybridization, he (1971, p. 97) observes:

> It is a now despised formula of "primitive" creolistics that pidgin is made up of the vocabulary of one language and the grammar of another. The observation may be faulty but it reflects a basic reality. It is, moreover, a description which fits very well certain linguistic phenomena ("secondary languages") associated with naive language learning.

At the least intense level of hybridization that he describes, Spanish lexical items (nouns, adjectives, verb radicals) are imported into an Italian morphosyntactical system without interfering with the native phonological system, a phenomenon that seems to parallel contact signing. Contact signing, however, appears to be unique in another way. In spoken language contact situations, speakers have at their disposal the phonological, morphological, syntactic, and discourse components of two or more languages, and it is possible to imagine a simultaneous mix of, say, the phonology of one language with the morphology of another, or the morphology of one with the syntax of another. It seems, however, the mixing *within* components, while possible, is necessarily sequential. That is, it seems impossible to simultaneously produce two phonological events from two different spoken languages. In the contact signing described here, however, in which a signer produces ASL lexical items on the hands and simultaneously mouths the corresponding English lexical items, the result is the simultaneous production of two separate codes. This appears to be a unique kind of code-mixing, different from what has been described for spoken language contact situations to date.[7]

The outcome of contact between ASL and English is not entirely predictable. The outcome *could* simply be a modified form of ASL, or it could be code-switching and code-mixing of the sequential type described for spoken languages. In fact, many of the instances of sequential switching observed in the present data are distinct from contact signing. An example is the following:

+mouthing ———————————————————————————→

THEY HAVE #KNOWLEDGE OF WHAT DEAF CULTURE #IS ABOUT

+mouthing ———————————→    −mouthing        +mouthing ——→

EXPOSURE TO #IT        SEE (inflected)   NOT IDIOTS

'They have knowledge of what deaf culture is about, exposure to it.
They have seen it for a long time. They are not idiots.'

In this example, the informant switches from contact signing (with mouthing of English lexical items) to an inflected form of the ASL sign SEE. This inflected form is a two-handed sign with a V handshape, produced in alternating elliptical circles away from the signer's face. It can be glossed as SEE FOR A LONG TIME. It is important to note that during the switch, the mouthing of English is interrupted and then resumed immediately following the sign.

There are also examples of simultaneous production of contact signing and ASL, such as the following:

Right hand

$\qquad\qquad\qquad\qquad\qquad\qquad\qquad$ + mouthing

ONE FRIEND POINT (to 1-CL on left hand) HEARING POINT (to 1-CL)

+ mouthing ———————————→

#ADOPT BY DEAF PARENT POINT (to 1-CL)

Left hand:

1-CL 'friend' ————————————————————————————————

'One friend was adopted by deaf parents.'

---

[7]The situation is somewhat analogous to the one described by Gumperz and Wilson (1971, p. 155) as convergence, where he claims that a single syntactic surface structure is the result of the extended contact between three languages. The outcome of the ASL-English situation is different, however, in that its basic syntactic structure is English. It should be noted that in spoken language contact, there could conceivably exist a simultaneous mixing of *features* within a single phonological segment, and it is this kind of mixing that probably accounts for certain kinds of accents. Our data are different, however, in that we see the simultaneous production of two complete segments (as opposed to features of segments) from two distinct phonologies, each segment retaining its integrity.

In this example, the informant starts out with ONE FRIEND and then points to a classifier predicate being produced with the left hand. (1-CL is the classifier predicate produced with a 1 handshape.) It represents the friend in question, and the use of that predicate is a feature of ASL. The left hand shaping the 1-CL, stays in place while the right hand produces contact signing with mouthing of English. (#ADOPT represents fingerspelling). That is, the left hand produces ASL, while the right hand and the mouth produce contact signing. A feature of contact signing is thus this simultaneous production of some ASL features, a phenomenon that must be distinguished from switches away from contact signing to ASL, as in the *SEE* example.

Contact signing is also clearly distinct from Signed English, as can be seen in Table VI. Although contact signing can involve the silent mouthing of English lexical items, for example, Signed English can involve spoken (voiced) English, including bound morphemes. Also, Signed English can include invented, non-ASL-like signs, and bound English morphemes can be represented manually.

We observed earlier in this paper that we are reluctant at this point to call the contact signing that we have observed a *variety* or a *dialect,* that is, a discrete and consistent linguistic system. Our examination of the linguistic features of contact signing would seem to justify our reluctance. Bob Johnson (personal communication) has observed that, due to the wide variety of language skills and backgrounds and educational backgrounds that signers bring with them to language contact situations, the best way to describe the outcome of language contact in the American deaf community may be as a collection of individual grammars. Further description of our data will shed light on his observation.

## *SOCIOLINGUISTIC FEATURES OF CONTACT SIGNING*

Sociolinguistically, the language contact situation in the deaf community also does not reflect a pidgin. It is clear that not all language contact situations result in pidginization. As Grosjean (1982, p. 38) succinctly summarizes this issue,

> The usual outcome of bilingualism . . . is a return to monolingualism: this may take the form of maintenance of the group's second language and the disappearance of the first language (often referred to as mother-tongue displacement or language shift); or the evolution to a new language through processes of pidginization and creolization.

In a review of the state of the art in interlinguistics, Muysken (1984) lists third-language creation, dialect shift, foreign accent, code-switching, relex-ification, code-mixing, and foreigner talk as possible outcomes in a language contact situation. Further, there has been continuous and vigorous debate about the fundamental nature of pidgins and pidginization at least since Hall's pioneering work in the 1960s, with DeCamp (1971), Alleyne (1971) Whinnom (1971), Bickerton (1975, 1977, 1981, 1984), Samarin (1971), Ferguson and DeBose (1977), Todd (1974), Kay and Sankoff (1974), Rickford (1981), Sankoff (1984), and Mühlhäusler (1986). However, there is apparently a basic convergence of opinion about the unique nature of pidginization in having at its inception a very particular set of sociolinguistic circumstances. As Barbag-Stoll (1983, p. 24) observes,

> The fundamental condition for the occurrence of pidginization is a contact situation involving two or more different languages. This should by no means imply, however, that any contact of two or more languages will result in hybridization. If the source languages are closely related, the output product is more likely to be a dialect, as the prevailing process will be substitution rather than simplification. If the spread of the source language is symmetrical when it is learnt through formal means, it is likely to result in bilingualism. Whether the output is a pidgin or a standard language depends on the degree of availability of target models and the extent to which they are exposed to the learners. If the standard language models are easily accessible and if the nature of the contact situation is such that the speaker interacts mostly with native speakers of the target language, he is most likely to learn the non-pidginized version of it. However, if the target language is spoken mainly with non-native speakers and the target models are rare, the output will most probably be pidgin.

Barbag-Stoll stresses the availability of target models and the extent to which learners are exposed to them as central to the pidginization process. Hall (1962) emphasizes that the language in question is not native to any of its users. DeCamp (1971, p. 15) defines a pidgin as "a contact vernacular, normally not the native language of any of its speakers. It is used in trading or in any situation requiring communication between persons who do not speak each other's native language." DeCamp goes on to say that pidgins are characterized by limited vocabularies, elimination of many grammatical devices such as number and gender, and drastic reduction of redundant features. But he cautions against equating this reduction with simplification. Bickerton (1975) states that at the inception of the pidgin-creole cycle, future pidgin speakers already have established grammars of their own and, in fact, are often multilingual. They are confronted by the grammar of the superstrate language and then removed both from their own language communities and from the target superstrate language. In later work, Bickerton (1977, pp. 49, 54) characterized pidginization as akin to

> second-language learning with restricted input . . . We can conclude that

> pidginization is a process that begins by the speaker using his native tongue
> and relexifying first only a few key words; that, in the earliest stages, even the
> few superstrate words will be thoroughly rephonologized to accord with
> substrate sound system and phonotactics; that subsequently, more super-
> strate lexicon will be acquired but may still be rephonologized to varying
> degrees and will be, for the most part, slotted into syntactic surface struc-
> tures drawn from the substrate; that even substrate syntax will be partially
> retained, and will alternate, apparently unpredictably, with structures im-
> ported from the superstrate.

Pidginization, then, is clearly the result of a unique kind of language contact, and the key elements in understanding the pidginization process appear to be the relative access to the target model, the lack of a mutually
intelligible language among interlocutors, the immediate need for communication, and the interruption of access to one's native language.

Although one result of language contact in the American deaf community is labeled Pidgin Sign English, the sociolinguistic situation in this community does not coincide with the "classic" pidgin situation or with any of
its key elements. Let us assume, for example, that English is considered the
superstrate language in the deaf community. Clearly it is the native language of hearing users of contact signing. But even deaf native ASL signers,
for whom English may not be a native language, have extensive exposure to
and contact with English in various forms, first in educational settings and
later in their adult lives through employment, interaction with hearing
people, and through print and broadcast media. This exposure to and
contact with English is accompanied by ongoing ASL interaction with other
native signers. The result for such native ASL signers in American society is
a maintained bilingualism, wrought from the many different kinds of contact situations occurring in the deaf community and dependent on the
participants' characteristics.

Again, we see parallels with Whinnom's (1971) description of cocoliche.
One reason for the occurrence of cocoliche is the resistance to full integration into the Spanish-speaking community. This invites speculation about a
signer's choice of contact signing, for example, over strict signed English.
Furthermore, because cocoliche represents a form of second-language
learning, Whinnom points out that the speech of any two individual cocoliche speakers can never be even nearly identical. This has clear parallels with the diversity of educational backgrounds of individuals in the deaf
community and what, as a consequence, they bring with them to a contact
situation. But Whinnom also points out that with cocoliche, the pressures
of formal language instruction do not contribute to language use. This
represents an important difference with the deaf community, as the role of
English in contact signing, owing directly to its role in the educational

system, cannot be discounted. The present study describes some of the linguistic and sociolinguistic outcomes of language contact in the deaf community, and reveals the situation to be considerably more complex than earlier descriptions have indicated. One interesting and perhaps ironic fact about the linguistic outcome is the occurrence of English structural features in contact signing, features which do *not* include the invented signs that are part of the manual codes for English that have been implemented in the educational system. One part of the irony lies in the fact that there is considerable use in the educational system of these manual codes, and it would not be unreasonable to predict that elements of these codes would occur in bilingual contact situations. However, very little evidence of those codes was found in the data described here. Another part of the irony has to do with the generally negative reception that these codes have received from members of the deaf community (Baker and Cokely, 1980). It should be clear from the present study that resistance to invented codes for English should not be mistaken for resistance to English per se, as the indigenous, natural signing that occurs as a result of the contact between bilinguals has many English features. Clearly the social stigma about invented systems does not preclude the occurrence of English features. The crucial difference is the difference between an invented representation of a language imposed on its users, and a naturally occurring form of language observed not only in deaf–hearing interaction, but also in the interaction of deaf native ASL users with each other.

Some final speculation about the future of language contact in the deaf community: In this study, we have described the occurrence of contact signing in situations where ASL might be predicted, i.e. between deaf individuals who are native ASL users. We have suggested that the occurrence of "other than ASL" can be accounted for by a variety of sociolinguistic factors, including lack of familiarity between participants or formality of the situation. Clearly, the choice of "other than ASL" is being made in some situations; "other than ASL" is clearly seen as more appropriate in some situations. If this were not so, native ASL users who choose ASL in some situations would use it in situations where they now choose "other than ASL." By way of conclusion, we suggest, as have other researchers (e.g. Stokoe, 1969), that the choice of "other than ASL" and the view that ASL is not appropriate for some situations are the direct results of a sociolinguistic situation in which ASL has been ignored and devalued, and in which the focus has traditionally been on the instruction and use of English. We suggest that, as ASL become more highly valued and becomes formally and fully recognized and used as a legitimate tool for communication in any situation, that the outcome of language contact in the American deaf community will change noticeably.

## ACKNOWLEDGMENTS

We are grateful to Scott Liddell, Walt Wolfram, and Bob Johnson for providing very detailed and valuable feedback on this chapter. This research has been supported since 1986 by the Gallaudet Research Institute, and by the Office of the Provost, Gallaudet University. We gratefully acknowledge this support, and in particular, would like to recognize Dr. Michael A. Karchmer, Dean of Graduate Studies and Research. We would also like to thank our informants and judges.

# 3

# Ethnicity and Socialization in a Classroom for Deaf Children

Robert E. Johnson and Carol Erting

> Society, identity and reality are subjectively crystallized in the same process of internalization. This crystallization is concurrent with the internalization of language. Indeed . . . language constitutes both the most important content and the most important instrument of socialization.—Berger and Luckmann, *The Social Construction of Reality*

The American deaf community and its language have been the subject of serious inquiry for about three decades. Many of the studies deal with some aspect of the grammatical structure of American Sign Language (see Klima & Bellugi, 1979; and Wilbur, 1987, for summaries of this research) and, collectively, the research demonstrates that American Sign Language (ASL) is a well-developed polysynthetic language, autonomous in structure from English. Additional extensive work by a number of scholars shows that ASL includes certain features exclusive to and well-adapted to language in a manual modality, as well as other features apparently shared among all languages (Fischer and Gough, 1978; Johnson and Liddell, 1984; Liddell, 1980, 1984; Liddell and Johnson, 1986; Lillo-Martin, 1986; Markowicz, 1980; Padden, 1983; Padden and Perlmutter, 1987).

It is also well-documented that sign language use in the United States is subject to broad variation, where signing ranges between varieties of ASL and varieties more reminiscent of English. The choice of language variety employed in a specific situation is reflective of membership in—and attitudes about—the deaf community. The situation has been described as one of bilingual diglossia (Markowicz and Woodward, 1978; Stokoe, 1969;

THE SOCIOLINGUISTICS OF THE DEAF COMMUNITY
Copyright © 1989 by Academic Press Inc.
All rights of reproduction in any form reserved.

Woodward, 1973a; Woodward and Markowicz, 1975) in which the more English-like varieties are used for out-group functions, specifically interaction with hearing people or interaction characterized by a strong social force for mainstream, hearing-oriented interpretations. ASL, on the other hand, is generally used for in-group functions, such as casual communication in an all-Deaf group.[1] Markowicz and Woodward (1978) propose that such variation indicates attitudes about membership in the American Deaf community and, as such, functions largely as a device for maintaining an ethnic boundary between hearing and deaf people. More recent treatments (Davis, this volume; Lee, 1982; Lucas and Valli, this volume) question the use of the term diglossia with reference to sign language variety in the American deaf community, proposing instead to describe the phenomenon as a combination of switching and mixing among varieties. The point remains true, however, that language users' perceptions of the social forces at work in a situation determine which varieties of signing are likely to occur.

These facts about language variation and contextual sensitivity of usage reflect the social constructions that in part constitute the deaf experience in the United States. It is these social constructions that are the subject of examination in this chapter.

This chapter has two major parts.[2] The first part proposes a theoretical framework for viewing social, linguistic, and cultural aspects of the American deaf community. In it, we focus on two kinds of social forces that have led to the constitution and maintenance of ethnic boundaries around Deaf people as a group. The first of these forces originates within the group itself and emerges from attitudes and values surrounding the use of ASL and notions of appropriate behavior for group members. The second force emerges from the interaction of Deaf people with mainstream society in their attempts to achieve access to socioeconomic benefits of that society. In our view, the dynamic tension between these two forces constitutes a

---

[1]We have adopted the use of "deaf" (with lower case *d*) as an adjective referring primarily to hearing loss, and the use of "Deaf" (with upper-case *D*) as an adjective referring to social collectivities and attitudes arising from interaction among people with hearing losses. This distinction was made first by Woodward (1972) and later explained by Erting and Woodward (1974). A similar distinction is standard in the literature on the "Deaf Community", although the distinction as we use it in this chapter is more narrowly drawn.

[2]An earlier version of this chapter was published under the title "Linguistic Socialization in the Context of Deaf Ethnicity" by the Wenner-Gren Foundation Working Papers in Anthropology, edited by Keith T. Kernan, in 1984. In addition, the earliest presentation of our classroom observations was made to a Plenary Session of the annual meeting of the American Anthropological Association in 1979 under the title "Sign, Socialization, and Solidarity." We are grateful to Hugh Mehan, Peg Griffin, James Woodward, Courtney Cazden, Carol Padden, McKay Vernon, Joshua Fishman, and Harlan Lane for their comments and criticisms of our formulations.

Deaf group that shares numerous characteristics with what are called ethnic groups. We argue that both kinds of pressure for group constitution are made evident through symbolic language use of the sort described above.

The second part of this chapter demonstrates the emergence of some elements of ethnicity among four-year-old deaf children. We suggest that symbolic language use has important implications for the socialization of deaf children and propose that evidence of the complex social and linguistic situation can be found in the linguistic interaction of deaf students with each other and with their teachers. Drawing on this proposition, we suggest that certain classrooms for deaf children reflect these structural properties of the adult deaf community. In addition, we propose that these properties will be most apparent in classrooms that are composed of a mixture of children with deaf parents and children with hearing parents and that involve both hearing and deaf adults. In the course of this discussion, we demonstrate that the interaction occurring in the classroom gives rise to and contributes to the continuity of the sociolinguistic properties of the adult deaf community; the classroom is at least in part the source of the adult sociolinguistic situation as well as a reflection of it. We examine these notions through the investigation of language variation and linguistic socialization in a day school classroom for deaf children.

## ETHNICITY, SOCIAL PROCESS, AND LANGUAGE

From the perspective of Deaf people in the United States, deafness must be viewed as more than just a physical disability; it is also a set of attitudes and behaviors. When Deaf people talk about being Deaf and about what Deaf people have in common, they have more in mind than audiological status. Even though it is true that some degree of hearing loss is necessary for a person to be Deaf, the loss of hearing *per se* is not the critical variable. Many individuals have only a minor hearing impairment in audiological terms but still are recognized as Deaf people according to social and cultural criteria. On the other hand, some people with very profound hearing losses are not considered to be Deaf according to those same criteria.

This observation is by no means new. A review of the literature reveals numerous references to Deaf people as a linguistic and sociocultural minority group (Carmel, 1976; Croneberg, 1976; Erting, 1978; Flournoy, 1856; Higgins, 1987a, 1987b; Jacobs, 1974; Lunde, 1956; Markowicz and Woodward, 1978; Meadow, 1972; Mow, 1970; J. W. Nash and Nash, 1981; Padden, 1980; Padden and Markowicz, 1975; Peet, 1871; Stokoe, 1960; Veditz, 1913; Vernon and Makowsky, 1969). These authors all emphasize the importance of American Sign Language as a unifying force in the composition of this group. Some authors, drawing upon Barth's (1969) theoretical contributions in the area of ethnicity, discuss the role of self-recognition and recognition by others as critical to the formation and maintenance of ethnic groups and highlight the role of ASL in the maintenance of the boundary between the Deaf group and outsiders (Markowicz and Woodward, 1978; Padden and Markowicz, 1975). Most discussions of the sociocultural aspects of deafness, however, in identifying the Deaf group, use the terms community, minority group, ethnic group, subculture, and culture virtually interchangeably. The status of this group is somewhat blurred by this proliferation of terminology. One treatment of the subject makes the now common distinction between a deaf community, a group of Deaf and hearing individuals who work to achieve certain goals, and a Deaf Culture, another group to which certain Deaf members of that community belong (Padden, 1980).

The treatments mentioned above have at least one characteristic in common: they are taxonomic.[3] They are basically labeling theories (Mehan and Griffin, 1979), which place people in groups on the basis of interpretations made by those who are doing the labeling. Sets of traits that define the behaviors and attitudes of the members of a Deaf group are identified, and individuals are labeled as Deaf or not depending upon the extent to which they exhibit those traits. Such labels can correspond to salient behaviors and values of a cultural group but they are unlikely to provide substantial insight into the processes that account for the emergence and maintenance of those values and behaviors as identifying features.

Our approach emphasizes interaction and process rather than taxonomic features. For this reason, we align ourselves theoretically with anthropologists who study phenomena similar to the Deaf sociocultural experience under the title of ethnicity. This framework appears to hold the most promise as a means of elucidating the social processes involved in the formation and maintenance of certain social groups. For our purposes, this approach provides the best means of studying the interaction of group members among themselves as well as the interaction of members with nonmembers.

## *Ethnicity*

Definitions of ethnicity abound. They vary widely in content and scope. This alone makes any discussion of ethnicity difficult. Our arguments and assumptions derive from the position that ethnicity is an intragroup as well as an intergroup phenomenon (Patterson, 1983; Royce, 1982). We will thus draw upon definitions of ethnicity that are concerned with processes internal to the ethnic group and also definitions that focus on interactional

---

[3]Padden and Humphries (1988) present another perspective, which emphasizes the centrality of ASL in the constitution of the group and focuses on its contribution to a Geertzian complex of interpretations that make up culture.

processes occurring at contact points between ethnic group members and outsiders. Barth (1969) and J. Fishman (1977) both argue that the notions of self-recognition and recognition by others are central elements in the definition of an ethnic collectivity; that is, members of such a collectivity recognize themselves as being members, and outsiders also recognize those members as being part of the ethnic group. As such, an ethnic group makes up a "field of communication and interaction" (Barth, 1969, p. 11), both for members with other members and for members with outsiders. This emphasis on communicative interaction within and between ethnic groups is especially relevant to this study. We will argue that sign language variety and socialization into the norms of bilingual language use are two of the phenomena that most strongly contribute to the formation and maintenance of the Deaf ethnic group.

Among the twenty-seven definitions of ethnicity examined by Isajiw (1974), biological aspects such as common ancestors or place of origin were mentioned most often as defining features of ethnicity. J. Fishman (1977) identifies the concept of biological continuity in an ethnic group as paternity, which relates to real or putative biological connections between generations. Paternity in turn is linked to another primary concept called patrimony, which concerns the ways in which members of ethnic collectivities behave and what they do to express membership. Patrimony might be viewed as the trappings of ethnicity, as opposed to paternity, which is the biological legacy of ethnicity. Although one would normally expect patrimony to be acquired with paternity, it is possible to acquire it without paternity, and it is also possible to have paternity without adopting patrimony. We will return to these issues later.

These two aspects of ethnicity, patrimony and paternity, are constituted to a large degree inside the group. They arise internally as a result of the persistence through time of biological and cultural phenomena and account for the internal composition and maintenance of the group.

A different perspective on ethnicity is presented by Cohen, who sees the phenomenon as "essentially a form of interaction between culture groups operating within common social contexts" (1974, p. xi). This corresponds to Barth's arguments for the importance of an interactional approach. Barth (1969, p. 16) suggests that there are rules governing interethnic encounters. These rules structure the interaction in ways that contribute to the persistence of cultural differences and thus exert pressure for group composition and maintenance. The pressure derives not from a focus on internal factors of composition and maintenance but from a focus on the boundaries between the ethnic group and other groups with which its members interact (Isajiw, 1974, p. 122). To the extent that such boundaries reflect and correspond to criteria for access to socioeconomic benefits controlled by the outside group, this kind of pressure for ethnic group maintenance is externally derived. Nonetheless, the values and the rules for behavior that pertain to this boundary or to interaction across it must be seen as significant parts of the cultural knowledge of a competent member of the ethnic group. Thus, the patrimony in an ethnic group must include attitudes and rules for behavior developed from both an internal perspective, relating to notions of the group as an atomic entity, and an external perspective, relating to notions of the group in the context of other groups.

Our theoretical orientation addresses both intragroup processes and intergroup processes in the constitution and maintenance of ethnic groups and the boundaries around them. Regarding intragroup processes, we are concerned with how it is that members recognize themselves and are recognized by other members as belonging to the ethnic group. Central to this concern are the concepts of paternity—involuntary, biological criteria for membership—and patrimony—voluntary, behavioral, and attitudinal indicators of membership.

Our concern with intergroup processes focuses on the boundary between the ethnic group and the outside world. We are interested in how interaction between members and outsiders is structured so that a boundary is formed and maintained, preserving the integrity of the ethnic group in the face of pressures from the outside.

It is important here to distinguish between culture and ethnicity. Ethnicity refers specifically to some degree of conformity to those customary values and rules for behavior that contribute to the social constitution and maintenance of a group. These customary values and rules then also represent the cultural aspect of ethnicity, but culture and ethnicity are not coterminous. Certainly, an ethnic group can persist despite changes in the content of its culture symbols (values) and categories of interaction (rules) (Barth, 1969, p. 29). Similarly, although members of an ethnic group embedded in pluralistic society can share many aspects of cultural content important to survival in generalized contexts of that society, much of that content may have little relevance to the actual constitution and maintenance of the ethnic group. We concur with Horowitz's (1985, p. 69) position that it is "ascriptive affinity and disparity and not some particular inventory of cultural attributes that found the group."

## Ethnic Boundaries Derived from Interaction among Group Members

At first glance, the notion of paternity seems to have little relevance to deafness, for only 3–4 percent of all deaf children are born to two deaf parents, and about 90 percent have two hearing parents (Karchmer, Trybus, and Paquin, 1978; Meadow, 1972; Rawlings, 1973; Trybus and Jensema, 1978). Thus, most deaf children do not share biological origins in the ethnic sense with their parents, but traditionally recognized transmitters of ethnicity. But just as paternity refers to an involuntary biological condition, so deafness involves an involuntary biological condition: hearing impairment.[4] Although the physical characteristic of impaired hearing is not sufficient to insure membership in the Deaf ethnic collectivity, it does appear to be a biologically necessary condition for membership. This biological condition and the experience it engenders constitute the involuntary link to past generations.

Although this somewhat revised notion of biological continuity is crucial to the definition of a Deaf ethnic group, the notion of paternity is applicable to some members of the group exactly as discussed by Fishman in terms of parentage. Many of the 3–4 percent of deaf children who are born to two deaf parents are born into a family with a history of deafness through several generations. These individuals can be seen as core members of the Deaf ethnic collectivity following J. Fishman's (1977, p. 17) argument that "ethnicity is, in part, but at its core, experienced as an inherited constellation acquired from one's parents as they acquired it from theirs, and so on back further and further, *ad infinitum*." Thus, in the case of Deaf ethnicity, we see that the concept of paternity has both an ordinary genealogical and an unusual biological component, with the latter being the necessary condition for membership and the former creating conditions contributing to the formation of a core of members of a diachronically continuous group (compare Becker, 1980, p. 58; Meadow-Orlans, 1987).

Royce (1982, p. 184) suggests that the ethnic identities that demonstrate ascription into a group by means of both birth and socialization are perhaps the most satisfying affectively. Those who meet the biological criteria for membership in ethnic collectivities thus typically also have an obligation to demonstrate particular patterns of behavior that are based on shared cultural knowledge and underlying values. They are evaluated by other members as good members, bad members, or nonmembers depending upon how well they exhibit the behavioral and attitudinal criteria of the group. This behavioral expression of membership in an ethnic collectivity (patrimony) is learned and has been referred to as a "common historical style" (Royce, 1982, p. 18). As such, it is a voluntary condition and is more negotiable and interpretable than the paternity side of ethnicity.[5] Both

---

[4]Isajiw's (1974, p. 122) final composite definition of ethnicity, based on his examination of twenty-seven definitions of ethnicity, refers to the involuntary nature of the ethnic group: "an involuntary group of people who share the same culture or to descendants of such people who identify themselves and/or are identified by others as belonging to the same involuntary group."

[5]While Isajiw's (1974) composite definition of ethnicity expresses this component of ethnicity as shared culture, J. Fishman (1977) is careful to point out that not all of culture is composed of collectivity-defining behavior. Thus, while patrimony and culture are highly interrelated, they are not coterminous. Barth (1969), too, distinguishes between an ethnic group and a culture, preferring to view the former as a form of social organization, a vessel for cultural traits that can change over time and are determined, in part, by ecology.

ethnic patrimony and ethnic paternity are necessary for membership in the Deaf ethnic group, but neither is independently sufficient. Several of the writers mentioned earlier suggest that it is not degree of hearing loss alone that determines membership in the Deaf ethnic group, nor is it strictly Deaf parentage. If a person clearly satisfies the paternity conditions (that is, is profoundly deaf and has Deaf parents) but does not "act like a Deaf person" according to the evaluations of group members, that person is not viewed by others as a member of the group, or at least not as a member in good standing. On the other hand, a person who is audiologically hard-of-hearing but who chooses to be a member of the group and expresses that choice by "acting as a member" might be accepted as a member. Conversely, hearing children of ethnically Deaf parents, whose socialization into Deaf ethnic patrimony may be extensive, may never be considered as members, no matter how "Deaf" they are able to act.

In each of these cases, the focus of patrimony is on certain behavior that symbolizes alignment with the values, attitudes, and norms of the ethnic group. The critical symbol of both paternity and patrimony in the Deaf ethnic group is language choice. As J. Fishman (1977) suggests, language is a trait typically aligned closely with ethnicity. Like ethnicity itself, language is often viewed as a biological inheritance and as a core identifying characteristic of an individual's feelings of belonging to a group. It is not uncommon for Deaf people to express the feeling that individuals who have a biological condition of hearing impairment also have a biological predisposition to communicate in sign language (Erting, 1982). For deaf children with one or two Deaf parents this inheritance of sign language is more apparent, for they learn ASL in an ordinary language acquisition situation, namely through interaction with their families and friends. For deaf children from Deaf families then, ASL is the vessel whereby ethnic patrimony is transmitted between generations. Thus, using ASL with other ethnically Deaf individuals is, in itself, a major part of ethnic patrimony. This is one reason that ASL has come to be a powerful symbol of ethnic group membership and its use a means of exhibiting personal commitment to ethnic group values. We will discuss later the means whereby this symbol is extended from people with Deaf parents to members of the Deaf ethnic group in general.

## Ethnic Boundaries Derived from Interaction with Nonmembers

Defining the deaf experience as primarily a visual experience is the key to understanding the constitution of the Deaf ethnic group (Erting, 1985; Sacks, 1988). As Horowitz (1985, p. 69) argues, the particular characteristics that most clearly define an ethnic collectivity will be those traits that members have in common as compared with the traits of other groups in contact in a single environment. The visual nature of the Deaf person's life experience, so clearly symbolized by the sign language that affirms and communicates Deaf identity within the group, also sets Deaf people apart from the hearing-speaking majority. It creates a "shared crisis of aliena- tion" upon which group consciousness is built and against which interac- tion across the boundary with nonmembers occurs" (Patterson, 1983, p. 25). While Deaf people experience the world and structure their lives ac- cording to a visual culture, they are required to interact with and to depend institutionally upon outsiders who know very little about the Deaf experi- ence and the culture of people who depend primarily upon vision for their knowledge of and interaction with the world.

It is here, in the cross-group interaction, that we see the second bound- ary around the Deaf ethnic group emerge. It defines a stigmatized group, socioeconomically embedded in American society and composed of indi- viduals with a hearing loss.[6] The boundary is created from and is sustained by evaluations of membership and nonmembership based on the degree to which individuals' values and behaviors correspond to those of normative mainstream American society.

Thus, a dynamic tension shapes the daily lives of Deaf individuals. The constraints imposed by deafness cause them to construct their lives in fundamentally different ways from the hearing majority while, at the same time, they must be institutionally dependent upon hearing people, who control their access to the socioeconomic benefits of society at large (Ert- ing, 1982). On one hand, a shared life experience based on a visual culture creates community among Deaf people. Values arising out of their common experiences, along with symbols that come to represent and recreate those experiences and reaffirm those values, unite Deaf people in a common social identity. On the other hand, everyday interactions with hearing peo- ple repeatedly remind Deaf individuals both of their daily struggle to over- come the threat to selfhood that deafness imposes and of their exclusion from full participation in mainstream life. Such interactions emphasize the impossibility of complete acceptance by the majority and therefore the impossibility of movement out of their stigmatized status.

Some of the most significant social values that underlie boundary-relat- ed evaluations of Deaf people are similar to those that affect other so- cioeconomic minorities. In the United States, there are a number of rela- tively rigid criteria for the assimilation of nonmainstream individuals into

---

[6]We are referring here to those individuals who have a hearing loss of relatively early origin and of sufficient severity to influence substantially their ability to communicate using vocal English. In addition, there are millions of people who have lost their hearing in adulthood. For these people, the loss of hearing may range from a minor inconvenience to a serious burden but they tend not to be socially stigmatized as a result of it. Such people have lost their hearing well after the establishment of their identity, which in most cases is only minimally influenced by the loss of hearing.

the mainstream socioeconomic system. One of the most powerful of these is the use of standard varieties of English.

Deaf people are subject to this criterion as well, but there are inflexible obstacles to their assimilation. The major block is the fact that most deaf people are unable to speak English at a level approaching even a minimal standard of vocal proficiency. Moreover, few are able to achieve a level of lipreading proficiency that would allow them to comprehend rapid, casual speech at a level approaching that of a hearing native speaker. These two standards of speech production and comprehension remain the primary criteria that prevent otherwise qualified deaf people from achieving access to a broad range of economic benefits. For deaf people in the United States, oral English proficiency is clearly the primary indicator of acceptability for assimilation and the primary condition for access to social mobility and the valued economic statuses associated with it (Miller, 1970; Northcott, 1981; Van Uden, 1968). In this sense, proficiency in spoken English, or lack thereof, is the major factor defining an externally constituted boundary around deaf people as a socioeconomic group.

The biological criteria for defining this boundary carry attitudinal valences opposite to those that define the Deaf ethnic group. Hearing loss, from the perspective of socioeconomic mobility, is a negatively valued characteristic, whereas, from the perspective of the ethnic group, it is positively valued.[7] It is significant also that while the degree of audiological hearing loss is largely irrelevant to the criterion of ethnic paternity, the degree of hearing loss of an individual generally is inversely proportional to that person's assimilability. Those who have heard more English and who hear more of their own speech are able more closely to approximate standard varieties of English speech. For this reason, with few exceptions, fully assimilated hearing-impaired people either have relatively minor hearing losses or became deaf well after their acquisition of vocal English.[8] Conversely, people with comparatively greater hearing losses often encounter more difficulty assimilating. Thus a person's audiological history is one characteristic defining that person's relationship to the socioeconomic boundary.

This externally derived boundary is also partially constituted and main-

[7]Padden and Humphries (1988, p. 17), in discussing this issue, point to the fact that the word "deaf" to Deaf people means "like us," whereas the same word to hearing people means "not like us." It is this sort of double-sided meaning, permeating the Deaf experience, that we refer to as a dynamic tension.

[8]Because our research deals with prelingually deaf children, we make only passing reference to adventitiously deaf people. To be sure, such individuals would be an interesting test case for the notion that patrimony is voluntary. The extent to which these deaf individuals are able to "act Deaf" and not "act hearing" would presumably be a measure of their ethnicity. Conversely, the extent to which they are unable or unwilling to throw off the attitudes and behaviors of hearing society would be a measure of the skepticism with which they are met by the Deaf ethnic group.

tained through certain patterns of interaction, which appear to be graded by degree of hearing loss. Because the boundary here is one relating to access to socioeconomic benefits, the significant interaction is between deaf people and members of mainstream hearing society. Clearly, people who successfully "cross" the boundary are accepted by virtue of being able to act properly in mainstream contexts. Proper behavior in this respect boils down to knowing and applying norms for the use of spoken English, because almost all Deaf people—assimilated or not—share a basic core of American values and behavioral norms with hearing people. Deaf individuals who have successfully assimilated often emphasize the positive ramifications of using English and the negative ramifications of not speaking and not assimilating. Such individuals, then, not only know how to interact successfully in encounters with hearing people but also exhibit attitudes closely approaching those of mainstream hearing norms. Thus, biological and interactional traits combine to provide an indication of ease of assimilation, defined in terms of the language and the values of normative mainstream society and the outsider's view of deafness as simply audiological hearing loss.

This situation results in roughly the same phenomenon as that encountered by many other American minority groups. The logic of this view contends that those deaf people who do successfully assimilate are those who can and will assimilate. This is taken as evidence that all deaf people can assimilate if they will and is seemingly verified by the successes of those who have assimilated. The outcome of this logic is that those who do not assimilate are said not to want to assimilate. Thus, the fact that many deaf people do not readily assimilate is often blamed on laziness, stubbornness, "negative effects" of using ASL, or excessive association with other Deaf people, rather than on the more realistic explanation of inability to learn acceptable spoken English.

Padden (1980) identifies a group she calls "the deaf community," which is composed of both hearing people and deaf people and is constituted around goals important to deaf people. She opposes this group to one she calls "the Deaf Culture." Although this insightful formulation is widely accepted, we do not find it useful to view communities as groups. In contrast, following our earlier discussion, the reference here is to an *interethnic contact community* that emerges from interaction among deaf and hearing people. This interaction takes place around the issues that arise as deaf people attempt to gain access to scarce socioeconomic resources and involves a wide variety of participants whose encounters tend to occur in society at large. These participants, however, do not constitute a well-defined group analogous to the Deaf ethnic group discussed earlier. Instead, their interactions come about more accidentally and randomly.

Padden (1980) implies that the deaf community is composed of deaf and hearing people who interact fairly customarily around the issues of access.

In this group would be included hearing service providers such as vocational rehabilitation counselors, interpreters, teachers, and the like. Our view of the interethnic contact community is much more broadly taken, and emerges from the totality of interactions between deaf people and hearing people, whether informed or naive.

Recently, it has been proposed that service providers constitute a "third culture" (e.g., Bienvenu, 1987). There is little evidence, however, to support this proposal. Although service providers constitute a fairly well-defined group of people—that is, all are at least moderately competent signers, all earn their living from service to the deaf, and all share certain normative behavioral and attitudinal values—this constellation of attributes, albeit "cultural," does not carry the force necessary to be labeled a "culture," except in the sense used to characterize groups such as longshoremen (Pilcher, 1972), heroine addicts (Agar, 1973), and cocktail waitresses (J. Spradley and Mann, 1975).

For a Deaf person, most interactions in the interethnic contact community involve hearing people, who very often control access to resources such as employment, education, and important services (Higgins, 1987a, 1987b; M. Sussman, 1965). For interactions in the interethnic contact community, the use of a language variety marked as English both enhances communication (hearing people, even those who can sign some, seldom know ASL) and symbolizes a deaf individual's suitability for access to resources. Such English-marked varieties can be any of three forms, depending on the linguistic background and attitudes of the participants and the features of the situation. In certain cases, the form can be vocal or written English, particularly if the hearing individuals in the contact situation have no access to signing. In other cases, the English-marked variety takes the form of sign-supported speech, which involves the use of a manual code for English and simultaneous speech or speech-like mouth movements. The third form of English-marked communication is a fluent contact variety of English signing (Lucas and Valli, 1987), previously called Pidgin Sign English (PSE).

In general, these three varieties represent choices with successively decreasing levels of symbolic salience with respect to ease of assimilation. That is, from the perspective of mainstream norms, vocal and written English are most highly valued, sign-supported speech is next, and English signing is least highly valued, although as a variety of signing marked as English it is symbolically superior to ASL.

Because of the socioeconomic necessity of using English in the contact community, those individuals who are ethnically Deaf in the sense described earlier find themselves tending to use ASL in ethnic group contexts and English-marked signing in contact community contexts. This type of variation was originally labeled as bilingual diglossia (Ferguson, 1959; Stokoe, 1969; Woodward, 1973c).

More recently, it is argued on both theoretical grounds (Lee, 1982) and descriptive grounds (Davis, this volume; Lucas and Valli, 1987) that the nature of the variation is not well characterized by the traditional concept of diglossia. The pattern of switching and mixing between ASL and English contact varieties, however, does follow the expected pattern whereby one variety—ASL—is used in in-group contexts and others—English contact varieties—are used in contexts invested with mainstream interpretations.

The norms for this kind of variation must be viewed as a part of the patrimony of Deaf ethnicity, for knowing when and with whom to use ASL and when and with whom to use English-marked varieties is an important part of being recognized as Deaf. Shifting between varieties according to social forces present in situations is fully appropriate and expected behavior for an ethnically Deaf person.[9] From the perspective of the aspects of patrimony, then, the use of either ASL or an English-marked variety accomplishes two things: (1) it symbolizes some of the values of the social group and the individual's conformity to those values (either of the Deaf ethnic group or of normative mainstream American society) and (2) it enhances communication among the individuals typically interacting in certain kinds of situations. Thus, in a situation including hearing people, either as participants or observers, and in other situations bearing interpretations related to socioeconomic mobility, some form of English-marked signing will most likely be the language of choice, even between two ethnically Deaf interlocutors. The use of ASL in such contexts might in fact be viewed as inappropriate. This situation has led to the frequent conclusion that a shift away from ASL to an English-marked variety, in effect, functions to restrict hearing people from easily learning ASL (Markowicz and Woodward, 1978). To the extent that this is true, ASL remains largely in the hands of Deaf people and the few hearing people who have obtained the ability to remain unnoticed in an otherwise all-Deaf group. This largely exclusive ownership of ASL is undoubtedly an additional factor in its symbolic attachment to Deaf ethnicity.

From the opposite perspective, the use of a symbolically salient variety of English by a deaf person in a situation with strong ethnic group interpretations will probably be viewed either as ironic or as inappropriate, if not as an outright demonstration of rejection of ethnic group values. In such a situation, the more salient the English symbol, the stronger the

---

[9]The frequent reference to a *diglossic continuum* in the literature represents the fact that, given strong contextual pressure for the use of English, the actual signed English sentences produced can vary in their closeness or approximation to the structure of spoken English sentences. This variation appears to be a function of a complex of factors, including the bilingual competence of the signer, the amount of attention given to the fact that English is being signed, the perceived linguistic and attitudinal orientations of the receiver, and the third persons present. For the purpose of this paper, we focus on the idealized varieties: ASL, English signing, and sign-supported speech.

potential for irony or implied rejection. Thus, from an internal perspective, the symbolic salience of the language varieties is the opposite of that in contact community interactions.

In summary, we have discussed two kinds of processes for constitution and maintenance of the boundary around the Deaf group: one emerging from interaction among Deaf people, and the other from interaction between deaf and hearing people. We have contended that the boundary is evidenced by the symbolic choice of sign language varieties. But the symbols resulting from one process originate within the traditions of the Deaf ethnic group, while those resulting from the other process originate in the norms of mainstream American society and the position of hearing-impaired people as a stigmatized group embedded within it. A given individual can participate in both the Deaf ethnic group and the deaf contact community, but it is not necessarily true that participation in the contact community implies membership in the Deaf ethnic group. The symbolism of language choice communicates where a person stands with respect to the values of the Deaf ethnic group and mainstream American society in given situations. Thus, individuals must be socialized not only into one or both groups but also into the norms for communicating their conformity to the values and rules of the group.

## Socialization and the Maintenance of Ethnic Boundaries

Our use of the word socialization follows Mehan's (1980, p. 134) definition as "the process by which culture is transmitted from one generation to the next." He suggests that culture is competent membership in a community, where competence is viewed as the skills and knowledge necessary for participation in that community. Socialization, then, becomes the "interactional and symbolic process involved in the transmission and acquisition of cultural knowledge" (Mehan, 1980, p. 134).

In contrast to more sociological views of socialization (e.g., Meadow-Orlans, 1987), this definition of socialization requires that we make social situations the units of analysis. This means that we must investigate cultural competence as it is learned in the context of specific kinds of social interactions. According to this view, socialization occurs as children learn to become competent participants in the various social situations in which they find themselves. This process of cultural acquisition (socialization) is parallel and analogous to the processes now identified as language acquisition. This is a departure from the more traditional view of socialization as a unidirectional process, from competent adult to incompetent child. It depends rather, on the view that adults are seen to present a competent model through everyday interaction while children seek to create their own cultural interpretations through their active participation in that interaction. This perspective is crucial because it leads us to ask questions about the contributions of both children and adults to the socialization process.

There are rules to be learned and followed if one is to act as a competent member of a group, and it is important to see all members as potential recipients and transmitters of social information. In fact, adults and children may socialize each other. Several studies of classrooms as culture-bearing communities (Griffin and Humphry, 1978; McDermott and Gospodinoff, 1981; Mehan, 1980; Schultz, 1976) demonstrate that children socialize teachers, teachers socialize children, and children socialize other children into competent membership. This is not a one-way process. It is a subtle, complex give-and-take between individuals, embedded in everyday participation in familiar events.

An interactional approach to socialization with its emphasis on competent membership is particularly suited to the investigation of the formation and maintenance of the Deaf ethnic group, since the peer group appears to be most responsible for socializing new members. It is in this respect that Deaf ethnicity diverges most from the ethnicity of traditionally recognized groups. For most deaf children, there is no model of competent cultural interaction available until contact is made with some arm of the educational system. The only deaf children who are socialized as early as infancy are those few whose parents are members of the Deaf ethnic group themselves. Deaf children of Deaf parents are thus important for two reasons. First, these children are being socialized into the Deaf ethnic group through interaction with their Deaf parents (Erting, Prezioso, and O'Grady Hynes, 1987), and, second, deaf children from Deaf families typically have both the paternity and patrimony of Deaf ethnicity.

Owing to this dual legacy, deaf children from Deaf families are the primary socializing agents available to potential members of the ethnic group, that is, individuals who have the paternity (hearing loss) but have hearing parents who cannot be agents for the transmission of Deaf patrimony. Moreover, the socialization of potential members typically begins only after these two groups come into contact in the educational system. In this way, Deaf patrimony is passed from one generation to the next within the core group and extended to the rest of the group largely through interaction among peers.[10] It is for these reasons that schools are especially relevant settings for the study of socialization into the Deaf ethnic group.

[10]The emphasis on peer socialization arises also from practices of the educational establishment. With only few exceptions, primary programs for deaf children employ an overwhelming majority of hearing teachers. Most deaf teachers are clustered in the higher grade-levels and at the secondary level. This is probably an artifact of the old belief that early exposure to ASL hinders the learning of speech. The indirect impact on socialization is the removal of many potential adult socializing agents from access to the youngest deaf children in the system.

# INTERACTION IN A DEAF CLASSROOM

The present study is concerned with the communicative interaction of preschool deaf children and their teachers in their day-to-day activities. Our interest is twofold: first, we attempt to isolate and verify manifestations of emergent Deaf ethnicity as constituted in the interaction between children and adults; second, we demonstrate some aspects of the mechanics of socialization into those parts of patrimony that pertain to the symbolism of language choice.

The group of individuals under study consists of eight four- and five-year-old children, all reported to be of normal or better intelligence and none exhibiting disabilities other than deafness. Four of the children are from Deaf families and four are from hearing families. Table I summarizes the characteristics of the children that are at least potential influences on their behavior in the context of the classroom. The teacher is hearing and communicates with the children through a localized variety of sign-supported speech (SSS).[11] She is assisted by a Deaf teacher's aide who uses ASL, fluent English signing, and SSS with the children.[12]

[11]In this study we distinguish three named varieties of signing: American Sign Language (ASL), sign-supported speech (SSS), and fluent English contact signing. ASL is discussed in the research cited in the introduction. Sign-supported speech is the generic label for a kind of signing that uses signs to represent each word or morpheme of a spoken English utterance. SSS productions are typically performed simultaneously with the spoken English sentences they are intended to represent, although some deaf people using SSS "mouth" the words of the English sentence without voice. SSS is usually used in association with school policies related to the teaching and modeling of English speech since the institution of Total Communication has become the predominant official form of communication in classrooms for Deaf children in the United States. The teacher and aide in this study use a localized variety of Signing Exact English (SEE2), which employs many specially invented signs for English words and morphemes combined with standard signs borrowed from ASL and fingerspelling. We refer to such signs as systematic signs. Even when the signs are ASL signs, however, the productions are not ASL sentences. In SSS sentences the signs are produced in uninflected citation form and as separate, largely unassimilated units.

Another variety of English signing is also employed by the aide in this study. For the sake of brevity, we refer to it as fluent English signing, although a more accurate label might be "fluent English-based, contact-variety signing (Lucas and Valli, this volume). Fluent English signing involves basically English grammatical structure but employs certain syntactic markers and certain features of discourse structure from ASL. In addition, the signs used are primarily ASL signs (rather than invented signs) and are typically subject to the kinds of phonological processes that typically apply in ASL sentences. Lucas and Valli (this volume) demonstrate that both switching and mixing processes account for the degree to which a particular production of fluent English signing approaches either English or ASL.

[12]Such a configuration for a classroom is probably quite unusual. Higgins and Nash (1987) point out that to have a classroom where half of the children have hearing parents and half have deaf parents is rare. It is also unusual to find a teaching team composed of a hearing signer and a lifelong Deaf signer in a classroom for very young deaf children. Residual fears about contamination of English by ASL still tend to confine deaf classroom workers to higher

**Table I**
Discriminating Characteristics of Children in Classroom Corpus

| Name | Age | Sex | Deaf Parents | Residential Institution | Skilled ASL | Degree of Hearing Loss |
|------|-----|-----|--------------|-------------------------|-------------|------------------------|
| R | 4:8 | M | + | − | + | Severe to profound |
| P | 4:3 | F | + | − | + | Profound |
| L | 5:9 | F | − | + | + | Profound |
| F | 4:6 | F | + | − | + | Profound |
| Sc | 5:11 | M | − | − | − | Severe |
| Su | 5:2 | F | − | − | − | Profound |
| T | 4:3 | F | − | − | − | Moderate to severe |
| J | 5:0 | M | + | − | − | Profound |

This situation is ideal for studying the interaction of the ethnic phenomena described earlier for at least three reasons. First, in the school there are traditionally strong and consistent pressures toward the use of English; sign-supported speech is the official "communication method" of the school and acceptable oral English communication is the primary goal of the educational program. Because of the characteristic power asymmetry between hearing and deaf decision makers, and because of the critical nature of English acquisition to social mobility for deaf people, deaf adults in the school are likely to perceive their formal roles from the perspective of teaching English and majority culture interpretations.

Second, the presence of the children of Deaf parents exerts a strong pressure toward ASL use and toward Deaf ethnicity interpretations of certain situations. Deaf adults can also perceive their informal roles in terms of collegiality with these children and thereby assign Deaf ethnicity interpretations to their interactions with the children under certain conditions.

Third, the presence of the deaf children of hearing parents implies the need for ethnic and linguistic socialization from both peers and Deaf adults. If socialization is interactional, as our general theoretical orientation predicts, then we should find ways in which the behavior in the classroom (by both adults and children) is structured to attend to all of these pressures. These three factors combine to make the classroom a microcosmic representation of the power and language issues at hand in the adult Deaf community.

---

grade-levels. This configuration, however, in spite of its relative uniqueness, provides a particularly appropriate setting for studying the dynamics of socialization and the emergence of certain details of ethnicity. In addition, it underscores the need for detailed ethnographic study of a variety of classrooms in order to even approach an adequate understanding of the linguistic and ethnic socialization of all deaf children.

Our analysis of classroom interaction examines the following two hypotheses:

1. Interaction among the participants reflects important structural properties of the adult deaf community.
2. The classroom is at least in part the source of the sociolinguistic aspects of Deaf patrimony.

We approach the first hypothesis through an examination of the linguistic interaction of the children and adults in the classroom situations we observed. As discussed earlier, because of the unusual notion of paternity active in the emergence of Deaf ethnicity, the presence of deafness itself, rather than biological parentage, is one of the necessary conditions to be ethnically Deaf. The second condition is the demonstration of Deaf patrimony, which in an all-Deaf group is the sufficient condition. Thus, if the deaf children in the classroom are acting in a way that reflects adult Deaf norms, we would expect them to affiliate on the basis of salient characteristics of patrimony. As we explained, the most salient feature of patrimony for American Deaf people is the ability to communicate in ASL and the knowledge of when to use it and when not to use it. For these reasons, we predict that the affiliation of the children centers more on characteristics of language use than on issues of parentage alone.

Much of the literature on ASL sociolinguistics makes it tempting to presume that collegial groups among these deaf children are established according to whether or not they have Deaf parents. From this perspective, we might presume that four-year-old children from Deaf families would demonstrate both native ASL proficiency appropriate to their age and some other aspects of Deaf patrimony. From this same perspective, the children with hearing parents might be presumed not to have acquired the same degree of linguistic and cultural competence and therefore might be presumed to display such behaviors to a lesser degree than the children with deaf parents. This approach thus derives the notion of a "native" group and a "nonnative" group from the criterion of parentage alone.[13] This assumption is one of the features shared by a number of the previous taxonomic studies mentioned earlier, many of which suggest that the notion of native versus nonnative can be significant in determining adult associational choices (e.g., Padden, 1980, p. 95; Stokoe, Bernard, and Padden, 1976).

Through an examination of the patterns of interaction among the children and adults in the classroom, we have isolated two interactional

---

[13]Recent research by Newport and Supalla (1987) examines the question of native versus nonnative competence in terms of certain complex morphological structures of ASL. Their work suggests the presence of persistent, lifelong structural differences between the grammars of signers who learned ASL at a very early age and those who learned it later in their lives.

groupings of children that show parentage alone does not predict interaction. Instead, the interaction of the children appears to be constituted around proficiency in ASL. Although ASL proficiency often derives from Deaf parentage, among these children (as in the community at large) it does not appear to correspond directly to parentage. Returning to Table I, notice that the four children who have deaf parents are not the same four children who have the greatest skill in ASL. Groupings constituted around deaf parentage distinguish children *R, P, F,* and *J* (henceforth *DP*) from children *L, T, Sc,* and *Su* of hearing parentage (henceforth *HP*). Alternatively, groupings based on skill in ASL distinguish *R, P, F,* and *L* (henceforth group *A*) and *Sc, Su, T,* and *J* (henceforth group *B*). The significant children in these two divisions are *L,* who has hearing parents but attended residential school,[14] and *J,* who has deaf parents but does not exhibit linguistic skills equal to those of his classmates who have deaf parents.

The issue of why *J* might be deficient in ASL is perplexing. Several hearing and deaf adults in the school commented that there is something different about *J*'s signing. The Deaf aide said that this child's signing seems "funny." In our corpus, we found several examples of *J* misarticulating common signs. Moreover, as discussed later, *J* fits well within group *B* in most of his classroom behavior, and the adults in the classroom typically interact with him in the ways that they interact with the other Group B children. An exception to this tendency is that the Deaf aide occasionally uses ASL or fluent English signing with him in situations where she would not with other group *B* members. On the whole, however, *J* acts as and is treated as a member of group *B.* Thus, *J* seems to fit the model of a child who is from a Deaf family but who, for some reason, has not developed the level of ASL proficiency normally expected for a child of his age.[15]

In an effort to determine preferred associational patterns, we first analyzed the seating choices made by the children throughout the entire videotaped corpus of our classroom study. For each situation in which the children were free to choose with whom they sat, we recorded all seating choices, including those of the adults present. The seating choices charted for all such situations in the videotaped corpus appear in Table II.

Our assumption in gathering these data was that the children's seating

---

[14]For deaf children with hearing parents, institutional residence before the age of six or so appears to be critical to their acquisition of ASL with full native competence. Meadow (1972, p. 24) and Woodward (1973c, p. 192) explain this effect in more detail.

[15]To our knowledge, no one has yet approached the subject of language disorders among children who are native users of ASL. It is reasonable to assume, however, that disorders exist in the sign language communities as they do in spoken language communities. The authors observed one case of an adult native signer who exhibits what might be called stuttering. It is possible that the traditional view of sign language use itself as a sort of pathology or aberration masks the occurrence of actual language disorders.

**Table II**
Seating Choices of Children and Adults[a]

| | R | P | L | F | Sc | Su | T | J | H | D | X | Y | Total Choices per Individual |
|---|---|---|---|---|---|---|---|---|---|---|---|---|---|
| R | — | 10 | 10 | 4 | 14 | 7 | 6 | 6 | 3 | 5 | 1 | 0 | 66 |
| P | — | — | 10 | 3 | 7 | 11 | 1 | 2 | 1 | 5 | 1 | 0 | 51 |
| L | — | — | — | 8 | 1 | 5 | 1 | 13 | 4 | 3 | 2 | 1 | 58 |
| F | — | — | — | — | 3 | 3 | 2 | 2 | 2 | 0 | 1 | 0 | 28 |
| Sc | — | — | — | — | — | 6 | 4 | 8 | 1 | 2 | 1 | 0 | 47 |
| Su | — | — | — | — | — | — | 3 | 3 | 6 | 1 | 2 | 0 | 47 |
| T | — | — | — | — | — | — | — | 9 | 9 | 4 | 0 | 0 | 39 |
| J | — | — | — | — | — | — | — | — | 6 | 3 | 0 | 1 | 43 |
| H | — | — | — | — | — | — | — | — | — | 0 | 0 | 0 | 32 |
| D | — | — | — | — | — | — | — | — | — | — | 0 | 0 | 22 |
| X | — | — | — | — | — | — | — | — | — | — | — | 0 | 9 |
| Y | — | — | — | — | — | — | — | — | — | — | — | — | 2 |
| Total | | | | | | | | | | | | | 454 |

[a]H, hearing teacher; D, deaf aide; and X and Y, adult visitors.

choices serve to predict their preferred associational groupings. Sociometric observations of this sort are widely used to obtain measures of affiliation. In this study, however, the seating data were not helpful.

The first apparent difficulty with these data is that, owing to absences, the children had differential opportunities to sit with each other. R, for example, had sixty-six opportunities to sit, but F had only twenty-eight. R sat ten times with L, and F sat eight times with L. But because of absences, F's eight seatings with L represent a larger proportion of her choices than do R's ten seatings with L. For this reason, the data for each child need to be weighted to reflect their proportional contributions to the child's total number of choices. The most effective means of doing this is to convert the choices to proportionally weighted percentages, as provided in Table III.[16]

Statistical examination of the values in Table III suggests that there are

[16]The values in Table III are derived by the following formula:

$$\frac{\dfrac{X_{ab}}{\Sigma a} + \dfrac{X_{ab}}{\Sigma b}}{n},$$

where $X_{ab}$ is the number of joint seatings between child $a$ and child $b$, $\Sigma a$ is the sum of seatings for child $a$, $\Sigma b$ is the sum of seatings for child $b$, and $n = 12$.

**Table III**

Proportionally Weighted Percentages of each Pairing to Total Number of Choices of the Interactants[a]

|     | R | P | L | F | Sc | Su | T | J | H | D | X | Y |
|-----|---|---|---|---|----|----|---|---|---|---|---|---|
| R   | — | 2.9 | 2.7 | 1.7 | 4.2 | 2.1 | 2.0 | 1.7 | 1.2 | 2.5 | 1.1 | 0.0 |
| P   | — | — | 3.1 | 1.4 | 2.4 | 3.7 | 0.4 | 0.6 | 0.4 | 2.7 | 1.1 | 0.0 |
| L   | — | — | — | 3.5 | 0.3 | 1.6 | 0.4 | 3.9 | 1.6 | 1.0 | 3.2 | 4.3 |
| F   | — | — | — | — | 1.4 | 1.4 | 0.9 | 0.7 | 0.9 | 0.0 | 1.1 | 0.0 |
| Sc  | — | — | — | — | — | 2.1 | 1.6 | 2.7 | 0.4 | 1.1 | 1.1 | 0.0 |
| Su  | — | — | — | — | — | — | 1.2 | 1.0 | 2.6 | 0.6 | 2.2 | 0.0 |
| T   | — | — | — | — | — | — | — | 3.3 | 4.3 | 2.4 | 0.0 | 0.0 |
| J   | — | — | — | — | — | — | — | — | 2.5 | 1.6 | 0.0 | 4.3 |
| H   | — | — | — | — | — | — | — | — | — | 0.0 | 0.0 | 0.0 |
| D   | — | — | — | — | — | — | — | — | — | — | 0.0 | 0.0 |
| X   | — | — | — | — | — | — | — | — | — | — | — | 0.0 |
| Y   | — | — | — | — | — | — | — | — | — | — | — | — |

[a]Total, 99.1% due to rounding error. Expected frequency for each cell, 1.502; $\chi^2$ (entire matrix), 72.605; df, 65; $p < .25$. H, hearing teacher; D, deaf aide; and X and Y, adult visitors.

no significant patterns of seating evident in the corpus. The chi-square test for the entire matrix is not significant, showing that the probability of randomness in seating choices is about one in four. More telling, a multidimensional scaling analysis of the figures was unable to isolate any significant seating groups in the sample.[17] Thus, the study of seating choices did not help to isolate associational groupings.

There are a number of possible intervening variables in seating choices that might have contributed to these results. We will discuss them here because the study of association in deaf children appears to be a potentially important source of insight into the structure of classroom interaction. Perhaps the failure of our analysis will help to inform a more successful study in the future.

The first difficulty with our data stems from our method of observation. We simply counted the raw number of times each child was next to each other child. In most of the situations, the participants were arranged in a near circle. Thus, most of the time each person was sitting next to two other people. In such a situation, it is probably quite frequent for a child to pick his or her affiliation with one child but to end up sitting next to an unfavored child on the other side. Because each seating dyad counts equal-

[17]We are grateful to Harlan Lane for performing a multidimensional scaling on these data and for his discussions with us concerning the generation and support of our hypotheses. It is largely his commentary that has been responsible for the substantive changes made in the second section of this chapter since its earlier versions.

ly, such arrangements tend to mask the actual choices made by the children and thereby to depress the chi-square value for the sample.

Second, the clustering of zero values in the lower right hand corner of Table III suggests that adults never sit next to other adults. This has the effect of lowering the possibility of two children choosing each other freely. Third, although we know of no substantiation of this claim, it is likely that the choice of seating may be less important in a classroom of eight children than in the larger classrooms typically found in public schools for hearing children. Fourth, probably most important is the possibility that deaf children affiliate in an entirely different manner than hearing children do. That is, because of the visual demands of sign language reception, it is quite possible that deaf children choose to sit across from favored affiliates in order to enhance communication, rather than next to them as we expect for hearing children. In order to control for all of these possible intervening variables, classroom seating studies will need to have much more sophisticated designs than that of the small study reported here.

Our examination of patterns of linguistic interaction was more informative about the children's groupings than the seating patterns were. We examined linguistic interaction among the children and adults in four different situations: one structured classroom lesson and three unstructured situations in the lunchroom, the first with the deaf aide serving food, the second with the deaf aide seated with the children, and the third with the hearing teacher seated with the children.

Table IV shows the initiations that occurred in the structured classroom situation. Several important patterns are discernible in this table. First, the children do not initiate interaction with one another, nor do the two adults

**Table IV**
Structured Classroom Situation: Initiations to and from Adults[a]

| | | | | | Receiver | | | | | |
|---|---|---|---|---|---|---|---|---|---|---|
| Initiator | R | P | L | F | Sc | Su | T | J | H | D |
| R | | | | | | | | | 6 | 7 |
| P | | | | | | | | | 4 | 3 |
| L | | | | | | | | | 4 | 2 |
| F | | | | | | | | | 3 | |
| Sc | | | | | | | | | 2 | |
| Su | | | | | | | | | 1 | |
| T | | | | | | | | | 1 | |
| J | | | | | | | | | 3 | 1 |
| H | 5 | | | | 1 | | | 1 | | |
| D | 5 | 1 | | | | | | | | |

[a] Time, 5 minutes; H, hearing teacher; and D, deaf aide.

talk to each other. All dyadic communication is between children and adults (monologic lecturing by the adults was not counted in these data), as might be expected in an American classroom. More significant for the purposes of this study is that the amount of communication in which each child engages is quite variable. *R* initiates talk with an adult thirteen times and *T* initiates talk with an adult only one time. The same observation applies to the differences between initiation and reception. Those children who initiate the most communication are (in general) the same children who receive the most communication. When these variabilities are compared across situations, patterns emerge that help to isolate the affiliative groupings of children and that support the contention that the children affiliate on the basis of sign language skill.

Tables V and VI reorganize the data from Table IV in two different ways, Table V grouping the children by parentage and Table VI by skill in ASL. In the structured classroom situation, there is no clear differential in the patterns of the groups constituted in this way, and thus the data are indeterminate as to which characteristic the children are using to affiliate. In both tables, however, a significant difference exists between what we might call the "more" Deaf group (either *DP* or *A*) and the "less" Deaf group (either *HP* or *B*). In each case, the more Deaf group has significantly more interaction with the adults than does the less Deaf group. Moreover, whereas for the more Deaf group the amount of communication with *H* (the hearing teacher) and with *D* (the deaf aide) is roughly the same, the less Deaf group engages in substantially less interaction with *D* than with *H*. This is a pattern we find repeated throughout the corpus: not only do the less Deaf children communicate less, a smaller percentage of their communication is with the Deaf adult present in the classroom.

This pattern is even more apparent in Table VII, where we record the

**Table V**
Structured Classroom Situation: Initiations to and from Adults by Parentage[a]

| Initiator | Receiver | | | |
|---|---|---|---|---|
| | DP | HP | H | D |
| DP | — | 0 | 16 | 11 |
| HD | 0 | — | 8 | 2 |
| H | 6 | 1 | — | 0 |
| D | 6 | 0 | 0 | — |

[a]Data recombined from Table IV. DP, deaf parentage; HP, hearing parentage; H, hearing teacher; and D, deaf aide.

**Table VI**
Structured Classroom Situation: Initiations to and
from Adults by Skill in ASL[a]

| | Receiver | | | |
|---|---|---|---|---|
| Initiator | A | B | H | D |
| A | — | 0 | 17 | 12 |
| B | 0 | — | 7 | 1 |
| H | 5 | 2 | — | 0 |
| D | 6 | 0 | 0 | — |

[a]Data recombined from Table IV. Group A, skilled
users of ASL; group B, unskilled users of ASL; H,
hearing teacher; and D, deaf aide.

total number of turns between children and adults in the structured classroom situation, compared for groups *A* and *B* only (the results for *DP* and
*HP* are almost identical). In Table VII it is apparent that not only do the
group *A* children have more opportunities to initiate conversation, but
their conversations on a topic also tend to include more turns. Accordingly, initiations to or from group *A* children result in exchanges that average
2.2 turns (40 initiations, 86 turns), and those to or from group *B* children
result in exchanges averaging only 1.9 turns (10 initiations, 19 turns). In
addition, the group *A* children engage *H* and *D* equally, whereas the group
*B* children share three times as many turns with *H* as with *D*. This issue is
pertinent to our observations of the processes of socialization in the classroom. We will return to the issue of differences in turn-taking later in this
chapter.

Overall, the data from the structured classroom situation, while not
illuminating the specific question of how the children affiliate, indicate
clear differences in communication patterns between those children we
would expect to be more ethnically Deaf and those whom we would not.

**Table VII**
Structured Classroom Situation: Total Number of
Turns Between Children and Adults[a]

| | H | D |
|---|---|---|
| Group A | 42 | 44 |
| Group B | 14 | 5 |

[a]Time, 5 minutes; H, hearing teacher; D, deaf aide;
group A, skilled users of ASL; and group B, unskilled
users of ASL.

Moreover, the data suggest differences in the ways in which the Deaf adult interacts with the two categories of children, presumably also a result of the values and expectations associated with Deaf ethnic patrimony.

We also examined three different situations in the lunchroom, where the children are more free to communicate as they wish. Tables VIII–XIII together present data on the initiations of interaction in the three unstructured lunchroom situations. Although we will present an analysis later that shows different patterns of interaction in each of these three situations, there are consistent patterns of interaction across the situations that illuminate the question of affiliation.

In all three situations, when the children are grouped by parentage the interaction patterns either tend toward randomness (as in Tables X and XI) or show patterns that indicate preferred affiliation with the opposite group (Tables VIII–IX and XII–XIII). Both types of pattern are inconsistent with our claims in the first part of this chapter.

When the children are grouped according to skill in ASL, the cells of the tables become considerably more distinct. The interaction patterns show substantial preference for group *A* children to interact with other group *A* children, for group *B* children to interact with other group *B* children, and for each group not to interact with the other. The interaction between the children and the adult present are patterned in ways we discuss later.

Clearly, these observations do not *prove* that the children are affiliating according to sign language skill. Such a demonstration would require a substantially larger sample of observations, subject to statistical analysis. If we can take as a given, however, that people tend not to act in random ways, and that Deaf adults tend to behave as we described in the early parts of this chapter, then these observations do indicate that the children in our study are beginning to act as Deaf people act. The strongest patterns of affiliation appear to be explained by the presence of the salient feature of

**Table VIII**

Unstructured Lunchroom Situation: Deaf Aide
Serving Food, Initiations by Parentage[a]

| Initiator | Receiver | | |
|---|---|---|---|
| | DP | HP | D |
| DP | 5 | 5 | 1 |
| HP | 13 | 0 | 3 |
| D | 9 | 9 | — |

[a]Time, 2:17 minutes; DP, deaf parentage; HP, hearing parentage; and D, deaf aide. Child F was absent.

**Table IX**
Unstructured Lunchroom Situation:
Deaf Aide Serving Food, Initiations by
Skill in ASL[a]

|  | Receiver | | |
|---|---|---|---|
| Initiator | A | B | D |
| A | 19 | 0 | 0 |
| B | 0 | 4 | 4 |
| D | 9 | 9 | — |

[a]Time, 2:17 minutes; group A, skilled users of
ASL; group B, unskilled users of ASL. Child F was
absent.

**Table X**
Unstructured Lunchroom Situation:
Deaf Aide Seated at Table, Initiations
by Parentage[a]

|  | Receiver | | |
|---|---|---|---|
| Initiator | DP | HP | D |
| DP | 3 | 3 | 12 |
| HP | 5 | 1 | 17 |
| D | 6 | 4 | — |

[a]Time, 8 minutes; DP, deaf parentage; HP, hearing
parentage; and D, deaf aide. Children F and Sc were
absent.

**Table XI**
Unstructured Lunchroom Situation:
Deaf Aide Seated at Table, Initiations
by Skill in ASL[a]

|  | Receiver | | |
|---|---|---|---|
| Initiator | A | B | D |
| A | 5 | 3 | 20 |
| B | 1 | 3 | 8 |
| D | 2 | 8 | — |

[a]Time, 8 minutes; group A, skilled users of ASL;
group B, unskilled users of ASL; and D, deaf aide.
Children F and Sc were absent.

**Table XII**
Unstructured Lunchroom Situation:
Hearing Teacher Seated at Table,
Initiations by Parentage[a]

|          | Receiver |    |    |
|----------|----------|----|----|
| Initiator | DP | HP | H |
| DP | 1 | 9 | 6 |
| HP | 3 | 0 | 7 |
| H  | 8 | 6 | — |

[a]Time, 8 minutes; DP, deaf parentage; HP, hearing parentage; and H, hearing teacher. Child F was absent.

**Table XIII**
Unstructured Lunchroom Situation:
Hearing Teacher Seated at Table,
Initiations by Skill in ASL[a]

|          | Receiver |    |    |
|----------|----------|----|----|
| Initiator | A | B | H |
| A | 9 | 2 | 4 |
| B | 0 | 2 | 9 |
| H | 7 | 7 | — |

[a]Time, 8 minutes; group A, skilled users of ASL; group B, unskilled users of ASL; and H, hearing teacher. Child F was absent.

ASL skill, and interaction patterns among groupings of children defined by this feature are similar to those one would expect from Deaf adults in similar situations. Put differently, if we use the characteristic of ASL skill to define groupings of children, we are better able to explain the behavior patterns that we observed in this study. If, on the other hand, we employ any other grouping, we must accept that the participants' behavior is largely unexplainable, an unlikely situation among human beings. For these reasons, we focus henceforth on groups *A* and *B,* rather than on groups *HP* and *DP*.[18]

[18]We give this special attention to ASL skills against the advice of more statistically inclined psychologist friends such as Harlan Lane, who pointed out that other, unconsidered factors could be causing the patterns that we observed in this study. Unfortunately, lacking a larger, controlled study, we are presently unable to determine if he is correct.

Tables XIV–XVI present an account of the number of turns occurring in each of the three unstructured lunchroom situations. For turn-taking behavior, the patterns we observed in the classroom are amplified here. Once again there is a strong tendency for group *A* to take longer turns and for most of the interaction to occur between members of the same group rather than between members of the two different groups.

We have been claiming that groups *A* and *B* are differentiated on the basis of ASL skill. Whereas the earlier described analysis dealt only with differences in patterns of interaction, the present analysis demonstrated that the group *A* children actually use more ASL features than do the group *B* children. For this analysis, we chose three bounded situations and examined in detail the actual productions of all the children.

The first of these situations is the segment represented in Tables VIII, IX, and XIV, in which the deaf aide is serving food in the lunchroom. We chose this segment because the children communicate so intensively during its 2:17 minute duration. During this time, we recorded 178 turns, all of which were either among children within the same group or between children and the aide. If ASL features appear anywhere, we would expect them to occur in the communication among the children in this situation because there is free communication and there are no hearing people immediately involved in the situation.

The second segment in which we counted all ASL features is bounded by the beginning and end of a lunchroom conversation about riding on a ferris wheel. The ferris wheel conversation itself is interrupted a number of times so that the entire segment involves a number of co-occurrent conversations. Moreover, the ferris wheel story, as originally related in ASL by *P*, presents the subsequent stimulus for a number of other children to make conversational use of the same ASL features employed in *P*'s story.

The third segment examined is bounded by the beginning and end of a lunchroom conversation about the lights blinking on and off. As was the case with the ferris wheel story, the topic is especially conducive to the use of the kinds of ASL features used by the children in the other two segments. The occurrence of inflected verbs and classifier predicates here operationally defines ASL use. These two features are not in themselves definitive of ASL, but they represent central components of ASL structure that are quite different from English and therefore are not derived from signed English input. For our purposes, utterances with such features are judged to be ASL and hence, at the same time, not to be English. Table XVII summarizes the use by each group of these two ASL features. Clearly, the group *A* children make greater use of these ASL features than do the group *B* children. This adds support to our contention that the groups are constituted around ASL skill and thereby are a reflection of an important structural property of the adult deaf community.

**Table XIV**
Lunchroom Turn Taking with Deaf Aide
Serving Food[a]

|  | Receiver | | |
|---|---|---|---|
| Initiator | A | B | D |
| A | 61 | 0 | 0 |
| B | 0 | 13 | 15 |
| D | 45 | 44 | — |

[a]Time, 2:17 minutes; group A, skilled users of
ASL; group B, unskilled users of ASL; and D, deaf
aide. Child F was absent.

**Table XV**
Lunchroom Turn Taking with Deaf Aide
Seated at Table[a]

|  | Receiver | | |
|---|---|---|---|
| Initiator | A | B | D |
| A | 8 | 5 | 42 |
| B | 1 | 8 | 18 |
| D | 3 | 12 | — |

[a]Time, 8 minutes; group A, skilled users of ASL;
group B, unskilled users of ASL; and D, deaf aide.
Children F and Sc were absent.

**Table XVI**
Lunchroom Turn Taking with Hearing Teacher
Seated at Table[a]

|  | Receiver | | |
|---|---|---|---|
| Initiator | A | B | H |
| A | 17 | 2 | 9 |
| B | 0 | 3 | 14 |
| H | 8 | 12 | — |

[a]Time, 8 minutes; group A, skilled users of ASL;
group B, unskilled users of ASL; and H, hearing
teacher. Child F was absent.

**Table XVII**
Children's Use of ASL Features in Three Lunchroom Segments[a]

| Informants | Inflected Verbs | Classifier Predicates |
|---|---|---|
| Group A | | |
| R | 3 | 10 |
| P | 2 | 26 |
| L | 1 | 6 |
| | — | — |
| Total | 6 | 42 |
| Group B | | |
| Sc | 0 | 5 |
| Su | 1 | 0 |
| T | 0 | 0 |
| J | 0 | 0 |
| | — | — |
| Total | 1 | 5 |

[a] Segment 1, aide serving food; segment 2, ferris wheel conversation; segment 3, lights-blinking conversation. Child F was absent in all three segments. Inflected verbs include inflections for subject-object agreement and distributive and adverbial manner. Classifier predicates include both locative predicates and stative size and shape predicates.

## ELEMENTS OF LINGUISTIC SOCIALIZATION IN THE CLASSROOM

Our second hypothesis is that the interaction observed in this study constitutes a major factor in the socialization of the deaf children with respect to certain aspects of Deaf patrimony. Although there are many reflections of adult patrimony apparent in the structure of the children's behavior, our interest here is limited to how the children learn to use ASL and how they learn to sign English. We have found three main processes of linguistic socialization in relation to ASL. These are (1) purposeful ASL teaching, (2) ASL imitation and practice, and (3) nonpurposeful transmission of ASL features.

Purposeful ASL teaching is exemplified in this study by the correction of signing errors. We have found several varieties of corrections. The first of these is represented by a number of clear instances of sign corrections from group A children to group B children. An example of sign correction appears in a conversation between R (group A) and J (group B) in which J first recognizes that the teacher's sign for hot-air balloon is incorrect and then also incorrectly makes the hot-air balloon sign. J is in turn corrected by *R*. He then adapts his own sign to look more like the correct sign. *R* then uses the correct sign with an inflection for large movements.[19]

| | |
|---|---|
| *H*: | YOU RIDE-IN-VEHICLE INSIDE $\underline{A}$ PARTY-BALLOON$_1$ |
| | *You ride in a balloon* (shows picture of hot-air balloon). |
| *J*: | BALLOON$_2$ [Incorrect hot-air balloon sign] |
| | 'It's balloon$_2$' |
| *R* to *J*: | BALLOON$_2$ WRONG BALLOON$_3$ RIGHT (on table) |
| | 'Balloon$_2$ is wrong. Balloon$_3$ is right.' |
| *J*: | BALLOON$_4$ (BALLOON$_2$ adapted to be more like *R*'s) |
| *R* to *J*: | BEAT-YOU BALLOON$_3$ (large movements) |
| | 'I got ya! It's balloon$_3$.' |

The second variety of sign correction involves the aide correcting baby signs to adult ASL signs, as illustrated in the following example.

| | |
|---|---|
| *R* to *D*: | WATER$_1$ |
| *D* to *R*: | WHAT? |
| *R* to *D*: | WATER$_2$ |
| *D* to *R*: | DRINK? NOT WATER$_2$ WATER$_3$ (adult form, with nodding) |
| | 'A drink? It's not "water$_2$". It's "water$_3$".' |
| *R* to *D*: | WATER$_3$ (adult form) |

The third variety of sign correction is quite similar to the second and so is not illustrated here. It involves the correction of what seem to be local or home signs into standard ASL signs.

The fourth variety of sign correction is represented in a number of

---

[19]We use the following conventions for representing the linguistic events that occurred in the classroom. The occurrence of a sign is represented by a simple gloss in upper-case. This gloss is not a smooth, syntactically well-formed translation into English but merely a label in English for the sign that occurred. If several variants of a sign are used in an exchange, subscripts distinguish them. An underscored upper-case gloss indicates the occurrence of a sign from an English signing system, for example, $\underline{IS}$. Glosses preceded by # are signs that have been lexicalized from fingerspelling. Upper-case letters separated by hyphens indicate fingerspelling. Speech is indicated by text in *italics*. If speech co-occurs with signing, it appears directly below the signed text. Parenthetical notations provide additional descriptions of ongoing events, for example, the occurrence of gestural deictics. Square brackets are used to enclose clarifications of particular signs. Finally, translations of the signing appear directly below the signed text and are framed by single quotation marks. These accompanying translations into well-formed or fluent English sentences are intended to complement the more abbreviated sign-glosses, which make the actual linguistic events appear impoverished. What we observed was, in fact, rich with nonmanual grammatical markers, inflections, located signing, and other features difficult to represent in a written textual format.

incidents in which children from either group recognize and attempt to correct misarticulated signs of the hearing adults present in the classroom. In the following example, the student teacher's (*ST*) misarticulated fingerspelling is recognized by *F* and successfully corrected by *R* and *J*.

*ST*:    (following Sesame Street alphabet game)    YAP-YAP
                                                   *oh* (the letter "o")

*F*:     (grabs *L* by the chin to get her attention)
         WRONG WRONG (face screwed up) YAP-YAP-YAP WRONG (points to *ST*)
         'That's wrong!'                 "yap-yap-yap!" She's wrong!'

*R* and *J*  *O*
   to *ST*:  'It's "O".'

*ST*:    (adjusts sign to *O*)

The extent of such teaching strategies localized within the classroom competence of the children is demonstrated by the repair of a content error made by the same student teacher. The next example shows that even when the teacher does not recognize the correction, the children conspire to communicate the mistake throughout the classroom. Although this is an example of the repair of a content error rather than an ASL error *per se,* it demonstrates the extent and the effectiveness of deaf children's repair strategies. Given that most of their teachers are hearing and hence nonnative signers, the need for such strategies is probably greater than in regular classrooms for hearing children. During the following segment of conversation, the class is in a semicircle doing calendar work. *ST* is off-camera so only her voice is indicated on the right side of the transcript.

                              *ST: F and L are not here today.*

*T*:     SICK *F L*
         '*F* and *L* are sick.'

                              This afternoon we will make Easter
                              baskets. We are going to make Easter
                              baskets.

*T*:     WRONG (points to calendar)
         'The calendar is wrong.'

                              WRONG (walks to calendar, points to it, looks at *ST*) WRONG
                              'Teacher, it's wrong.'

                              *Remember*

*P*:     WRONG (points to calendar)
         'The calendar is wrong.'

*J* to *T*:    (walks to calendar) WHERE?

*T*:     (shakes head and points to another place on the calendar)
         WRONG

'No, not there. It's wrong over there.'

|  |  | *yesterday* |
|---|---|---|
| *J* to *ST*: | WRONG | |
|  | "Teacher, it's wrong.' | |

*yesterday*

| *J*: | (pointing to *ST* and sticking tongue out) (points to *H*) |
|---|---|
|  | YESTERDAY-YESTERDAY-YESTERDAY |

| *Su*: | (walks to calendar and points) |
|---|---|
|  | 'There!' |

| *R*: | (walks to calendar) |
|---|---|

*yesterday was*

| *Su* to *R*: | WRONG |
|---|---|
|  | 'It's wrong.' |

| *Su* to group: | (takes seat) | WRONG WRONG WRONG |
|---|---|---|
|  |  | 'It's wrong, wrong, wrong!' |

*Tuesday. Who can find Tuesday? P?*

| *R* to *H*: | (pointing to *ST*) WRONG WRITING-ON-BOARD WRONG |
|---|---|
|  | 'She's wrong. The writing up there is wrong.' |

| *Su* to *H*: | WRITING-ON-BOARD WRONG |
|---|---|
|  | "The writing up there is wrong.' |

*Can you find Tuesday?*
*Yesterday . . . Tuesday.*

| *J*: | (puts wastebasket over head) |
|---|---|

It is unclear from our tapes exactly what error the teacher made. But her inability to recognize and respond effectively to the children's attempts to clarify it made it necessary for the children to communicate about it among the group. Significantly, it may have seemed to *ST* that the class was in chaos and uncontrollable, but the children were actually reasonably well on task.

The second process of ASL socialization is apparently imitation and practice of ASL features by group *B* children. In these cases, group *A* children (and possibly the aide) are models for ASL use but are not attempting directly to teach ASL principles or signs. For example, *P* introduces the bent-*V* (legs sitting) classifier to demonstrate some of the finer points of riding a ferris wheel. *L* joins the discussion and adds two new uses of that classifier, thereby demonstrating that she can competently use its inflected forms. *P* and *L* then begin a favorite game of repeating a sign—in this case the bent-*V* classifier moving on a ferris wheel—in exaggerated form, each claiming to be stronger than the other. *R* is attracted by the game, asks what the sign is, and changes it to another classifier, which is also acceptable in this context. When asked later by the deaf aide what he is talking about, he explains by returning to the original classifier and using it in a completely new way, claiming that he went around on a really big ferris wheel. The aide responds with 'Good.' Meanwhile, *Sc* joins the game by repeating *R*'s new classifier, but he does not demonstrate competent knowledge of how to use it. He is using *R*'s handshape but is incorrectly moving it. Apparently, he is merely copying the sign in order to join in the game.

We propose that such instances of copying behavior, which occur with great frequency, represent ASL practice for the group *B* children. In the case of the bent-*V* classifier, the context of the game makes their use of the sign acceptable without complete knowledge of how to use it and provides them the opportunity to refine their skills in producing the sign. This proposal is supported by the fact that a majority of the cases of sign copying in the corpus involve group *B* children copying group *A* children.

The third aspect of linguistic socialization in relation to ASL norms of use demonstrates the characteristics of ordinary language acquisition, where everyday language use stands as a model for the language learner. Such nonpurposeful transmission of ASL features can be divided into two categories. The first is the everyday use of ASL by the group *A* children serving as a model of ASL usage for group *B* children. Virtually all of the group *A* children's communication can be assigned this function. For the most part, it is logically impossible to distinguish their contribution to the socialization of group *B* from that of the Deaf aide or any other Deaf adults in contact with the children. One instance, however, demonstrates the contribution of the group *A* children conclusively.

The children in this school regularly use a sign that means 'I like you.' The sign is produced with an *H* handshape with the thumb extended. It can show agreement with subject and object, that is, it can be directed at anyone or anything and is articulated by sharply flexing the extended thumb, as in the sign GUN. As such, it is clearly not an English verb so would not have been taught as a part of the curriculum. Moreover, it is not a sign that Deaf adults use; it appears to be used exclusively by the children and is probably transmitted and maintained among the children of the school. In the entire lunchroom corpus, group *A* children use the inflected form of the I-LIKE-YOU sign seven times and the group *B* children use it six times. This is one of only a few signs that is not only subject to a decidedly ASL inflection but also used about evenly by group *A* and group *B* children. In addition, this sign and its opposite, #NO (used in inflected form to demonstrate dislike), are salient and frequently used symbols in the interactional constitution of social relationships for the children. We propose that the use of these signs by the group *B* children provides grounding and practice in the critical ASL grammatical principle of subject-object

agreement. That I-LIKE-YOU is not used by adults can be taken as con-
clusive evidence of the group *A* children's contribution to ASL socialization. By extension, we can conclude that all of the classroom signing of
group *A* children similarly affects the signing of group *B* children and thus
can logically assume that the group *A* children are among the primary
agents of ASL socialization.

The second aspect of nonpurposeful transmission of ASL features results
from the structure of communication in the classroom and in the lunchroom. In the course of isolating groups *A* and *B,* we discovered that, in
every situation, group *A* children initiate communication and receive responses much more frequently than group *B* children. In our sample of
twenty-three minutes of interaction, group *A* children account for almost
67 percent of the children's turns. Given the importance of group *A* as a
model for linguistic socialization, this greater percentage of turns can be
seen to reflect an interactional structuring of time that provides increased
exposure to skilled signing and thus represents a kind of nonpurposeful
teaching of ASL by children.

Socialization in relation to the usage norms of English signing can also
be divided into several processes. In the first, the Deaf aide communicates
that some situations bear heavy hearing-world interpretations and thus
require the use of English signing. The second process is translation between English and ASL. The third is the purposeful teaching of English by
the adults.

It is important for deaf children to learn to recognize features of situations that call for certain language varieties. As explained earlier, situations
with strong in-group interpretations, such as the maintenance of solidarity
within the Deaf ethnic group or the transmission of ethnic patrimony, are
usually invested with strong pressures for the use of ASL. Conversely, those
situations associated with out-group interpretations, particularly those
concerned with socioeconomic mobility and assimilation into mainstream
society, are invested with strong pressure for the use of a variety marked as
English.

Although we do not have sufficient space here for the documentation,
analysis of our interactional data shows that the serving of food tends to
elicit varieties of English-marked signing from *D,* the aide. Sometimes the
marked variety is a form of sign-supported speech and, other times, it is a
form of fluent English signing. The following example is an exchange between *D* and *J* while food is being served. After being asked in fluent English
signing if he wants some bread, *J* touches three pieces before making his
choice, which brings an etiquette lesson down on him.

*D* to J:    #D$_D$-O$_a$ YOU$_a$ WANT(one-handed) #BREAD (loan sign from
fingerspelling)

*J*:            (touches three pieces before deciding on his choice)

*D*:            (sets plate down and grabs *J*'s arm)
            NOT TOUCH (one-handed, high)
            'Don't touch it!'

            NOT TOUCH (distributive, over bread) NO ONE PICK
            'Don't touch every one. No!' 'Pick one.

            NOT TOUCH (distributive, on hand) NOT
            Don't touch them all.'

            (hands *J* a slice of bread)
            THAT-ONE
            'Take that one.'

The breach of etiquette involved in touching the food redefines the situation. It began as a food-serving situation, heavily invested with hearing interpretations. After *J* touches the food, it is not just a food-serving situation that requires English; it is now a situation that pertains to the transmission of cultural values, in this case table manners. *D* switches to ASL for this purpose. Her sentences now are not in English word order and are not in citation form (she uses three different inflections of the verb TOUCH). Instead, they contain a number of features of ASL. After handing *J* the proper piece of bread (the first one he touched), *D* turns to *T* and reestablishes the food-serving situation, producing the following sentence in careful English word order with full citation form signs.

$D_p$-$O_p$ YOU    WANT (two-handed)    BREAD (citation form)

Such rapid and complete switching underscores the strength of the food-serving situation in eliciting English-marked sentences. The use of English by Deaf adults is usually elicited in the context of some sort of economic exchange. If Deaf adults want access to resources of the society, they must use English. It is not unreasonable to suggest that the most common economic exchange in the classroom, the serving of food and snacks, is invested with the same kind of language symbolism.

What we have here is an example of the way in which the aide switches between English signing and ASL according to situational pressures. There is also some evidence that the children themselves are beginning to understand that food-serving situations in the school bear English pressures. We previously demonstrated a consistent pattern of differences in the interaction of group *A* and group *B* children in the three lunchroom segments (Tables VIII–XVI). If we examine more carefully the behavior of group *A* and group *B* independently, we see important differences among the three situations. Specifically, the situation in which the aide is serving food (Tables VIII, IX, and XIV) and the situation in which the hearing teacher is seated at the table (Tables XII, XIII, and XVI) are very similar in terms of how each group acts. Correlating each cell of Tables VIII and IX with the corresponding cells of Tables XII and XIII yields a correlation (Pearson) of 0.7285, significant at below the 0.05 level. Similarly, the correlation between these two situations in terms of the number of turns (Tables XIV and XVI) is 0.7015, again significant at the 0.05 level. From this, we conclude that the patterns of interaction that occur while the deaf aide is serving food are very similar to those that occur when only the hearing teacher is present.

The application of the same procedure to the third situation—that in which the deaf aide is seated at the table with the children—yields correlations that are insignificant. This demonstrates that the patterns of interaction in this situation are different from those in the other two situations.

That the children alter their patterns of communicative behavior according to the situation is strong evidence that they have already begun to internalize some understanding of the role of English in their lives. They are not yet able to effectively switch to fluent English signing, but in certain situations they demonstrate their understanding that English is required. One such situation is snack time in the classroom, a period traditionally specified as English-learning time in teachers' lesson plans. In this situation, the children serve the juice and cookies. As they do so, they require that the other children produce sentences carefully rendered in English word order and with the "English signs" recommended by the school's sign-supported speech system. They typically withhold the snack until they receive a request in the appropriate form. The following excerpt is from the interaction recorded during juice and cookie time.

| | |
|---|---|
| *Su* to *D*: | FALL-DOWN<br>'[Something] fell.' |
| *D*: | WHAT <u>IS</u> FALL? |
| *Su*: | COOKIE |
| *D*: | COOKIE FALL?<br>'A cookie fell?' |
| *T*: | (begins passing out cookies; holds one out to *P*) |
| *P*: | (with eye gaze diverted) <u>I</u> WANT <u>A</u> COOKIE<br>(*T* gives her the cookie.) |
| *Su*: | ME-ME-ME-ME (*T* gives her a cookie across the table.) |
| *T*: | (gives cookie to *L* but holds on to it) |
| *L*: | (with eye gaze diverted) <u>I</u> WANT COOKIE<br>(*T* releases cookie) |
| *D*: | (pouring juice) |
| *P*: | ME-ME-ME |
| *D*: | (stops by *P*) |
| *P*: | <u>I</u> . . . <u>I</u> WANT . . . SOME . . . OJ |

*D*:         OK (pours juice)

*Su*:        (looking at *D*) ME WANT . . .
            (diverts eyes from *D*) I̲ WANT SOME OJ (eyes back to *D*)

*D* to *L*:   *L* WHAT WANT?

*L*:         I̲ WANT WHAT? SOME OJ

Although all of the children are apparently able to produce coherent sentences in coded English, it also appears that they are simply reciting lines. When the children use such sentences, they either divert their eyes (as if trying to remember) or they hesitate between signs. Both of these styles are unusual for all the children in ordinary conversation. Additionally, in our data corpus, all of the instances of English-marked signing are in situations involving food. It may thus be the case that they are not learning productively competent English from such exercises. Still, they are certainly learning that such a thing as English exists and that it is required if they want certain desirable things in the world.

A second process involved in learning to use English can be recognized in translations by and for the children. The group *A* children, by virtue of their more extensive contact with the adult Deaf community and its norms for language use, appear to be developing a more competent understanding of English than the group *B* children. Although this English competence is not yet fully productive, they are able not only to understand certain English sentences produced by their hearing teacher but also to translate these sentences into sentences that the group *B* children can understand. Once such instance is the following:

            (lights flicker)

*Sc*:        (points to ceiling) LIGHTS
            'Look at the lights.'

*H*:         LIGHTS LOCATED-ON AND O-F-F

*R* to *Su*:  OVERHEAD-LIGHT-ON-AND-OFF
            "The lights on the ceiling are flashing on and off.'

*R* to *H*:   OVERHEAD-LIGHT

*H* to *R*:   FROM RAIN RAIN RAIN

*R* to *Su*:  THUNDERSTORM RAIN (intensive) OVERHEAD-LIGHT-ON-AND-OFF
            'There's a thunderstorm. It's raining very hard. It's making the lights blink.'

Here the teacher uses two English constructions built from mistranslated signs. This is a common occurrence in the use of sign-supported speech, which characteristically employs one sign for one English word even when that word corresponds to several signs in ASL. For example, when the teacher uses the sign LOCATED-ON to mean the English word *on,*

*R* translates her misuse of that sign into the proper ASL sign OVERHEAD-LIGHT-ON-AND-OFF. He then attempts to show the teacher the appropriate sign LIGHTS. He does the same thing when the teacher incorrectly uses the preposition FROM to indicate causality. His translations are made directly to *Su,* who turns to him for the translations after the teacher finishes each sentence.

It also appears that *T,* who has a fair amount of residual hearing, has been able to develop a primary competence in oral English. In interacting with the hearing adults, she depends heavily on her hearing to understand. Also, she has some difficulty understanding ASL as the other children use it. This may, in part, account for her relative isolation from the other children (except *J*) and her tendency to sit next to the teacher. We have found that she receives carefully signed English productions in all situations, and that she must often look to the teacher for translations of the other children's signing. In the following example, the teacher translates *R*'s ASL into sign-supported speech. Each time *R* addresses *T,* *T* turns to the teacher for assistance. The teacher responds with an English-like explanation, after which *T* responds to *R.* When *T* apparently does not understand *R*'s game, the teacher helps her discover the appropriate response. It is significant, however, that *T* does not respond to *R* without first looking at the teacher. That is, she does not ask *R* for an explanation and may be depending heavily on the teacher's spoken English.

| *R*: | (In bunny hat, is passing out imaginary candy Easter eggs. Each child is to pick a color.) |
|---|---|
| *R* to *T*: | COLOR<br>'What color?' |
| *T*: | ORANGE |
| *R*: | ORANGE ZERO<br>'There's no orange.' |
| *T*: | (puzzled, looks at *H*) |
| *H*: | ZERO ORANGE SORRY      OUTSIDE ORANGE<br>*No orange. He's sorry, but he's out of orange.*<br><br>PICK OTHER COLOR<br>*Pick another color.* |
| *T*: | PURPLE |
| *R*: | ZERO PURPLE |
| *T*: | (looks at *H*) |
| *H*: | ZERO PURPLE WHAT WRONG TOGETHER-WITH EASTER DEVIL<br>*No purple?    What's wrong with this Easter bunny?* |
| *T*: | BLACK (*R* gives her an imaginary eg.) |

These observations point to the third process for learning English, namely, the purposeful teaching of English by the adults in the classroom. Sign-supported speech is supposed to provide the children with an exact and consistent model of spoken English so that they are able to develop English competence. Therefore, the use of sign-supported speech on any occasion can be interpreted as the purposeful provision of a model for learning English. The model of English presented by the teacher in the last example is inexact, incomplete, and incongruous with her speech. It is possible that only a child with a fair amount of hearing or with almost complete competence in English could understand her. The translations into English speech are helpful to *T* because she has enough hearing to pick up the meaning. But for the children who have less hearing, the translations can be confusing since the signing itself often makes little sense. Moreover, the children with less hearing do not have the advantage of being able to hear English so have little basis for the kind of competence necessary to infer a coherent English sentence from the jumble of signs presented to them.

The last example is not unusual in its inaccuracies, either for this teacher or for hearing teachers in general. The extreme cognitive and physical demands placed on a hearing individual while attempting to sign and speak simultaneously typically cause adjustments in either the signing signal or the speech signal. Because we are accustomed to auditing our vocal output to ensure that our outgoing stream of signals is acceptable, most hearing people use their vocal output to audit the quality of their sign-supported speech productions as well. Thus, adjustments made to ease the overload are generally made in the signed portion of the utterance, and misarticulations, incorrect signs, and deleted signs are not noticed. It is our impression that most hearing people who sign in this manner would claim that their signing is accurate and temporally congruent with their speech signal.

After examining in more detail the teacher's sign-supported speech productions during the earlier cited segment, we found several patterns. In the following transcript excerpt, the elipses ( . . . ) indicate intervening sentences by a child. As a reminder, vocal English is in italics; sign glosses are in upper-case italics.

TELL    SAY          HORSE RABBITT    NO       ALL OUTSIDE
*Tell . . . tell the Easter Bunny . . . He said, "No, he's all out.*

          DIFFERENT COLOR PRO-3rd
*You can take a different      color.*

          FORGET TELL              THANK-YOU YOU
*. . . You forgot to say you've . . . say thank      you . . .*

T    YOU FORGET HER          VOICE PLEASE
*T says you   forgot   her. Use your voice   please . . .*

ZERO ORANGE  SORRY        OUTSIDE ORANGE PICK OTHER COLOR
*No orange. He's sorry but he's out of    orange.  Pick another color . . .*

ZERO PURPLE WHAT WRONG TO GETHER-WITH EASTER DEVIL
*No purple? What's    wrong      with this        Easter Bunny? . . .*

          PRO-3rd CAN'T HEAR YOU PRO-3rd CAN'T HEAR YOU
*Well, tell him. He     can hear you.      He     can hear you . . .*

I THINK I    FREEZE GREEN TOGETHER-WITH YELLOW FLOWER LOC-ON I-T
*Ah, I think I want a green one with        yellow    flowers on        it.*

[————unintelligible————]    YELLOW FLOWER [————] OTHER ONE
*Those are purple flowers. I said yellow    flowers. Get another one.*

EAT EAT WAIT                OTHER ONE   CAN  OTHER ONE
*Okay.    Wait a minute. Can I have another   one? Have another one?*

I FREEZE OTHER ONE CAN I HAVE TWO      PINK ONE GOOD
*I want another one.   Can I have  two? Oh. A pink one.*

I GET TWO              MAYBE ASK GOOD

*I got  two . . . I don't know, maybe.    Good. Okay, let's change.*

          GOOD EASTER DEVIL
*You were a good  Easter  Bunny.*

The teacher consistently misarticulates signs, a problem compounded by the fact that her misarticulations often result in signs that actually mean something else, for example, DEVIL and HORSE for RABBIT, CAN'T for CAN, and FREEZE for WANT. But more problematic is the incongruity of her signs with her spoken English. It is clear that her signing is not in any sense an exact representation of English speech. Many English words are not represented by signs, and there is no consistent pattern to what is eliminated. The end result is signed sentences that are mostly incomprehensible, often contradictory in relation to the intended meaning, and largely incomplete. Even at best, the teacher's sentences are not accurate representations of English. To expect children with little or no hearing and with little previous contact with English to learn English from this kind of model is unrealistic.

Again, this is not an isolated instance and this teacher is not to be vilified for her performance. Such signing is typical of what children see in classrooms today. It is typical of hearing people attempting to speak and sign at the same time (Baker, 1978; Crandall, 1974, 1978; Kluwin, 1981b, 1981c; Marmor and Pettito, 1979) and appears to be more related to modality interference than to individual neglect.

The English signing of the Deaf aide stands in sharp contrast to the sign-supported speech of the hearing teacher. She seldom mistranslates an English word and she includes a sign for each of the words critical to the understanding of sentences. Her most common errors from an English perspective are mistakes in subject-object concord in the verb BE, and tense and aspect errors, such as we saw in her hyper-English sentence: WHAT *IS* FALL? These are more like classic second-language learner errors and are relatively minor in comparison to the errors that appear in the signing of the teacher. In this respect, we propose that the Deaf adult presents a more consistent and accurate model for the learning of English than does the native English speaker.

This classroom is unusual in that it contains an adult who is proficiently bilingual in ASL and English signing and who can make active use of both languages in teaching. In several instances, she effectively contrasts a structure or lexical item from English signing with the corresponding structure or item from ASL. The following example illustrates two instances of the contrastive use of ASL and English signing. In the first sentence, *D* employs English word order and the separate lexical item NOT. She immediately provides the ASL translation, which employs the incorporated negative and a construction typical of ASL. In the second sentence, she uses English word order. She begins to fingerspell H-I-S, stops and uses the systematic sign H̲I̲S̲, and then provides the ASL sign HIS. Such contrastive and comparative uses of English signing and ASL cannot help but reinforce the learning of English in children.

*D* to *R*:    *J* NOT WANT EAT CHOCOLATE PUDDING
'*J* doesn't want to eat [his] chocolate pudding.'

(turns) DON'T-WANT CHOCOLATE PUDDING DON'T-WANT
'[He] doesn't want his chocolate pudding, [he] doesn't.'

*D* to *Su*:    *J* NOT WANT TO EAT H- H̲I̲S̲ (systematic sign)
'*J* doesn't want to eat "H" his [in system]

HIS (ASL sign) CHOCOLATE PUDDING
his [in ASL] chocolate pudding.'

Our purpose in this section of the chapter has been to document and discuss several processes of linguistic socialization that emerge from the interaction among deaf children and their teachers. Specifically, we are concerned with the socialization of the children in relation to norms of use for ASL and fluent English signing, an important aspect of Deaf patrimony that contributes to the formation and maintenance of the Deaf ethnic group. We chose to study the processes of linguistic socialization in the classroom rather than in the home because we are interested in discovering how and by whom the majority of deaf children—those who do not have Deaf parents—are socialized. We concur with Berger and Luckmann's (1966, p. 153) claim that "language constitutes both the most important content and the most important instrument of socialization." Because most deaf children do not have parents who can communicate fluently with them, they learn and use language, and thus are socialized, primarily within the school environment.

The processes of linguistic socialization that we identified in this study indicate that both the form of the language and the content of the conversational interactions are important in the socialization of deaf children. The choice of a particular variety of signing—ASL, fluent English signing, or sign-supported speech—in particular situations with particular people carries social meaning in and of itself. The content of communication— what people are talking about—is also an independent component of the socialization process. For example, recall the scene in which the aide taught *J* something about table manners. The content in this case can be viewed as having an independent socializing function. In addition, when important content that relates to the structuring of the child's social world and identity is transmitted through a particular language variety, that language itself becomes an integral part of the child's social identity. Recall that the Deaf aide switched from English to ASL to communicate her point. In our study, the deaf children proficient in ASL choose to associate and communicate more with each other than with the children who are less proficient in ASL. This suggests that the form of their language is already related to who they are, both in their own and other people's eyes. Thus, through their daily face-to-face conversations with each other and with the Deaf aide, the children continually reaffirm and reconstruct their social world and their places within it.

The children who are less proficient linguistically are passive participants in this process unless they attempt to join a conversation by imitating parts of it or are corrected by the ASL-proficient children when they misarticulate a sign. At least one very salient ASL construction is already used productively by the less proficient children: I-LIKE-YOU. It is significant that the content of this linguistic construction allows a child to symbolize his or her understanding of the very immediate and salient social category friendship. Moreover, since the children are at an age when peers ordinarily replace parents as primary linguistic models, it is significant that the linguistic construction used to talk about a salient peer relationship is one of the few morphologically complex constructions used by the children. It is a construction created on a central structural principal of ASL. The use of ASL is the salient linguistic symbol of identity in the Deaf ethnic group, which is the group into which the children are being socialized. This again emphasizes the connection between linguistic content and form involved in these processes of socialization.

# 4

# Distinguishing Language Contact Phenomena in ASL Interpretation

Jeffrey Davis

## INTRODUCTION

The major linguistic outcomes of prolonged language contact, namely, code-switching, code-mixing, and lexical borrowing, are well documented in the research on bilingual communities (e.g., Di Pietro, 1978; Gumperz, 1976; Gumperz and Hernandez-Chavez, 1971; Poplack, 1980; Poplack, Wheeler, and Westwood, in press). The outcomes of language contact between ASL and English, however, are only in the early stages of systematic description. Lucas and Valli (this volume) discuss the complexity of the ASL-English contact situation in terms of the variety of participant characteristics and the varieties of language available to the participants. The complexities and vicissitudes of the situation raise a myriad of issues for signed language interpreters, who function at the point of interface of these two languages and cultures. The question of what constitutes acceptable or accurate English-to-ASL interpretation emerges as a frequent topic of debate in the field of signed language interpreting. Judgments about interpreted ASL output are based not only on how well the source language meaning is conveyed but also on how closely the interpreter approximates ASL grammatical structure and the degree to which interlingual transference—that is, code-switching, code-mixing, and lexical borrowing—is used appropriately. The appropriateness of the interpretation is determined according to the topic, setting, and participants. The primary questions addressed in the present study are (1) in what ways is interlingual

THE SOCIOLINGUISTICS OF THE DEAF COMMUNITY
Copyright © 1989 by Academic Press Inc.
All rights of reproduction in any form reserved.

transference manifest in the target language output of ASL interpreters and (2) what is the nature and the structure of these contact phenomena in terms of the ASL-interpreted output and how can they be distinguished from each other?

## INTERPRETING IN THE DEAF COMMUNITY

In order to study interpreting in the ASL-English contact situation, it is necessary to understand the nature and structure of sign language variation in the deaf community of the United States. In sociolinguistic terms, the language situation in the deaf community is most often described within the framework of a bilingual-diglossic continuum between American Sign Language (ASL) and English-based signing, with the intermediate varieties of sign language along the continuum labeled Pidgin Sign English (Stokoe, 1969; Woodward, 1973b). More recent research, however, suggests that alternative analyses are needed to describe the ASL-English contact situation. In fact, the situation cannot be adequately described by the traditional model of a bilingual-diglossic continuum. Researchers also suggest that the varieties of sign language found along the ASL-English continuum are not accurately described in terms of signed pidgin varieties (Cokely, 1983, 1984a; Davis, 1987; Lee, 1982, 1983; Lucas and Valli, this volume). The accuracy of the PSE cover term is thus challenged, exposing the need for systematic studies of the linguistic outcomes of prolonged ASL-English contact.

In the deaf community, we do not find the usual outcomes of bilingualism, namely, a shift to the group's first language and the disappearance of the second language, a shift to the group's second language and the disappearance of the first language, or the evolution of a new language through processes of pidginization and creolization (Grosjean, 1982). The linguistic outcomes of prolonged language contact in the deaf community seem to be influenced in a large part by the phenomenon of deafness. That is, deafness restricts linguistic input by way of the auditory channel. Furthermore, the parents of most deaf children do not use sign language. As a result, acquisition of the group language (ASL) and acculturation into the deaf community are achieved, for the majority of deaf individuals, on a deaf child-to-deaf child basis rather than on a parent-to-child basis. This feature of language contact appears to be unparalleled among bilingual communities in the world and serves as a model for understanding language acquisition outside the traditional bounds of the parent-child relationship, the phenomenon of bilingualism, and language variation in general.

Bilingualism in the deaf community is well documented in the literature (Grosjean, 1982; Kannapell, 1985; Stokoe, 1969; Woodward, 1982). A major issue in these studies is the use of the bilingual label, since most deaf people do not demonstrate native competence in English and the "dominant" language for most members of the community is ASL or contact signing. Grosjean (1982, p. 235) points out that "most bilinguals use their languages for different purposes and in different situations, and hence 'balanced' bilinguals, those who are equally fluent in both languages, are probably the exception and not the norm." The English-ASL contact situation is parallel to cases of societal bilingualism where one language (English, in this case) enjoys greater prestige and wider use than the other (ASL, for example). These contact situations, because of uneven situational and functional allocation of the codes, result in different configurations of bilingualism, for example, dominance in the majority language, balanced bilingualism, and dominance in the minority language (Mougeon, Beniak, and Valois, 1985). At the societal level, then, the deaf community in the United States can probably be best described as multilingual, since ASL, English, English-based signing, and contact signing are used to varying degrees in the community. At the individual level, the majority of deaf Americans are likely to be bilingual, since it appears that most members of the community probably have some degree of proficiency in signed, written, or even spoken English in addition to proficiency in ASL.

A unique characteristic of interpreting in the English-ASL contact situation, then, is that some degree of bilingual proficiency can often be found in the deaf audience who are the consumers of English-to-ASL interpretation. In other words, while interpreting into the target language (ASL), the interpreter can assume that the deaf audience has some degree of written or spoken proficiency in the source language (English). Based on this assumption, the interpreter has the option to encode spoken English words or phrases in the visual mode. That is, English words or phrases could be fingerspelled, a visual representation of English syntax could be given in the sign modality, or ASL signs could be accompanied by the mouthing of English words. The audience, however, may not always be bilingual. There are situations where the deaf consumer(s) may be an ASL monolingual. In this case, a different interpreting output would be expected (i.e., ASL with minimal transference from English).

The field of language interpretation represents an excellent forum for research in language contact phenomena. The linguistic study of interpreters, however, remains a neglected area of research. The primary goal of this study is to examine one form of signed language interpreting—English-to-ASL—in order to determine the nature and structure of interlingual phenomena such as code-switching, code-mixing, and lexical borrowing. As a first step, it is important to provide at least preliminary definitions of the major terminology used here. As discussed later, the present research demonstrates that it may be necessary to modify these definitions in order to accurately characterize the contact between signed language and spoken language.

## *DEFINITIONS*

English-to-ASL interpretation is the focus of this study. English is thus the source language or the language from which the interpreters work, and ASL is the target language or the language into which the interpretation is made. Interpretation refers to a interlingual process, that is, interpreting between two different languages. Translation, in contrast, implies changing a written message from one language to another. Whereas interpreters are most often required to simultaneously interpret the message from one language to another, translators have the "luxury" of time to accomplish their task.

Since interpretation is a process whereby the source language message is immediately changed into the target language, the task requires comprehension of the source language input, immediate discarding of words from the source language, analysis of the source message for meaning, and restructuring of the source message into the target language output (cf. Seleskovitch, 1978). This endeavor is even more difficult when the two languages involved are highly divergent structurally, such as English-Russian, Finnish-Spanish, English-ASL. The last example, English-ASL, not only involves two structurally diverse languages but also two different linguistic modalities (aural/oral vs. visual/gestural). If the situation were not complex enough, it is further complicated when one language traditionally enjoys greater status and wider use than the other. That is, English (the majority language) is heretofore the primary language used in deaf education and is construed as the language needed for purposes of upward mobility. ASL (the minority language), is traditionally relegated to use in informal settings and intragroup activities.

ASL interpretation must also be distinguished from sign language transliteration, that is, changing an English message from one form of English to another. In transliteration, it is conceivable to produce a morpheme-to-morpheme correspondence between spoken English and sign language. In a broad sense, this is a visual representation of English. An interpreter who transliterates, then, renders spoken English into a visually accessible form. Deaf individuals who are fluent in English may prefer transliteration over ASL interpretation (Frishberg, 1986). Winston (this volume, p. 148) argues that transliteration is "more than a simple recoding of spoken English into signed English. It is a complex combination of features from ASL and from English."

Code-switching, code-mixing, and lexical borrowing are typical in the conversational style of bilingual communities (De Pietro, 1978; Gumperz, 1976; Kachru, 1978a; Poplack, 1980). In bilingual communities where there is prolonged and intensive language contact, code-mixing occurs in both the home and the community at large. This type of bilingual community is referred to as a code-mixing community (Gumperz and Hernandez-Chavez, 1971). Switches that are motivated by a change in the speech event or situation are referred to as situational code-switching (Gumperz, 1976). When bilinguals switch for stylistic or rhetorical purposes, this is referred to as conversational code-switching (Gumperz and Hernandez-Chavez, 1971). Lee (1983) found that, depending on the topic, situation, and participants, signers switch from ASL signing to signing that is more like English (that is, situational code-switching). At other times, usually for stylistic purposes or as a rhetorical device, ASL signers manually encode an English word or phrase (that is, conversational code-switching). Lee's (1983) research supports the contention that the types of code-switching found in bilingual and multilingual hearing communities are also evident in the signing of bilinguals in the multilingual deaf community.

Code-switching refers to any stretch or portion of discourse where there is alternation between two languages. In other words, *there is a complete switch from one language to the other,* including a switch in the phonology and the morphology. By this definition, code-switching between ASL and English can only refer to cases where someone signing ASL stops *signing* and starts *speaking* English, or vice versa. In this study, however, the meaning of code-switching is extended to include a switch from ASL signing to English-based signing, that is, switching within a modality. How the interpreters in this study mark or "flag" a switch from ASL to English-based signing is described later.

Code-mixing, on the other hand, is much more difficult to distinguish. The term refers to "pieces" of one language being used while a speaker is basically using another language. The language used predominantly is the base or primary language, while the language from which the "pieces" originate is the source language. There is debate in the literature about the appropriate use of the code-mixing/code-switching labels. The debate arises out of how to differentiate switches *within* sentences (intrasentential) from switches at or *between* sentence boundaries (intersentential). Some researchers argue that the term code-mixing rather than code-switching should be used to refer to intrasentential phenomena—that is, the embedding or mixing of linguistic units from one distinct grammatical system to another *within* a sentence, clause, or constituent (Bokamba, 1985; Kachru, 1978a; Sridhar and Sridhar, 1980; Thelander, 1976). Lucas and Valli (this volume, p. 34) discuss how code-mixing in the ASL-English contact situation must be distinguished from cases of code-mixing described for spoken language situations:

mixing *within* components, while possible, is necessarily sequential. That is, it seems impossible to simultaneously produce two phonological events from two different spoken languages. In the contact signing described here, however, in which a signer produces ASL lexical items on the hands and simultaneous mouths the corresponding English lexical items, the result is the simultaneous production of two separate codes.

Code-mixing in the present study, then, is used to describe the interpreters' simultaneous mouthing of English words while signing ASL.

Lexical borrowing is different from code-switching and code-mixing. In the case of lexical borrowing, words from one language are repeatedly used in another language until they eventually become indistinguishable from the native vocabulary. That is, the borrowed lexical item becomes assimilated into another language. The borrowed form gets used longitudinally across speakers until it takes on the phonological and morphological characteristics of the borrowing language. Nonce borrowings, in contrast to established loanwords, are words that do not have frequent or widespread use in the borrowing language (Sankoff, Poplack, and Vanniarajan, 1986; Weinreich, 1953). They can be used only in one context by one speaker. Similar to established loanwords, however, nonce borrowings share the phonological and morphological characteristics of the borrowing language.

Linguistic interference is the *transfer of rules* from one language to another. This is in contrast to the interlingual *transfer of material* from the source language while the rules of the base language are maintained, that is, transference (Mougeon *et al.,* 1985). If the switch from ASL to English-based signing were sporadic and unsignaled, it might be considered a form of interference. In spoken language interpreting, for example, if a monolingual English audience were depending on an interpreter to understand the lecture of a visiting Russian scholar, and the interpreter used an occasional Russian word or sentence construction, it would probably be considered interference by the English audience. Cases of interference in signed language interpretation are the inappropriate use of English mouthing during ASL interpreting or the spoken glossing of ASL signs during ASL-to-English interpreting. Interference between the contact languages during English-to-ASL interpreting must thus be distinguished from transference. In the present study, the interest is ultimately in describing when interlingual transference (code-switching, code-mixing, and lexical borrowing) is used as an interpreting strategy for clarifying what is being said by the speaker.

Since signed language interpreters are usually required to *simultaneously* interpret between spoken English and ASL—two highly divergent languages—some interference between the languages can be expected. Unfortunately, it is notoriously difficult to ferret out factors that contribute to interference, for example, difficulty of the topic, lack of linguistic proficiency in one of the languages by the interpreter, simultaneous versus consecutive interpretation of the message.

It is conceivable that a lack of ASL proficiency on the part of the interpreter can significantly contribute to linguistic interference. For example, an interpreter who learned ASL as a second language might use idiosyncratic grammatical constructions. In order to separate outcomes of language contact that are the result of second-language acquisition from such regular and rule-governed outcomes as code-switching and lexical borrowing, the data used in the present study are from interpreters who are native ASL signers. Since the interpreters are interpreting into their native language (ASL), it is assumed that interference from English is minimal. The questions addressed in this study can thus be restated as follows: Are there instances in which the interpreters visually or manually represent source language forms (English) in the target language output (ASL)? If so, what is the nature and the structure of the interpreters' representations of English forms in the visual-manual modality of ASL? Finally, when is interlingual transference between ASL and English appropriately viewed as code-switching, as code-mixing, and as lexical borrowing?

## THE DATA BASE

Sign Media Inc. (SMI) (1985) has produced and marketed a videotape entitled *Interpreter Models: English to ASL [lectures]*. Because this tape is specifically designed to present models of English-to-ASL interpretation and is commercially available through SMI, the interpreting performance of the two models in this tape was examined. Both of these interpreters are native ASL signers and are considered "master" interpreters by professionals in the field of signed language interpreting. There are two interpreted lectures on the tape. The tape first shows one of the spoken English lectures, followed by the two ASL interpretations of that lecture, then both interpreters and lecturer are shown simultaneously. This is the format for both lectures. Following a preparatory meeting with each speaker, the two interpreters are asked to simultaneously interpret, without interrupting the speaker, the same two unrehearsed, thirty-minute lectures. The source language is English and the target language is ASL. There are fourteen people in the audience, five deaf and nine hearing. The audience is divided so that each interpreter is interpreting for a separate audience: the speaker can see all members of the audience, the interpreters can see the speaker but not each other, and each half of the audience can see only one interpreter.

In the videotape, we see approximately three-fourths of a full-body camera view of each interpreter. The videorecording includes a digital display of hours, minutes, seconds, and tenths of a second at the top of the visual frame. The viewer does not see the first ninety seconds of the lecture or the interpretation, then approximately six and one-half minutes of the lecture are shown. The final twenty or so minutes of the lecture are not shown on the videotape. For the present study, the first spoken English lecture and simultaneous ASL interpretations were transcribed. The topic of this lecture is radio and television measurement services, for example, Arbitron and Neilson. (These measurement services determine which radio and television programs consumers are tuning in.)

The spoken English lecture was transcribed using conventional orthography. The interpreted ASL was transcribed into gloss form and includes information pertaining to the use of ASL grammatical features, for example, nonmanual behaviors, use of space, indexing, and mouthing. All three sets of transcriptions (that is, the spoken English and both ASL interpretations) were done by the author. Two graduate assistants verified the English transcriptions. Two deaf, native ASL consultants and one interpreter consultant verified the ASL transcriptions. All transcriptions, verifications, and analyses were done with the aid of videoequipment that allows forward and backward slow motion viewing and full stop viewing with minimal distortion. Following verification of the transcripts, the spoken English text was matched with the interpreted ASL.

The data were then analyzed to determine if and when the interpreters use code-mixing, code-switching, and lexical borrowing. There are three major ways in which source language forms (English) are represented in the visual modality during ASL interpretation: (1) pronounced mouthing of English words (without voicing) while simultaneously signing ASL; (2) prefacing or following an ASL sign with a fingerspelled word; and (3) marking or flagging a fingerspelled word or the signed representation of an English form with certain ASL lexical items, for example, the index marker, the demonstrative, and the quotation markers. In the following discussion, each of these three categories is examined and illustrated with examples from the data corpus. How the visual representation and flagging of English may or may not qualify as instances of switching, mixing, or lexical borrowing is in turn considered.

## *Mouthing English Words while Simultaneously Signing ASL*

Because of the differences in linguistic modality (visual-gestural vs. aural-oral), interlingual transference between ASL and spoken English is different from transference between two spoken languages. Specifically, the constraints on the auditory channel imposed by deafness prevent the use of vocalization to convey linguistic meaning in ASL. The mouth, however, is used to convey linguistic meaning, whether in the ASL articulation of adverbs or in the visual representation of certain English words. The latter is a salient characteristic of intensive language contact between ASL and English and appears to be a type of simultaneous code-mixing. That is, rather than sequential switching from one language to the other, features of both languages are simultaneously produced. Over time, many of these mouthed English words are no longer recognizable as English. In many cases, native ASL users do not even recognize mouthing as a phonological remnant of English. Through the use of forward and backward slow motion and full stop videoequipment, and through verification by the deaf consultants, the interpreters' mouthing is included in the present data corpus.

In the following examples, the spoken English input is provided first, followed by each ASL interpretation. The transcription overscoring the glosses of the ASL signs is the interpreters' mouthing. The following diacritics are used: *ENG* ↑ indicates the clear use of English mouthing, *ENG* ↓ indicates reduced English mouthing, and *ASL MOUTH* refers to the use of adverbials (e.g., *MM, TH, PAH, CHA,* etc.). A switch from English mouthing to ASL mouthing, or vice versa, is indicated by a double solidus (//). In the case of reduced English mouthing, the part of the gloss that is mouthed is indicated with underscoring. Finally, in this study, fingerspelling is indicated by the symbol # preceding the example, the + symbol indicates sign replication, and * means the sign is articulated emphatically.

| Speaker: | *most households in the United States* | | |
|----------|----------------------------------------|--|--|
| | ENG ↑ | //ASL MOUTH | |
| Interpreter *A*: | MOST #US HOME (hesitates) IN-GENERAL | | |
| | ENG ↑      //ASL MOUTH //ENG ↑ | //ASL MOUTH | |
| Interpreter *B*: | HERE #US ALL-OVER   HOME-HOUSE OPEN 5-CL PLURAL | | |

In this first example, interpreter *A* simultaneously uses English mouthing and ASL signs for the interpretation of "most households" and then switches to ASL mouthing (*MM*). Interpreter *B* alternates between ASL mouthing and simultaneous English mouthing with ASL signing. *B* interprets "households" as HOME-HOUSE and later reverses the order to HOUSE-HOME. In both instances, *B* mouths the English gloss of what is being manually articulated. Both ASL consultants pointed out that, in their experience, ASL signers rarely, if ever, use the English word *households* in conversation. They agreed, however, that the concept could be conveyed by signing HOUSE following by a plural or possessive marker (e.g., HOUSE++, HOUSE OPEN 5-CL PLURAL, or HOUSE 3rd-POSS). The consultants also said that they had never before seen the configuration HOME-HOUSE or HOUSE-HOME.

It appears, based on these data, that a word such as *household* that does not have a one-to-one equivalent in ASL is "flagged" by the interpreters. Interpreter *A* signs HOME, then hesitates briefly before adding IN-GENER-AL. Interpreter *B* uses a different strategy. Since *household* has two sylla-bles, *B* represents the English word with what appears to be two-syllable compound sign in ASL, that is, HOME-HOUSE. This analysis is supported by the fact that the sign is later reversed to HOUSE-HOME by the same inter-preter. Again, it is important to emphasize that *B* never mouths the English word *households*. Also note that *B* does tag the anomalous HOME-HOUSE with OPEN 5-CL PLURAL, that is, the way in which the consultants reported that ASL signers typically convey the concept.

In the data corpus, there is only one case where one of the interpreters mouths something that is heard, as opposed to glossing what is signed with the hands. When the speaker uses the word *cartoons* in the lecture, *B* signs

Speaker: *Lots of people have heard about Neilson television rating services which is in the television side of the fence and we are a, ah, kind of share that market in terms of providing measurement data for the television services. But in radio, Ar-bitron is the "major book."*

|  | ENG ↓ |  | //ENG ↑ | //ASL MOUTH// | ENG ↑ | // |
|---|---|---|---|---|---|---|
| Interpreter *A:* | MANY PEOPLE KNOW NAME | #NEILSON, | FOCUS | #T.V.++, |

//ASL MOUTH　　　　　　　　　　//ENG ↑　　ENG ↑
(left space) POSS-PL, (shift to right space) THAT #ARBITRON, #NEILSON (shifts

////ASL MOUTH　　　　　　　　　//ENG ↓　　//
back to left space) #TV++, HAVE SHARE PL=POSS (hesitates) BUSINESS (shift

//ENG ↑ //　　　　　　　　//ASL MOUTH //ENG ↑　　//ASL MOUTH
back to right space) #IDRADIO (left indexic marker), REALLY #ARBITRON TOP

　　　　　　　　　ASL MOUTH　//　ENG ↓　　　　　　//ASL MOUTH//　ENG ↓
Interpreter *B:*　UNDERSTAND, PEOPLE-INDEXIC-PL, FAMOUS KNOW NAME

//ENG ↑　　　　　　　　　　　　//ASL MOUTH//
WHICH #ANIELSON (interpreter self corrects) THAT (right indexic marker)

ENG ↑　//ASL MOUTH　　　　//ENG ↑ //　ENG ↓　　　　　//ENG ↑
#NEILSON, STRONG CONNECTION #TV++, FAMOUS SAME-AS #ARBITRON

//ENG ↓　// ASL MOUTH// ENG ↑　//ENG ↓　　　　　　　　　　//ASL MOUTH
SAME-AS FOCUS　#TV++++ MEASURE PEOPLE WATCH, HOW-MANY SO-FORTH,

　　　　　　　　//ENG ↑　　　　　　　　　//ENG ↓
UNDERSTAND++ FOCUS RADIO (left indexic marker), #ARBITRON *STRONG

**Fig. 1** Sample of English-to-ASL interpretation and mouthing that accompanies ASL signs.

SILLY-STORY but mouths "cartoons." The two ASL consultants said that deaf signers commonly fingerspell *cartoons*. This is the strategy that interpreter *A* adopts. Interpreter *B*, in contrast, again uses syllabification, that is, a two-syllable word in English (*cartoons*) is interpreted as a two-sign compound (SILLY-STORY).

The excerpts in Figures 1 and 2 show how each of the two interpreters simultaneously use English mouthing, reduced English mouthing, or ASL mouthing during the course of English-to-ASL interpretation. Analysis of these data suggests a range of mouthing, as outlined in Figure 3. At one extreme is what can be aptly described as a unique kind of code-mixing, the use of ASL simultaneously with the mouthing of English words, for example, nouns, question words, numbers, and fingerspelled words. At the other extreme is ASL mouthing, which does not encode English. In some cases, the mouthing is strictly and purely a feature of ASL, such as the mouthing of ASL adverbial markers that bear no synchronic or diachronic relation to English. In other cases, such as the mouthing that accompanies the ASL signs LATE, HAVE, and FINISH, English words have apparently been

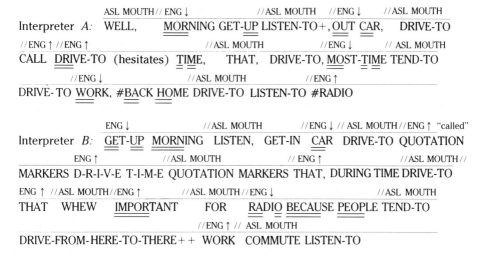

Speaker: *So you listen to it in the morning as you're getting up, then you go out in your car and the drive times as they refer to them, are the major times that people listen in the United States to the radio, is when they're driving to work, and when they're coming home.*

```
                   ASL MOUTH// ENG ↓              //ASL MOUTH   //ENG ↓    //ASL MOUTH
Interpreter  A:   WELL,     MORNING GET-UP LISTEN-TO+,OUT CAR,    DRIVE-TO
//ENG ↑ //ENG ↑                    //ASL MOUTH           //ENG ↓   // ASL MOUTH
CALL  DRIVE-TO  (hesitates)  TIME,     THAT,   DRIVE-TO, MOST-TIME TEND-TO
        //ENG ↓              //ASL MOUTH          //ENG ↑
DRIVE-TO WORK, #BACK HOME DRIVE-TO  LISTEN-TO  #RADIO
```

```
                 ENG ↓              //ASL MOUTH        //ENG ↓ // ASL MOUTH//ENG ↑ "called"
Interpreter  B:  GET-UP  MORNING  LISTEN,  GET-IN  CAR  DRIVE-TO  QUOTATION
          ENG ↑             //ASL MOUTH             // ENG ↑             //ASL MOUTH//
MARKERS D-R-I-V-E  T-I-M-E  QUOTATION MARKERS THAT,  DURING TIME DRIVE-TO
ENG ↑ //ASL MOUTH//ENG ↑        //ASL MOUTH//ENG ↓                  //ASL MOUTH
THAT   WHEW   IMPORTANT      FOR   RADIO BECAUSE PEOPLE TEND-TO
                                        //ENG ↑ // ASL MOUTH
DRIVE-FROM-HERE-TO-THERE++  WORK  COMMUTE LISTEN-TO
```

**Fig. 2**  Additional sample of English-to-ASL interpretation and mouthing that accompanies ASL signs.

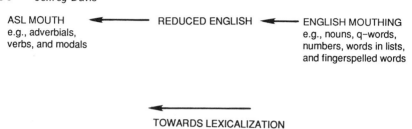

**Fig. 3**  A range of mouthing during English-to-ASL interpretation.

borrowed and subsequently lexicalized into ASL by way of mouthing. Between these two extremes of full English mouthing and ASL mouthing, there is reduced English mouthing, which for now is best described as a kind of lexical borrowing. On the whole, further research is needed in order to adequately analyze and describe the formal-functional range of mouthing and its linguistic underpinnings.

## ASL Signs Prefaced or Followed by a Fingerspelled Word

Fingerspelling is a system for representing the English alphabet manually by varying handshapes. It is used primarily to represent proper nouns and English terms that do not have ASL lexical equivalents. Fingerspelling is usually articulated in the space between the face and dominant shoulder and the palm orientation is toward the addressee. Clearly, fingerspelling forms an integral part of ASL (as opposed to being a part of English). In contrast to individual ASL signs, which usually involve one or two handshapes, a fingerspelled word often involves many different handshapes.

Battison (1978) suggests that the representation of English orthographic events with fingerspelling, as such entails phonological and sometimes morphological restructuring and is an example of lexical borrowing in ASL. He claims that fingerspelled words, which are structurally different from ASL signs, are restructured systematically to fit the formal patterns of ASL. By this account, some of the systematic changes a fingerspelled word undergoes in this process are deletion of handshape letters, dissimilation of handshapes and assimilation of number of fingers involved, location changes, movement additions and orientation changes, and semantic restructuring of the signs. The lexical items that result from this process are referred to as fingerspelled loan signs (Battison, 1978, pp. 218–19).

It can be argued, however, that the fingerspelling of English words is not lexical borrowing in the strictest sense (S. K. Liddell and C. Lucas, personal communication). That is, in the lexical borrowing that takes place between spoken languages, a lexical item, or form-meaning pairing, in one language is borrowed into another language. When this happens, there are typically phonological and semantic adjustments that make the form-meaning relationship in the borrowing language different from that in the source language. For example, the Spanish lexical item *junta*, [*húnta*], was borrowed into English and is now pronounced [*ǰ'ʌntə*].

That is not exactly what takes place in the ASL-English situation. For example, the orthographic representation of the English word *date* occurs as a fingerspelled lexical item in ASL, consisting of a sequence of four ASL morphemes (d-a-t-e), what earlier analyses might have described as a sequence of four handshapes. The salient relationship here is not between the respective phonological systems of two languages but rather between the orthographic system of one language, (English), and the phonological system of another, ASL. Furthermore, the relationship between the phonological systems of spoken languages is truly one of *borrowing*—one language *borrows* the sounds of another and the result is a *loan*. At no point, however, can the relationship between English orthography and ASL phonology be characterized as borrowing. ASL morphemes are never borrowed from the orthographic English event; they are simply used to *represent* the orthographic event. An example of a proper analogy from spoken languages for the relationship between ASL fingerspelling and English orthography is a speaker's pronunciation of the English letters used to orthographically represent a Spanish word, such as [*ǰe-u-ɛn-ti-e*] for *junta.*

A fingerspelled word, then, can never technically be described as English. Fingerspelling, by its very nature, is an ASL phonological event. In a pattern similar to lexical borrowing, a fingerspelled word can get used repeatedly and eventually become lexicalized into ASL. In other words, a fingerspelled word can undergo systematic phonological, morphological, and semantic changes like those described by Battison (1978). And through this process of lexicalization, the word can eventually become an integral part of the ASL lexicon. This usually happens when the fingerspelled word is used longitudinally across speakers, but lexicalization is also evident when words get fingerspelled repeatedly in a single context.

The interpreters in this study make extensive use of fingerspelling. The examples in the data corpus fall into three categories: (1) lexicalized fingerspelled signs, which have been lexicalized into ASL through the processes described earlier; (2) nonce fingerspelling that is context and topic specific but eventually follows the pattern of lexicalization already described; and (3) full fingerspelling, wherein each "letter" (i.e., ASL morpheme) is clearly represented. Some examples of the first category are presented in Table I. These particular examples of lexicalized fingerspelled signs are not only used extensively by the two interpreters in the present study but are also used throughout the ASL community at large.

**Table I**
Examples of Lexicalized Fingerspelled Signs

| Interpreter A | Interpreter B |
|---|---|
| #BACK | #ALL |
| #CAR | #BUSY (two-handed) |
| #CARTOONS | #CO |
| #CO | #NEWS |
| #DATE | #OR |
| #DO-DO | #SHOW |
| #HOBBY (speaker says "hobbies") | #SPORTS |
| #IF | #TV |
| #NEWS | #WHAT |
| #SPORTS | |
| #TV | |
| #US (speaker says "United States") | |
| #WHAT | |

Some fingerspelled signs are used like nonce events. Typically, these start out as examples of full fingerspelling, that is, the signs are produced in the area typically used for fingerspelling, with all morphemes represented and with palm orientation away from the signer. Examples include #RADIO, #ARBITRON, and #NEILSON. These words are context and topic specific. Both interpreters, following repeated use by the speaker, eventually treat these words as an ASL lexical item, as opposed to a fingerspelled representation of an English orthographic event. For example, there is either deletion or assimilation, or both, of the number of handshape letters involved during the production of these repeated fingerspelled words.

Sometimes the interpreters preface or follow an ASL sign with a fingerspelled word. Examples are as follows:

| Speaker: | *public affairs* |
| Interpreter *A*: | DISCUSS #PUBLIC AFFAIRS |

| Speaker: | *cartoons* |
| Interpreter *A*: | FUNNY #CARTOONS |

| Speaker: | *billboards* |
| Interpreter *B*: | #BILLBOARDS OPEN C-CL |

| Speaker: | *drive times* |
| Interpreter *B*: | QUOTATION MARKERS, #DRIVE TIMES, QUOTATION MARKERS, THAT DURING TIME DRIVE-TO THAT |

In each case, it appears that an English orthographic event is fingerspelled because there is no ASL counterpart for that event. The fingerspelled word is often "flagged" with an ASL lexical marker, for example, a classifier, demonstrative pronoun, or quotation mark. In other instances, a multi-meaning ASL sign, for example, DISCUSS or FUNNY, is tagged or prefaced with a fingerspelled word. In the first two cases, for example, the interpreter chooses to tag the ASL signs with the fingerspelled representation of the words used by the speaker.

From a preliminary analysis of the data corpus, there appears to be a range of fingerspelling used in English-to-ASL interpretation, as outlined in Figure 4.

Fingerspelling entails event marking in very particular ways by the interpreters. For example, mouthing of an English gloss accompanies all fingerspelled words, even lexicalized fingerspelled signs. Indexing, eye-gaze, and support of the active arm with the passive hand also mark the fingerspelling used. In their use of fingerspelling, the interpreters appear to follow a pattern of movement toward lexification of fingerspelled signs into the structure of ASL.

Overall, fingerspelling serves a variety of purposes in ASL. Personal communication with deaf consultants indicates that ASL signers sometimes use fingerspelling for stylistic purposes. For example, an ASL signer can opt to fingerspell a word rather than sign the ASL equivalent. An ASL sign can be prefaced or followed with a fingerspelled representation of that sign. What is also evident in these examples is the simultaneous use of two phonologies, that is, an ASL representation of an English orthographic event is accompanied by English mouthing. The processes involved in fingerspelling need further elucidation before accurate labels can be attached, although it is suggested that the expression *fingerspelled representation* characterizes the phenomenon more accurately than the expression *fingerspelled loan sign* or *lexical borrowing*.

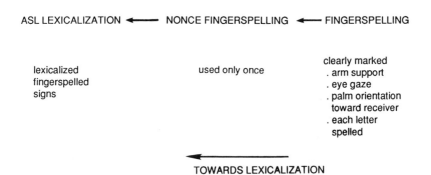

**Fig. 4**  A range of fingerspelling during English-to-ASL interpretation.

## *Marking or Flagging a Fingerspelled or Signed English Form with Certain ASL Lexical Items*

In this category are English forms that are visually represented and flagged in very specific ways. Consider the following example:

| Speaker: | *A lot of parents, young parents, use television as a babysitter.* |
| --- | --- |

ENG ↓                   //ENG ↑       //

Interpreter A:    MANY MOTHER-FATHER YOUNG, FINE #TV++,

ASL MOUTH            //ENG ↑//ASL MOUTH

                TAKE ADVANTAGE-OF, BABY TAKE-CARE-OF, SO-TO-SPEAK

In this example, the interpreter marks the speaker's metaphoric use of the television as a babysitter with the ASL sign SO-TO-SPEAK. This sign is similar to the one for QUOTATION MARKERS, except that the former is done lower and more rapidly than the latter in sign space.

Observe how the QUOTATION MARKERS sign is used in the following excerpts:

| Speaker: | *then you go out in your car and the drive times as they refer to them* |
| --- | --- |
| Interpreter *B*: | GET-IN CAR, DRIVE-TO, QUOTATION MARKERS, #DRIVE-TIMES, QUOTATION MARKERS, THAT DURING TIME DRIVE-TO THAT |
| Interpreter *A*: | OUT CAR, DRIVE-TO, CALL DRIVE (hesitates) TIME, THAT DRIVE-TO |

Interpreter *B* fingerspells *drive times* and marks this segment before and after it is spelled with QUOTATION MARKERS. It is as though the interpreter is setting this form off as a lexical item that is not ASL. Interpreter *A* prefaces DRIVE TIME with the labeling sign CALL, hesitates, then marks the segment with a demonstrative followed by a glossing of *drive times* with DRIVE-TO. Interpreter *B* also incorporates the use of the demonstrative.

## SUMMARY AND CONCLUSIONS

This study has described how spoken English lexical items are represented in the visual modality. The possibility that these visual representations of English qualify as code-switching, code-mixing, or lexical borrowing has been discussed. The results of intensive contact between two structurally diverse languages like ASL and English are extremely complex and point to a need for modification of the terms traditionally used to characterize language contact phenomena. For example, with a strict definition of code-switching, a complete switch to another language is required, including a switch in phonology. According to this definition, a "true" switch occurs only if an ASL signer stops signing and begins speaking English (or any other language for that matter). In order to understand the underlying linguistic and sociolinguistic processes involved in code-switching, the strict definition of the phenomenon must be extended to include switching from ASL to English-based signing, that is, switching within modality.

The term code-mixing also should not be loosely applied. It does not imply that the two contact languages are thrown together in a random and ungoverned fashion. Code-mixing, in the form of simultaneous use of English mouthing and ASL, appears to be highly rule-governed. This is demonstrated by the very similar ways in which the two native ASL interpreters simultaneously produced features of both languages. Code-switching and code-mixing also must be strictly distinguished from interference (often a result of inadequate second-language acquisition) and lexical borrowings common even in monolingual speech.

The movement toward lexicalization within the target language (ASL) is evident in these data. The manual representation of English forms is primarily an intrasentential phenomenon. That is, the use of English by ASL interpreters is restricted to single or double lexical items within what otherwise is an ASL text. That English mouthing sometimes marks the ASL interpreting output has to do with the cross-modality nature of the ASL-English contact situation, that is, visual-gestural and oral-aural. Because of the phenomenon of deafness, the auditory channel is not available for linguistic input. As a result, vocalization is not used for linguistic encoding purposes in ASL. The mouth, however, because it is highly visible, is used to convey linguistic meaning (e.g., adverbials). One of the characteristics of intensive contact between ASL and English, then, is that the mouth is sometimes used to visually represent certain English words. In the vast majority of cases, the interpreters do not mouth what they hear. Rather, they gloss, by way of mouthing, what is articulated with their hands. This is apparently a type of simultaneous code-mixing, rather than sequential switching from one language to another. The present research and the research by Lucas and Valli (this volume) appear to be the first studies to describe simultaneous code-mixing in this way.

The use of mouthing seems patterned, in that both native ASL interpreters in this study produce mouthing in very similar ways. English mouthing marks fingerspelled words, most lexicalized fingerspelling is used for emphasis, lists, numbers, and question words. The deaf consultants in this study agreed that both interpreters use mouthing in a way appropriate to ASL. In fact, it was only through slow-motion viewing that the two native ASL signers recognized some of the mouthing as pronounced English. Both consultants felt that deaf signers use mouthing in much the same way as the interpreters. In this chapter, it is proposed that there exists a range of mouthing in ASL. At one extreme, English words are clearly mouthed; at the other, mouthing no longer represents English. It appears that some English words are borrowed by way of mouthing and subsequently lexicalized into ASL (that is, native ASL signers see the use of mouthing as a part of ASL).

The use of fingerspelling also appears to follow a pattern toward lexicalization into ASL. The interpreters in this study make extensive use of fingerspelling. Sometimes an English orthographic event is fingerspelled because there is no ASL counterpart for that event, or a multimeaning ASL sign is tagged or prefaced with a fingerspelled word. In such cases, the fingerspelled words are flagged in very specific ways, for example, mouthing, eye-gaze, indexing, labeling, quotation markers, and palm orientation. When a fingerspelled word is used repeatedly in a single context, it begins to be lexicalized in ASL according to patterns similar to those found with lexicalized fingerspelled signs. The mouthing and fingerspelling of English events by the interpreters in this study does not appear to be sporadic or unsignalled, but rather patterned and rule-governed. Both devices serve to disambiguate and elucidate the interpreted message.

It appears that the degree to which there is interlingual transference during English-to-ASL interpretation is determined by the participants, topic, and setting. In many interpreting situations, the deaf audience has some degree of written or spoken proficiency in the source language (English). In a sense, the interpretation is needed not because the deaf audience members do not understand English, but because they cannot hear it. Based on the assumption that the audience is bilingual, the interpreter has the option of encoding spoken English words in the visual mode. That is, English words, phrases, or syntax are sometimes represented in fingerspelling or through a morpheme-to-morpheme representation using ASL signs. Further research is needed to elucidate these processes.

## ACKNOWLEDGMENTS

I would like to thank Ceil Lucas and Scott Liddell for providing significant feedback during the preparation of this chapter; Susan Walker, Mary Ann LaBue, and Patricia Saylor for the many hours they spent working on the ASL and English transcriptions; and Barbara Riggs, Steve Collins, Clayton Valli, Kathy Jankowski, Jean Lindquist, and Cindy Roy for invaluable input. All interpretations, as the saying goes, are my own.

# 5

# *Sociolinguistic Aspects of the Black Deaf Community*

Anthony J. Aramburo

## *INTRODUCTION*

The black deaf community can be described as a group of individuals who live in a "hearing and color-conscious society" (Anderson, 1972). They are continually striving to overcome the communication problems faced in everyday living while still having to contend with racist attitudes that govern society. They are a group of individuals that appear to be immersed in both the black and deaf cultures.

At least three issues surface as a result of this "double immersion." One issue concerns the actual reality of a black deaf community, as distinct from both the black community and the deaf community. A second issue concerns identity. That is, given the double immersion in both black and deaf cultures, the question is whether the individual's identity is primarily as a member of the black community, the deaf community, or the black deaf community. A third issue concerns communication patterns as defined in terms of differences between black signing and white signing, and in terms of sign variation and code-switching. Casual observation reveals that the signing of black deaf individuals varies as a function of the race of other participants in a conversational setting. That is, black signers sign differently with white signers than they do with other black signers.

This study investigates all of these issues and presents empirical data that permit a clearer sociolinguistic perspective than has heretofore been possible. Data relating to the issue of identity consist of the results of a

THE SOCIOLINGUISTICS OF THE DEAF COMMUNITY
Copyright © 1989 by Academic Press Inc.
All rights of reproduction in any form reserved.

survey conducted with sixty black deaf individuals. For the issue of communication patterns, data consist of videotapes made of the conversational interaction of seven dyads controlled for race, audiological status, and signing skills.

## THE BLACK DEAF COMMUNITY

As defined by Hillery (1974), a community is a general social system in which a group of people live together, share common goals, and carry out certain responsibilities to each other. Loomis (1983) states that communities strive to protect the resources that will serve to inform future generations of their cultural past. Padden (1980) distinguishes between culture and community and refers to the former as a set of learned behaviors of a group of people who have their own language, values, rules for behavior, and traditions. She goes on to point out that a community can not only have individuals who are culturally deaf but also hearing and deaf people who are not culturally deaf yet still interact with culturally deaf people and see themselves as working with them in various common concerns (Padden, 1980, pp. 92–93). Evidence for the existence of both a black community and a deaf community is presented elsewhere (e.g., Higgins, 1980; Padden, 1980).

The first issue here concerns the reality of the black deaf community, as distinct from both the black community and the deaf community. The contention here is that there does indeed exist a black deaf community, and that it shares the characteristics and values of both the black community and the deaf community. In addition, it has some characteristics and values that are unique. For example, members of the black deaf community share with the black community the obstacle of overcoming societal prejudices against black people. The high unemployment rate is felt more in the black community than the white community. The unemployment rate is even higher among blacks in the deaf community. Indeed, underemployment is rampant in both black communities (Christiansen and Barnartt, 1987). There are few black political leaders in the black community. They are nonexistent in the black deaf community. Both the black community and the black deaf community declare their black heritage, and the struggles that blacks endured in obtaining their civil rights are salient in both communities.

Features shared by the black deaf community and the deaf community are largely in the domain of communication. Their language, American Sign Language, is an important factor in the socialization process within the deaf community. Social activities such as sports events (where the teams are comprised of deaf players), deaf club activities, deaf-related conferences and meetings attract deaf individuals because all involved can identify with the mode of communication used, ASL. Stereotypes classifying the deaf as dumb, uneducated, and unable to work, to name a few, are realities both the general deaf community and the black deaf community have to overcome in a "hearing world." The black deaf individual must also overcome some additional stereotypes that society at large places on blacks. Lower-class whites have similar stereotypes placed on them.

Characteristics and values that are unique to the black deaf community can be identified by looking at patterns of social interaction, education, and use of sign language. For example, many of the clubs where the black deaf go for social purposes cater primarily to the black deaf community. This is true in most cities (Higgins, 1980). There is also, in most cities, a meeting place where the white deaf go for their social activities. No law or rules laid down by the deaf community mandates this occurrence, it is simply something that happens. The separation of social meeting places is evidence of the existence of a black deaf community. The clubs where the black deaf meet are their places for disseminating key information about how they will carry out certain functions as a group. Club meetings, sports meetings, dances, card socials, and personal celebrations such as birthdays and anniversaries all happen at the club house. Information related to jobs, problems that members are faced with, new laws pertaining to the deaf is all available at the deaf club.

Not many black deaf individuals have the luxury of owning a telecommunication device for the deaf (TDD), so the telephone is not a viable means for relaying information. Members of the black deaf community do not all live in the same area of the city. For those who do live in close proximity, the club house is the most convenient place for meeting in order to discuss and pass on information. Observation of the black deaf community confirms that black deaf marry other black deaf. Judging from married couples in the black deaf community, an individual tends to marry another black deaf individual who attended the same residential school. When a black deaf individual does marry a hearing person, that hearing spouse is usually also black.

Educational patterns also provide evidence of the existence of a black deaf community. In recent years, the black and deaf communities have made significant achievements in the area of education. Blacks no longer must settle for an education that is "separate but equal" and can freely attend any school or university for which they are qualified. During the days of racial segregation, however, most elementary school programs for black deaf children were set up on campuses that accommodated an all black student population. The programs were mediocre (Hairston and Smith, 1983) and in most cases, the administrative personnel had no expertise in the field of deaf education, a topic on which information was scarce.

Although there were good intentions for educating this special group of students, the reality was that the tools and personnel needed to achieve the best results were not available. Teachers in black schools for the deaf were not required to have college credits or course work related to the education of deaf children. College programs that provided blacks with a degree in education offered no course work specifically geared to educating the deaf. Teachers used their knowledge and expertise in these schools to work with deaf students and provide them with a decent education. Still, the problem of communication surfaced.

Then as now, educational programs for the deaf do not require the teacher to be versed in American Sign Language. Programs designed to teach sign language to teachers are rare. The manual alphabet was the predominant mode for teaching in many of the schools with black deaf students. Often entire lessons were fingerspelled. In many schools, sign language was not permitted in the classroom. Teachers cannot understand their students, so they insist on fingerspelling (in English) as the sole means of communication. Needless to say, the student has to have a good grasp of the English language in order to comprehend what is being taught in the classroom. In many cases, the home environment was not the ideal place for learning English. Today, black deaf children who are born to hearing parents face the same predicament of their peers in the past, namely, many hearing parents refuse to communicate with their children through sign language. Parents leave the burden of educating their child solely to the school system.

Black deaf children born to deaf parents have an advantage over their peers with hearing parents, since deaf parents communicate with their children through sign language. When these students go back to the residential schools, they bring sign language with them. This provides a means of communication other than fingerspelling. Outside the classroom, students converse using sign language. Playground activities or other non-school-related activities permit students to develop their language and social skills. During the years that black schools were not permitted to compete with white schools in athletic activities, black students had to travel in order to compete with rival schools. During these visits, black deaf students shared their language and taught each other new signs. Upon completing school, most black deaf students chose to learn a trade in order to make their living, and it has been suggested that a correlation exists between this choice and inadequate English skills. Moreover, this choice of vocational training greatly lessened the number of black deaf students entering college (Christiansen and Barnartt, 1987). The number of black deaf students entering colleges and universities today is still small. Many students, whether in the residential schools or special education programs for the hearing-impaired in local school districts, are graduating with a high school certificate and not a high school diploma. Facilities and services offered to black deaf students are becoming better, but the number of black deaf individuals possessing a doctoral degree is very low when compared to the overall deaf community.[1]

Although a certain level of achievement has been attained within the majority deaf and the majority hearing communities, black deaf individuals are still behind in terms of advancement. The black deaf person is doubly affected insofar as being labeled black, poor, and disabled amounts to simultaneous placement in two devalued worlds (Alcocer, 1974). Blacks in general have made considerable gains for the black community, but members of the black deaf community have had a difficult time emulating their success. Deaf people in general did not participate in the movement to improve their civil rights until the 1970s, when they actively joined other organizations of disabled people in transforming their own special civil rights issues into the 1973 Rehabilitation Act (Boros and Stuckless, 1982). The black deaf community, having missed the opportunity to gain advancement alongside the black community, must now advocate for themselves. As stated by many black deaf individuals, they have noticed no real improvements overall in the black deaf community. Deaf people, like other minorities, are subject to categorical discrimination (Schowe, 1979). Being discriminated against on the basis of deafness is difficult enough to overcome, but the joint impact of handicap discrimination and ethnic discrimination compounds the hardship and increases the barriers to success.

Further evidence of the existence of a black deaf community comes from differences observed between black signing and white signing. Later in this chapter, evidence is provided of how black signing differs from white signing, mainly in the area of lexical choices.

On the whole, members of the black deaf community are aware of both their black culture and deaf culture. Much as members of the black community pass on to future generations cultural resources such as black art, black folklore, and black spirituals, members of the black deaf community pass along similar cultural resources. For example, an oral history about residential school experiences from the era when schools were segregated parallels the oral history of the black community about slavery.

## BLACK OR DEAF?

As discussed earlier, black deaf individuals are immersed in both the black and deaf cultures. It appears that the black deaf individual can be part of

---

[1]These observations come from in-depth interviews with administrators and teachers at the Southern School for the Deaf in Baton Rouge, Louisiana (closed in 1978). The interviews covered the educational situation for the black deaf in Louisiana, Mississippi, and Texas in particular.

both cultures, so a question of identity arises. That is, does a black deaf individual identify primarily with the black community or with the deaf community. In an attempt to answer this question of identity, a survey was conducted among sixty members of the black deaf community in the Washington, D.C. area. The majority of the persons who participated were high school and college students attending the Model Secondary School for the Deaf (MSSD) and Gallaudet University. Approximately one-third of the individuals interviewed lived in Washington, D.C. and surrounding areas. Twenty individuals were targeted from three age groups: eighteen to twenty-five years old, twenty-six to thirty-five years old, and thirty-six years old and above. A representative sample of ten men and ten women was targeted for each age group. Older members of the black deaf community from Washington, D.C. were sought for representation of the adult black deaf population.

In actuality, a total of thirty-three men and twenty-seven women participated in the study. The median age of the participants was 27.1 years. The age at which each respondent acquired sign language was recorded: fourteen participants (23 percent) learned sign language before age six, and forty-six participants (77 percent) learned sign language after age six. The majority of those surveyed attended a residential school, that is, fifty participants (88 percent). The remaining seven participants (12 percent) attended either public or parochial schools, or both. Four of the participants (7 percent) are children of deaf parents. The remaining fifty-six participants (93 percent) are children of hearing parents. In disclosing their competence in using ASL, fifty-five participants (92 percent) described themselves as native signers of ASL. The remaining five participants (8 percent) did not provide an assessment of their skills as native ASL signers.

The interviews were conducted with participants on a one-on-one, informal basis. A comfortable setting was agreed upon by both the interviewer and the respondent. Interviews averaged thirty minutes in duration. In the initial part of the interview, respondents were briefed about the nature of the study. These preliminaries also enabled the interviewer to gain familiarity with the communication skills of each respondent. ASL was used throughout the interview as the primary mode of communication. First, respondents were asked background questions concerning age and onset of deafness, deaf family members, and educational history. Once comfortable with the interviewing process, the respondents were next questioned about black culture and the black community in general. The questions were as follows: (1) Who are some black leaders you recognize as influential in the black community? (2) Where did you acquire your knowledge of black history? (3) Have you ever felt you were discriminated against or treated differently not because you are deaf but because you are black? (4) In terms of upward achievement, where do you see the black community headed? (5) What contribution(s) do you feel black deaf people can make in bringing about racial equality?

This session on black culture and the black community in general was followed by questions about deaf culture and the black deaf community. The questions included the following: (1) Just like we talked about a black culture, do you feel there is a deaf culture existing in the deaf community? (2) Who are some deaf leaders you identify with? (3) What is the most significant achievement obtained by deaf people? (4) When in school, were you taught deaf culture in class? (5) Did you ever feel you were discriminated against or treated differently because you are deaf?

Subsequent to the discussion of the individual topics of black culture and deaf culture, the two topics were combined in order to inquire about the participants' feelings on being black and deaf. The participants were asked to conjoin their knowledge and experiences of being black and deaf in order to comment on what they perceived to be black deaf culture. The questions leading into this discussion were the following: (1) How does black culture and the black community differ from deaf culture and the black deaf community? (2) What are advancements you notice that have been made by black deaf individuals? (3) Do you feel black deaf culture is alive and strong in the black deaf community? (4) What do you see as the most significant barrier black deaf individuals have to overcome in order to be considered equal with the black community and also with the deaf community? (5) What do you hope to contribute to the black deaf community? (6) Which do you identify with first, your black culture or your deaf culture?

## RESULTS

The survey provided a general answer to the question of identity. Eight participants (13 percent) said that they identify themselves as deaf before they identify as black; the remaining fifty-two participants (87 percent) identified themselves as black first. Among those participants that identified with their deafness first, the majority have deaf parents and were educated in a residential school for the deaf. These people are more integrated into the deaf community than those who identified with their blackness first. As hypothesized, when compared to the responses of the black-identified participants, the responses of the deaf-identified participants were broader in scope with questions about deaf culture and more limited in scope with questions about black culture. This deaf-identification does not serve to preclude knowledge about black culture, but the responses of the deaf-identified do indicate much greater enthusiasm for questions related to deaf culture than to those related to black culture.

In contrast, the respondents who identified with black culture first said that they see their color as more visible than their deafness and that they want respect for their ethnicity before their deafness. One comment was typical of many of the black-identified participants: "You see I am black first. My deafness is not noticed until I speak or use my hands to communicate." Members of this group, as expected, gave more detailed answers than the deaf-identified group to questions about black culture. All were able to identify with famous black leaders such as Martin Luther King and Jesse Jackson. When asked to identify the person who invented the cotton gin or the person who discovered plasma, they were not able to produce the names. Many of the participants were babies during the time blacks fought for their civil rights, so their knowledge was not first hand. When asked where they acquired their knowledge of black history, the majority said that they did not learn about black culture in school. They were informed about their black heritage from what parents and siblings taught them in addition to what they learned on their own. Most could identify with present problems facing blacks. Many of the answers focused on racial discrimination. In response to a question about how they would achieve racial equality, these participants spoke about blacks working together. Their common goal was to see blacks and whites, both deaf and hearing, interacting on the same level.

In response to questions about deaf culture, all of the participants agreed that there is a deaf culture. When asked about prominent deaf leaders, Thomas Hopkins Gallaudet was named most frequently and nearly exclusively by a majority of the participants. No contemporary deaf leaders were identified as making a substantial contribution to the deaf community. Many of the participants, however, provided names from their school or local community when discussing who they felt made a contribution to the deaf community. On the whole, all of the participants agreed that the deaf community has progressed in recent years. Areas of achievement were noted in the field of employment opportunity and education. All participants felt that they were discriminated against or treated differently because of their deafness or their blackness, or both. Many of the participants also mentioned that they felt they were being discriminated against or treated differently by members of the deaf community, in addition to the general hearing community.[2]

[2]This issue was raised by Dorothy Gilliam in an article in the *Washington Post* (18 April 1988), appearing a month after the Gallaudet protest. The article remarked that "it is tempting to think that within their own world, every person who is hearing impaired is totally visible, absolutely equal. But according to some black and white parents of students in Gallaudet's Model Secondary School for the Deaf, the institution over the years has sometimes displayed marked insensitivity to black students." One parent describes the racism she witnessed as "horrific, shocking." Some parents formed a Black Concerns Committee, which organized

In the final battery of questions, participants were asked to comment on the black deaf community. In many of the responses, participants mentioned parallels between the black community and the deaf community. Also mentioned were notable accomplishments that blacks have made since the civil rights movement began. The barrier of communication was seen as the most prevalent obstacle separating the black deaf community from the black and deaf communities. This topic of communication often surfaced in the interview segments on the black deaf community. Individuals in the black deaf community feel that their communication skills are not on the same level as hearing members of the black community. Communication is facilitated when individuals have something in common, but it is hampered when differences exist among individuals (Glenn and Glenn, 1981). Members of both the black deaf community and the black community share black culture. But the members of each group lack, to a certain degree, the ability to communicate effectively with each other through either American Sign Language or spoken English. Black deaf individuals often find themselves alienated from the dominant black culture. The lack of cross-cultural communication between members of the black deaf subculture and members of the majority black culture places both cultures at a distance. The participants who strongly identified with their black deaf culture also noted that differences exist in the ways of signing between black deaf and white deaf individuals. They mentioned too the separation of black deaf clubs and white deaf clubs as an ongoing dilemma that explains why both cultures are not totally cohesive.

The following are some not-so-flattering excerpts from the interviews. They provide an outline of what some of the participants said about the harsh realities facing members of the black deaf community.

> The black community in general has more opportunities for advancement than the black deaf community.

> Black deaf women have a much harder time at success than their male counterparts.

> Progress within the black deaf community has seen little or no improvements within the last ten to fifteen years.

---

discussion groups between black and white students, and workshops on race relations. One goal of the committee is the appointment of a black deaf person as one of the deaf board members guaranteed in the student victory. A further example of the racism that exists in the deaf community was provided by a white foreign student studying at Gallaudet for one year. This student inquired about shopping at a market near the campus and was told by a white deaf university administrator that it might not be wise to shop there, because "that's where all the black people shop."

The total number of blacks seeking higher education has increased, while the number of black deaf individuals seeking higher education is still comparatively low.

The deaf community has made progress, but the black deaf community still lags behind.

Communication is important in terms of socializing skills.

Black deaf individuals' communication skills are weak when relating to the general black community.

Sign language skills are an important tool in functioning in the black deaf community.

Upward achievement is difficult for black deaf persons without sufficient role models.

We have just begun to see a focus on black culture and black history in the education setting.

Much of what black deaf people learn about black culture is through readings they do on their own or what family members teach them. We learned nothing in the schools.

A black deaf person has to identify with their blackness first because of its visibility. Deafness is invisible. You do not notice I am deaf until I begin to communicate.

Members of the black deaf community have well-developed feelings and sentiments towards each other. They behave according to well-defined norms on what is proper and improper in their black deaf culture. Throughout the interview, the sense of identity and the feeling of belonging were apparent in the comments and behavior of the participants. To be sure, a person who is black and deaf is not automatically a member of the black deaf community. Black individuals who become deaf late in life are examples of this. They have not yet experienced the deafness aspect in the combination of what it means to be black *and* deaf. Many of the examples of discrimination cited by the participants were not very encouraging in terms of the comparisons made between where black deaf individuals were ten years ago and where they are today. Still, the participants expressed a commitment to positive change. Although the greater percentage of participants identified themselves as black first and deaf second, the black deaf community is nonetheless a cohesive, highly motivated culture. They demonstrate a desire for self-improvement. Prevalent in their responses is a need to educate the black deaf community. In order to find ways of improving their

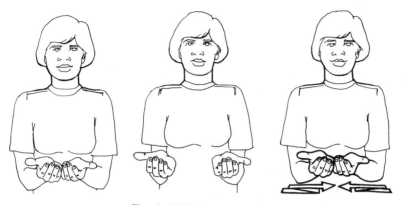

**Fig. 4**   SCHOOL, black form.

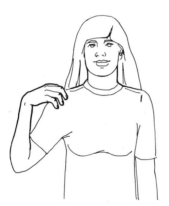

**Fig. 5**   BOSS, citation form.

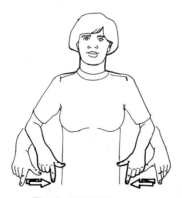

**Fig. 6**   BOSS, black form.

less exaggerated facial expressions, fewer body movements, and a smaller signing space when conversing with the white deaf participant than when conversing with each other.

Other studies provide additional evidence of variation in ASL that is related to ethnic background (e.g., Woodward and De Santis, 1977; Woodward and Erting, 1975). Other findings of the present study suggest that the two sociolinguistic oppositions of deaf-hearing and black-white (i.e., variables of participant social identity) can have interlocking effects on discourse. For example, in dyad 6, the black deaf participant $X$ is more of a passive listener when conversing with the white deaf participant than in his other conversations. Although black participant $Y$ is far from passive in his conversation with this same white deaf participant in dyad 7, the only instances where $Y$ interrupts his coparticipant in order to speak are all in dyad 3, when he is conversing with $X$, the other black deaf participant.

There is a general observation in the literature that native ASL signers use a more English-like signing when conversing with hearing signers than when conversing with other deaf signers (Lucas and Valli, this volume). In dyad 1 of the present study, black deaf participant $X$ produces a greater degree of English-like features in his signing when with the black hearing participant than occur in any other conversation in the data corpus. For example, in many instances, participant $X$ uses an ASL sign and then "corrects" the sign with an English equivalent, such as ME TRY in ASL followed by I T-R-Y, in an effort to conform to English style. Participant $X$ also uses more copulas in this conversation than occur in any other conversation in the corpus. Additionally, in one instance, he uses the emphatic form of WORK, which, with nonmanual features, means 'working hard'. He also uses the sign VERY to indicate emphasis. In contrast, when $X$ converses with the other black deaf participant (dyad 3), copulas, as well as the initialized sign for 'I', are not used at all. When these same two participants converse with the white deaf participant (dyads 6 and 7), their conversational styles include English-like features. Finally, throughout his entire conversation with the white hearing participant (dyad 5), black deaf participant $Y$ keeps his responses short and uses almost perfect English word order. When with this same white hearing participant (dyad 4), black deaf participant $X$ does not correct toward English as frequently as he does with the black hearing participant (dyad 1), but he still incorporates English-like features in his signing.

## SUMMARY AND CONCLUSIONS

The existence of a black deaf community is in part evidenced by the survival of all-black clubs for the deaf, where members go to socialize in a setting that satisfies their communication needs. The existence of this community is reinforced by a history of segregated schooling. The lack of adequate facilities and qualified personnel needed to prepare black deaf individuals for the future is reflected not only in the high levels of unemployment and underemployment found in the black deaf community but also in the small number of black deaf individuals who enter institutions of higher learning.

In the present study, a survey was used to answer the question of which community black deaf individuals identify with first, the black community or the deaf community. The majority of the respondents identified themselves first with the black community. They believe that they are seen by others as black first, since, unlike skin color, their deafness only becomes visible when they communicate in sign language. In contrast to these respondents, the remaining respondents who identified themselves first with the deaf community are more immersed in this community than the black-identified group. That is, the deaf-identified respondents are from deaf families, grew up in residential schools for the deaf, and socialize mostly within the deaf community as adults.

The language of the black deaf community is ASL. Yet, variations of ASL occur when members of this community engage in conversations among themselves, as opposed to conversations with others who are outsiders or nonmembers of the black deaf community. Specifically, as found in the present study, black deaf individuals commonly use signs that are unknown to outsiders. These "black signs", used mostly by black deaf individuals when the schools were segregated, are used when conversing with other deaf blacks, but standard ASL signs are used when conversing with white deaf individuals. This sociolinguistic variation also evidences the existence of a black deaf community.

Overall, as an essential part of the deaf community, the black deaf community faces the challenges of securing better education, more promising employment opportunities, and social advancements similar to those already acquired by members of the black community at large. Both in drawing attention to these issues and in describing some sociolinguistic features of black deaf discourse, the overriding aim of this chapter is to stimulate further research on the black deaf community. It is hoped that future studies will increase our understanding of this particular minority group as well as other minorities within the deaf community at large.

# Part II

## LANGUAGE POLICY

# 6

# Language Planning
# in Deaf Education

Claire L. Ramsey

## INTRODUCTION

This chapter is about the emergence of Signing Exact English (SEE), one of
the widely used manual codes for representing English (MCEs) to deaf
children (Gustason, Pfetzing, and Zawolkow, 1972).[1] This system is known
as SEE 2, to distinguish it from another signed code for English, SEE 1 or
Seeing Essential English (Anthony, 1971), which also grew out of the original planning effort that Gustason and her colleagues embarked upon. Although structural details of the various MCEs differ, the systems are similar
in that they are all intended to represent English manually. This is accomplished by assigning each English word and affix a sign in accordance with
a set of principles. The developers built the requisite MCE lexicon by
borrowing ASL signs, modifying ASL signs with handshape features from
the manual alphabet, and inventing signs specifically to represent English
derivational and inflectional morphemes.

Within a sociolinguistic framework, the development of SEE 2 is analyzed
in the present study as an example of language planning. From this perspective, language is defined as a social resource through which people
make and share meaning and define and order their social world. The

[1]Most of this paper is based on published accounts of the development of SEE 2. Other
portions of the data were collected during an interview with Gerilee Gustason in April 1987. I
thank her for her very helpful, personal account of the development of SEE 2. It would not
have been available from any other source.

Copyright © 1989 by Academic Press Inc.
All rights of reproduction in any form reserved.

following discussion is not aimed toward an evaluation of the correctness or effectiveness of the structure of SEE 2 (or other MCEs), although these are unresolved issues with serious implications. Specifically, there is widespread acceptance of these systems despite questions about their effectiveness as models of English and their utility as modes of communication (S. Supalla, 1986). Rather, the goal here is to examine and assess a more fundamental sociolinguistic issue, namely, the place of signed codes for English in the repertoire of the speech community of signers and in the speech community of English speakers.

This chapter focuses on several language-planning issues that are pertinent to the special case of deaf education in the United States. Both the rationale of the SEE 2 group for developing the system and the social forces accounting for its ready acceptance and propagation through the vehicle of schools are discussed. Finally, the appeal of SEE 2 to monolingual English speakers and the antagonism that the system has generated within the deaf speech community are considered.

This discussion of SEE 2 begins with the assumption that signing, speaking, reading, and writing in deaf education are all value-laden activities that are embedded not only in the specialized social context of the classroom but also in the larger context of a hearing, fundamentally monolingual English-speaking nation. Those who seek to manipulate language for instructional purposes in the classroom must take into account the social dimension of language and consider the ways that language functions for individuals in the broader world outside the classroom, for it is in these two social contexts that their plans and development work will ultimately be enacted.

## *ISSUES IN LANGUAGE PLANNING*

Language planning is characterized as deliberate decision making in response to language problems (J. Fishman, 1974). The work consists of proposals that are intended to influence the development of language (Haugen, 1972) and to guide decisions about alternatives in nonhomogeneous settings. Fasold (1984) points out that planning efforts explicitly make or promote certain choices among alternatives available to speakers. Such proposals and decisions have social meaning. Attempts at reforms, such as the recoding of Standard English into signs, aim toward the standardization of norms. Written norms are generally taken as the standard in reference to which planners work, as done in the case of SEE 2.

Haugen (1972) provides a useful descriptive framework for the process of language planning. He observes that planning efforts begin with the recognition of a language problem framed against a set of social facts. The planners' interpretation of the facts and their definition of the nature of the language problem result in the setting of a goal. Next, the technical details of planning are carried out, and the results propagated. Although schools are often the major vehicle for implementing the results of language planning, schools do not exist in a vacuum. Any language developments introduced through schools are also introduced into a wider social context. The final stage is evaluation of the results of the plan, although many planning efforts are never evaluated (Rubin, 1984).

Fasold (1984) contrasts two approaches to language planning. One, the "instrumental" view, construes language in the society at large and in the classroom as a "tool." Planning efforts that take an instrumental approach are directed toward making language suitable and efficient for its uses. This approach emphasizes planning to improve or modernize languages or to replace less suitable languages with those considered better-suited for specific uses. An alternative approach begins with the recognition that language problems have interacting linguistic and social dimensions. Fasold uses the term "socio-linguistic" to describe this approach. Planners working in this framework assess the broader social context in order to identify alternatives that can be applied to the language problem, rather than to try to improve the functional characteristics of a language perceived as unsuitable for some reason.

Although the term "planner" has a bureaucratic ring to it, and language planning is often the responsibility of government agencies or official language academies, groups or individuals at a grassroots level initiate language-planning efforts as well. J. Fishman (1974, p. 26) notes some of the social forces that influence conventionally accepted views of appropriateness within language communities are the "mass-media, the writer, the popular hero, . . . the clergy, [and] the elite." He suggests that their language behavior constitutes planning that occurs without academic or governmental sponsorship. Haugen (1966, p. 11) notes that there is no tradition of language academies in England and the United States. An eighteenth century proposal to establish an American English language academy apparently conflicted with early values on liberty and was not accepted (Heath, 1981). Rather, in our tradition, standards are set by private enterprise, through dictionary writers and publishers.

SEE 2 creation occurred in response to a "language problem." Its designers wanted to influence use and choice of language for a set of special purposes: communication in monolingual English-speaking families with deaf children, communication and English instruction in schools with deaf students, and participation in and access to the English-speaking nation. In carrying out their reforms, they followed a standard already operative in the classrooms of the United States, namely, the norms of written English. The goal was to make this variety of English visible to deaf students through signs. In the tradition of language planning in the English-speaking world, the route to this goal of teaching standard English to deaf children was development of a set of norms and publication of a dictionary.

Although the language-planning issues involved in the development of SEE 2 are general issues that would play a role in any effort directed at manipulated linguistic change, they take on a new shape when applied to the social situation of the majority of deaf children educated in the United States. The unique demographic situation of deafness presents a sociolinguistic complication. Most deaf children are born to hearing monolingual English-speaking parents. As discussed later, a view of deafness as an ethnic phenomenon (Johnson and Erting, this volume) illuminates the minority language-community status of deaf Americans. But the community of deaf Americans who share this ethnicity, into which most deaf children are eventually socialized (Meadow, 1980; Padden, 1980), is not often involved in the raising or schooling of young deaf children. Although SEE 2 encroaches on the linguistic territory of the deaf community by utilizing the medium of signing, the primary user-group for this sign system is composed of teachers and parents (Gustason, 1974–1975, 1983); its use is not widespread among deaf adults (Wilbur, 1987). Deaf children who reside with their hearing families are thus different from their parents in important ways, even though they may not yet be full-fledged members of the deaf community. This set of circumstances creates the unusual possibility that deaf students not only do not share the speech community of their parents and their teachers during their school years; they will not share it as adults.

## SOCIOLINGUISTIC BACKGROUND

SEE 2 was introduced into a highly complex sociolinguistic and historical context. Although deafness as a handicap is by definition a complex phenomenon on both an individual and a societal level, its common medical definition will be left aside here and deafness will be taken to be an ethnic phenomenon (Johnson and Erting, this volume). Still, the etiology of deafness and its pattern of occurrence in the population contribute to the community's unique demographic situation.

ASL-signing deaf people constitute an unusual speech community embedded in a larger, normally hearing, and essentially English monolingual society. Both social and biological factors contribute to the structure and maintenance of the deaf group. "Ethnically deaf" children, that is, the fewer than 10 percent of deaf children with at least one deaf parent, are socialized into the signing deaf community from birth. The majority of deaf individuals, however, have both hearing parents and siblings. (Additionally, once parents themselves, they will most likely have hearing children.) These deaf children traditionally are socialized into the signing deaf community either when they enter residential school or at some later point as adults (Meadow, 1980). This socialization into and eventual membership in the signing deaf community occur despite the formal educational efforts directed toward as thorough a socialization as possible of deaf children into the hearing monolingual speech community. This objective is reflected in the historical focus on speech and on English and in the current focus on integration with the hearing society through educational mainstreaming. But the complete linguistic socialization of deaf children into the hearing speech community is exceedingly difficult to accomplish since these children are different from mainstream members in such a crucial way.

Sociolinguistically, the society that surrounds deaf Americans as students and as adults is a hearing monolingual nation for whom the standard varieties of spoken and written English language serve symbolically as a unifying social thread. Although many Americans accept the existence and use of "signing" in a generic sense, no sign language has equal status with standard English. To be sure, competence in ASL is valued and admired by some members of the English-speaking community, but signing is still generally seen as a supplement to competence in English, which is considered both socially and educationally necessary (Gustason and Zawolkow, 1980). Additionally, competence in standard varieties of English indicates membership both in the American English speech community and, implicitly, in the broad group of "normal" human beings. Finally, as defined by the values of the surrounding, English-speaking community, education through standard English is promoted as the key to economic and social mobility, as well as to intellectual growth.

In a historical context, the essentially local efforts of the SEE 2 group were influenced by the broader and radical changes taking place in the field of deaf education. When the group began their project, the tradition of oral education was giving way to the Total Communication (TC) approach, which was, by then, spreading across the country.[2] This move away from oralism was drastic and swift. A survey on communication in educational programs for the deaf, conducted in 1975 (Jordan, Gustason, and Rosen, 1980), found that 43 percent of the 796 programs responding had recently changed the medium of communication in the classroom, mostly to Total

[2]In 1976, the Conference of Executives of American Schools for the Deaf agreed on the following definition, cited in Gustason (1980, p. 37): "Total Communication is a philosophy requiring the incorporation of appropriate aural, manual, and oral modes of communication in order to ensure effective communication with and among hearing impaired persons."

Communication. A sharp increase in the number of programs reporting change occurred in 1970, and this increase was steady from 1972 to 1975.

Although incorporation of "manual modes of communication" is part of the definition of TC, "manual modes" are not clearly defined. Despite the seemingly radical changes in philosophies and methods for educating deaf children that occurred during this period, the central focus of their education was still the development of proficiency in English. The ideological shift away from oralism, coupled with the common sense notions about English and signing current at the time, made it seem that the language problem around which deaf education was structured could be solved with manually represented forms of English. SEE 2, the system Gustason and her group had developed, and other manually coded English systems devised around the country (e.g., Anthony, 1971; Bornstein, 1974) found what was apparently a readymade niche in the homes and classrooms of parents and teachers who adopted the TC approach.

G. Gustason (personal communication, April 1987) reflects both the historical context and the societal value on English in the following recollection:

> We had absolutely no idea that the frustration throughout the U.S. had made the time ripe for a TC explosion. I believe our book appealed to people because it was still English and like us, they were frustrated in that regard. And it was a supplementary visual code to the language we were trying to teach. Not a different language like ASL. So things kind of went BOOM overnight. Looking back, I think we had no idea, actually I know we had no idea what was going to happen.

SEE 2 appealed to common sense definitions of current needs in deaf education in an intuitively reasonable way. A signed supplement to spoken English, if it were possible to create one, would clearly be more accessible to deaf students than spoken English alone had been. If, at the same time, the signed code appeared to actually be English, it could further educational goals for deaf students and, at the same time, gain acceptance with its target group of users, educators and parents. Thus, SEE 2, officially sanctioned signing in deaf education classrooms, took hold during a shift in pedagogy in deaf education that not only led to a major change in methods but also maintained the field's historical ideological focus on Standard English.

The original SEE 2 group, whose members collaborated from the winter of 1969 to the fall of 1970 and then split into three groups, each designing somewhat different systems (Gustason, 1983), worked within a framework of ten "basic tenets." These ten statements served to outline their interpretation of the educational context in which were working and to argue in support of their goal.[3] Gustason (1983) provides an elaborated list of these notions, documenting the group's definition of language acquisition—based on the notion that "normal input must precede normal output" (Gustason, 1983, p. 37)—and their concern about the problems that deaf children encounter when learning "good English". The group built an argument against oral-only methods and, in the end, proposed their solution, the addition of the "patterns or structure of English to the sign language" (ibid., 40). From their definition of the problem of teaching English to deaf children and their understanding of the facts that surrounded it, their stated goal was "the consistent, logical, rational, and practical development of signs to represent as specifically as possible the basic essentials of the English language" (Gustason, 1974–1975, p. 11).

Embodied in their statements is an expectation that their system would be useful in three quite distinct contexts. In addition to the school, where SEE 2 was expected to be useful both as a medium of instruction and as a basis for developing literacy skills in English, SEE 2 was also expected to be useful in homes and in the broader social context. In the home, it was expected to be appropriate and useful for a deaf child's first encounter with language, ensuring that "comfortable parent-child communication be established as early as possible in a language readily perceivable by the child" (Gustason and Zawolkow, 1980, p. 7). Finally, in the English-speaking society at large, SEE 2 was expected to count as English for purposes of access and assimilation.

Yet, the SEE 2 group's notions, intuitively reasonable on the surface, merit a close examination. From the point of introduction, SEE 2 has met with some antagonism, particularly from the deaf community. The goals and values of signing deaf adults are not entirely consistent with those of

---

[3]The ten basic tenets (Gustason, 1983, pp. 36–41) are as follows:

1. Acquiring good English is a tremendously difficult task for a child born deaf.
2. The most important factor in acquiring good English is an understanding of its syntax and structure.
3. Normal input must precede normal output. Aural input being blocked, visual input must be used.
4. The visual cues of speechreading are too small and ambiguous to make possible normal, natural language learning.
5. Sign language is easier to see than speechreading or fingerspelling.
6. The feeling for structure is more important than the ability to spell a word in question immediately.
7. The patterns or structure of English may easily be added to the sign language.
8. It is easier to sign all parts of a sentence than to sign some and spell others.
9. Any specific sign should mean one thing, and one thing only.
10. English should be signed as it is spoken. This is especially true of idioms.

hearing parents and educators. Additionally, there is growing evidence that SEE 2 in use is not functioning as its developers predicted it would.

Hearing parents of deaf children hold certain values and expectations regarding the education and language use of their deaf children (Erting, 1982). Central among these values is the currently widespread conviction that deaf children can and should learn English from their parents through a manual code for English (T. Spradley and Spradley, 1980). Deaf adults, while sharing many core values with other Americans, do not necessarily share these expectations and values concerning signed codes for English. As a community, they greatly value ASL as a marker of group identity and share a certain proprietary feeling about the mode of signing itself (Padden, 1980). They express reservations about all the manual codes for English (Kannapell, 1978). For example, a former executive secretary of the National Association of the Deaf (Schreiber, 1974–1975, p. 5) reflected the feelings of many deaf Americans when he referred to MCEs as "a facelift [on] the signs that belong to the deaf community." The deaf community's concerns for the educational and linguistic well-being and betterment of the next deaf generation are somewhat different from those of the hearing parents and teachers who constitute the target group for SEE 2 and whose expectations SEE 2 is designed to fulfill.

SEE 2 has proved to be less effective than expected for its intended uses (S. Supalla, 1986). In assuming that deaf children with hearing parents who use SEE 2 with simultaneous spoken English would experience "normal" language learning, the developers of SEE 2 believe that "if a deaf child is exposed to consistent, continuous English in his home and school environment in a visual form, he will develop English as comfortably and naturally as a hearing child does" (Gustason, 1974–1975, p. 12). They envision a typical home for young deaf children, with a family, particularly a mother, able and willing to master and to simultaneously and consistently use spoken and manual English (Gustason, 1983). Although they recognize that deaf children may be initially exposed to SEE 2 at a somewhat later age than their hearing peers are to spoken English (Gustason, 1983), the developers of SEE 2 expect that consistent use of a signed morpheme-by-morpheme model of English will create a situation analogous to that encountered by hearing children who are natively acquiring the language of their environment. But there is no evidence that the situations of the hearing and the deaf language learner are analogous.

Although, in principle, the SEE 2 planners hoped that hearing parents would be able to pass their native language on to their deaf child through SEE 2, the use of manual codes for English, particularly with the simultaneous production of spoken English, is in practice quite difficult to accomplish (Erting, 1982). Swisher and Thompson (1985) report that hearing mothers of deaf children have difficulty consistently producing complete signed and spoken utterances, and they identify two factors that contribute to this difficulty. First, the complexity of simultaneously producing signs and spoken English is typically underestimated. Second, the language-learning situation faced by hearing mothers of deaf children is far from ideal. The opportunity for language learning is constrained because there is no community of native MCE users with whom the mothers can interact in order to learn. Also, these mothers must learn to produce an MCE system with spoken English amidst the set of painful and generally unexpected circumstances that surround the birth of a deaf infant.

Finally, neither the technical linguistic details nor the social context of the planning that produced SEE 2 are as straightforward as might appear. On the structural representational level, SEE 2 resulted from an attempt to design a manually coded representation of English, which evolved as a spoken language. As S. Supalla (1986) argues, the related issues of modality and naturalness in signed languages are crucial to understanding both the problems of MCEs and their relation (or lack thereof) to spoken English as well as the failure of MCEs to serve as useable means of communication among those who depend on vision for communication and for learning. Because native monolingual speakers of English can utter an English word and simultaneously produce a sign that has many features of meaning in common with the English word, they are led to believe that the signs they are using actually represent English words and that the signed strings they produce are in fact English sentences. Yet given the interaction of modality and linguistic structure found in ASL, there is no deeper way that signs and spoken words could be related.

On the level of phonology, it is apparent that ASL signs are quite unlike spoken English words. Signs are constructed not of sequences of sounds but of sequences of movement and hold segments with attached bundles of articulatory features (Liddell, 1984). The more crucial and problematic distinction between spoken English and the lexicon of signs borrowed from ASL for use in SEE 2 occurs at the level where morphology and syntax interact. ASL uses a system of morphology in which sign-internal features such as points in space or handshapes can act as morphemes. This is in striking contrast to the system of sequential affixes and the prominence of word order in English. For example, in an ASL sentence, the morphologically complex verb glossed 'give' is produced with a subject marker on the first segment and an object marker on the final segment. These two markers are produced at points in space that constitute the beginning and the end of the movement. An additional morpheme, a sign-internal classifier handshape that marks direct object and occurs through all segments, can also be present. Thus, it is possible in ASL to utter one morphologically complex sign that is glossed in English as 'she gives the cup to him'. This sign resembles English only in the coincidental SVO order.

Native speakers know that subjects, objects, and indirect objects in English are not marked on the verb itself but are realized as separate words, and that sentences generally take the SVO word order. In order to reflect this, SEE 2 requires the production of a sequence of morphemes, a combination of citation-form signs borrowed from the ASL lexicon and signs invented for SEE 2. This brings up a difficulty in the interaction between ASL and English. Although there is an uninflected form of the ASL sign *GIVE*, it remains on an abstract level and is not producible without subject and object markers on the initial and final segments. Points in space, which in ASL are always potentially meaningful, are required because in order to constitute a movement, the sign must begin and end at some points. With this requirement in mind, consider what the SEE 2 version of the earlier English-glossed sentence must include in order to reproduce the spoken English version manually. This version attempts to use the citation form of GIVE and separate signs for each of the other morphemes in the sentence. Invented SEE 2 signs for English SHE, third person singular -S, TO, HIM, THE and CUP are required. The issue is not that these invented signs are impossible to produce. They clearly are possible, and many teachers and parents can produce them in isolation and in strings. The question is the extent to which SEE 2 utterances, such as the example here, represent useable information about English and meaningful communication to deaf children who, because they are not proficient in English, cannot derive either the meaning or the grammatical information that any signed message is intended to convey.

Each MCE, SEE 2 included, is the result of arbitrary decisions about how to represent the morphology of English through signs. Although each system can reflect the word order of English, the representation of morphology presents a problem. To briefly take another example, the affixing system used by SEE 2 uses the ASL sign PAST to mark tense on all verbs, although many English irregular verbs undergo a spelling change when the past tense is formed. Thus, GIVE + PAST, the SEE 2 rendition of 'gave', provides no accurate information about the spoken and written English versions. Rather, it gives information that would lead to an incorrect prediction of how to write the past tense of this irregular verb.

Deaf children who are encountering language through the SEE 2 code must have a way to make sense of the manual production and to relate it to spoken English, a language they do not know and have no real access to. S. Supalla (1986), using morphologically complex verb signs such as GIVE, found that deaf children who had been exposed to a "pure SEE 2" environment appeared to be making use of a hypothetically more signed language-like morphology to reanalyze SEE 2 utterances into more natural, that is, more spatially sensible, utterances in their own signing. This suggests that the SEE 2 to which they are exposed cannot function well as a model of

English for these children, since they reanalyze what they see into a system even less English-like than SEE 2. It further suggests that SEE 2, as it is designed, cannot function as a means of communication for the children unless they reanalyze it. These examples of the vast differences between signed and spoken modes point out the unresolvable problems inherent in attempting to combine them to produce MCEs.

On the social level, the SEE 2 planning effort represents a troublesome interaction between, on the one hand, social and educational goals for deaf children defined by one group, parents and educators, and, on the other hand, the linguistic resources and values of another group, the mode and lexicon of the deaf speech community. In essence, developers of MCEs attempted to create a language for which no sociolinguistic niche exists. The style of discourse introduced by MCEs, namely, simultaneously produced signed and spoken English, appears to have neither a genuine function among signers nor a useable form.

These issues point to the contradictory facts of deaf education. Although the education of deaf students is structured to a great extent by concern about language and language instruction, a broad understanding of language as a social resource is often lacking. To recall Fasold's (1984) term, the instrumental view of language predominates. In line with this view, the goal of the SEE 2 planning effort and the strategies devised for accomplishing it were primarily instrumental. Planners believed that they were creating a tool that would enhance English language instruction for deaf children in homes, schools, and the monolingual society. The SEE 2 group understood very well the history of deaf education and the implications of the decline of strict oralism. They had no way to assess the complex sociolinguistic situation in which deaf education and their own work was embedded.

Several aspects of the SEE 2 planning effort can help us better understand its development, use, and symbolic value for deaf children and their parents and teachers, as well as its impact on the ASL-using speech community. SEE 2 is based on a rationale with implicit definitions of language, language use, and language communities. Additionally, SEE 2 was expected to foster certain goals for deaf students.

## DEFINITIONS OF LANGUAGE

The SEE 2 group focused on developing competence in English syntax in deaf children, implicitly equating language with syntax. This definition of language grew out of the theoretical climate in which the selection and the codification of English-based SEE 2 signs were made. At the time, psycholinguistic accounts of language acquisition were primarily concerned with the development of syntax (Wells, 1981). Language learning was frequently analyzed out of the contexts of use in homes and schools. The child's developing ability to understand and create meaning through conversation with others, which grows as young children begin to produce linguistic structures, was not often the focus of attention.

Given the times in which they were working, it is not surprising that the SEE 2 group considered the task of acquiring English synonymous with gaining "an understanding of its syntax and structure" (Gustason, 1983, p. 36). Since the SEE 2 group defined language acquisition as the acquisition of linguistic structures, their stated concern was with the kind of "input" that would promote "output" of these structures. They felt that SEE 2 addressed this concern directly by providing a medium that would make the structures of English visible and explicit to deaf language learners. Accordingly, when students produce strings of signs from the SEE 2 lexicon, teachers (and parents) take it as evidence that their students are gaining proficiency in English. The definition of language as syntax and the input-output model of language acquisition are inherent in much explicitly structured language instruction in the education of deaf students. It is the concern with acquisition of linguistic forms that explains the instrumental focus of SEE 2. In educational contexts, there is a lack of appreciation for the all-embracing quality of language as a social resource, the nature of language variation, the relation between spoken and written language, and the role spoken language plays in developing literacy skills.

As we would expect of a natural language spoken in a nation full of diversity and used as a worldwide medium of communication, English is subject to much regional and social variation. Although there are no linguistic grounds for claiming that any particular variety of spoken English is better than another, socially-recognized prescriptive norms do exist in relation to the written standard. This social fact influenced the SEE 2 planners, who focus their efforts on an idealized notion of "good English." They place value on the idealized English that, for most Americans, symbolizes the shared language of the nation and is represented by the written standard. The SEE 2 group's framework indicates that they, like many members of the literate American speech community, believe that genuine good English can be found in the written forms of the language. Thus, "good English" means written standard English. This is consistent with the social prestige enjoyed by standard languages in general. As Stubbs (1980, p. 30) points out, "once a written language has developed in a community, it characteristically takes on something of a life of its own, and characteristically is regarded by its users as important and often superior as a form of language."

The SEE 2 planners state that "the most important principle in Signing

Exact English is that English should be signed in a manner that is as consistent as possible with how it is spoken or written" (Gustason and Zawolkow, 1980, p. 9). By assuming that spoken and written language are formally and functionally the same, they, like many English speakers, overlook the varying forms language can take when it is put to use in social contexts. As Chafe and Danielwicz (1987) observe, although spoken and written modes allow many styles, some more "written-like" and others more "spoken-like," factors such as context, purpose, and subject matter also influence the shape of language in actual usage. Thus, there is not one form of English that can be made useful in all contexts. It is crucial for parents and teachers to recognize that the form of language varies systematically between homes and classrooms. As Heath (1978) has suggested in her discussion of "teacher talk," these powerful contexts constitute distinct domains where distinct language varieties are used.

Although SEE 2 was designed to reflect spoken English, it was modeled on the written variety of English (Bornstein, 1973; Johnson, 1983).[4] The framers of SEE 2 developed the system in the hope that it would instill English reading and writing proficiency in deaf children, something that other educational methods had been unable to accomplish. This raises important questions about the use of SEE 2 in the local social contexts of home and school.

The attempt to use a morpheme-by-morpheme model of written language for face-to-face communication introduces developmental and language-learning issues. Johnson (1983, p. 50) points out that affixes in English are not equivalent to whole words in either form or function. The SEE 2 principle of creating separate signs to represent affixes and "adding" them to the sign language lexicon (Gustason, 1983, p. 40) gives them a salience unwarranted by the structure of English.

There is an additional developmental issue regarding salience. Use of SEE 2, much like the production of written language, requires analysis of language into lexical units (words and derivational and inflectional affixes). Yet, most hearing children are unable to segment the stream of speech into

---

[4]The original SEE group began work with a set of signs developed by David Anthony and based on Basic English (Gannon, 1981), a simplified written English devised by C. K. Ogden in 1930 as an international language that would be easy to learn to write and to read. Large (1985) considers Basic English a "modified natural language" rather than a strictly artificial language. He notes similar goals shared by attempts at natural language modification and language invention, particularly attempts at developing completely regular linguistic systems with small vocabularies for specific purposes. Basic English was intended for use as an international auxiliary language but, in its time, was not well received. Basic English was not intended to serve as either an introduction to language or as an instructional medium for Standard English.

conventional "words" until well after they have begun to develop literacy. The lexical units that proficient adult language users are able to identify are not salient to children in the streams of speech that constitute language in face-to-face situations (Stubbs, 1980).

Metalinguistic awareness of language is an artifact of literacy learning. As a consequence, SEE 2 is not constructed from the point of view of a learner but from that of a user. The system thus makes intuitive sense and works best for users who are already proficient in adult literate English. Its relation to written English is likely to remain outside of the awareness of deaf children, the group for whom the system was designed, just as the relation of spoken English to written forms is beyond the awareness of most young hearing children.

This prerequisite of proficiency in English has implications for the use of SEE 2 in educational settings. It is not clear that the items that proficient adult signers are able to identify as salient lexical units—inflected signs, for example—are equally salient to deaf children. It is not even known how young deaf children who learn ASL as their first language understand the stream of signs. More importantly for the use of SEE 2, it is also unclear what the salient segments are for deaf children who are trying to learn a signed code for English produced simultaneously with spoken English.

Again, SEE 2 depends on very young children being able to conduct relatively sophisticated "written-like" analyses of language in order to develop language in the first place. That this kind of explicit reflection on language is normally required only at the point where children begin their formal instruction *about* language and literacy makes developmental sense. The helpful analytic distinction between learning language, learning about language, and learning through language is made very clearly by Halliday (1980). In Halliday's terms, children do not regard language as an object. Under normal developmental circumstances, they construct their knowledge of language through the process of using it to communicate with others. The process of learning to accomplish social functions and to communicate linguistically must therefore be distinguished from the process of gaining conscious awareness of language. The two are confused in the SEE 2 literature, where it is not only assumed that written and spoken "good English" are identical systems but also that learning language and developing metalinguistic awareness of language structure are the same process.

## IDEAS ABOUT LANGUAGE USE

There is a fundamental distinction between the functions of spoken language and those of written language, a distinction that interacts with situational and social factors to produce language variation (Chafe and Daniel-wicz, 1987).[5] What is pertinent here is the variation that arises in relation to the contexts and purposes of language use. Since this kind of variation is an inevitable part of the sociolinguistic context of any language-planning effort, planners must take into account the differences between the forms and functions of language in face-to-face interaction and those of language in written communication.

Members of speech communities call on a broad range of linguistic resources, a repertoire that forms the basis for communicative competence. A sociolinguistic examination of functions of spoken and written language in literate speech communities, for example a society like the United States, would find differences between language used in face-to-face domains and language used in written domains.

This contrast in domains of use defines the conflict between the fundamentally "written-like" nature of SEE 2 and the fundamentally "spoken-like" purposes it is intended to accomplish at home and at school. SEE 2 is expected to serve face-to-face functions as the deaf child's first medium for encountering language, both in the home and in the educational programs that deaf children enter at unusually early ages, some as early as twelve months old (Meadow, 1980). Yet, the use of SEE 2 as a form of English assumes the previously discussed analytic, reflective awareness of language, its structure, its constituent parts, and their relative saliency that few native speakers of English and even fewer children actually command. Members of speech communities are rarely called upon to bring details of their communicative competence to conscious awareness and make them explicit. Ironically, according to the SEE 2 principles, deaf language learners, who are less proficient language users than their hearing peers both because they are still learners and because they do not learn English under normal circumstances, are expected to take a relatively sophisticated literate stance toward language. This excessive demand on user abilities has serious implications for the viability of SEE 2 as a language variety and thus for its usefulness as a medium of communication.

In a home or school setting with young children, written-like language does not well serve everyday face-to-face interaction. This incompatibility

---

[5]A dichotomy between "oral and written" language is sometimes presented. I am diverging from this usage since the terms "oral," "spoken language," and "speech" have narrow technical definitions in the context of deaf education. When referring to contexts of language use that involve signing, I have substituted the term "face-to-face communication" where the terms "oral" or "spoken language" might otherwise have occurred. In this discussion, the functions and domains of language use are more pertinent than the mode of linguistic expression. In the context of a young child's home and school, face-to-face communication predominates, and it is for this kind of interaction at home and at school that SEE 2 is recommended.

causes representational problems (Johnson, 1983) and can contribute to the production problems associated with the simultaneous use of manual codes for English and spoken English (Kluwin, 1981a; Marmor and Pettito, 1979). It is possible that these problems are caused by the difficulty of forcing a written form of language into the oral domain, a factor that did not enter into the SEE 2 group's interpretation of the language problem that they set out to solve.

The general function of face-to-face linguistic (or prelinguistic) interaction between adults and young children under normal circumstances is communication. Caretakers and teachers do not use written-like language to satisfy the need for prelinguistic and early communication with young children. Rather because they want to communicate, develop mutual understanding with their young interlocutors, and give and receive information, adults who converse with child language learners carefully (and relatively unconsciously) construct both the form and the meaning of their talk. Adults are able to take account of the perceived level of the child's linguistic development (Snow, 1986). Through this kind of interaction, children learn how to use language to accomplish a variety of needs. It is developmentally reasonable that the primary purpose of the interaction is communication and not the provision of explicit models of English. Since deaf children also encounter language for the first time and learn about its forms and functions through face-to-face communication, varieties of language used in this domain need to support the communicative needs of both children and adults. It is possible that SEE 2, developed to provide a model of "good English" and recommended for use because it can provide one, is constrained by its roots in written English to such a degree that it cannot fit into the functional sociolinguistic niches for which it was developed.

The production problems with MCEs, particularly omissions, may be a result of the difficulty of simultaneous production. In a sense, these problems serve to make the MCE more spoken-like. Although Gustason (1983, p. 62) attributes the "tendency to drop signs" to a lack of signing skill and emphasizes that consistent use of SEE 2 is crucial, she seems to recognize the pressure to "maintain normal speaking speed" (Gustason, 1983, p. 44), that is, the need to use the system in a more spoken-like way. She cautions parents and teachers that should they decide to delete signs, they should do so with the awareness that a child cannot use words or constructions that are never seen. Although it seems that the planned development of a more spoken-like MCE might overcome these problems, the planners of such a system would have to take into account both the pressures of modality and the problems inherent in simultaneous production. Thus, this hypothetical system would have to conform to the naturalness constraints for signed languages and thus would be limited to production on one channel only, a sign language with no simultaneously spoken component. Additionally, the developers of the system would have to redefine its functions and place the emphasis on the system's inherent capacity for creating and transmitting meaning between interlocutors, rather than on its potential as a model of English. Finally, to be ideal, such a system would have to have a sociolinguistic niche in a community of users. ASL can presumably fulfill these requirements, as can the indigenous form of "fluent English-based signing" in use among bilingual deaf Americans in contact situations (Johnson, 1983). Unfortunately, it seems unlikely that any of the MCEs as they are now used in deaf education in the U.S. can be useful as systems for signing English in face-to-face contexts.

The development of SEE 2 was also based on the assumption that exposure to an exact signed model of the idealized written form of a language is crucial for literacy learning. Yet, it is not clear that a precise, completely analyzed, morpheme-by-morpheme signed English utterance is necessary or even helpful for a deaf child's literacy learning. As discussed earlier, deaf language learners are not fully able to take advantage of the system's explicit coding of English precisely because they do not yet know English.

For hearing children, a determination of what written language is, and if or how it might relate to spoken language, is not accomplished by following a straight path from oral to written language. These children not only need to develop sufficient levels of metalinguistic awareness and analytic skill, they must also reconcile their confusion about engaging in this new relationship with language. Stubbs (1980) suggests that the motivation for carrying out this kind of linguistic analysis is vague and confusing to children. This is an additional reason why the use of a written model for face-to-face communication can increase the difficulty of the sense-making task that deaf children have to engage in as they encounter language through SEE 2.

Hearing children often make use of several symbol systems (including drawing) as they work their way toward literacy (Dyson, 1986). It is not surprising that deaf children are doing the same as they build up their symbolic resources while learning about fingerspelling (O'Grady, van Hoek, and Bellugi, 1987; Padden, in press; Padden and Le Master, 1985) and written language (Ewoldt, 1985; Staton, 1985). An additional factor in literacy learning is that it is surrounded and supported by talk, both the supportive talk of adults and older children and the stream of peer talk that children engage in as they play, dramatize, draw, read, and write. If SEE 2, together with simultaneous spoken English, cannot be reasonably learned and used for face-to-face interaction, then it cannot foster literacy learning at all. Studies of both hearing (Dyson, 1986) and deaf children (Ewoldt, 1985; Staton, 1985) suggest that literacy evolves from purposeful meaning making through manipulation of symbols from the different systems that the child has access to. Consequently, it would seem more fruitful to construe communication and development of meaning through natural language as the primary early educational need of deaf children, rather than to continue the focus on providing models of English (Brannon and Livingston, 1986; Livingston, 1986).

## IDEAS ABOUT LANGUAGE AND COMMUNITIES

The questions about the use of SEE 2 as an introduction to English at home and at school lead to the consideration of language use in community contexts. In the case of SEE 2, we must consider the complex phenomenon of "English" in the broad social context of a nation that perceives itself to be English speaking and essentially monolingual. The hearing community at large uses many social and regional varieties of spoken English, and most citizens read and write the standard written variety of English. Although SEE 2 was expected to fit into this sociolinguistic context, English produced in a signed code is not an authentic national language. As yet, there is not even an authentic community of speakers of SEE 2 (or any of the MCEs). Such codes are not the idealized native language of the nation. This basic fact is lost in optimistic descriptions of SEE 2, such as Gustason's (1980, p. 15) claim that it provides deaf children with "some way to communicate with anyone, and to assimilate with both deaf and hearing people and to choose their mode of communication accordingly." As difficult as it may be to face, hearing parents who attempt to use SEE 2 with spoken English are not passing their native language on to their deaf children but rather are using a secondary system based on a functionally constrained variety of their native language.

The complexity of the relationship between spoken and written language in itself calls into question the usefulness of SEE 2 in the education and literacy learning of deaf children. Once this point is combined with the recognition that we are not a nation of English signers but of English speakers, the expectations for SEE 2 as an educating and assimilating tool can only be viewed as overly optimistic. Just as the assumption that signed English will "work" as English to achieve educational goals is questionable, the assumption that signed English will count as English and "work" socially and culturally in a hearing nation is also questionable.

## GOALS FOR DEAF PEOPLE

Educators' and parents' widespread faith in SEE 2 (and other MCEs) brings up fundamental questions about the educational goals for deaf children in the United States. These questions center on the ways that we define deaf children and their unconventional encounters with language at home and at school. Traditionally, deafness is considered a medical, educational, and linguistic emergency. For educational purposes, deaf children are considered the disabled offspring of English-speaking parents in an English-speaking nation, and their educational needs are accounted for within this framework. In practice, although educators are increasingly aware of the existence of the deaf community, they are rarely able to seriously consider the real educational implications of their students' future membership in the deaf ethnolinguistic minority. Currently, the context of deaf education is sufficiently different from both hearing homes and the adult deaf community that it apparently constitutes a third linguistic community composed solely of deaf children and hearing adults (Stokoe, 1985). The seriousness of this situation is evident in light of one unintentional consequence of mainstreaming deaf students. There is informal evidence that sign language interpreters, often the only signing interlocutors available to deaf students, serve informally as language teachers. In essence, nonnative, hearing signers who may have a limited command of an MCE and no ASL competence at all are teaching deaf children, who are also nonnatives in that they do not have native command of any language when they enter school. This is certainly not an optimal situation for language and literacy learning.

The exploration of language use in deaf education involves a question of perspective, and a decision about how to define the problem. Is language a tool for instruction with little symbolic value to users? Or, is it a group resource deeply embedded in social and cultural life? Is the central problem of deaf education one of identifying an efficient methodology for language instruction? Or, is it the effort to foster communication, reflection, and learning through language? Is the focus of education for deaf students best narrowed to instruction that leads to mastery of a set of language skills? Or, should it be expanded to wider language problems with both social and linguistic aspects? These are not neutral choices. In making these choices educators define and represent the hearing society's goals for deaf Americans as students and as citizens.

Certain slogans that represent the assimilationist spirit of the mainstream American value system remind deaf Americans of what is expected of members of linguistic minorities. Deaf people are expected to be able to get along in the "real" world and are told that "English" is the key to vocational and educational success in this world. Although it would be hard to deny that deaf people get along in the hearing world, the way in which they accomplish this is not necessarily a silent replication of the hearing way.

Literacy holds great symbolic cultural power in the United States. English literacy skills are highly valued by both hearing people and deaf people. But, they contrast with "literate behaviors" that are equally crucial and not guaranteed by the acquisition of literacy skills such as spelling, mechanics, and the ability to construct English sentences from a workbook model (Heath, 1984). In their discussion of deafness as an ethnic phenomenon, Johnson and Erting (1982) consider the boundary that separates the deaf community from the hearing mainstream society. For deaf people, access to social and economic benefits depends on successfully crossing the ethnic boundary. In Johnson and Erting's (1982, p. 12) view, demonstrating acceptability "boils down to knowing and applying the norms for the use of spoken English." Unfortunately, it is quite likely that this highly valued literate behavior, the use of spoken standard English in the manner of educated Americans, is still out of reach for many deaf Americans, despite pedagogical shifts in the field of deaf education. Although the mainstream belief system holds that education and standard English are the upward path for ethnolinguistic minorities, we are forced to ask if such mobility can ever be the outcome of manual codes for English in deaf education.

American deaf children are raised in a monolingual society where the value on literacy and literate behavior is implicit in everyday activities, both at home and at school. It is unlikely that they will grow up to be adult deaf Americans who are not aware of the social value of English. The painful questions, controversies, and conflicts center on the kind of English that deaf children and their hearing families use, the range of language varieties and registers that deaf children should command, and the best ways to foster linguistic growth. In the early years of education, the examination of the probable future status of deaf children and their need to develop the linguistic and interactional competence required for life as signing deaf Americans may prove to be as critical as the response to their deceptively immediate problems in developing English syntax. SEE 2 attempts to address the seemingly more immediate language need. Its widespread acceptance by parents and teachers indicates that they perceive the problem of teaching English as more urgent than the problem of fostering the broad-based communicative competence needed to be a deaf American.

## APPEAL OF SEE 2
## TO PARENTS AND TEACHERS

A surface level explanation of SEE 2's widespread acceptance in deaf education is that it holds promise as an instructional tool that is more accessible to students than oral English. In a more profound sense, however, its broad appeal rests on its compatibility with the sociolinguistic values of its main clientele, hearing parents and teachers. J. Fishman (1974) offers a broader point of view than this by taking into account the power of social context in the promotion and acceptance of the results of language-planning efforts. He (1974, p. 23) observes that "every one of the system-building or revising triumphs of language planning has been carefully cloaked in sentiment, has appealed to authenticity rationales, [and] has claimed indigenousness." Viable efforts to manipulate language depend upon appeals to the wishes of the speech community to maintain, revive, or create a language that is authentically their own and that reflects their history and guarantees their future as a unified people. These features of social context have implications for the viability of systems like SEE 2 in both hearing and deaf speech communities.

Discussions of language use in deaf education include the use of manual codes for English as well as the traditional methodological issues regarding the permissibility of signing and the relative focus on speech development and use of residual hearing. These issues summon forth intense feelings of language loyalty on all sides. This indicates that the precise sentiments to which Fishman refers are deeply enmeshed in this particular situation of language planning. SEE 2 makes the strongest appeal of indigenousness to its target group, namely, hearing parents of deaf children and teachers of the deaf, who are mostly well-educated white women with unimpaired hearing (Corbett & Jensema, 1981). The mainstream institutions where these teachers receive their training are also part of the target group. To this group, English articulated in a signed channel represents the "indigenous" or national language.

Yet indigenousness in the context of the deaf ethnolinguistic group has a different meaning. The indigenous language to which the deaf community assigns value and loyalty is ASL. The use of SEE 2, representing manipulation of the indigenous language of the deaf community, is thus accompanied by a conflict of loyalties. Gustason (1983) suggests that antagonism toward SEE 2 among ASL signers is the result of unfortunate timing, since SEE 2 emerged just as deaf ethnic and linguistic awareness began to grow. In important ways, the development of SEE 2 and the emergence of deaf awareness grew out of the same political and historical atmosphere of the 1960s. The antagonism goes deeper than coincidental "bad timing." J. Fishman's (1974) observation sheds more light on the sociolinguistic complications of the situation. The materials used to construct SEE 2 are highly valued linguistic resources in the deaf community: ASL lexical items and the medium of signing itself. These resources are being used to promote the linguistic values of another community. It should come as no surprise that this sociolinguistic situation is viewed with pain and anger.

There are social aspects to any language-planning project, particularly the codification of new norms and lexical changes. Language is a powerful symbol. People in modern speech communities may never consider the complex ways that language, culture, and society interact. Nevertheless, they hold on to their own language with loyalty because they believe that it reflects something about who they are. The paradox of SEE 2 is that it appeals to the hearing language values of its hearing target group while creating conflict with the language values of the deaf group. It succeeds in reflecting both the essence of the hearing society and its goals for education, both who the idealized "we" are as a society and who our intuitions tell us deaf children should be. This powerful sentiment underlies the widespread propagation of SEE 2 despite its so far unproven usefulness in instilling broad-based literacy in deaf students.

Citizens of the United States are still expected to behave as hearing monolingual speakers of English, and schools are expected to propagate, protect, and maintain Standard English. SEE 2 represents an intuitively reasonable solution to the problem of teaching English to deaf children. The system is, in effect, a compromise that has been worked out for educating deaf children in the hypothesized ideal image. But as sociolinguists and educators learn more about ASL and other varieties of signed languages in the signing speech community, they learn more about where to seek empirical evidence of actual social and linguistic niches for English among deaf Americans. Rather than design a speech community for deaf students, induct them into it through schooling, and then expect them to maintain it, it may be more fruitful to begin by asking who young deaf American students are, linguistically, socially, culturally, and educationally. This latter approach holds more promise of uncovering the ways that varieties of English and ASL interact and serve the needs of young deaf children, their hearing families, and their deaf culture mates in their homes, schools, and social lives.

## CONCLUSION

The development of SEE 2 and other MCEs bears a resemblance to the language-planning activities carried out on a national scale that appear to require instrumental solutions. Rather than attempt to create standard written norms, SEE 2 planners aimed to mold another language (ASL) into a system of signs that recode the standard. This is a unique problem in language planning. Nonetheless, by analyzing SEE 2 as an instance of language planning, rather than as a more or less effective tool for teaching English to deaf children, we are forced to consider the broader issues that make SEE 2 and other MCEs controversial and problematic in relation to the complex sociolinguistic situation that surrounds deafness and the minority language community so engendered in the United States.

The most provoking and potentially problematic issues in any language-planning effort grow from the social context that planners work in and into which their developments are introduced. In the case of SEE 2, the social and historical context of deaf education defines the problem. Traces of this history are seen in the basic principles and goals that guided the project. Although the social context into which the SEE 2 developments were introduced and propagated is unique, the factors of loyalty and sentiment that both promote and discourage acceptance are much like the forces that shape the success of language planning in other settings.

For all the criticism and controversy surrounding systems like SEE 2, they are still perceived as a step forward. Until relatively recently, the common ideal image of a deaf person was one of a citizen orally educated and fully assimilated into the English-speaking mainstream. To many deaf adults and concerned observers of the deaf education scene, the introduction of official, permissible signing in educational contexts constitutes a minor miracle. One deaf individual, who was educated in the 1920s in a residential school where older students were permitted to sign after their required oral primary years, provided the following observation on the relatively recent reintroduction of signing into deaf education: "The young deaf people seem to take it for granted as a right, whereas we older deaf people had to fight like hell to get it in the classroom." This same informant identified what he considers the weakness in actual practice of the total communication philosophy: "the students' lingo—call it ASL if you will but it is non-English" should be used as a medium of instruction for English and other subjects (Ramsey, 1984, p. 24).[6] G. Gustason (personal communication, April 1987) has also expressed her feelings about the differences she sees in the lives of deaf students: "When I first started working as a dorm counselor in a school for the deaf, my kids didn't want to go home weekends because no one in their family could sign, nor any of the hearing kids. It is such a completely different ballgame now."

Nonetheless, it is difficult to overlook the sociolinguistic situation in which English and SEE 2 in deaf education are embedded. J. Fishman's (1974) observation about the relationship between social sentiment and language accurately describes the heart of the language issues in deaf education. Language takes on a life of its own as human beings use it to symbolize and represent themselves as members of social groups. Just as

---

[6]These personal reflections were collected during a life history study of an ethnically deaf American, Steve Adams. The study traces the conflict and tension brought about by the pressures inherent to being both deaf and American. The course of Adams's life is followed from childhood in a large deaf extended family, through residential school and Gallaudet College, and finally to his search for professional employment. In each phase of his life, he was influenced by the tension between the idealized American value of self-reliance and the reality of deafness, namely, dependence on the benevolence of the individuals and institutions of hearing society.

language problems are not isolated phenomena, the activity of designing language changes in order to address problems cannot be considered apart from social context. Attention to context is especially important with regard to language problems in schools. Rubin (1984) points out that language problems in educational institutions can be symptoms of larger problems with causes and effects that extend far beyond the classroom.

SEE 2 emerged in response to a set of real problems with multiple definitions and thus many potential solutions. In this context, it appeared to represent change. Yet, as Lane (1980) makes clear in his historical discussion of the interaction of signing deaf communities in the United States and France with majority language groups, there are striking similarities between problems wrought from the use of MCEs and those from the sole use of spoken English as a medium of instruction for deaf students, precisely the situation that SEE 2 was designed to remedy. The attempt to create manual forms of English by restructuring ASL signs and Standard English is a logical extension of the hearing monolingual definition of the language problems that deaf children encounter and that deaf education is charged with resolving. Unfortunately, the solution offered by MCEs serves the symbolic needs of the hearing society much better than it does the linguistic and educational needs of deaf children.

# 7

# Transliteration: What's the Message?

Elizabeth A. Winston

## INTRODUCTION

Transliteration is a specific form of sign language interpreting. It is the process of changing one form of an English message, either spoken English or signed English, into the other form. Interpreting, in contrast, refers either to the general process of changing the form of a message to another form, or to the specific process of changing an English message to American Sign Language (ASL), or vice versa. The assumption in transliteration is that both the spoken and the signed forms correspond to English, the spoken form following the rules of standard English and the signed form being a simple recoding of the spoken form into a manual mode of expression. The guidelines for the spoken form are relatively clear. It is the signed form that lacks any sort of standardization at the level of systematic recoding of spoken utterances. Indeed, the signed forms themselves are variously referred to as Pidgin Signed English, Manually Coded English, and even foreigner talk.[1]

[1]These terms represent a few of the terms used to describe the contact varieties of signing and speaking (or mouthing without voice) that are used when deaf people who rely on signing and hearing people who rely on speaking wish to communicate. Pidgin Signed English (PSE) is discussed by many authors, including Marmor and Pettito (1979). Manually Coded English (MCE) refers to forms of signing that encode various formal features of spoken English in manual signs. These features are generally morphemic: copula, tense agreement, inflectional and derivational morphemes, as well as root morphemes of English. They are intended to be

THE SOCIOLINGUISTICS OF THE DEAF COMMUNITY
Copyright © 1989 by Academic Press Inc.
All rights of reproduction in any form reserved.

147

It is not the aim of this chapter to discuss the labels used for the forms of the signed message. Rather, the goal is to describe some of the features of the signed forms in relation to the strategies used to produce a message match in the target language. The focus in this study is on the form of the signed message when it is the target form because it is the form often requested by those using a transliterator. The question of the form of the signed message when it is the source language is equally significant, and a similar study centered on this aspect will be invaluable to our understanding of the English forms of signing and transliterating.[2] The present study proposes that the signed form is more than a simple recoding of spoken English into signed English. It is a complex combination of features from ASL and from English and is accomplished by conscious strategies employed by the transliterator. The form of the target message is analyzed here in terms of these conscious strategies, conscious in that they are planned by the transliterator as opposed to being either randomly or erroneously produced.

## DEFINITIONS OF TRANSLITERATION

The form of signed transliteration is vaguely defined in a few texts. In fact, it is not actually the form of the message that is described but the process of transliteration that produces the form. Frishberg's (1986, p. 19) text, which is used for teaching sign language interpretation, defines transliteration as "the process of changing an English text into Manually Coded English (or vice versa)." This definition is only marginally helpful in understanding transliteration and the forms of the signed message since there are several signed codes for English, each with its own distinct principles for encoding English. (See S. Supalla, 1986, for a discussion of these forms.)

In the process of transliteration, any of these codes, or any combination of these codes, might be used. The effectiveness of these codes for transliteration has not been studied. However, their effectiveness for everyday communication has been seriously questioned. Marmor and Petitto (1979) found that even skilled users of these codes did not accurately represent

---

literally represented on the hands through the use of signs, many of which are borrowed from the lexicon of American Sign Language (ASL). Further description of these forms is in S. Supalla (1986). Cokely (1983) describes the contact varieties as forms of foreigner talk. For a broader understanding of the complex nature of the manually signed versions of English, the reader is referred to the literature already cited as well as to various items listed in the reference section.

[2]A study of this kind is now in progress at Gallaudet University, under the direction of Ceil Lucas and Clayton Valli. The data collected and the results of this study will provide much-needed information in the area of transliteration.

the spoken message on their hands in one-to-one communication. If this is a problem for speakers who control both the speed and the content of the communication, it is logical to assume that an even greater problem in message match develops for the transliterator. In a transliterated setting, it is the speaker who has control of the speed and content of the source message, not the transliterator. Since the transliterator does not have control of either speed or content, the use of such coding systems for transliterating must also be seriously questioned. Thus, this first definition of transliterating as a simple encoding process inadequately describes both the form of the message and the production process.

The instructional text of Caccamise *et al.* (1980, p. 3), describes transliteration as changing "'only' the *mode* of the sender's communication or message . . . e.g., English speech to a signed or manual code for English." This definition allows for more flexibility in the form of the message since it allows for more of the contact varieties of signing. This increased flexibility, however, leads to the question of which variety or varieties can be used or expected by any given consumer and transliterator. There are no comprehensive descriptions of any of the contact varieties that are in use among English speakers and ASL signers. The variety of forms is multiplied when deaf consumers whose native language is some type of signed English, rather than ASL, are included in the group of target consumers. This definition, while allowing for more flexibility, thus does not provide a clear description of the signed output.

One approach to the description of transliteration entails analysis both of the problems faced during the transliteration process and of the strategies used by transliterators to deal with these problems or constraints [Conference of Interpreter Trainers (CIT), 1984]. This perspective describes transliterating as English-like signing, which by its very nature does not have a standardized form. This lack of standardization of sign forms results in "intermediate varieties" of signing that are "incapable of fully conveying the grammatical/syntactic information" (CIT, 1984, p. 95) of the source language. This perspective views the target form as a less than complete message, more in the form of a pidgin that can provide a means of communication but cannot provide all the subtleties of either language. The CIT discussion of transliteration centers on strategies used by transliterators to add clarity and meaning to the inadequate form of signed English, these strategies being various borrowings from ASL. Their discussion also provides many insights into the problems of making an inadequate form (signed English) more meaningful and clear. It stresses the need for borrowing features from ASL in order to produce this clarity.

S. Supalla (1986) approaches the question of signed forms of English from a slightly different perspective. His discussion centers on the occurrence of features of visual languages in signed forms of English, not because of the inadequacy of English but because of the adequacy of signed languages in dealing with visual needs. This is a different but important perspective in an analysis of transliteration. Since the goal is to provide a visual target form that not only resembles to some extent spoken English structures but at the same time is also comprehensible, it is appropriate to use forms that are specific to visual languages such as ASL in order to achieve clarity and meaning. It is also appropriate to include features of English that are visual, such as mouthing. The present study is conducted from the perspective that visual features from ASL, borrowed to clarify an English message, can be expected in the target form; their occurrence is a logical result of trying to use a visual mode for a spoken language. Any definition that precludes or ignores the features of visual communication in favor of English structure cannot adequately describe transliteration.

It was helpful during the course of this project to consider perspectives on interpretation that are not specific to sign language per se but make pertinent reference to the principles and practices of interpreting between various spoken and written languages. Many of these descriptions and discussions can be extended to include sign language interpreting, and specifically, transliterating. Nida (1976) discusses the question of translatability, in general, and whether any sort of information transfer by means of interpreting is even feasible. He concludes that, while exact equivalence of meaning, including all the linguistic and cultural nuances of one language transferred completely to another, is not possible, functional equivalence is possible. By functional equivalence, he means the production of a message that is pragmatically similar. He (Nida, 1976, p. 63) includes the following reminder about the general nature of communication, a factor often forgotten by those who discuss the "correctness" of an interpreted message:

> Even among experts discussing a subject within their own fields of specialization, it is unlikely that comprehension rises above the 80 percent level. Loss of information is a part of any communication process, and hence the fact that some loss occurs in translation should not be surprising, nor should it constitute a basis for questioning the legitimacy of translating.

This statement does not excuse inadequate transliteration but simply reminds us that there are many aspects of the process that need further study and improvement. Interpreting and, more specifically, transliterating, can still be successful. The point is that we must analyze successful transliterated messages and describe how and why they are successful. Nida's comment serves as a reminder that there are limitations on even the most effective forms of communication. The legitimacy of transliterating is often questioned on the basis of its inadequacy. But perhaps the rather limiting definitions of transliteration make the process appear inadequate; perhaps, also, expectations about the capabilities of any sort of information transfer are higher than normally expected of even direct communication processes.

Another valuable discussion of interpreting, specifically, translation from one written form to another, is provided by Casagrande (1954). He describes four possible goals of the translator when producing a text, each of which can affect the final form of the message. These goals are the following:

1. Pragmatic: the goal is to translate a source message as efficiently and as accurately as possible, with a focus on the meaning rather than on the form of the message.
2. Linguistic: the goal is to "identify and assign equivalent meanings" (Casagrande, 1954, p. 337) between the source and target languages; the form of the target is directed by grammatical concerns rather than by meaning.
3. Aesthetic-Poetic: the goal is to produce the message in a form that is aesthetically similar in both languages.
4. Ethnographic: the goal is to include cultural background and explanations of text from one language to another.

These goals are not mutually exclusive; each translator works to achieve a final text that reflects the original message by balancing the requirements of each goal. Transliterators likewise work to achieve a final message that is a balance of these goals. Transliterators are more constrained by the linguistic goal than are other kinds of interpreters because they are expected to produce a form that resembles the source English message. They also deal with the pragmatic goal of producing a message simultaneously with the speaker, as well as with the final two goals.[3] The balancing of these goals results in a form that resembles English in some of its features, ASL in other of its features, and a blend of both that may be specific to the contact varieties and the effects found whenever a spoken message is recoded in a visual-manual mode.

---

[3]Another interesting assumption made about transliteration is that this English also reflects the form of the speaker's message. It is assumed that, even though many of the spoken English morphemes such as tense marking and plurals are omitted from the signed version, the structure and order of the signs produced follow the structure and order of the speaker. The data of the present project indicate that this is not necessarily the case. Although the form produced can reflect an English order, it is not necessarily the order of the speaker. This difference is described in this chapter under the section about restructuring.

## THE PRESENT STUDY

The output, or target form, of any interpreted message is always determined by those consumers directly involved in the communication. Even interpreters working between languages with very standardized forms can produce different interpretations of the same message. When dealing with forms that are not standardized, the variety of interpretations can be even greater. The present study describes the form of a transliterated message that occurred in one setting with one transliterator and one consumer. The objective is not to assess this form in terms of the appropriateness of its use in transliteration. Rather, the objective is to analyze the form in terms of the strategies used by transliterators. These strategies are reflected by the features of the transliterated target form. Transliterators use these strategies to produce a target form that conveys most of the information of the source language message. A basic assumption of this study is that a transliterated message is not simply a codified, inadequate version of a spoken English message. On the contrary, it is proposed that transliteration is a process that includes a combination of English and ASL features capable of conveying the source message as clearly and unambiguously as any other form of interpreting. It is necessary to reiterate that this is true when the client is to some extent bilingual in ASL and English. The features from English include word order and mouthed English words.[4] ASL features include lexical choice, head and body shifting for marking phrases and clauses, and use of location.

The hypothesis of the present study is that transliterators produce signed target language messages that contain a mixture of English and ASL features. This mixture of features, rather than causing confusion to the watcher, provides enough detail to produce a message that is clear and unconfusing to the watcher.

In addition, it is proposed that these features reflect conscious strategies used by transliterators during analysis and production of the target form, rather than random productions or errors. This is evidenced by the transliterator's feedback and comments about the target forms during an interview conducted after the data were analyzed. The strategies discussed here and the features that they reflect are (1) conceptual sign choice, (2) addition, (3) omission, (4) restructuring, and (5) mouthing. Additional features of the data corpus are not analyzed in comparable detail. The target form features are categorized in terms of differences from the source form of spoken English. In the evaluation of the data, the features that added to the clarity of the message are analyzed; those portions of the form that con-

---

[4]It may be that the word order is not English word order per se but an order that is shared by both English and ASL.

tained mistakes or errors are not analyzed or described. This determination is subjective in the same way that any discussion of "correct" interpretation is subjective. In addition to the researcher's judgment, the transliterator was consulted in many of the cases about her reasons, or strategies, in using specific features. There are other measures that can and should be used to further determine the adequacy of any transliterated message, for example, the consumer's comprehension, the comprehension of other consumers, other interpreters' agreement with the form choice. For the preliminary description presented here, the researcher's judgment, the interpreter's judgment, and the apparent satisfaction of the consumer with the transliteration are relied upon in assessing the adequacy of the message form.[5]

## DATA COLLECTION AND TRANSCRIPTION

The data for this study were collected from a university-level course that was regularly transliterated by the same person. The transliterator and the deaf consumer had, at the time of the videotaping, worked together in this course once a week over a span of eleven weeks, as well as in another course during the same semester and over the same amount of time. The topic of the course was familiar to both the transliterator and the consumer; they were accustomed to working with each other and with the instructor, as well as experienced with the procedures for the class and the vocabulary and content. The purpose in choosing these particular data was to exclude, as much as possible, the type of transliteration that occurs when the transliterator is unfamiliar with the topic, the consumer, and the vocabulary. In the present case, the goal is a processed, analyzed form of the target message, as opposed to a more mechanical reproduction of the English sounds. This, of course, reflects the assumption that this type of transliteration is appropriate and does provide an accurate portrayal of the source message. In addition, the consumer is not a native ASL signer but an English signer in the process of learning ASL. The consumer expected the transliteration to be patterned on English but also "conceptually accurate," that is, effective in conveying the meaning of the speaker as well as the form. This represents a balancing of two of the goals outlined earlier: pragmatic and linguistic transliteration. It is assumed, for this particular situation, that the need for efficiency and clarity motivates use of ASL features, and the need for English structures motivates use of English features.

---

[5]Consumer satisfaction, apparent or real, is an issue that is often only superficially discussed at best. It is an area of extreme importance that warrants serious attention.

The transliterator in this study is a nationally certified transliterator. In addition to her qualifications as a transliterator, she has a Master's degree in the academic specialty in which she transliterated for the data corpus of this study. Information about the strategies used in the transliteration process was gathered in an interview with the transliterator after the data were analyzed. The researcher's experience as a transliterator, as well as discussions with other transliterators, provided additional insights about features found in the data and their relation to the strategies employed.

A transcription of approximately twenty-five minutes of the classroom lecture was analyzed. Segments of the text from two different time periods were selected for the analysis. Constraints on the choice of text segments included high audibility of the source message, for purposes of comparison, and high visibility of the transliterator. One important area excluded from this study is teacher-student interaction. The description of features used by transliterators both to indicate the speakers and to include as much information as possible is essential to understanding transliteration. Unfortunately, most of the student participation is unintelligible on the videotape. The present analysis is thus limited to the transliteration of the instructor's lecture.

The transcription of the data consists of three parts: transcription of the source message; transcription of the manual signs by means of a gloss and any additional description needed to identify the form of the sign produced; and a transcription of the mouthing that accompanies the signs. Only the mouthed words and parts of words that are clearly recognizable on the videotape are included in the transcription. This leaves many gaps in the mouthed transcription since many parts of the words are not visible, especially with a two-dimensional videotape picture. Mouthing, however, is an important part of transliteration and is included in the analysis whenever possible. In discussing data from the tapes, and in presenting examples, the following conventions are used: first, the original spoken message is orthographically represented, in italics; next, ASL signs are represented with an English gloss-label, in uppercase (any further description needed to clearly identify an ASL sign is added parenthetically after the ASL sign citation); finally, the mouthed form that accompanies the manual signs is framed with double quotation marks, all within square brackets. An example of this transcription technique is the following:

*Go to the store.* → GO (to the right) STORE ["go to the store"]

The analysis focuses on the five categories, or strategies, earlier described as sign choice, addition, omission, restructuring, and mouthing. Although several additional features were identified in the target form that added clarity to the message, these are not discussed in detail here. They appear to be very important, but there is not enough information about these features, as they are used in ASL, to be able to analyze their uses when borrowed for transliterating. A more detailed description of these features and many others is needed.

## ANALYSIS OF STRATEGIES

### Sign Choice

The first strategy, sign choice, was originally defined in this study as the use of a conceptually accurate sign in place of a literal translation of the English word. Although the idea of conceptual accuracy is somewhat elusive, the reference is to the appropriate portrayal of meaning in each language involved in the transliteration process. To claim that a manual sign is more or less conceptually accurate depends entirely on one's understanding of the meaning of the sign and of the intended word. In sign language interpreting, however, the term "conceptual accuracy" is used most often to refer to the use of a sign that portrays the meaning of the word rather than the form of the word. An example of this is the English word *get.* A literal linguistic transliteration of this word would use the sign GET, which in ASL means to actually take something into one's possession. In English, the word *get* is used with many different meanings, only one of which corresponds to the ASL sign GET, as in the sentence, "I got the book." A literal transliteration would use the same sign in sentences such as the following:

1. "I got sick."
2. "She got hit."
3. "They got there."
4. "I got it," meaning 'I understand'.

None of the verbs in these four sentences uses *get* to mean to take into one's possession. A conceptually accurate transliteration would entail representation of the word *get* with a manual sign that has the meaning of the sentence rather than the form of GET. The verbs in the listed sentences might be conceptually transliterated with the following signs:

1. BECOME
2. something HIT her
3. ARRIVE
4. UNDERSTAND

An example of this strategy in the data is found in relation to the spoken utterance: *the person might <u>wonder</u> if they should happen to turn around and see you checking things off.* Here, the transliterator uses the sign PUZZLE 'to be puzzled' instead of the sign WONDER, which corresponds to the actual English word *wonder*. The transliterator's comment about this choice is that the sign PUZZLE reflects the meaning of the speaker better than the sign WONDER. This is clearly a conscious decision of the transliterator to use a lexical item from ASL that matches the meaning of the speaker rather than the English lexical item of the speaker.

Another example is the spoken utterance: *I want you to take a few minutes now*, where the transliterator uses the sign USE instead of the sign TAKE, which would have matched the English word. In English, the word *take* is similar to the word *get* in the earlier examples. It has many different meanings, only one of which corresponds to the ASL sign TAKE. The transliterator again chooses an ASL sign that matches the meaning of the speaker rather than the words of the speaker. The following spoken word-manual sign pairs from the data also demonstrate this sign choice strategy. In each case, it is the underlined portion of the spoken English message that is recoded to achieve a meaning-match, as opposed to a lexical correspondence:

*for speech varieties which correspond to solidarity*
Signed: WITH

*it looks like everyone*
Signed: YOU-*plural* A-L-L

*because it doesn't work as well as*
Signed: SUCCEED

*could you make it up*
Signed: INVENT

*and turn it in so you can get credit for it*
Signed: GIVE-TO-ME

Another example of this strategy is the use of reduplication for pluralization, which is a feature of ASL, rather than the use of a plural -*s* marker added to a manual sign, which is a feature of signed English. This use of reduplication was classified as a sign choice rather than an omission from the English message because the latter label would make the actual signed form seem less than adequate. The ASL feature, as part of the form of the transliterated message, shows the richness of the actual form. One example from the data is the following:

*many societies* → MANY SOCIETY-*plural*

As discussed in the next section, reduplication can also be aptly described as an addition of an ASL feature to the English message. The categories of omission and addition are not discrete; they overlap, and several features can be found in any given sentence. They are divided here into separate categories for discussion, but they are not so easily divided in a message.

The definition of conceptual sign choice, then, is the use of a conceptually accurate sign instead of a sign that portrays the English word form. This definition is extended to include not only words for which both a literal and a conceptual sign could be used, but also those English words that have no exactly comparable form in ASL. These words are occasionally represented by fingerspelling of the exact word and, more frequently, by the use of a manual sign with a similar meaning together with simultaneous English mouthing of the word. An interesting aspect of this is the choice of the word that is mouthed. It is sometimes the speaker's original word and, at other times, the word that is often used to gloss the sign itself. An example of this is the word *versus*. The sign that is generally gloss-labeled OPPOSITE is used for this word in the data. In this instance, the transliterator signs OPPOSITE and simultaneously mouths "versus" to match the speaker's choice of words. Other examples are the following:

| Source word | Sign | Mouthing |
|---|---|---|
| *assignment* | → HOMEWORK | ["assignment"] |
| *wonder* | → PUZZLE | ["wonder"] |
| *brilliant* | → SMART | ["brilliant"] |

In these instances, the transliterator chooses a conceptually appropriate sign while mouthing the exact form of the source English word to achieve clarity in the target form.

This strategy of conceptual signs plus mouthing is used in a second way by the transliterator. Rather than mouth the word choice of the speaker, a word that is usually associated with the sign is mouthed:

| Source word | Sign | Mouthing |
|---|---|---|
| *appear* | → SHOW-UP | ["show up"] |
| *data sheet* | → DATA PAPER | ["data paper"] |
| *normally* | → MOST TIME | ["most time"] |
| *stuff* | → EVERYTHING | ["everything"] |

No particular pattern is discernible in the data in terms of mouthing of the speaker's word versus the transliterator's own word. It is noteworthy that both are used and that the speaker's word choice does not completely dictate the mouthed form, as is widely assumed. The transliterator suggested a possible explanation for her choice of mouthed form. She feels that it is more natural for her to mouth the word that she associates with a sign. But her training, which defines transliteration as a sign-to-word correspondence, leads her to use the speaker's words. She also stated that choice of mouthing is partly determined by the amount of processing that a message requires. In a difficult passage that requires a great deal of analysis, her mouthing is much more likely to be her own. When a passage requires less analysis to provide a clear target form, she can give greater attention to reproducing the original words on her mouth. This insight supports the suggestion that both pragmatic and linguistic goals determine the form of the transliteration.

Sign choice, as a feature of transliteration, reflects a strategy used by transliterators to achieve the pragmatic goal of the task, the efficient production of a functionally equivalent message. At the same time, the addition of mouthing seems to be an attempt to more closely approximate the English form of the message.

## *Addition*

The second strategy, addition, refers to the use of a conceptually accurate sign either before or after a more literal equivalent. An example of this is the use of the more literal sign equivalents for the phrase "don't want," where a transliterator signs DON'T, follows it with WANT, and then signs the ASL form typically used, DON'T-WANT. This configuration expresses both the form and the meaning of the source message, thereby achieving both pragmatic and linguistic representation. Included in this category of addition are a number of ASL features that are added to signs in the target message. These features include the use of space to establish a referent (a feature used in ASL but not in English) and the addition of a negative headshake to negative signs, a nonmanual form that is used syntactically in ASL to mark negative clauses. The transliterator in the present study adds head shaking to negative signs. The addition of ASL adverbial markers with verbs occurs in one case as well.[6]

Examples of additions of signs are found in the following discourse fragments from the data corpus. In each case, the transliterator produces the addition after signing the source message fragment:

*that place has to be within sight*
Addition: an index 'in this area'

*that doesn't happen one right after the other*
Addition: NO plus a negative marker

*a week from today*
Addition: MONDAY

These additions occur after a restructuring of the spoken phrase. Because these data do not provide a sufficient base for generalizing about processes of transliteration, it is important to continue the search for patterns of addition in the data bases of other, similarly designed studies.

An example of the addition of a negative headshake with negative signs

---

[6]A discussion of ASL adverbial markers can be found in Liddell (1980).

occurs in the sequence I-F NOT. A negative headshake is added to the sign NOT. This is not a grammatical feature of English. It is used in ASL to mark clauses rather than single signs, but it appears to have been added here for clarity in the message.

The use of space in ASL is a feature that adds clarity to information by locating objects and entities in the signing space. For example, the speaker talks about a person who, after walking away, might turn around and look back. The transliterator, when signing this stretch of the discourse, adds a classifier predicate indicating that the person walked away to the right. When the speaker talks about the person turning back around, the transliterator signs LOOK-AT-the signer 'looking back at me' and places the sign in the same location on the right where the person had already been established as walking toward. This use of space is a feature that is not available in English but that seems to add clarity to the signed version of the source message. This entire sequence appears to combine the substitution of ASL classifier signs for the more literal signs that could have been used and the addition of signing space used as an established location for a referent.

A second example of use of signing space in the data is the establishment of a person referent to the right of the signing space. Each time the speaker refers to this person, the transliterator points to the previously established location, thereby clearly referring to the person.

Only one example of the addition of ASL adverbials was found in the data corpus. ASL uses specific nonmanual behaviors for expressing an adverb. For example, "to walk carelessly" is expressed by the sign WALK plus the simultaneous addition of the *-th* adverbial produced by the mouth, meaning 'careless'. Specifically, with this adverbial, the mouth is slightly open and the lips and the tongue protrude slightly. The example found in the present data is the *-mm* adverbial, meaning 'casually, in an off-hand way'. In this adverbial, the lips are together and protruding. The nonmanual sign *-mm* is added to the verb WRITE when the speaker discusses the possibility of recording data on a sheet without really doing any of the research. The actual spoken English words are *to mark down at random.* There are no literal equivalents of these words in ASL that express the same meaning that *-mm* expresses so clearly. With the addition of *-mm,* the goal of efficient, pragmatic transliteration is achieved.

Another feature added to transliteration is facial expression. ASL, as a visual language, relies much more than spoken English on facial expression. The kind of facial expression referred to here is in addition to the facial expression that accompanies nonmanual adverbs in ASL. A frequent complaint of consumers is that transliterators are monotone, that is, they lack any sort of facial expression. This aspect of a visual language, although not always a grammatical feature of ASL, adds clarity to the visual message and is often missing in a transliterated message. This use of facial expression appears to be one way of representing stress and intonation. It is usually assumed that these spoken language features cannot be adequately transferred to a signed language. This is another area requiring much more investigation. The first of this type of addition in the present data is the use of an exaggerated facial expression with the sign BIG to portray the meaning 'very big'; the second example is the facial and body expression added to the signs SELF RESPECT. An expression of pride on the face and an expanded chest accompanies this sign sequence.

It can be argued that some of the features classified as additions are not additions at all but are required elements in an appropriate and accurate transliteration. The elements add clarity to the message and portray meaning in ways that are not necessarily represented by literal recoding of English words into manual signs. They are classified here as additions only because they are not generally discussed as part of the output of signed transliteration. The use of addition as a strategy is perceived as necessary for clarity in the visual message, both by the transliterator in this study and by other transliterators who served as consultants.

## Omission

The third strategy consists of the omission of portions of the source language in the target form. This strategy is used to achieve the goal of efficiency: pragmatic transliteration. Many parts of English words and phrases are not necessary to the overall meaning in context; they are redundant. For example, across a stretch of discourse in English, the use of the past tense marker on each verb is unnecessary from the standpoint of context-bound, referential-and-predicational effectiveness. ASL users mark tense at the beginning of a topic and then do not mark it again until the tense needs to be changed. The transliterator in the present data deletes tense markers in recoding the English message even though there exists a set of literal sign equivalents. Likewise, English plural markings are deleted, as are affixes, such as *-ful* in the word *powerful.* The copula is also almost entirely missing from these data. Although there is a full set of literal sign equivalents for the forms of the English copula, there is only one instance of use.[7] When the speaker emphasizes the phrase *should be,* the transliterator includes the copula, not by using the sign for 'be' but by spelling B-E and emphatically mouthing it at the same time.

Another omission that occurs less consistently than those already noted is the omission of prepositions not necessary to the message. The phrase

[7]Copula is not used in ASL; the sign equivalents are based on a single sign meaning 'true' or 'real'. This basic form is assigned specific modifications in order to provide sign equivalents.

*groups of people* is signed GROUP PEOPLE.It is significant that even though the sign is omitted, the word itself is often mouthed by the interpreter. This provides a more linguistic, literal representation on one set of articulators (oral) while providing a more efficient message with the other set of articulators (manual). Mouthing seems to provide a much more consistent reflection than the hands of the literal English message.

Omission of previously established subject pronouns also occurs. The English sequence *I'm not* is transliterated as WILL NOT. This type of structure, with the pronoun omitted, is not a feature of formal English. It is a feature of ASL that is borrowed by this transliterator as a strategy to achieve the goal of efficiency in the transliteration.

## *Restructuring*

The fourth strategy, restructuring, refers to the replacement of one grammatical structure with another. This is different from the sign choice category because sign choice mainly involves one or two-word sequences; restructuring involves changes in longer utterances. Restructuring can occur in combination with any and all of the earlier-mentioned strategies. Examples of restructuring occur within the following discourse fragments. In each case, it is the underlined portion of the spoken English message that is restructured:[8]

*which is voiced 'th'*
Restructured to: T-H WITH VOICE (' "th" with voice')

*I'm giving you a week from today off*
Restructured to: NEXT-WEEK MONDAY

*more friendly and more trustworthy.*
Restructured to: CAN TRUST MORE

*it has to be a location which is within sight*
Restructured to: PLACE YOU CAN SEE

*All you're after is one word.*
Restructured to: ONLY WANT ONE WORD

*if it's within sight then people will*
Restructured to: I-F CAN SEE THAT PLACE

These restructured discourse fragments are accompanied by mouthing of English words that correspond to the restructured form and not to the source message. This is another indication that transliteration involves more than a literal representation or recoding of spoken English.

---

[8]Note that the second example of restructuring here is also cited earlier, in the section on the strategy of addition. The sign MONDAY is an addition embedded within a restructuring.

It is noteworthy that three of the source forms are structures involving the copula, a feature not used in ASL. It may be that one cause of restructuring is forms or configurations in the source message that cannot be comparably recoded in ASL. The present transliterator, although aware that she uses this strategy, could not identify any particular feature of the message that caused restructuring. Her explanation was limited to an express awareness that some of the English utterances, as structured, would not provide a clear visual message when recoded into the target form, and, therefore, she restructured them.

## *Mouthing*

The fifth strategy, mouthing, is described earlier in relation to sign choice. There are instances in the data when the mouthing matches the source form, and other instances when it matches the transliterated form. A match with the transliterated form is also seen in the mouthing that accompanies restructuring in the transliteration. In addition to these uses of mouthing, there is another use that occurs in the data when a specific sign that occurs can serve to recode more than one English word. On these occasions of potential ambiguity in the manual mode, mouthing is used to indicate which English word is being transliterated. The following examples show the many-to-one relationship between mouthed English words and, in each case, the co-occurring manual sign:

| Sign | Mouthing |
|------|----------|
| RELATE-TO | ["correspond"] |
|  | ["associated"] |
| SITUATION | ["situation"] |
|  | ["domains"] |
| MUST | ["will"] |
|  | ["should"] |
|  | ["have to"] |
| SMART | ["smart"] |
|  | ["intelligent"] |
|  | ["brilliant"] |
| VARIOUS | ["variety"] |
|  | ["variable"] |

Not all of these mouthed English words have literal sign equivalents. The transliterator, rather than using a different sign for each meaning, uses the same sign and simultaneously mouths the English form. In each instance, the mouthing serves to distinguish the intended meaning of the manual sign. This use of mouthing, which presupposes consumer reliance on speech-reading, is an important strategy in transliterating. The effectiveness of this strategy, like the effectiveness of all the other strategies, is dependent on the consumer's skills and knowledge of the target form. It is one more strategy for producing both a conceptual and a literal message at the same time.

The transliterator agreed that the mouthing strategy was important for the particular consumer in the present study. Although some of the strategies, such as restructuring, are chosen because of structural incongruities between languages, the use of mouthing is determined by the consumer's needs. For different consumers, the transliterator can employ different techniques, such as fingerspelling, to provide the English equivalent.

An additional aspect of transliterating that is not described here is the phenomenon of pacing or phrasing. This includes the features used by transliterators to mark the separation of clauses in the target form. This type of marking is achieved through stress and intonation in English and through various features in ASL, some of which are described in this chapter. These features include body shifts, head nodding, signing space, and facial expressions. These features appear in the transliterated data of this study, although not necessarily in combination with ASL sentence structures. These features, in ASL, are used with entire phrases or clauses. In the transliterated message, nonmanual features similar in form to those of ASL appear to mark the beginning and ending points of the English structures. This combination of ASL and English features is a transliteration strategy that adds clarity to the message.

## *SUMMARY AND CONCLUSIONS*

Although the analysis and description of the target message examined in this study are preliminary, the findings indicate that the form of transliteration is different from what is assumed by both transliterators and consumers. On the whole, it is apparent that at least some forms of transliteration include not only English-like signing of the source message but also many features of ASL. This type of transliteration requires skills in both ASL and English in order to achieve and blend pragmatic and linguistic goals in the production of a target message. Analyzing the source message and producing a target form that is both functionally equivalent and structurally similar to the source is a complex process and requires more than the simple recoding of English words.

This study, in the tradition of preliminary investigations, raises more questions about transliteration than are answered. It is hoped that as we understand more about the structure of ASL and the process of interpreting in general, the process of transliterating will also be better understood.

Areas of research suggested by this study include a description of the source message when it is a signed form of English and a description of different varieties of transliteration, including the varieties requested by bilingual ASL and English users as well as the varieties primarily understood by English signers. It will also be important to study the effects of a variety of speakers on the form of the signed output produced by one transliterator for one consumer.

## *ACKNOWLEDGMENTS*

Funding for this research was provided through the Small Grants Fund, Gallaudet University, Washington, D.C. I thank all of those who participated in the data collection for this study: the deaf and hearing students, the instructors, and, most especially, the transliterators.

# 8

## Visually Oriented Teaching Strategies with Deaf Preschool Children

Susan A. Mather

## INTRODUCTION

The purpose of this study is to describe how a native signer teaches in a preschool classroom with five deaf children who entered with minimal communicative competence. None of the children had acquired linguistic skills (either in sign language or in English) before entering school at the age of three.

The study involves the review of a story, "Three Little Kittens," which had been read to the students. In this review, the teacher does not read the story but rather asks the children about the story. The study demonstrates how the teacher helps the students adapt to the classroom situation. Specifically, it focuses on how the teacher uses questions; elicits answers; responds to answers; uses classifier predicates, role playing, and "miniature" signs; adapts signs to the specific actions depicted in pictures; and changes English words that show sound-related concepts to signs that show visual concepts. The findings suggest that to communicate effectively with those students who are prelingually deaf and have minimal language competence, a teacher must be competent in the use of different forms of American Sign Language (ASL).

## LANGUAGE IN DEAF EDUCATION

Administrators of educational programs have only recently recognized that a bilingual approach to teaching prelingually deaf students may be neces-

Copyright © 1989 by Academic Press Inc.
All rights of reproduction in any form reserved.

sary, that is, teaching students ASL as a first language and English as a second. Traditionally, educators view ASL either as a symptom of a deficiency to be avoided whenever possible or only as a method of teaching, rather than as a language (Stevens, 1980).

Deaf teachers are traditionally placed in the classrooms where students are either older than most other students or are low-achievers academically, while hearing teachers are placed in the preschool classrooms and in the classrooms of deaf students with good English skills. One reason for the selective placement of deaf teachers is the widespread notion that normal deaf children should be protected from the "poor English" of deaf teachers. Any signing that is not equivalent to English is considered harmful to deaf students. Another reason is that deaf teachers can communicate with "less capable" deaf students while the hearing teachers cannot (Stevens, 1980).

A vast majority of teachers for the deaf sign in English word order, that is, use Signed English (Jordan and Karchmer, 1986). Signed English is completely different from ASL. ASL is not based on or derived from English. Signed English, on the other hand, is not a separate language but rather a manual code for English, since it attempts to manually represent the spoken language English. This code uses signs in a sentence in the same way that they are used in English, as opposed to how signs are used in ASL. Some examples of this type of code system are Seeing Essential English (Anthony, 1971), Linguistics of Visual English (Wampler, 1972), and Signed English (Bornstein, 1973). All are designed for use by teachers and parents of deaf children.

A continuing debate revolves around how students who are prelingually deaf and have minimal communicative competence should acquire English, whether as a first or as a second language. On the one hand, Quigley and Kretschmer (1982) contend that the primary goal of education for prelingually deaf children should be literacy in English. On the other hand, Livingston (1986) asserts that in order for deaf children to become literate in English, they must first develop their meaning-making and meaning-sharing abilities. She contends that in order to develop these abilities, educators of the deaf should use the linguistic system that best represents meaning for deaf children; in many cases, that system is ASL.

These recommendations are complicated by certain attitudes arising from the debate, attitudes that create problems for the actual use of languages in the classroom setting. For example, there is evidence that in classrooms where ASL is used, native ASL users often correct the errors made by "nonnative" teachers (Chesterfield, Barrows, Hayes-Latimer and Chavez, 1983; Erting, 1980; Johnson and Erting, this volume). As discussed later, the students in this study also often interrupt when the teacher violates the grammatical rules of ASL, that is, fails to correctly reflect in sign the intended meaning of concepts or information in the story view. The students' attitudes toward the teacher are apparently affected adversely by the teacher's seeming lack of respect for the importance and appropriateness of transmitting correct information.

## Cultural Norms and Classroom Discourse

Language use in deaf education needs to be considered within the broad context of the relationship between cultural norms and classroom discourse.

In a classroom setting, at least two sets of behavior rules and discourse rules are operating: the teacher's rules and the students'. The teacher brings to the classroom his or her own socially conditioned ways of behaving and a value system through which the teacher interprets the role of teacher and accepts, refuses, or tries to modify the behavior of the children. Students bring to the classroom socially conditioned ways of behaving both verbally and nonverbally. They learn the language of their parents and of other significant persons in their environment. Communication problems can arise when a teacher uses a different linguistic repertoire than those of the children in the classroom (Matluck, 1978).

La Forge (1983, p. 3) suggests that language as social process is "different from language as communication." Thus, education in the classroom is viewed as a cultural process (Richards and Rodgers, 1986). Inherent to this view is that learning is a social act. The process is shared by the teacher and students who cooperatively accomplish their social affairs. Members of a culture share "a system of standards for perceiving, believing, evaluating and acting" (Goodenough, 1971, p. 41).

Stevens (1980, pp. 180–81) argues that the suppression of signing deprives deaf children of a language and this, in turn, deprives them of a culture:

> Language and culture cannot be separated. It is not possible to learn a language without knowledge of the culture. Conversely, it is not possible to acquire the culture without knowledge of the language because the language is the major vehicle by which culture is transmitted from one individual to another and from one generation to another. When deaf children were not allowed to learn Sign Language, many of these children were deprived of the only communication system which could effectively transmit the culture to them. Consequently, the natural bonds between these children and their hearing parents, the community, and, ultimately, the general culture were not established. These children then entered school in a cultural "limbo," without language, and unable to ever again have the preschool experiences so crucial to success in school and adulthood. Fairy tales, cops and robbers, ring around the rosey, church and table talk left no marks on the great

majority of deaf children. Thus, these children entered school without a knowledge of their culture because of linguistic suppression and remained in this cultural limbo because of the educational system itself.

To achieve social ends in the classroom, the teacher and students must behave in patterned ways and know the behavioral strategies required to gain the teacher's attention or to obtain entry into a place of study and secure cooperation of the peer group (Gumperz and Cook-Gumperz, 1981, p. 433). This knowledge makes it possible for them to make sense of what it is they do together. What is reality to one culture—what is right and wrong, what is wise and ignorant—can be nonsense to another culture.

## *Language at Home and at School*

Ochs and Schieffelin (1984) identify at least two basic attitudes toward child language acquisition. The first is to adapt situations to the needs of young children, for example, caregivers simplify their own speech in order to make themselves understood when talking to young children, so-called baby talk. The second is to expect children to meet the needs of the situation by modeling adult utterances, that is, caregivers instruct children on what to say and to whom.

Recent research suggests that a child's home-based interactive style affects the quality of collaboration between teacher and child. For example, Michaels and Cazden (in press) state that when a child's home-based interactive style does not match the teacher's style and expectations, interaction between them is "often disharmonious and not conducive to effective help by the teacher or learning by the child." Heath's (1983) study suggests that the upbringing of children in the home environment affects their success in school systems. This study compares two working-class neighborhoods, one black (Trackton) and one white (Roadville). Both neighborhoods are working class, and while members of both neighborhoods are not highly educated, Roadville's inhabitants tend to finish high school more often than Trackton's. Trackton parents often expect their children to adapt to their situations. An example of these expectations is found in the types of questions used by Trackton parents. The parents use four common question forms. The first form is an analogy by eliciting comparisons. The response called for is nonspecific comparison of one item, event, or person with another, such as "What's that like?" (referring to a flat tire on a neighbor's car). The second form is a story-starter; the aim in its use is to encourage children to start a creative story, such as by asking "What did you do with Maggie's dog yesterday?" The third form is an accusation question involving explanation and excuses, for example, "What is that all over your face?" The fourth form includes questions to which the respondent is assumed to have the answers, for example, "What do you want?" Another form of question, rarely used by Trackton parents, is one to which the questioner knows the answer, for example, "What is your name?" This last form is also known as a very common type of "school" question. While Roadville parents use this fifth type of question, Trackton parents regularly use only the first four types of questions. Heath claims that although Trackton children are often creative in school, they are not specifically prepared at home to answer "school" questions.

The question-answer format is the most prevalent method of turn-taking in American classrooms. The goal of this communication is to be correct as often as possible and incorrect as seldom as possible. Often inherent to this form of communication is an assumption that incorrect answers are the fault of the child. If a teacher asks a question and the child answers incorrectly, it is often assumed that the problem is the child's. Recent research such as Heath's suggests, however, that part of the problem can be traced to the form of the teacher's question (see Shuy, 1979).

The form of the teacher's question is not limited strictly to the verbal or manual components. Another important feature in the regulation of classroom turn-taking, for example, is eye-gaze. Mather (1987) compares eye-gaze behaviors in two preschool classrooms for deaf children. The teacher in one classroom is a native signer; the teacher of the second is a skilled signer who acquired sign language as an adult. This study finds that, in these classrooms, rules for using eye-gaze and for sending appropriate nonmanual signals to mark utterances are necessary to regulate effective turn-taking. Improper use of eye-gaze by the "acquired" teacher confused her deaf students; they did not know whether and how to answer.

Clearly, issues raised in spoken language situations concerning the relationship between cultural norms and classroom discourse, as well as the discontinuities between home and classroom interactive styles, have implications for sign language situations and for deaf education. One goal of this study is to define these implications.

## A STUDY OF TEACHING STRATEGIES

### Preliminary Observations

In the data corpus of the present study, the native signer follows certain patterns for asking questions, eliciting answers, and responding to answers. With respect to questions, the native signer does not use the "school" questions, but rather uses questions that require the students to think about important parts of the story. In eliciting answers, she works with students who incorrectly answer the questions by giving clues until they answer correctly. In responding to students' answers, she avoids saying that an answer is incorrect, so as to encourage students to answer the questions without being penalized for giving incorrect answers.

The native signer also makes special efforts and follows certain patterns to convey correct information in terms of cultural values. For example, instead of exactly signing printed words only, she employs several techniques in ASL in order to give the intended meanings of concepts.

## *Background*

The data for this study consist of videotapes of two teachers reviewing the same story with two classes of hearing-impaired preschool students. The first teacher is hearing-impaired and a native signer. She is fluent in ASL and uses it with her class. Her class consists of five children whose parents are hearing and whose sign language exposure is through the school. The other teacher is a hearing native English speaker. Her students entered school with language. Most of their parents are deaf and use sign language. She has learned a manual code for English as a second language, namely, Signed English as an adult. In her class, she uses Signed English as the primary mode of communication.

In the two classes, the exercise is a review of the story "Three Little Kittens." Because this study focuses on the techniques that the native signer uses to teach the students, only the native signer's data are analyzed in detail. The "acquired" signer's data are mainly used for comparison of the techniques that the two teachers use in reviewing the story.

Some information on the background of the native signer's students and their families was obtained from the teacher through an interview. The students entered school with little or virtually no language. They grew up in home environments where there was no language for them to acquire. The parents of these children are hearing and none of them learned how to sign with their children. The children did not sign until they entered school. The teacher said during the interview that some of the children communicate with their parents by using gestures and body language. Owing to the restrictions in their communication modes, the parents are not able to have a good conversation with their children, such as during meal times or story reading. At the time of the videotaping, some of the parents were learning sign language, primarily Signed English.

The five students are three black males and two South American females. Four of them are from low-income families, the other from a middle-class family. According to the teacher, at the time of entry, the students did not have any concept of "who I am" when they were shown pictures of themselves. When the teacher asked them individually who was in the picture, they just gave blank stares. The teacher had to show the students their pictures and ask them to state their names. Eventually they responded to who was in the pictures. They generally had a very short span of attention, so the teacher had to make everything short and simple. At the time of the videotaping, they were three years old and in the preschool class. Two of the students were considered highly active (high) in class participation and the other three relatively inactive (low) (Gearing and Epstein, 1982).

The teacher who is a native signer is hearing-impaired and comes from a deaf family. She prefers to sign without voice and does not accept using voice without signs because she believes it is important that she and her students fully understand each other. She feels that she equally emphasizes the form and content of communication. Accordingly, one of her goals for the review of the story reading with her class is to have the students understand the picture descriptions of the story and respond correctly to her questions. As another goal, she encourages them to respond in any way to the pictures in order to help them build their self-esteem. To catch the students' attention, she touches or points at the students, waves a hand in front of them, uses other sharp movements in body motion, or signs "ah" or "oh" when the students become restless.

## Strategies and Devices

As noted earlier, the native signer uses different strategies and special linguistic devices of ASL in reviewing the story with the students who had little or no communicative competence. These strategies and devices include: using questions; eliciting answers; responding to students' answers; using classifier predicates, role playing, and "miniature" signs; adapting signs to the specific actions depicted in pictures; and changing English words that show sound-related concepts to signs that show visual concepts.

### Using Questions

At the beginning of the review of the story, the teacher asks what the title of the book is about. There is no response. Then the teacher rephrases the question and signs "What is this book about?"[1] The children respond "Cats." The teacher nods. She asks "How many cats?" When there is no response, she quickly repeats the question with an additional clue by quickly signing "1, 2, 3, or 4?" She then has the students participate actively in counting the cats in the book. The first two "high" students count while the teacher nods. Then the teacher takes the hands of one of the "low" students to help her count the cats. She then repeats herself by counting

[1]In this and following quotes, what the person signed is translated into English sentences. This applies to the nonnative signer as well as to the students.

**Fig. 1**    Mother cat. From *Three Little Kittens,* illustrated by Lilian Obligado. Copyright ©
1974 by Random House, Inc. Reprinted by permission.

three cats in order to reinforce the question and signs emphatically,
"These are three little kittens."

In contrast, the questions used by the teacher who is a nonnative signer
are "school" questions. As a teacher trained in the educational system, the
nonnative teacher uses questions to confirm that students have learned
something. The first three questions are: "What is the title?", (to a particular student) "Do you know the title?", and (to the same student) "Do you
remember the title?" When there are no responses from the students, the
teacher eventually gives the answer herself.

Another contrast between the native and the nonnative signers' types of
questions revolves around a picture showing the mother cat frowning and
turning a timer (see Fig. 1). The native signer asks "What did Mom say?"

The nonnative signer asks "Do you think Mom was crabby? The native signer's question is the type of question that requires information. It requires the students to participate and think actively in a discussion either with other students in the group or with the teacher. The nonnative signer's question requires only a yes or no answer.

Unlike the native signer, the nonnative signer uses different types of questions, similar to the ones described by Heath (1983) in the Roadville case. The nonnative signer asks questions that require specific information, such as "What is the title?" Throughout the review of the story, the native signer asks Trackton-type questions, such as "What happens?", "What kind of pie does Mother make?", or "Where is one more kitten?" The students are very active in discussing or discovering what kind of pie the mother cat made, in trying to find where one more cat was, and in counting the numbers of cats.

**Eliciting Answers**

In the course of reviewing the story, the native signer demonstrates how she prepares the students to adapt when they are expected to meet the needs of the situation. She says what they should say and directs them to participate by encouraging them to talk with her. Before the native signer asks any particular student a question, she always asks the class the question. Often the "high" students volunteer to answer her questions. After those students answer, she asks the "low" students questions with additional clues, such as pointing to the picture. If there is no response or an incorrect answer from the students, instead of giving an answer, she helps the students adapt to the situation by giving even more clues, pointing more to the picture, or playing a role to help the students grasp the idea of what the kittens in the story did. In contrast, the nonnative signer does not attempt to have the students adapt to the situation by indicating what she expects them to say or by directing them to what they should say. Instead, after one or more questions with slight modification or rephrasing, she provides the answer herself.

This difference in teaching strategies appears to have an impact on the process of eliciting answers. Throughout the initial portion of the review session, the native signer asks forty-one questions and all of them are answered by the students themselves. In contrast, the nonnative signer asks only nine questions and only two are answered by the students.

The different ways in which the two teachers discuss the story's opening illustrate the contrast in strategies between them. Specifically, the native signer opens the book. The picture on the opening page shows the kittens' footprints, a bike on the floor, and a ball on the bench (see Fig. 2). She orally exclaims "Ah" with a surprised look. She gazes at all the students and asks "What happened?" Sasha (high) responds "Bike." The teacher

Illustrated by Lilian Obligado

Three

Copyright © 1974 by Random House, Inc. All rights reserved under International and Pan-American Copyright Conventions. Published in the United States by Random House, Inc., New York, and simultaneously in Canada by Random House of Canada Limited, Toronto. ISBN: 0-394-82771-6. Library of Congress Catalog Card Number: 73-16858. Manufactured in the United States of America.
15  16  17  18  19  20

**Fig. 2**  Opening pages, *Three Little Kittens.* From *Three Little Kittens,* illustrated by Lilian Obligado. Copyright © 1974 by Random House, Inc. Reprinted by permission.

signs "Yes, you remember" to the student and then shifts her gaze to the class. She shows the book around and then puts the book on her lap. She rephrases her question and asks whether the house is clean or dirty. She repeats the question, "Is the house clean or dirty?" Kevin (high) responds by putting his hands on the floor, in pantomime, as if he is a cat walking all over the floor. The teacher nods and responds "Yes, there are dirty footprints all over the floor." Then she asks Barb (low) the same question, "What happened?", and points toward the picture of the dirty footprints. The student responds "Dirty footprints." The teacher acknowledges her answer with "Yes, there are dirty footprints all over the floor." The teacher then asks the same student another question, "Whose footprints?" There is no response from that particular student. Then she rephrases the question

# Little Kittens

Random House
New York

by saying "Barb's [one student's name] footprints?" That student responds but her signs are unclear on the videotape. The teacher answers "No, whose footprints?" to the same student but there is no response.

The teacher next shifts her gaze to Ted (low) and asks the question "Whose footprints?" The student responds "Ball." The teacher nods and responds "See the ball." She then points to the picture of footprints and signs: "The cats went out to play. Later they were ready to come in the house again." Then the teacher gets up and repeats the first statement, "The cats went out to play." She starts to play the role of a cat and signs "Played outside and then entered the house." Portraying a cat again, she uses her legs and hands and bends forward with her hands on the floor. Using the nonverbal gesture of "knowing nothing," she acts as if she walks without knowing that her paws are dirty. She then signs that the floor became dirty all over. She then sits down, looks at everyone, and smiles. The students respond "Dirty floor." The teacher nods.

In contrast, the nonnative signer elicits an answer from a particular student to a question about the title of the story. When asked, the student does not have a chance to answer the question because the teacher switches her gaze to the student on her right side and repeats the last part of the question, "Title of?" Another student sitting in the middle replies "Cats" several times, but the teacher does not see him. Then the teacher asks if someone can help the first student and repeats the question "What is the title?" Shortly thereafter, she gives the answer herself. Unlike the native signer, the nonnative signer does not use any means to elicit answers from the group, such as giving a clue or playing a role, as the native signer does. She simply repeats questions a few times with little modifications, such as "What is the title of this story?", "Do you remember the title?", or "You forgot."

## Responding to Students' Answers

In responding to answers, the native signer encourages the students to take "risks." When a student gives a wrong answer, the teacher does not penalize the student for it. Instead, she focuses both on the answer and on the intended meaning. In the earlier example, when the teacher asks "Whose footprints?," the student responds "Ball." Instead of penalizing the student for the incorrect answer, the signer nods and responds "See the ball." She then goes back to the original topic and performs the role of a cat playing outside and then entering a house with dirty paws. Then the student answers "Dirty floor." The intent of the teacher is to acknowledge what the student says or to request clarification.

The following example shows that the native signer repeatedly responds by acknowledging the student's utterance and clarifying it. When one student plays the role of a kitten, he uses the BITING-FROM-THE-PLATE classifier predicate, which is not correct (see Fig. 3). Then the teacher imitates his classifier with a slight modification, producing the CHEWING-FROM-THE-PLATE classifier predicate.

Later, another student corrects the teacher indirectly by using her mouth movement to indicate licking, not chewing. The teacher responds positively and says that the student is correct. Then the teacher uses the LICKING-THE-PLATE classifier predicate to show that the kittens were licking their plates. Then all of the students excitedly imitate the teacher's actions.

Consistent patterns appear in the native signer's ways of responding to students' answers throughout the story review. The teacher usually responds positively to students' answers, whether they are correct, partially correct, or incorrect. For example, if a student's answers are incorrect, the clamation but, as actually signed, indicates size; and PRINT, an already existing sign meaning the printed word, used here to mean "footprints."

What is most striking about the native signer's use of classifier predicates is the positive impact on the students' responses. Despite their initially low communicative competence, the students are encouraged by the teacher's use of the classifiers to take risks in answering questions and developing language. One possible explanation is that classifiers involve the use of certain handshapes, locations, and movements that not only serve to clearly convey the intended meanings but also to present them in an active sense as opposed to a passive sense. In any case, classifier predicates seem to be an effective strategy in promoting linguistic risk taking among the students.

## Using Role Playing

Another technique that the native signer uses to transmit the information from the pictures is role playing. Rather than utilize the printed word, the native signer uses role playing to expose the students to the actions portrayed in the pictures. For example, the teacher pretends to be the mother depicted in one of the pictures (see Fig. 4). To explain that the mother is mad, the teacher starts by detaching her eye-gaze from the group and looking down, her head and body leaning forward as if three kittens are standing before her. In this manner, she shifts her role from that of a teacher to that of a mother cat. Imitating the picture exactly, she puts her hand on her hip, pretends to scold with the rolling pin, and signs "I am mad." She scolds each kitten once and, while gazing down at the three kittens, signs: "Three little kittens, you (you-plural) lost your mittens so you won't have pie. You (you-plural) go and look for your mittens." She puts her hands on her hips and frowns. Returning to the role of teacher, she shows the picture to the students and points to the picture of the mother cat. She then repeats the role of the mother cat in the picture. [She asks if the] mother cat is happy. "No," she signs (with both hands), "she [is mad." She] shows the picture around again and signs "The mother cat is [mad."]

[As she u]ses the role playing of the mother cat, scolding the kittens, [it i]s important to emphasize that the teacher deliberately [scold]s to reflect the number of kittens.

[Another examp]le of role playing used by the native signer occurs when [she shifts he]r role to that of the mother cat kissing the kittens (see [Fig. 5). She begin]s this role by leaning forward and pretending to kiss the [kittens.] By leaning back, she returns to the role of teacher and [commen]ts." She then shows the picture around. One student [signs somethin]g that is unclear on the videotape. The teacher re[sponds: You hug]ged the three kittens. Mom said you can have some

---

And soon ate up the pie.

**Fig. 3** Three little kittens. From Three Little Kittens, illustrated by Lilian Obligado. Copyright © 1974 by Random House, Inc. Reprinted by permission.

teacher says "Yes, you remember" or "Yes, I see that." She then restates the question or points to the picture in the book to give another hint for a correct answer. If the student gives a partially correct answer, the teacher repeats the student's answer and clarifies it with additional information. For instance, when asked what happened on the opening page, one student answers "Footprints." The teacher responds "Yes, there are dirty footprints all over the floor." If the student answers correctly, the teacher acknowledges it. Then she either repeats the previous question to other students or moves on to the next question or page.

The nonnative signer, on the other hand, does not create an environment that promotes risk taking on the part of the students. This teacher responds negatively to answers when they are partially correct or incorrect, for example, "No, don't you remember?," "You forgot," or "Could someone else help?" She often responds to the students' answers by saying "Oh, you think so." And, if a student answers correctly, she sometimes fails to acknowledge the correct answer.

## Using Classifier Predicates

Consciously or not, the teacher who is the native signer respects the importance and appropriateness of transmitting information that conforms to the grammatical rules of ASL. Moreover, she adapts her signs to the specific actions depicted in the pictures rather than to the printed words that accompany each picture. To adapt the signs, she uses one of the features of ASL structure, classifier predicates.

One picture shows the mother cat using her rolling pin to scold the kittens (see Fig. 4). The standard sign for the word *naughty* entails the use of one index finger to scold, but the teacher does not use this sign. Instead, she uses an instrumental classifier predicate, where her handshape signals holding onto the rolling pin and scolding at the same time, to mean 'naughty'. Since Signed English does not involve the use of classifier predicates, the nonnative signer correctly signs the form that means 'naughty' in Signed English, but the signing does not exactly convey the intended message of the picture.

Another example of the native signer's use of classifier predicates occurs when she discusses the picture that shows one cat sliding down a rail (see Fig. 5). She uses a RAIL classifier handshape to convey 'slide', together with her left hand serving as a rail. She also uses the HOLDING-GLOVES classi-

"What! Lost your mittens, you naughty kittens!

**Fig. 4**  Mother cat and her kittens. From *Three Little Kittens,* illustrated by Lilian Obligado. Copyright © 1974 by Rnadom House, Inc. Reprinted by permission.

And they began to cry,

"Oh, mother dear,
See here, see here,

**Fig. 5**  Rail, bicycle, and kittens with mi⁄
Lilian Obligado. Copyright © 1974 by Rand⁄

fier predicate and says "I fou⁄
cat riding the bicycle, she⁄
portray the cat's speed i⁄
found my mittens." Ther⁄
am so happy that you⁄

The nonnative sig⁄
native signer becar⁄
feature. She doe⁄
does not use the⁄
with their intendea .⁄
fiers include GREAT (an⁄

Our mittens we have found."

**Fig. 6**  Mother cat kissing her kittens. From *Three Little Kittens,* illustrated by Lilian Obligado. Copyright © 1974 by Random House, Inc. Reprinted by permission.

pie but take the pie outside." She then shows the picture around again. In other portions of the story review, the teacher accurately uses the mathematical concept of three when playing the role of the mother cat hugging or kissing the kittens three times. The same student corrects the teacher when she plays the role of a mother cat kissing the three kittens separately, which conflicts with the picture portraying the mother cat hugging all the kittens at the same time.

Unlike the native signer, the nonnative signer violates the mathematical concept of three several times. Sometimes the students who are native ASL signers interrupt the teacher to correct signing that is not consistent with the mathematical concept. For instance, in playing the role of the mother cat, the nonnative signer kisses each of the five students directly as if all of them are the three kittens. The three students whose native language is

ASL discuss among themselves the teacher's act of kissing each of them, and one student counts the five students. Another student whose native language is ASL then protests the number of kisses and says that it is three, not five. The nonnative signer, throughout the story review, often plays the role of the mother cat in a way that is inconsistent with the specific actions portrayed in the pictures.

## Using Miniature Signs

Both teachers show the book to the students and then put it down before they sign, since it would be impossible for them to look at the book and pay attention to their signing at the same time. Unlike deaf students, hearing students can read or look at the pictures and listen to the teacher at the

"What! Found your mittens,
Then you're good kittens!
Now you can have some pie."

"Purr-r, purr-r, purr-r,

**Fig. 7**  Mother cat, kittens, and pie. From *Three Little Kittens,* illustrated by Lilian Obligado. Copyright © 1974 by Random House, Inc. Reprinted by permission.

same time. In her classroom, the native signer accommodates the students' visual needs by employing a special signing technique that can be termed "miniature" signs. This technique enables the students to see the book and the teacher's signs at the same time.

An example of miniature signs occurs when the teacher is explaining two particular pages of the story (see Fig. 7). The teacher rests the book on her stomach with the pictures facing the students. She looks around and then bends her head down and signs on the book using very small signs. The picture fills two pages of the book and depicts the kittens getting dishes down from a cupboard as the mother cat carries pies that she has just taken from the oven. The teacher signs "The cats get the dishes." She repeats the statement three times to portray the number of the cats per-

Yes, yes, let's have some pie."

forming the stated action. Using miniature signs and moving her hands to her right, from the page with the three kittens to the page with the mother, she shows how the cats carry the plates to their mother. Then she signs on the page, "Mom put a pie on each plate." With her right hand, she acts as if she is an actual mother cat holding pies. With her left hand, she portrays a little kitten holding a plate. She then moves her right hand to the left to show how the mother distributes the pies. Then she shows the picture around, tries to get the students to settle down, and signs "The cats got the pies and brought them outside." Overall, as she explains the pictures in the book, she directs the students' attention to both the miniature signing and the pictures in the book at the same time. By using miniature signs, she is able to explain the events from one page to another without having to stop at each page.

Unlike the other teacher, the nonnative signer has to stop at each page before she can go to the next page. This teacher does not use any miniature signs throughout the exercise.

## Adapting Signs to the Specific Actions Depicted in Pictures

The native signer often adapts her signing to reflect what is portrayed in the pictures. For example, the teacher points to the picture of a snowman and asks "What is that?" One student responds "Snowman." The teacher says "Yes." Looking down at the picture, she orally says "Oh" and signs "Excuse me." She points to the picture of the snowman's ears and whiskers and signs: "Snowcat, I am mistaken. Look at the cat's ears and whiskers." She shows the picture around and signs "It's a snowcat!"

Unlike the native signer, the nonnative signer uses the Signed English sign SNOW-MAN. (Note that the sign SNOW-CAT is an invented sign; there is no standard sign meaning 'snowcat'.) When one student asks the teacher about the sign, she ignores the question and proceeds to the next page.

For this pedagogical task of adapting signs to describe pictures, these data indicate that in cases of conflict between a printed word and its intended meaning, the native signer chose the latter, and the nonnative signer chose the former. As discussed earlier, the nonnative signer's choices are in part limited by Signed English, which does not provide devices that enable the teacher to recode intended meanings instead of English lexical items.

## Changing English Words That Show Sound-Related
## Concepts to Signs That Show Visual Concepts

The native signer chose signs that had relevance to the visual background experience of her deaf students. For example, in Signed English and ASL, there is no standard means (except fingerspelling) for recoding the English word *meow*. Instead of fingerspelling it, the native signer translates the

"Mee-ow, mee-ow, mee-ow."

"No, you shall have no pie."

**Fig. 8**   Crying kittens. From *Three Little Kittens,* illustrated by Lilian Obligado. Copyright © 1974 by Random House, Inc. Reprinted by permission.

word as *cry* (in the sense of 'whimper'). Compared with the word *meow,* the sign *cry* appears more consistent with the intended meaning of the picture. The native signer used signs that show visual concepts (see Fig. 8). First, the teacher signs three times, "The cats cry." Later, she changes her choice of mouthing from "Cry" to "Meow" and signs while meowing orally, "The cats cry," repeating the sign *CRY* three times.

Unlike the native signer, the nonnative signer signs the printed sentence "They began to cry" and then says "Meow" several times while not manually signing. This shows again that the nonnative signer literally follows the printed words in Signed English. Whether she is aware that her signing codes a meaning different from the intended one is not known.

## CONCLUSION

This ethnography of the native signer's review of the story shows at least eight different patterns in her ways of communicating with the students. First, in asking questions, the teacher uses wh-questions that encourage the students to think about important parts of the story. Unlike the nonnative signer, the native signer does not address yes/no questions even to the students with minimal communication competence. Second, in eliciting answers, the native signer asks questions of the class first. After some students (high) volunteer to give answers and the answers are correct, the teacher asks other students (low) questions with additional information. Third, unlike the nonnative signer who does not promote risk taking by the students, the native signer encourages students to take risks. When a student gives an incorrect answer, the teacher does not penalize the student for it. Instead, she encourages the students to answer without worry of being criticized or negatively corrected. Fourth, the native signer uses a feature of ASL structure, classifier predicates, to adapt her signs to the specific actions depicted in the story pictures. In contrast, the nonnative signer produces classifier predicates in her signing but does not use them appropriately.

Fifth, the native signer uses role playing to expose the students to the visual concepts in the pictures. In contrast, perhaps owing to limited training or experience, the nonnative signer does not use role playing that is consistent with either the mathematical concepts or the specific actions depicted in the pictures. Sixth, the native signer uses the technique of miniature signs in reviewing the book. This technique enables the students to see the book and the teacher's signs at the same time. The nonnative signer signs normally throughout the review so that the students cannot see the signs and the book pages at the same time. The students thus receive only certain portions of the message, not the whole message. Seventh, the native signer adapts her signs to the specific actions portrayed in the pictures, but the nonnative signer literally reads the words without using the appropriate sign to recode the intended meaning of the words and pictures. Finally, adapting to the needs of the students, the native signer changes English words that show sound-related concepts to signs that show visual concepts. In contrast, the nonnative signer again just recodes the printed words into Signed English.

As mentioned earlier, deaf and hearing teachers are unfortunately assigned to different groups for specific reasons, including those that relate to the teachers' and the childrens' communication skills. As in spoken language situations, language use and choice play critical roles in successful classroom interaction between the teacher and the students, but both features also must be considered in the broader context of cultural norms.

This study demonstrates the potential for discontinuity between home and school styles. There is some evidence, from the nonnative signer's class, that this discontinuity impedes the classroom discourse between teacher and students. The student's home-based style must be carefully considered.

The study also shows clear differences in strategy used by native and nonnative signers, especially in eliciting answers from the students. The native signer asks forty-one questions and all of them are answered by the students. On the other hand, the nonnative signer asks only nine questions and only two are answered by the students. These differences are especially important since, unlike the nonnative signer's students, the native signer's students entered school with little or no language input. These findings suggest that there is a need for ASL in the classroom. This does not mean that nonnative signers should not teach. Rather, the suggestion is that teachers of the deaf should develop and demonstrate competence in ASL (albeit the competence of an adult second-language learner), and training in ASL should be a required part of the preservice training. Also, more teachers who are native ASL users should be trained and hired. It is important to stress that the present study compares the teaching strategies of only two teachers. Individual differences can certainly play a role in the choice of strategies, and further examination may reveal that nonnative signers also successfully use the strategies chosen by the native signer in this study.

In short, this study demonstrates the need for communicatively competent teachers to teach deaf students, whether the students have minimal language or have already acquired a language before entering school. Specifically, the teacher must be able to use the special linguistic techniques of ASL, such as classifier predicates, miniature signs, and role playing. The study also shows the need for appropriate strategies in using questions and eliciting answers from students, and in responding to the students' answers. For despite initially low communicative competence, students are capable of answering wh-questions and of developing language in an environment where risk taking is promoted.

## ACKNOWLEDGMENTS

The author wishes to thank Dr. Ceil Lucas and Dr. Paul Epstein for their support and guidance. She also thanks Dr. Carolyn Ewoldt for permission to use the data videotaped in the Gallaudet Research Institute Literacy study.

# Part III

## LANGUAGE ATTITUDES

# 9

# An Examination of Deaf College Students' Attitudes toward ASL and English

Barbara Kannapell

## INTRODUCTION

The problems in the American educational system for deaf people are complex. The current system addresses deaf people as if they were monolingual in English (Gilbert, 1982). English, either in spoken or in signed form, is the predominant language used in educational programs, while the language of the Deaf community, American Sign Language (ASL), is overlooked.[1] The educational system has documented its own failure to educate deaf people, who are expected to be two or three years behind their hearing peers by present measurements, and its own failure to teach English skills to many deaf people (COED Report, 1988; Paul, 1972; Schein and Delk, 1974; Stevens, 1980; Vernon, 1968).

A basic problem of this educational system concerns two assumptions of educators of the deaf about deaf children. One assumption is that deaf people are monolingual in English. The other assumption is that deaf people are expected to identify with hearing people and accept enculturation into mainstream American culture or society. In other words, deaf people are expected to acquire the same rules of cultural and communicative competence that hearing people have.

[1]The term "Deaf" in this paper refers to sociological deafness; the term "deaf" refers to audiological deafness. The term "Hearing" refers to those (deaf) people who identify with oral language communities and their values; the term, "hearing" means the ability to hear (Woodward, 1982, p. 1).

THE SOCIOLINGUISTICS OF THE DEAF COMMUNITY

Copyright © 1989 by Academic Press Inc.
All rights of reproduction in any form reserved.

In theory, some educators of deaf people may acknowledge ASL as the natural language of Deaf people. In practice, however, teachers of the deaf are not required to be competent in ASL in order to teach. With the two assumptions mentioned earlier, the educators' attitudes affect deaf students' language choice and identity choice. Deaf people may use English or speech and/or identify themselves as hard of hearing as a way of not being so deaf, or they may use ASL as a way of not being so hearing. Thus, language choice reflects identity choice. Deaf people are deprived of their culture and their identity when their language is not accepted, valued, or taught.

Educators of the deaf also often fail to accept the fact that deaf students already have a diverse linguistic and communicative repertoire. Ironically, many educators in the United States accept English as a Second Language (ESL) as a method of teaching deaf students. In such cases, what does English as a Second Language mean? Logically, the assumption should be that ASL is the first language of many deaf students, but many educators do not look at it this way. Others assume that if deaf students are not proficient in using English, this means they are proficient in using ASL. This is also not true of all deaf students. Some are "semilinguals" who are not proficient in either English or ASL.

The educational system of the deaf has sophisticated tests for evaluating each mode of communication in English for each deaf student—reading, writing, lipreading, speech, and audition. There are only minimal tests for sign language or sign systems in terms of a continuum of ASL and English. This is treated in depth later.

These current measurements do not, therefore, give a complete picture of the linguistic and communicative repertoires of each student in an educational program for deaf students. What is often overlooked is that the students' attitudes about deaf culture and mainstream American culture make a major contribution to their choices of modes of communication with deaf and hearing people.

## THE NEED FOR A SOCIOLINGUISTIC PROFILE

Ideally, educational institutions of the deaf should have a sociolinguistic profile of each deaf student. The sociolinguistic profile should consist of three components (see Fig. 1):

1. Rating by professionals of each communicative/linguistic skill, including ASL and English.
2. Students' self-evaluation of communicative and linguistic skills.
3. Students' attitudes toward all forms of sign systems, English, and the cultures of deaf and hearing people.

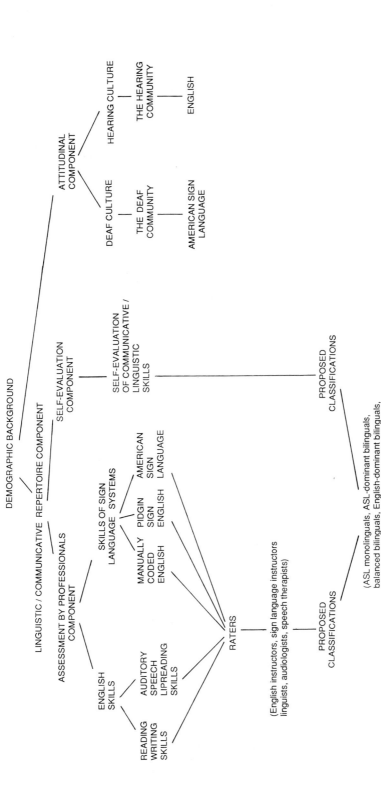

**Fig. 1** Sociolinguistic profile.

The goals of an educational program for deaf students should be to maximize each student's skills in using both ASL and English. In this way, the student can develop communicative competence and positive attitudes about the languages and the cultures of both Deaf and hearing people. A sociolinguistic profile would help professionals understand the students' linguistic competence in relation to their attitudes about the languages and cultures.

This study focuses on all the components of such a profile, except the subcomponent of sign language skills. The reason for not evaluating sign language skills is that Gallaudet University, the site of the study, has not yet devised an adequate system of evaluating these skills in the undergraduate population.[2] Gallaudet University was chosen because it provides a rich source of data for a sociolinguistic study of deaf students. Research conducted at Gallaudet University can be applied to other educational institutions of the deaf in America.

The general goal of this study is to describe the sociolinguistic characteristics of a representative sample of Gallaudet students. The specific objectives are presented in the following outline:

I. Description of the demographic background of a representative sample of the students.
II. Investigation of the diverse linguistic/communicative repertoires of deaf students.
  A. Self-evaluation
    1. English skills
      *a.* Reading and writing
      *b.* Speech and lipreading
    2. Sign language/systems skills
      *a.* Manually Coded English (MCE)
      *b.* Pidgin Sign English (PSE)[3]
      *c.* American Sign Language
  B. Self-identity as deaf or hard of hearing.
  C. Self-classification of linguistic skills as ASL monolinguals(?)[4], ASL-dominant bilinguals, balanced bilinguals, English-dominant bilinguals, English monolinguals, semilinguals.

---

[2]The School of Communication at Gallaudet University was in the experimental stage of evaluating simultaneous communication skills of incoming students in the fall of 1983. Simultaneous communication means mouthing or voicing English words while signing in English order. This does not reflect the true linguistic repertoire of each student in ASL.

[3]This is what one outcome of language contact in the deaf community is labeled (see Lucas and Valli, this volume).

[4]This question mark is warranted because all students are required to pass a minimum English examination. It is thus unlikely that an actual, as opposed to self-described, ASL monolingual would even be enrolled at Gallaudet University.

III. Investigation of social variables that make major contributions to student attitudes about ASL, English, and deaf and hearing people. Primary social variables:
   A. Hearing status of parents and siblings
   B. Time of onset of hearing loss
   C. Number of years at residential school
   D. Age when sign language learned
   Secondary social variables:
   A. Self-identity
   B. Self-classification of linguistic skills
IV. Investigation of relationship between self-reported data of student communication skills and assessment by professionals.
   A. Reading and writing skills
   B. Auditory, speech, and lipreading skills
V. Investigation of students' feelings and thoughts about ASL, English, and language users.

Linguistic and sociolinguistic concepts and theories indicate that there should be varying degrees of bilingualism and biculturalism among deaf people. Deaf people have a language, ASL, and a culture of their own. Deaf people are bilingual in ASL and English in varying degrees and some are either ASL or English monolinguals. They are identified with the Deaf culture, American mainstream culture, both cultures, or neither culture. Their attitudes about the languages and cultures involved depend largely on several sociolinguistic factors: the functions of the languages, language choice, group reference, and cultural identity. Clearly, in the United States, the system forces deaf people to choose one language or culture over the other. Deaf people may feel ambivalent toward the competing languages and cultures.

The sociolinguistic profile in this study indicates the variation in communication and linguistic skills of a significant number of Gallaudet University students. It also shows the variation in their attitudes about ASL and English, and the cultures that surround them. The aim is to clarify some of the reasons for this variation as well as the implications of linguistic variation for the educational system.

This study is presented as a contribution toward the development of an adequate methodology for sociolinguistic profiles of deaf students at Gallaudet University and at all school programs for deaf students in the United States. Based on the sociolinguistic profile of deaf students, the study examines the relationship between self-reported data of linguistic skills and the assessment of professionals.

Finally, the implications of the profile for institutions that educate deaf people are explored in terms of curriculum, teacher preparation, and attitudes about and awareness of proficiency in ASL as a prerequisite for participation in Deaf culture. The positive attitudes that result from recognition of the full, rich culture of Deaf people are also discussed.

## RELATED WORK

Research on language attitudes indicates that individuals in spoken language situations internalize associations between features of language variation, dialects, or individual linguistic cues, and features of social stratification that consist of combined differences in income, occupation, and social class between groups of people. There is much research that focuses on a structural analysis of ASL and its variations, but there is a lack of research on language attitudes among deaf people.

Several studies examine misconceptions about ASL and English among deaf high school and college students (Berke, 1978; Curry and Curry, 1978; Lentz, 1977). General misconceptions include the strong association of poor English with inferior intelligence, the association of ASL with negative attributes of users, and the association of MCE with positive attributes of users. These studies are similar to studies of South American attitudes about Indian languages and the dominant languages (Rubin, 1968), and Canadian attitudes about French and English and their respective users (Anisfeld and Lambert, 1964; Lambert, Hodgson, Gardner, and Fillenbaum, 1960; Preston, 1963).

Other studies discuss deaf students' attitudes about English and English learning (Bergman, 1976; Meath-Lang, 1978; Meath-Lang, Caccamise, and Albertini, 1982). Reasons for poor writing are associated with the misconceptions of deaf people and ambivalence is revealed in their attitudes about English.

Studies of the self-evaluation of communication skills of deaf people are strongly associated with the norms of hearing people, that is, the greater their speaking ability the more positive their self-concept (Schein, 1968; A. E. Sussman, 1973).

The prior studies that relate to deaf people and their attitudes about ASL and English focus on only one component of these attitudes. The present study attempts to examine deaf students within the entire scope of their linguistic repertoire from a sociolinguistic perspective.

## METHODOLOGY

This study was conducted in three phases. The first phase examines social variables and language attitudes of subjects by means of a questionnaire.

Included here are the construction and revision of the questionnaire as well as the selection of social variables and attitude subscales incorporated into it. A pilot study was conducted to test the reliability and validity of the original format. Fifty subjects participated in the pilot study. A description of the demographic background of those subjects included their academic status, school and family backgrounds, and self-evaluation of communication skills.

The reliability of attitude subscale items was tested and found acceptable for the major study. There were 110 items in the original questionnaire. A statistic-corrected item-total correction was used to determine whether to retain or to delete each item of each subscale. The number of items was reduced to 69 for the revised questionnaire. These items are grouped into three major subscales: attitudes about languages, ASL, English, and forms of English; and three other subscales: attitudes about deaf people, hearing people, and speech. The data were then collected, processed, and analyzed.

The second phase—self-report data—includes the self-evaluation of linguistic and communication skills in two areas: competence and performance in the use of ASL and English. Based on the self-evaluation of competence in ASL and English, the participants are classified into six groups: ASL monolinguals, ASL-dominant bilinguals, balanced bilinguals, English-dominant bilinguals, English monolinguals, and semilinguals. The types of performances are grouped as sign language skills, speech and lipreading skills, and reading and writing skills. The self-evaluations of communication skills were then compared with the ratings by English instructors and faculty and staff members of the Audiology Department at Gallaudet University.

The third phase consists of videotaped interviews with sixteen subjects. They were selected on the basis of four social variables: the number of years spent at a residential school for the deaf, the hearing status of parents, onset of hearing loss, and the hearing status of the subjects. The interview schedule has six sections: demographic information; demonstration of knowledge of different sign systems and of Total Communication; feelings about sign systems and the use of ASL and English in degree of comfort; perceived attitudes of students, teachers, and administrators about sign systems; communication methods used in the education of deaf children; and students' feelings toward deaf and hearing persons' correction of their ASL and English. The data from the taped interviews were transcribed and translated into English.

## ANALYSIS OF FINDINGS

This section presents the statistical analysis of findings in three phases:

Phase I:   The results of the study of the relationship between social
           variables and language attitudes
Phase II:  The results of the study of the relationship between self-
           reported data and the ratings by professionals
Phase III: The results of interviews with the subjects

## Phase I Results

A total of 205 subjects participated in the survey. The subjects are almost
evenly distributed by class year. The mean age of the subjects is 22.07.
Approximately 66 percent of the subjects are female, and 84 percent of the
subjects are American citizens. In educational background, 38 percent of
the subjects spent all their lives at a Deaf School, 36 percent spent some
years at a Deaf School, and 26 percent never attended a Deaf School.
Slightly less than 75 percent of the subjects were born deaf and a majority
of them have parents who are both hearing. Only twenty-eight subjects
have parents who are both deaf. A full 75 percent of the subjects identified
themselves as deaf and less than 25 percent identified themselves as hard-
of-hearing. The subjects use two main communication modes with their
deaf relatives, friends, and teachers—ASL and the simultaneous method
that includes fingerspelling. The subjects are versatile in their use of communication modes with their hearing relatives, friends, and teachers—
speech and lipreading, the simultaneous method of communication, fingerspelling, writing, and gestures.

The first phase of this study in part examines the relationship between
primary social variables and the linguistic attitudes of the subjects. Using
the *t*-test analysis, the most significant social variables, contributing to
attitudes about ASL, the forms and status of English, speech, and deaf
people, are the number of years spent at a Deaf School and the age of onset
of hearing loss of the subjects. The next most significant social variable,
contributing to attitudes about deaf people, forms of English, English, and
speech, is the age when sign language was learned. The third most significant social variable, contributing to attitudes about Deaf people, forms of
English, and ASL, is the hearing status of parents. The fourth most significant social variable, contributing to attitudes about deaf people, is the
hearing status of siblings.

Based on the results of an analysis of variance, the most significant
social variables, contributing to the subjects' attitudes about all subscale
topics except the attitude about hearing people, are the number of years
spent at a Deaf School and the age when sign language was learned. A
second most significant social variable, contributing to the subjects' attitudes about the forms and status of English and ASL, is the age of onset of
hearing loss. The third most significant social variables, contributing to the

subjects' attitudes about the forms of English and about deaf people, are the hearing status of parents and of siblings.

The first phase of this study also examines the relationship between secondary social variables and the linguistic attitudes of the subjects. The secondary social variables are self-identity and self-evaluation of linguistic and communication skills of the subjects. The subjects who identified themselves as deaf or hard-of-hearing have positive attitudes about ASL. Deaf subjects have borderline attitudes about the forms and status of English, and speech and hard-of-hearing subjects have positive attitudes toward those subscales.

Approximately 124 subjects (61 percent) classified themselves as balanced bilinguals, 44 subjects (22 percent) classified themselves as ASL monolinguals or ASL-dominant bilinguals, and 32 subjects (16 percent) classified themselves as English monolinguals or English-dominant bilinguals. Only two subjects (1 percent) classified themselves as semilinguals. Analyses of variance indicate that the ASL group has more positive attitudes about ASL and deaf people than the two other major groups; the balanced group and the English group have positive attitudes about the forms and status of English and speech. The findings do not reveal any significant social variables that contribute to the subjects' attitudes about hearing people.

## Phase II Results

The second phase of the research, involving self-report data, examines the relationship between self-ratings of communication skills and ratings by professionals. Analysis of the subjects' self-evaluations of communication skills reveals that 68 percent rate their ASL skills highly; 78 percent rate their PSE skills highly; 22 percent rate their MCE skills highly; 47 percent rate their speech or lipreading skills as good or very good; 74 percent rate their reading skills as good or very good; and 81 percent rate their writing skills as good or very good. Based on the correlations between self-evaluations, the higher the subjects evaluate their own skills in using ASL, the lower they evaluate all of their other skills, except PSE proficiency. There are very high correlations between speech and lipreading skills and between writing and reading skills.

The correlations within the ratings of students' skills by professionals reveal high positive correlations between speech skills and lipreading and hearing skills. There are also, as expected, high correlations between the ratings of the reading and writing skills of the subjects by English instructors. Based on twenty-three subjects, the better the rating of the speech and hearing skills of the subjects by professionals, the better the rating of the writing and reading skills of the subjects by the English instructors.

Pearson correlations were used to examine the relationship between the ratings by professionals and the self-ratings of communication skills. The higher the subjects evaluate their own ASL skills, the lower all of the other communication skills, except "hearing aided," are rated by the professionals. There is not a significant relationship between PSE skills rated by the subjects and all of the other communication skills, except for "lipreading aided and unaided," rated by the professionals. There is also not a significant relationship between MCE skills rated by the subjects and all other skills, except writing skills, rated by professionals. The higher the subjects evaluate their own speech and lipreading skills, the higher the professionals also evaluate their communication skills. There is a direct correlation between the rating of reading and writing skills by subjects and professionals. Overall, for the second phase of the project, the conclusion is that there is a direct relationship between the self-evaluated English skills of the subjects and the assessment by professionals.

## Phase III Results

The data from the videotaped interviews provide a wealth of information on the subjects' attitudes about languages and language users, in contrast to the data from the questionnaire. That is, the subject reveal their thoughts and feelings about languages and language users more in the face-to-face videotape interviews than in their responses to the written questionnaires.

Sixteen subjects are interviewed on videotape. The demographic information shows diversity in the family and school backgrounds and in the self-evaluation of communication abilities and language skills of these subjects.

In terms of their understanding and knowledge of sign systems and Total Communication, the students seem to have good information about the differences among ASL, PSE, and MCE. They know that there are two separate languages, ASL and English, but they still have misconceptions about ASL, for example, the view of ASL as broken or bad English. Most of these students easily associate ASL users with those who come from Deaf families and Deaf Schools, but their responses to PSE users are widely varied. They associate MCE users mostly with hearing people who are learning sign language and teachers who try to teach deaf children proper English. Moreover, they still associate these sign systems with their own preconceived notions about the status of people who use them, that is, ASL users are less-educated deaf people, PSE users are college educated, MCE users are highly educated deaf people.

In explaining Total Communication, the responses of the students are divided into two categories. One group explains that there are various ways of communicating with deaf people in order to convey ideas, and the other group merely defines Total Communication as talking and signing at the same time, which is also called "simultaneous communication" or "simultaneous method."

Most of the students have learned about sign systems and Total Communication through their courses at Gallaudet University and at their schools prior to coming to Gallaudet. In response to the question of how they feel about different sign systems, none of them expresses clear feelings toward the support of English only and the rejection of ASL. Only one subject reveals sufficiently strong feelings about ASL to reject all signed forms of English. Varying degrees of ambivalence in their feelings toward the languages and language users are shown in their responses. They associate specific languages with specific social standings of the language users. That is, the subjects do not care whether or not hearing people are very skilled in using English, but they look up to deaf PSE users because using English features is a mark of status.

The degree of comfort in using both ASL and English is related to self-classification of linguistic skills from the questionnaire. Eleven subjects classified themselves as balanced bilinguals, four as ASL-dominant bilinguals, and one as an ASL monolingual. Six of them did not agree with their initial self-classifications and later chose other classifications. Three changed from balanced bilingual to English-dominant bilinguals, two changed from balanced bilingual to ASL-dominant bilingual, and one changed from ASL-dominant bilingual to balanced bilingual. Among the unusual findings are the change in self-classification of a hard-of-hearing postlingual from balanced bilingual to ASL-dominant bilingual, her main reason being that she grew up in a Deaf family; a college-educated subject who classifies herself as ASL monolingual; and a person who learned sign language at age 20 who classifies himself as an ASL-dominant bilingual.

Most of the subjects report that they feel comfortable using ASL, PSE, or both with deaf friends. Their communication modes with hearing friends encompass many different forms, including the use of English or fragments of English such as mouthing English words. Gestures are also reported as a means of communication. Language use with deaf relatives is more varied than originally expected. Most of the subjects use English in writing but use voice and gestures with their hearing relatives.

The subjects' perceptions of student attitudes about sign systems are varied. Instead of discussing the students' attitudes, the subjects characterize ASL users as extroverted members of Deaf culture, PSE users as introverts, those who use signs and voice at the same time as "heafies," and English and PSE users as "oralists". ASL users are proud of their language and perceive the oralists as being against ASL because it is broken English and not proper. One self-described ASL monolingual believes that the students are confused about sign systems and are strong support- ers of PSE; the English-dominant bilingual believes that students have much more supportive attitudes about sign systems than before and that the oralist students are willing to learn ASL.

The subjects also have varied perceptions of faculty use of sign systems and faculty attitudes about sign systems. Namely, by the subjects' account, deaf faculty and staff members use ASL; deaf and hearing faculty use PSE or straight English and sign and talk at the same time; deaf faculty and staff use more ASL than did hearing faculty; faculty support ASL, but it is not used much in classrooms because ASL negatively influences deaf students' writing skills; students would not understand ASL if faculty did use it; and faculty are not able to adapt to ASL. Some of the subjects think that deaf and hearing faculty have different attitudes about ASL and English. The students have concerns about the lack of sign language skills among hear- ing faculty.

The subjects have mixed feelings about speech being taught to deaf children. Two subjects believe that speech should be taught only after children first learn ASL or sign language. Other subjects believe that speech could be taught, depending on certain conditions, such as the ability to hear, the desire of deaf children to learn to speak, and the use of signing with speech.

There is a general absence of response to the question of whether or not Cued Speech should be taught to deaf children. Most of the subjects simply know too little about this method and how it works to have an opinion. Some of them do express strong reactions to the method, such as "dumb," "joke," or "embarrassing." One subject says that it is all right to use the method for speech therapy, but it should not be used in the deaf community.

The subjects' responses to the hearing status of people who correct the English or ASL of others provide an unusually clear picture of how the subjects would feel if a hearing person should happen to correct their English. Some of them would unconditionally accept a hearing person's correction of their English, and some of them with conditions, such as in writing only or with discussion first or if assistance with English is re- quested. Some subjects feel intimidated by a hearing person's correction of their English. In regard to a deaf person's correction of their English, some would accept such correction only if the deaf person has a good command of English. Some have never even thought of the possibility that a deaf person would correct their English. Some say that they would discuss the matter first or that deaf people should help each other with English rather than correct each other. Most of the subjects also have strong reactions, mostly negative, to how they would feel if a hearing person should happen to correct their ASL, for example, point out that ASL signs should be initialized. In relation to the question of how they would feel if a deaf person corrected their ASL, some of them say that they would discuss it and compare different signs if the two of them are from different Deaf schools. Some say that they would resist such correction, and others, after initial hesitation, say that they are willing to accept correction of their ASL.

All subjects are in favor of the idea that students take a course on languages in order to understand more about them. Different reasons are cited, such as increasing their awareness of their own language, explaining ASL to hearing people, feeling less inferior, clearing up confusion among new students, protecting their rights, and wanting to learn ASL in depth.

Analysis of the videotaped interviews indicates that most subjects are not aware of their own contradictory statements. Clearly, varying degrees of ambivalence toward the languages and language users are shown through these contradictions. The following are different content areas of contradiction extant in the interview corpus:

1. The status of ASL as a language and misconceptions about ASL, specifically about its linguistic features.
   *Example:* The subjects say that ASL is a language in its own right. At the same time, they think that ASL has no rules, is just pictures, and is broken English.
2. The role of ASL and speech in the education of deaf children.
   *Example:* A subject supports the use of ASL in classrooms with deaf children but also says that speech is important too because the world is filled with hearing people.
3. Self-rating of linguistic skills and the status of ASL or PSE users.
   *Example:* A subject rates herself as an ASL-dominant bilingual and yet labels ASL users as non-college-educated deaf people or as vocational deaf people.
4. Status of Cued Speech and experiences of speech only.
   *Example:* A subject says that she does not support the idea of teaching only through speech because of her negative learning experiences in this kind of situation. At the same time, she thinks that Cued Speech is wonderful as a method for parents to communicate with deaf children.
5. Hearing status of the person correcting ASL and the degree of comfort using ASL with deaf friends.
   *Example:* A subject says, "I experience full communication in ASL and feel comfortable using it. With ASL, I do what I want. Be myself. No one criticizes me. Be myself." Later, she is asked how she would

feel if a deaf person corrected her ASL and she responds "Sometimes a deaf person criticizes my signing. In spite of it, I feel great socializing with them."

Clearly, the subjects have developed an internal or subconscious ability to adapt their communication modes or languages and to make choices from their linguistic repertories. Most of their responses to most questions during the interviews are framed by "depending on." For example, the question of who tends to use ASL yields "depending on": their family and school backgrounds, students' communication preference, the situation, etcetera.

## CONCLUSION AND DISCUSSION

The key findings of this study are as follows:

1. There is a wide spectrum of linguistic/communication repertoires among the students and these reflect a diversity of family and school backgrounds.
2. Students are aware of their own bilingualism and classify themselves on a continuum of bilingualism.
3. Students are conscious of their language choices, as such depend on the hearing status of participants and other sociolinguistic variables, for example, the educational or social setting.
4. Students rate their own communication skills higher than expected.
5. There is a direct relationship between the self-evaluations of English reading, writing, and speech skills and the assessments by professionals.
6. Students have positive attitudes about ASL, but they also are ambivalent toward it and have misconceptions of it.
7. The number of years spent at a Deaf School, the onset of hearing loss, and the age when sign language is learned are the most significant primary social variables contributing to the students' attitudes about sign language, English, and language users.
8. Self-identification as deaf or hard-of-hearing and self-classification of linguistic skills are very significant secondary social variables contributing to the students' attitudes about sign language, English, and language users.
9. There is a strong relationship between the attitudes of students about ASL and those about deaf people, but there is no relationship between their attitudes about English and those about hearing people.

**Table I**
Attitudinal Typology of Deaf People

| Type | English | ASL | Hearing Persons | Deaf Persons |
|------|---------|-----|-----------------|--------------|
| 1 | + | + | + | + |
| 2 | + | + | − | + |
| 3 | − | + | − | + |
| 4 | + | − | + | + |
| 5 | + | − | + | − |
| 6 | + | − | − | + |

# An Attitudinal Typology of Deaf Persons

Based on the findings of this study, an attitudinal typology of deaf people is presented in Table I. The typology encompasses cultural identity, attitudes about ASL and English, and self-classifications of linguistic skills. The positive and negative values of Table I pertain to the following descriptions of each attitudinal type:

1. These are individuals with positive attitudes on all scales. They are balanced bilinguals with harmonious identities in both Deaf culture and American mainstream culture. Some are the hard-of-hearing children of deaf parents and attended public schools.
2. These are individuals with positive attitudes about English, ASL, and deaf people, but negative attitudes about hearing people. They are balanced bilinguals who identify with Deaf culture and reject hearing people. A majority are the deaf children, and some are the hard of-hearing children, of deaf parents and attended Deaf schools.
3. These are individuals with positive attitudes about ASL and deaf people, but negative attitudes about English and hearing people. They are ASL monolinguals and ASL-dominant bilinguals who identify with Deaf culture and reject hearing people. Many are deaf children of hearing parents and some are the deaf children of deaf parents and attended Deaf schools.
4. These are individuals with positive attitudes about English and hearing and deaf people, but negative attitudes about ASL. They are English-dominant bilinguals with harmonious identities in both Deaf culture and American mainstream culture. This type refers to those who lost their hearing at an early age, have hearing parents, and attended Deaf schools. In the Deaf community, Deaf people label people of this type "heafies".
5. These are individuals with positive attitudes about English and hearing people, but negative attitudes about ASL and deaf people.

They are English-dominant bilinguals who identify with hearing people and reject Deaf people. This type includes those who lost their hearing at a late age and attended public schools, as well as attitudinally hard-of-hearing and deaf persons who were trained in oral schools.

6. These are individuals with positive attitudes about English and deaf people, but negative attitudes about ASL and hearing people. They are English monolinguals who identify with deaf people and reject hearing people. This type refers to those who identify themselves as deaf but prefer to use English. An example is a deaf person who runs a meeting in English and does not want to include hearing people. The meetings are to be run by deaf people only.

## *Implications for the Education of Deaf Children*

This study indicates that language control is a powerful tool in the education of deaf children. Language planning means identity planning. The school systems utilize the "English only" method to teach deaf children. This method causes the confusion of identity among deaf children.

The decade of the 1980s can be aptly called the era of ambivalence and chaos in communication system values and choice because the meaning of Total Communication is ambiguous or open to several interpretations. In a powerfully written article comparing the use of language choice in Israeli and American programs in deaf education, Glickman (1984, p. 26) reiterates the central tenets of the present study:

> Despite the bitter opposition between these two schools of thought, the interesting question is not how oralism and Total Communication differ, but how they are the same. Beyond the question of whether or not deaf children should be allowed to sign, the two approaches share a fear of exposing deaf children to the Deaf Community and deaf cultural values. . . . Both approaches share the belief that the most successful product of deaf education is the person most able to integrate fully into the hearing world.

Organizations such as the Alexander Graham Bell Association express explicit goals of teaching oralism to deaf children and expect them to become members only of mainstream American culture. Citing a speech presented by Dr. Leo Connor, past president of the Alexander Graham Bell Association, to its 1972 convention, Glickman (1984, p. 25) observes that "the real issue in deaf education is not teaching methodology (manual versus oral) but identity and community. The purpose of deaf education, he said, is to give deaf children the identity of hearing and to insure that they do not affiliate with the Deaf Community."

Does a majority of schools using Total Communication express the goals of teaching only English to deaf children and expecting them to be members of mainstream America culture? The main goal of educating deaf children is to prepare them to live in the hearing world. Educators are ambivalent toward deaf people who chose to identify with the Deaf community. They feel that such an identification undermines the education and preparation of deaf children to live in the hearing world. But at the same time, some educators attend events sponsored by deaf people and give support to the organizations run by deaf people. As Glickman (1984, p. 25) states:

> When hearing educators of deaf children forbade the use of sign language, it was not sign language, per se, to which they objected. Behind their objection to sign language was their fear that, if permitted to sign, deaf children would become culturally deaf. Their real objection was to the Deaf Community. Educators felt that the existence of the Deaf Community was an embarrassment and proof that they had failed at their job of integrating deaf children into the hearing world. For the past 100 years, education of the deaf has had the central purpose of making deaf children speak, lipread, and use their residual hearing; in short, to identify with, and resemble, hearing people. Deaf children who became culturally deaf were thought to have failed and to have been lost to the Deaf World.

Where are the schools that express the explicit goals of teaching both English and ASL as media of instruction and that expect deaf children to be members of both cultures? Where are the schools that express the explicit goals of teaching ASL only and that expect deaf children to be members of Deaf culture only, in opposition to the Alexander Graham Bell Association? Glickman (1984, p. 27) addresses these questions:

> If Total Communication shares the oral bias against the Deaf Community and Deaf Culture, why have so many people and responsible organizations like the NAD defended it? The answer is partially that deaf people also differ on the degree to which they feel that an affirmative deaf view of deafness should be presented to deaf children. For some deaf people, this is going too far. More importantly, from a historical point of view, it has been easier to combat oralism from a Total Communication rather than a bicultural approach precisely because Total Communication does not challenge the fundamental assumptions of oralism. Both approaches value speech over sign, listening over seeing, English over ASL, hearing over deaf identities. Neither approach attempts to make deaf children bicultural.

Educators are powerful agents of change, with a powerful influence on deaf students' use of languages. One subject in a videotaped interview in the present study says that PSE is his true sign language and explains how he decided to use PSE:

> I started to sign in English sentences. People began to say that I always talked

in sentences. I thought I always signed right while those who used ASL were wrong. Why? Because I observed that the teachers called ASL users names like "stupid" or "dumb" while they praised me. I was their pet, just because I used English sentences. That's how I thought my signs were right and ASL signs were wrong. I was smarter than they were, etcetera. Too bad. All my life, I rarely saw deaf students using PSE. Whenever they used PSE, I identified with them and became good friends. We thought we were better than others. We were high class.

Apparently, educators are also ambivalent toward deaf children who wish to develop their own identities as Deaf people. They feel that they know what is the best identity for deaf children, as Glickman (1984, p. 26) observes:

> Dr. Connor believes that the horizons of culturally deaf people are more limited than those of hearing people and of hearing-impaired people who identify with hearing people. He does not see how having a strong deaf identity can be an asset for a deaf person, how it can enable a deaf person to function successfully with hearing people. Instead, he sees a deaf identity as, essentially, a personality flaw. *Deaf people,* he suggests, *are themselves too biased to define their own identity.* (Italics added.)
> It would be difficult to find a more perfect example of the paternalistic idea that hearing people know what is best for deaf people. Hearing people are objective and broad-minded. Deaf people are biased and narrow-minded. Deaf people need hearing people to tell them which kind of identity is the healthier one.

Carol Erting, a researcher of culture and communication at Gallaudet University, studies the interaction of deaf children with hearing and deaf people in the school environment. Erting (1982, pp. 7–8) describes this ambivalence as arising from a contradiction between the deaf person's personal identity and social identity:

> This basic contradiction between the deaf individual's social identity, constructed, in part, out of the need for community with others who share fundamentally similar experiences and can communicate them, and the individual's personal identity, resulting, in part, from the physical and emotional bonds between parents and children, very often manifests itself as ambivalence toward both deaf society and hearing society. The challenge to integrate these two identities and resolve the tension these competing and conflicting categories and their symbols generate is perhaps the greatest and most constant challenge faced by the deaf individual.

Most deaf people do not realize how enmeshed they are in the competition between two identities with separate languages and cultures. It is only when deaf people develop an awareness of their situation and face it maturely that integration and resolution of the two identities become possible.

Deaf students should learn about themselves as deaf people so they can deal with and maturely resolve the ambivalence that binds them. One way to achieve this is through the implementation of Deaf Studies programs in higher education. We can only imagine the enormous gains that could be made in the education of the deaf if the system sought to *build* on deaf culture, language, and identity instead of to ignore or squash these elements. All the positive energy that is now consumed in ambivalent struggles could then be channeled in one positive direction for deaf people and for the educational system. The current system is producing deaf people who pay a high price for rejecting their own culture, language, and identity in order to assimilate with hearing people.

In a system that officially ignores the existence of ASL and Deaf culture, the miracle is that there remains a strong core of deaf identity and of students who feel positive about that identity. This speaks to the vitality of Deaf culture and its transmission in spite of the system.

The educational implications of this study are well-articulated in Erting's (1982, p. 25) following observations:

> Intelligence, degree and type of hearing loss, etiology, and age at onset of the deafness are all variables which have educational implications; these types of considerations are usually taken into account in educational programming. However, schools have failed, by and large, to take account of the sociocultural aspects of deafness and their implications for education. Factors such as parental hearing status, membership in the deaf community, linguistic socialization experiences, socio-economic status, and parental goals and expectations are usually not treated as critical variables affecting educational programming. Nowhere is this inattention to sociocultural variables more evident and more problematic than in the area of policy decisions and everyday interaction around language issues.

The message is that deaf people must have an educational system that is bilingual and bicultural. Ideally, such a system would implement the following directives:

1. Develop balanced bilingual students, competent in both ASL and English and comfortable in both cultures.
2. Develop positive attitudes about ASL, English, and the language users among deaf children and their teachers and dispel the myths and misconceptions about ASL.
3. Require teachers to be bilingual and bicultural.
4. Review and redesign the curriculum to incorporate the contents of Deaf culture.
5. Design a curriculum to meet students' diversified linguistic/communication backgrounds, for example, if a student is fluent in English and demonstrates an excellent knowledge of mainstream American

culture, then instruction on ASL and Deaf Culture is needed, and vice versa for ASL monolinguals.
6. Develop a tool to evaluate students' ASL fluency.
7. Construct a sociolinguistic profile of all deaf students as they enter school and monitor the profile as it changes.

The thesis of this study is that language choice reflects identity choice among deaf people. The deaf college students in this study are aware that they are bilingual in varying degrees. The study documents their ambivalence toward ASL and English. Deaf people will continue to feel ambivalent toward both languages and cultures as long as educators feel ambivalent toward deaf people. It is important for deaf people, educators, and parents to work for a bilingual and bicultural educational system where the identity and reality of deaf persons are fully accepted.

# 10

# An Examination of Language
# Attitudes of Teachers
# of the Deaf

Julie Ward Trotter

## INTRODUCTION

Language attitudes clearly affect relationships with others. Stereotypes of people are based on language; generalizations and judgments of individuals are based on language form and use. For example, in their study of the language attitudes of Jewish and Arab adolescents toward Arabic and Hebrew, Lambert and Yeni-Komshian (1965, p. 87) observe that

> it is of particular interest that the Jewish and Arab Ss responded to representatives of one another's groups in mutually antagonistic manners in the sense that both samples of Ss saw their own group as more honest, friendly, good-hearted and more desirable as relatives through marriage. Mutual distrust of this sort would certainly restrict social interaction since members of neither group would initiate a friendly overture if they anticipated the others to act in a relatively dishonest, unfriendly, and selfish manner.

The study of language attitudes originates with the discipline of psychology. Perhaps one of the earliest operational definitions of attitude is a "quantified set of responses to bipolar scales" (Osgood, Succi, and Tannenbaum, 1957, p. 190). Williams *et al.* (1976, p. 83) suggests that "perhaps a person's attitude might also be accurately assessed as a range of ratings of a particular stimulus." Shuy and Williams (1973, p. 94) comment that

> a person's reactions to a dialect may not only reflect his attitudes about the social stratum of that dialect, but may also include clusters of attitudes

THE SOCIOLINGUISTICS OF THE DEAF COMMUNITY
Copyright © 1989 by Academic Press Inc.
All rights of reproduction in any form reserved.

related to apparent quality of the dialect or of the people who speak that dialect. . . . Such attitudes . . . may begin to reveal the affective dimension of dialect stereotyping.

The applications of language attitude studies are as important as the research itself. Fasold (1984) divides the applications of language attitude studies into the social and educational realms. The social realm of language use encompasses all language use except that occurring in educational settings. Although language use related to identity and diglossia is included in the social realm, these two linguistic phenomena appear to at least indirectly play a role in the educational setting as well.

One type of study in the social realm of language attitude studies concerns the instrumental versus the integrative orientation of language learners. An integrative orientation is defined as a desire to learn a new language as a vehicle for participating and perhaps even gaining membership in a new cultural group. An instrumental orientation, on the other hand, is defined as learning a new language to fulfill an educational requirement, to get a new or better job, or to prove oneself as a "successful, cultured person." Language attitude studies, conducted with people learning a second language, repeatedly state that an integrative orientation toward the new language (and culture) is important in successful language learning (Cohen, 1975; Hodge, 1978; Krashen and Scarcella, 1978). In other words, people who desire to learn a second language in order to function in another language or cultural group are more likely than instrumentally oriented people to approach or achieve fluency in their second language.

Fasold (1984) also discusses how language attitudes affect learning. He divides this educational area of application into two subcategories: (1) teacher attitudes about students' language and culture and (2) student attitudes about language.

Fasold cites Frederick Williams as a primary researcher in the area of language attitudes in education. Besides renown for his meticulous methods, Williams's studies on teacher attitudes have produced some interesting results. In one particular study, teachers are not presented with speech samples but rather are simply given ethnic labels and asked to evaluate the speech qualities of students based on their personal experiences. As Fasold (1984, p. 174) reports, "Not only was it possible to elicit stereotypes, but there was evidence that the results were highly reliable." Williams' initial research did not determine how these stereotypical attitudes influence actual teacher behavior or evaluation.[1] But Lucas and Borders (1987, p. 138) provide some insight: "If interaction between teachers' language attitudes and assessment can be demonstrated in experimental situations, it stands

[1]As in other correlation studies, it is difficult, if not impossible, to establish cause and effect.

to reason that the same interaction may be operative in actual everyday classroom situations, as a function of the occurrence of dialect diversity."

Language attitude studies and their applications have clear relevance in the deaf community, and a number of studies have investigated the attitudes of deaf students toward ASL, English, and manual codes for English (e.g., Bergman, 1976; Berke, 1978; Curry and Curry, 1978; Lentz, 1977; Meath-Lang, 1978). A good case in point is Kannapell's (1985) study on how language choice reflects identity choice among deaf college students at Gallaudet University (see Kannapell, this volume). Through questionnaires and videotaped interviews, she discusses with students their attitudes about ASL, English, and a language contact variety that is labeled Pidgin Signed English (PSE). She (1985, p. 295) concludes that students are aware of their situational language choice and of their own bilingualism and have "positive attitudes toward ASL, but they are ambivalent toward it and have misconceptions about it." On the surface, these conclusions may seem unrelated to issues in education; however, Kannapell discusses how her research has implications for the education of the deaf. Language, specifically, preferred and skilled use of ASL, serves as a vehicle to membership in the Deaf community. Thus, to the extent that an absence of skills in using ASL hinders participation in the Deaf community (Markowicz and Woodward, 1978), Kannapell (1985, p. 297) interprets her data as evidence that "language control is a powerful tool in the education of deaf children. Language planning means identity planning."

## THE MATCHED-GUISE METHOD

The present study examines the language attitudes of prospective teachers of the deaf through the use of a modified matched-guise method. The method was developed by Wallace Lambert in Quebec in the late 1950s as a tool for assessing attitudinal reaction to language (dialects, accents, styles, and different languages). The method uses "judges" to attend to speech samples and then rate the speaker. A "guise," that is, a person fluent in two languages, produces language samples of identical content, one in each of the person's two languages. The judges are unaware that the language samples are produced by the same person. After attending to each language sample, the judges rate it on a semantic differential scale, a six-point scale with bipolar adjectives (e.g., intelligent/unintelligent, confident/not confident, friendly/unfriendly). Because judges do not know that the samples are produced by the same person, differences in the judges' evaluations of the guises are said to be the result of different attitudes about the different language varieties (Cooper, 1975). Significant agreement in the judges' ratings of one language variety is interpreted as stereotyping of users of this language variety by the judges. In addition to the use of the matched-guise method to assess attitudes about two distinct languages, the method is also widely used among sociolinguists to assess attitudes about varieties of spoken languages (J. R. Edwards, 1977; El-Dash and Tucker, 1975; Lambert, Hodgson, Gardner, and Fillenbown, 1960; Tucker and Lambert, 1969).

The study that introduced the matched-guise technique was conducted by Lambert *et al.* (1960) in Montreal with French Canadian and English speakers. The judges were all Montreal residents, sixty-four English speakers and sixty-six French speakers, ranging from "not at all" bilingual to "fluent" bilingual. Four bilingual individuals served as guise speakers and read identical passages in English and French. Two filler sections were also used for a total of ten passages presented to each judge. To rate the tapes, the judges were asked to complete a fourteen-item semantic differential, guess the occupation of each model, and complete cloze sentences covertly addressing language attitudes. The researchers found that there was a tendency for judges to rate members of their own language group more favorably than nonmembers, but the general trend was to rate English speakers as having higher status than French speakers and to rate French speakers as more likable than English speakers.

In a subsequent study also by Lambert and Yeni-Komshian (1965), two bilingual models each produced two guises, in this case, Arabic and Hebrew. The judges were forty Jewish students fluent in Hebrew and twenty-nine bilingual Arab students. The only indication that the Jewish students had Arabic fluency was that they lived in Tel-Aviv and were enrolled at their Jewish school in an Arabic language course. Both Jewish and Arab judges saw members of their own language group, compared to nonmembers, as more honest, friendly, good hearted, and desirable as relatives through marriage.

In a variation of the matched-guise technique, Gibbons (1983) set out to assess the attitudes of bilingual speakers of Cantonese and English about "MIX" (i.e., code-switching). In this study, the MIX data were taken from three segments of actual conversation. Translations were then made of this conversation into Cantonese only and into English only. The judges were bilingual users of both languages. English was seen as a symbol of high status and Westernization. Catonese was seen as an indicator of Chinese humility and solidarity. In previous, overt studies of language attitudes, MIX was rated very negatively. This study indicated that in comparison to covert attitudes about Cantonese, the negative rating of MIX might reflect actual attitudes. Compared to English, however, MIX is a neutral language variety and perhaps on some traits, more favorable than English. Subjects also confirmed that MIX is very functional.

In Wales, a study was conducted to see if previously gathered overt attitudes about Welsh and English matched with covert attitudes obtained through the matched-guise technique. Bourhis and Giles (1976) chose male bilinguals to tape three sections each: one in Welsh, one in English with Received Pronunciation, and one in English with a mild English accent. Judges were from three separate groups: Welsh-English bilinguals, Welsh learners, and Welsh individuals who were English monolinguals. It was found that, although the Welsh overtly express reservations about the Welsh language, they appear to covertly possess positive attitudes.

In another Welsh study by Price, Fluck, and Giles (1983) models read identical passages in three guises. The judges were sixty-four children, ranging from ten to twelve years of age. These children were defined by their teachers as bilingual, but 86 percent of them claimed Welsh as their native tongue. This study also found that there can be a difference between overt and covert attitudes about Welsh. These studies use two or three guises. In a modification of the technique, J. R. Edwards (1977) hired a professional actor to produce samples of five regional accents of Irish. Typical of matched-guise studies, each of these samples was read aloud.

Giles proposes some of the most drastic modifications to the matched-guise method. He was interested in using this method to get beyond attitudes and into the realm of observable behavior. For example, Bourhis and Giles (1976) conducted a study with one model producing four guises. The guises were English, Welsh, English with a heavy Welsh accent, and English with a light Welsh accent. These taped sections were randomly played one at a time on various nights in a theatre. Patrons were asked to assist the management by going out into the foyer and completing an informational survey. The use of Welsh in this request for assistance was more effective than the use of English, as measured by the number of surveys completed.

Giles and Bourhis (1976) conducted another study that used a modification of their earlier technique. English Canadians heard tapes of French Canadians describing a picture. The English Canadians were instructed to draw a picture based on the verbal descriptions (the quality of drawing not being important). The judges (the English Canadians) were all monolingual. The guise segments played to them were: totally in French, mixed in French and English, fluent in English but with a French accent, and nonfluent in English. After hearing the tape and drawing their picture, judges were asked to fill out a questionnaire about the speaker they had heard and about the speaker's performance on the tape. Speakers adopting the dominant language of the judges (English) were perceived more positively than the French speakers.

In a recent modification of the matched-guise method, Petronio and DeKorte (1984) asked Gallaudet Prep students to act as judges and rate videotapes of ASL-like and English-like signers. These judges had varied language backgrounds. Out of the total pool, 48 percent were presumed native signers (children of deaf parents or children who attended residential school prior to the age of thirteen), 32 percent had attended day schools where "some kind" of sign language was used, and 20 percent had not used sign language prior to attending Gallaudet. Contrary to what might be expected from intuition and from the literature, Petronio and DeKorte (1984, p. 23) found that judgments of "a person's intelligence, educational background, economic status, or honesty were not influenced (for these deaf judges) by the languages used (ASL-like or English-like)."

## THE LANGUAGE ATTITUDES OF TEACHERS

Research has also been done on how teacher attitudes about children's speech choice and language choice affect a teacher's interaction with and evaluation of students, thus affecting the overall quality of a child's education (Crowl and MacGinitie, 1974; McDermott and Gospodinoff, 1981; Pellegreno and Williams, 1973; J. B. Taylor, 1983; Williams, 1973). Attinasi (1983) studied how Puerto Ricans in New York City regard their own language and culture. Interview data from ninety working-class people living in Puerto Rican neighborhoods and from forty teachers employed in bilingual programs in the same neighborhoods show that both groups have strong loyalties to the Spanish language and Puerto Rican culture.

Rey (1978) investigated the effect of accent on teachers' evaluation of potential educational success. The subjects were nineteen adults (white Americans, black Americans, and Cuban nationals). The judges were forty-one high school teachers and twenty-five university teachers. In terms of social classification, school success, and employment opportunities, judges rated the white American accent first or most favorable, the black American accent second, and the Cuban accent third or least favorable.

V. Edwards (1978) suggests that there are strong links between attitudes about a language and attitudes about the speakers. The tape-recorded speech of four individuals in high school was examined: a British born Barbadian female who spoke first with a working-class reading accent and then in Creole, a working-class male who spoke in a working-class reading accent, a middle-class male who spoke with Received Pronunciation, and a Jamaican female who spoke in a very marked Creole. Teachers were asked to evaluate the speech in terms of probable behavioral characteristics and academic achievements and to indicate if they would want each student in their classes. Teachers were found to discriminate between middle-class and working-class speech and to discriminate further between working-class and West Indian speakers.

Although each of these cited studies examines a distinct social group and the corresponding attitudinal responses of teachers, the general message is summed up by Saville-Troike (1973, p. 3): "If an English-dominant social group puts a stigma of inferiority on a child's native language, it can easily create a barrier to learning. Teachers need to be sensitive to their own attitudes . . . Unrecognized, such feeling must create a source of negative identity and conflict."

In terms of the deaf community, Kannapell (1985) discusses what appear to be results of this very type of negative influence among students at Gallaudet in their ambivalence toward ASL and in how language choice reflects their identity choice. The present study provides data to document the language attitudes of teachers of deaf children.

## TEACHERS OF THE DEAF

Although by no means comprehensive, the previously cited literature suggests the value of attitudinal studies and the need to replicate these studies in relation to deafness, particularly in the area of education. Language attitudes are an integral part of each person's life. These attitudes within the educational process are often the basis for choosing teaching methods, for selecting a communication mode, and at least an indirect way of evaluating students.

The oral-manual versus Total Communication controversy among educators of the deaf is far from complete resolution. In addition to this controversy, there are debates over the use of Signed English and ASL in the classroom and the proposal by some to include deaf children in bilingual education programs (Baker, 1978; Cokely, 1978; Kannapell, 1974; Livingston, 1986; Lou, 1988; Luetke-Stahlman, 1983). Members of the educational profession vary widely in their stands concerning the medium of instruction. Whatever the stand, however, attitudes seem to be deeply ingrained and are vehemently defended.

Because language attitudes have an impact on classroom interaction and on a child's overall education, the current study focuses on the language attitudes of teachers of the deaf. It is hypothesized that many prospective teachers of the deaf enter teacher-training programs with little to no knowledge of deaf culture, deaf people, or the nature of sign language.

The attitudes of these teachers about ASL and deaf people are primarily acquired in teacher-training programs. Some of the attitudes currently pervasive in deaf education in both students and teachers are no doubt counterproductive in the learning process. This observation is based in part upon direct experience in a training program for teachers of the deaf.[2]

[2]I attended a four year NCATE university-training program for state certification in teaching K-12, hearing-impaired students. The curriculum was heavily weighted in experience, totaling more than two hundred hours in the classroom prior to student teaching. Content areas taught by teacher trainees were language (English) and speech.

Battison (1978, pp. 3–11) examines four prevalent beliefs about sign language: "These beliefs, or more accurately myths, are related to: (1) universality of sign languages; (2) coding based on oral languages; (3) iconicity and transparency; (4) restricted content or range of expression". The training program in question assumed that myths 2, 3, and 4 are true. Students are taught (by example) to believe that sign language is a coding system based on oral language. There were no deaf instructors in the teacher-training program or in the lab school where training took place. As a result, everyone used some kind of simultaneous communication, consisting of spoken English and (primarily) Signing Exact English (SEE) signs. A course was offered entitled "American Sign Language," primarily a vocabulary course in legal, religious, and sexual signs, and signs related to drug use. There was minimal acknowledgement and discussion of the differences in word order between ASL and English and of Stokoe's (1960) important identification of three parameters of signs. *No* discussion was provided of grammatical facial expression, use of signing space, classifiers, inflections, or the distinction between ASL and non-ASL initialized signs. Nor was it ever made clear that voicing or mouthing of English words is not part of ASL. Students never saw ASL on the hands of a signer in person or in videotape.

Students were also encouraged to look for iconicity or transparency in signs. While learning sign language vocabulary, students were given "reasons" as to why a particular sign was made in a particular way (e.g., *GIRL* is made on the chin because, historically, females wear bonnets). When working in the classroom for practica, if a particular sign needed was not listed in any available sign language books, students were encouraged to use the handshape of the initial letter of the English word and "create" their own sign. This sign was supposed to iconically represent the concept of the English word or perhaps bear sufficient similarity in form to a related sign.

The most damaging myth advanced in the training was that sign language is restricted in content. As future teachers of the deaf, students were told that (1) the biggest obstacle of deaf people was their lack of language (in contrast to lack of skills in the English language); (2) all deaf children enter school with no language (similar to the prevalent view in the 1960s that black children enter school with no language, see Labov, 1972, p. 201); (3) those deaf persons who use sign language still operate at a deficit, because sign language, with its limited vocabulary, is incapable of discussing abstract ideas; and (4) it is the rare and brilliant deaf person who is capable of abstract thought.

Based on the association among graduates of teacher-training programs nationwide, it appears that the teaching of these beliefs about sign language and deaf persons is not atypical. If the teacher-training program described here is at all representative of programs that train teachers of the deaf, there is clearly a need (1) to refute the myths perpetuated by the professionals who train teachers of the deaf and (2) to begin exposing the language attitudes of teachers of the deaf and those who train these teachers.

## THE LANGUAGE ATTITUDES OF TEACHERS OF THE DEAF

Using a modification of the matched-guise technique (Lambert, Hodgson, Gardner, and Fillenbaum, 1960), the present study examines the language attitudes of prospective teachers of the deaf. The purpose of the study was to determine the covert and overt language attitudes of subjects about ASL and Signed English. In addition, comprehension and language identification of signed sections was assessed.

Data collection for the study consisted of having fifty-five student teachers from three different teacher-training programs in the Midwest rate the videotaped output of signers on a semantic differential scale. In addition, subjects completed a demographic questionnaire, wrote summaries to show their comprehension of the signed sections, and responded to a questionnaire about the use of ASL and Signed English in the classroom. Student teachers were chosen for the study, rather than experienced teachers, because it was hypothesized that student teachers would be the most idealistic and flexible. If they enter the classroom with negative attitudes, they are unlikely to see the ethnically nonstandard child in their classroom as a child with potential to have great educational success (Williams *et al.,* 1976).

The tapes have two passages of ASL-like signing and three passages of English-like signing. The videotapes were made with the matched-guise technique in order to insure that subjects respond to language use and not to the signer. That is, because of the matched-guise design, subjects are not rating signer appearance, word choice, or topic choice but rating ASL and Signed English.

The research design used differs from the "classic" matched-guise study (Lambert, Hodgson, Gardner, and Fillenbaum, 1960) because in the original design judges are not aware that both language sections are produced by the same speaker. This type of design ensures reliability. Since ASL and Signed English are visual, rather than auditory, languages, the original design had to be adapted to a visual mode. The particular modification employed insures that each group is rating users of ASL similarly, that each group is rating users of Signed English similarly, and that each group sees both types of signing in the process of data collection.

One of the first steps in this study was to choose models for the matched-guise videotapes. Three individuals were chosen on the basis of their perceived bilingual skills. The first model, a fluent bilingual, produced an adequate amount of quality data. In contrast, the second model was not comfortable using English-type signing and her Signed English segments are replete with signs, word order, use of space, and facial expressions from ASL. Also significant is that the first model was very linguistically aware of her own language use and of the structural differences between ASL and English. The second model was more linguistically naive. The third model, a sibling of the first, exhibited approximately the same bilingual skills and linguistic awareness of the first.

The actual process of videotaping was set up to secure as natural a production as possible of the languages in question. The ASL interview was conducted by a deaf native user of ASL. The Signed English interview was conducted by a hearing signer who used SEE signs.

The guise segments were selected on the basis of the quality of the signing in each language and also with consideration to discourse content.[3] The aim was to have the same general topic or level of topic in common across all of the segments. As suggested in Williams *et al.* (1976), each signed segment is approximately two minutes in duration. Two separate tapes were made utilizing the experimental design depicted in Figure 1. The encircled segments of each tape are identical.

Group 1 (half of the subjects) viewed tape 1 and group 2 (the other half of the subjects) viewed tape 2. Segment *A* was used as a sample or practice section for the judges. Segments *B* and *C* were used as the identical segments needed to test the validity of the matched-guise. That is, if the experimental design is a true matched-guise, then there should be no statistical difference in how the two groups of judges rate identical segments of ASL (segment *B*) and identical segments of Signed English (segment *C*). Segments *D* and *E* are the actual guises where attitudes are examined and assessed.

The data on attitudes were collected using a semantic differential scale. The input for the semantic differential was formulated by modifying information from the following sources: Petronio and DeKort (1984), Williams *et al.* (1976), and W. Wolfram (personal communication). This scale was used to measure covert language attitudes. In addition, an overt attitude questionnaire was built on a modification of the radical Language Attitude Scale in O. Taylor (1973), used there to test language attitudes of teachers about the Standard English and Black English of their students. The aim of the

---

[3]To compensate for some inadequate data, videotapes from the matched-guise study conducted by Karen Petronio were used to supplement the present data corpus. I thank Karen Petronio for sharing her data with me.

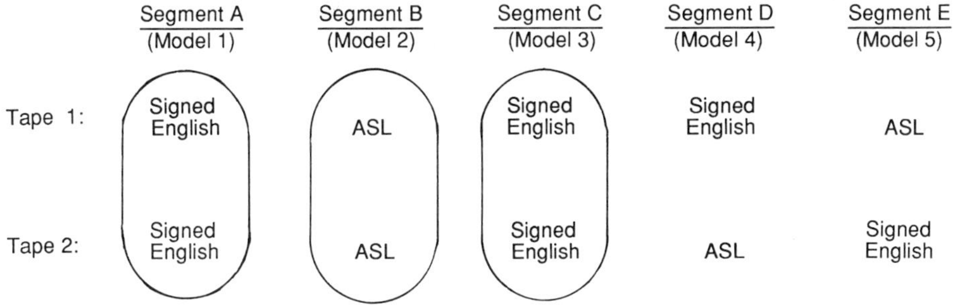

|  | Segment A (Model 1) | Segment B (Model 2) | Segment C (Model 3) | Segment D (Model 4) | Segment E (Model 5) |
|---|---|---|---|---|---|
| Tape 1: | Signed English | ASL | Signed English | Signed English | ASL |
| Tape 2: | Signed English | ASL | Signed English | ASL | Signed English |

**Fig. 1** Experimental design, showing order of presentation of language segments on each tape. For segments D and E, see footnote 3.

present application of a modified form of this scale was to compare covert attitudes about ASL and Signed English (obtained through the matched-guise) to overt attitudes about the same languages. Finally, demographic information about each judge was obtained.

Since it was questionable whether the students from the teacher-training programs would understand ASL, it was suggested by Walt Wolfram (personal communication) that a comprehension index be included in the study. The subjects were simply asked to write out a summary of what was said in each of the discourse segments. The subjective reactions of expert judges were used to rate the comprehension skills of the student teachers. Three interpreters fluent in ASL and Signed English rated the written summaries. The written summaries were judged on the basis of how they compared to the actual content of each ASL segment. Specifically, each expert judge viewed the tapes and then rated the written summary of the content using the following scale: 0–1, no response; 1–3, no comprehension; 3–5, little comprehension; 5–7, some comprehension; 7–9, full comprehension.

## ANALYSIS

Segment *A* was a practice segment, so no written data was obtained. Segments *B* (ASL) and *C* (Signed English) were used as controls. Because both groups of subjects saw both of these identical segments (each containing the exact same signers, signing the same information), no significant difference was expected in the way that the subjects rated the signer. Any items on the semantic differential that, for some undetermined reason, elicited a significant difference (two-tailed *t*-test, $p > .05$) were eliminated at this point in the analysis.[4] The items actually eliminated were those

---

[4]Probability to *t* (two-tailed test) was used. A probability level of $p < .05$ was deemed significant. Further data are available, upon request, from the author.

measuring the clarity, organization, efficiency, and beauty of the signed message.

The remaining items on the semantic differential were analyzed using *t*-tests to determine which items elicited a significant difference in the ratings. Excluding the items just listed, a number of variables elicited a significant difference between the ratings of ASL and Signed English ($p < .05$).[5] Since signers are the same and the discourse topics are similar, the differences can be attributed to differences in reactions to ASL and Signed English. The range of the semantic differential is 1–7, where 1 is the highest positive value and 7 is the lowest negative value. The mean range is 1–2, positive; 4–5, neutral; and 6–7, negative.

ASL was rated as more expressive and exciting than Signed English ($p < .01$). The only other item where ASL was rated higher than Signed English was on the basis of speed ($p < .05$). Signed English was rated more grammatical than ASL on the basis of "grammar quite good" ($p < .001$) and fluency ($p < .05$); more accurate than ASL on precision ($p < .001$) and completeness ($p < .05$); and more useful than ASL on functional value ($p < .05$), message adequacy ($p < .05$), and effective use of language ($p < .01$). Finally, users of Signed English were judged to have better educations and to be more culturally advantaged than users of ASL ($p < .05$).

The responses of the subjects to overt attitude statements about the use of ASL and Signed English in the classroom were measured for mean values. The responses range from 1 to 4. A mean value of 1 indicates a positive response, where the subjects either strongly agree with a positive statement (e.g., strongly agree that ice cream is delicious) or strongly disagree with a negative statement (e.g., strongly disagree that ice cream is sickening). A mean value of 4 indicates a negative response, where the subjects either strongly agree with a negative statement (e.g., strongly agree that ice cream is sickening) or strongly disagree with a positive statement (e.g., strongly disagree that ice cream is delicious). The score ranges are 1–2, positive; 2–3, neutral; and 3–4, negative.

The overall mean response value for questions about ASL is 2.07. This value indicates that the student teachers, overall, had neutral-to-positive responses to direct questions about ASL. The specific responses in the favorable range indicate the subjects' disagreement with the following assertions: ASL is too imprecise to be an effective means of communication, allowing ASL to be used in schools will undermine the schools' reputations, and notwithstanding the possible benefits to be gained from approval of ASL, such approval would be basically wrong. The seven remaining assertions about ASL were more neutrally (although not unfavorably) responded to by the subjects as a whole. Of all the overt attitude questions,

---

[5]Unless otherwise noted, *p* is probability of *t* in a two-tailed test.

including those about ASL and Signed English, the assertion most positively responded to is that ASL is a language. The assertion least favorably (although not unfavorably) responded to is that if the use of ASL was encouraged, speakers of ASL would be more motivated to achieve academically.

The overall mean response value for questions about Signed English is 2.09. The responses indicate the subjects' agreement with the following assertions: there is much danger involved in rejecting Signed English, allowing and accepting the use of Signed English in the classroom will encourage the academic progress of the class, and when the use of Signed English is encouraged, deaf children are more motivated to achieve academically. The remaining four assertions about Signed English were more neutrally (although not unfavorably) responded to by the subjects as a whole.

Overt response to ASL and Signed English is basically the same, with Signed English being slightly favored (a .002 difference in the standard deviation values). This small difference indicates that in terms of overt responses to ASL and Signed English, subjects showed no preference between ASL and Signed English.

After viewing each segment of signed discourse, the subjects were asked to identify the language that the signer had used. Responses were made on a seven-point scale with ASL at one end and English on the other. Responses were evaluated as: 1–2, ASL; 3–5, neutral response, mixed (ASL and English), or midcontinuum language variety (Woodward, 1973c); 6–7, English. Tables I and II present the frequency distributions of subject responses in identifying (and misidentifying) ASL and Signed English.

As shown in Table I, the ASL signing in segment *B* is not misidentified as Signed English by any of the subjects. The ASL signing in segment *D* is about equally identified as ASL and as a mixed or midcontinuum language

**Table I**
Frequency Distribution of Identifications, ASL

| Response Scale | Segment B (Both Groups) | Segment D (Group 2) | Segment E (Group 1) |
|---|---|---|---|
| 1 (ASL) | 15 | 5 | 7 |
| 2 | 16 | 5 | 9 |
| 3 | 15 | 6 | 5 |
| 4 (mixed) | 7 | 5 | 7 |
| 5 | 1 | 1 | 0 |
| 6 | 0 | 2 | 3 |
| 7 (Signed English) | 0 | 0 | 0 |
| Total *N* | 54 | 24 | 31 |

**Table II**
Frequency Distribution of Identifications, Signed English

| Response Scale | Segment C (Both Groups) | Segment D (Group 1) | Segment E (Group 2) |
|---|---|---|---|
| 1 (ASL) | 3 | 0 | 0 |
| 2 | 1 | 2 | 0 |
| 3 | 10 | 5 | 3 |
| 4 (mixed) | 11 | 6 | 7 |
| 5 | 15 | 11 | 5 |
| 6 | 11 | 6 | 7 |
| 7 (Signed English) | 2 | 1 | 1 |
| Total $N$ | 53 | 31 | 23 |

by the subjects in group 2. The ASL signing in segment $E$ is correctly identified by most of the subjects in group 1. On the whole, the ASL segments are correctly identified by approximately 50 percent of the subjects, with only minimal misidentification of ASL as Signed English.

In contrast, as shown in Table II, most subjects (about equally divided between groups 1 and 2) identified the Signed English in segments $C$, $D$, and $E$ as a mixed or midcontinuum language, commonly referred to as Pidgin Signed English (PSE). Only about 25 percent of the subjects correctly identified the signing in these three segments as Signed English, but there is only minimal misidentification of Signed English as ASL.

The subjects were also asked to write down a summary of what had been said by the signer in segments $B$ through $E$. As described earlier, these responses were rated by expert judges and a mean value of comprehension was calculated for each of the segments on each videotape (except for segment $A$, the practice segment). As shown in Table III, all of the scores

**Table III**
Subject Comprehension of Discourse Segments

| Segment (Group) | Language | Mean[a] | Standard Deviation |
|---|---|---|---|
| E (1) | ASL | 3.03 | 1.08 |
| C (1/2) | Signed English | 3.21 | 1.50 |
| D (1) | Signed English | 3.58 | 1.31 |
| E (2) | Signed English | 4.12 | 1.64 |
| B (1/2) | ASL | 4.47 | 1.79 |
| D (2) | ASL | 4.70 | 1.23 |

[a]Subject comprehension was rated on a scale ranging from 1 to 9: 1, no comprehension; 9, full comprehension.

are in the middle range of comprehension, indicating only partial comprehension by the subjects of both the ASL and Signed English segments.

## DISCUSSION

Using the matched-guise method of assessing language attitudes, Signed English is in general rated higher than ASL, although responses to both languages were generally in the neutral range. What do these neutral attitudes indicate? They may indicate that attitudes have not yet been either fully taught or fully developed. They also may indicate that further modifications of the matched-guise methodology is needed.

ASL is rated more expressive, more exciting, and faster than Signed English. Signed English is rated as having greater precision, more complete sentences, more consistently correct sign usages, grammar that is better, signs that are more functional, and a more complete message than ASL. English signers are rated as using language more effectively, having better educational backgrounds, and being more fluent than ASL signers.

In response to overt questions regarding ASL and Signed English, the subjects did not overtly show any preference for ASL over Signed English, or vice versa. The responses to both ASL and Signed English are in the favorable-to-neutral range, definitely not unfavorable. An understanding of this apparent contradiction (covert preference for Signed English versus overt absence of preference between ASL and Signed English) may eventually be found through use of a more sensitive behavioral measure of attitudes. Since the hypothesis was that subjects would respond more favorably to Signed English on all counts, a number of explanations for the overt equality of the languages are possible.

One possibility is that these prospective teachers of the deaf are sophisticated enough to know that an overtly negative response to ASL is not widely and uniformly acceptable behavior. In the context of the present study, they may even have sensed the researcher's bias. It is also possible that student teachers from these programs have, at some level, sufficient information about ASL to know that it is an equally acceptable choice for communication, alongside Signed English. This information, however, may not be fully accepted at the unconscious level of attitudes, where Signed English is preferred.

Each passage of ASL was correctly identified as ASL by 50 percent of the respondents. Only a small percentage of respondents misidentified ASL as English. The remaining respondents identified the ASL segments as a language in the middle or neutral category. In contrast, each Signed English passage was correctly identified by approximately 25 percent of the respondents. Only a small percentage of respondents incorrectly identified

Signed English as ASL. The majority of subjects identified the Signed English segments as a language in the middle category.

This drop-off in percentage of correct identifications may say something about the use of the word "English" in the language label. Teachers may not perceive Signed English to be English but rather a code for English; teachers may not expect deaf people to use "good English." Student teachers may be idealistic prescriptive evaluators rather than sign language users.

The subjects' comprehension of the discourse segments was within the neutral range, with one ASL segment being the least understood passage and another ASL segment being the most understood passage. The Signed English in segment $D$ was understood better than the same signer's ASL segment, and the ASL in segment $E$ was better understood than the same signer's Signed English segment. It seems that comprehension is not exclusively tied to the particular language used but is dependent on other variables not isolated in this study. These factors could be the frequency of contact with deaf adults, the number of years that the subjects have been signing, and the orientation of the subject to the language (recall the distinction between instrumental versus integrative orientations of language learners, discussed earlier). At this point, however, a description of these factors is conjecture. All of the signed segments were only moderately understood by the student teachers, implying that their receptive sign language skills are mediocre.

If receptive skills truly precede expressive skills, the fact that this group of student teachers have low receptive skills speaks negatively about their ability to communicate effectively in sign language. This limited ability may relate to the number of deaf instructors, deaf students, and the size and visibility of the local deaf community.

Does lack of comprehension yield negative attitudes? Covertly negative and neutral attitudes (obtained through matched-guise) about ASL, coupled with the correct identification of the type of signing (e.g., ASL or Signed English) and the low degree of comprehension of ASL, appear to indicate that attitudes are taught and learned away from rather than developed through actual interaction with deaf people. It is highly probable that these prospective teachers have received their information about deafness, and learned their non-positive attitudes about ASL from their teacher-training programs.

Hewett (1971), in a study of teacher attitudes, found that prospective teachers were ready to devalue the speech of black lower-class speakers, suggesting that such stereotyping exists before the teacher actually has extensive contact with the children. Americans *do* grow up with attitudes and stereotypes about racial and socioeconomic groups. The proposal here, however, is that, in general, people are not socialized into stereotypes and attitudes about deafness, Deaf people, or the deaf community. Owing to the relatively small number of deaf people, the essential obscurity of deafness as a handicap, and the relative difficulty hearing people have in approaching the deaf community, some prospective teachers may have actually met only one or two deaf people prior to assuming their roles in the classroom. The majority of prospective teachers have little or no information about deafness and Deaf people and have had no contact with the deaf community. Indeed, it is very likely that they have no idea a deaf community or subculture exists. Deaf people are often seen by the population at large simply as culturally hearing persons with abnormal audiograms and less than full hearing. So, whereas teacher experience plays little role in Williams' factor analysis (Williams *et al.,* 1976), it seems that teacher-training programs probably serve as the vehicle not only for informing prospective teachers about deafness, the Deaf, and deaf community, but also for initially shaping prospective teacher's attitudes and stereotypes about the deaf experience.

## Implications for Education and Teacher Training

Just as students of French go to France to develop full fluency, students of sign language need contact with the deaf community. And just as French courses are best taught by people fluent in the language, sign language courses should be taught by native signers. Signed English *and* ASL should both be taught to teachers of the deaf. Without knowledge of the deaf community, teachers are essentially trying to prepare deaf children for what, from the teacher's perspective, is "the unknown." The vehicle for learning about deaf community and culture is language, in particular, ASL.

The present study also has implications for Signed English. The student teachers in this study did not think that the signers' use of English was "English-enough" as indicated in their language identification responses. Are their expectations about Signed English based on prescriptive descriptions of this language? And, more importantly, does skill in producing Signed English directly correlate with skill in reading and writing English?

The student teachers have obviously been exposed at some level to information about ASL. But the discrepancy between overt (conscious) attitudes and covert (unconscious) attitudes suggests that, at this point, the apparent change toward equality between ASL and Signed English may be only superficial. The matched-guise findings reveal that Signed English is still "more equal" than ASL.

Students in teacher-training programs must not only learn about the theory and method of ASL but also interact with users of ASL and have contact with the deaf community. Initial steps have been taken toward educating student teachers and teacher trainees about the function of ASL in the deaf community and the (potential) bilingualism and biculturalism of the children who will be in their classrooms. This process must continue.

Prospective teachers may be led to believe various principles about deafness and sign language through their teacher-training programs. If, as anticipated by research among hearing pupils and their teachers, teacher attitudes do affect students and the educational process, then it is the responsibility of teacher-training programs to present attitudes and perspectives about deafness that enhance the potential of deaf students and the teacher-student relationship.

## *ACKNOWLEDGMENTS*

This study was funded through a grant from the Gallaudet Research Institute, Department of Graduate Studies and Research, Gallaudet University, Washington, D.C. I owe thanks to Dr. Ceil Lucas, Dr. Robert Johnson, and Dr. Walt Wolfram for their assistance and patience with me in developing and completing this research.

# Part IV

## DISCOURSE ANALYSIS

# 11

## Features of Discourse in an American Sign Language Lecture

Cynthia B. Roy

### INTRODUCTION

A videotaped talk in ASL about stickleback fish was described by users of American Sign Language (ASL) as "terrific" and "interesting." This chapter describes what kind of talk this was, explores why the talk and the speaker were received so favorably by the audience, and presents an analysis of some features of ASL discourse produced by a single speaker.

Discourse analysis in ASL is a recent development and most of the research to date concentrates on aspects of the structure of conversation and the exchange of talk in ASL (Baker, 1976, 1977; Baker and Padden, 1978; Wilbur and Pettito, 1983). For the most part, these studies focus on macrofeatures of turn-taking, linguistic functions of nonmanual behaviors, and utterance boundaries and topic-flow. For example, Baker (1977) describes in detail devices that control turn-taking procedures in ASL dyadic conversations. Wilbur and Pettito (1983) describe the flow of discourse topics in a dyadic conversation and the devices that are used to accomplish the initiation, maintenance, and termination of topics within an ASL conversation. McIntire and Groode (1982) discuss, from their own experience, what are conversational differences in greetings, ongoing conversation, and leave-takings between Deaf and hearing interactions. Prinz and Prinz (1985) describe the acquisition of conversational behavior in the sign language of twenty-four deaf children between the ages of three and eleven.

In studying the discourse of a single speaker, Gee and Kegl (1983) give a

THE SOCIOLINGUISTICS OF THE DEAF COMMUNITY
Copyright © 1989 by Academic Press Inc.
All rights of reproduction in any form reserved.

detailed stylistic analysis of two narratives. They claim that narrative structure in ASL can be revealed via an analysis of the pause structure at each word boundary. One of the narratives, which had a known story structure, namely, "Goldilocks and the Three Bears," was analyzed in the opposite direction to see if its pause structure matched the narrative structure. Although there are other descriptions of features in ASL narratives (Baker, 1983; Liddell, 1980), there are no studies of the features of ASL discourse that occur in a lecture or speech.

Although brief in length, the talk described here is best labeled a lecture, for reasons explained later. Informal interviews with audience members, as well as the researcher's own experience, suggest that in a good lecture, the content is of high quality, it is well organized, and it is "interesting." Lectures are discourses with particular goals in mind, goals that are both informational and social. Although lectures tend to be monologues (as opposed to dialogues or dialogic conversation) by nature and do not require interaction in the form of talk, good lecturers are aware of the audience's needs to both follow the flow of the talk and enjoy the experience of listening.

Lectures of a scientific nature are generally expected to provide objective knowing which is created, in part, by a presentation of known facts. Lectures are thus expected to be more content-oriented than, say, conversations. Since lectures are discourses of retention, they also require the use of linguistic devices that give the listener a firm idea of how an utterance fits into the lecture process as a whole (Lebauer, 1984, p. 42). These are the kind of linguistic elements that are not a part of the content of the lecture, per se, but do guide listeners in how to interpret the information that they are hearing. These words or phrases are cohesive, structural devices that contribute to a listener's ability to distinguish between major and minor points, old versus new information, and turns or shifts in the flow of topics. These elements contribute significantly to the gestalt of a lecture. In this chapter, the use and function of two such discourse devices found in an ASL lecture are explored.

Content and organization are necessary but not sufficient characteristics of a good lecture. Thus, in this chapter, a third criterion is also addressed, that which makes a lecture vivid and interesting. It is a sociolinguistic assumption that not only the strategies and devices typical of ordinary conversation but also the elements of good storytelling are used to create vividness and audience interest (Goffman, 1981). Lecturers involve their audiences by having them participate as much as possible in the development and understanding of the information presented; this is achieved by creating the impression of immediacy and forcing the listener to make sense out of what is being said. One aim of this chapter is to examine one of the features that contributes to this involvement between the speaker, the audience, and the lecture itself.

# THE LECTURE

A five-minute discourse by an ASL user on the mating habits of the stickleback fish was elicited. This user is a Deaf man in his thirties. He attended residential schools from the age of four, has hearing parents, earned a Master's degree, and was tutoring deaf college students at a technical institute in a Southwestern state. His discussions with the researcher about ASL led to a decision to make a videotape demonstrating that ASL could be used to talk about scientific subjects. Since fishing is one of his lifelong hobbies, he read about the mating habits of a particular fish in a college freshman biology book and reproduced this information on videotape, in a studio, with an audience of two people, a Deaf man and a hearing woman. He was told to picture his audience as college freshmen.

ASL speakers who have never seen this man before tell me that the lecture is fascinating and the speaker is good and clear. They also identify the language used as ASL. When asked who the potential audience is for the videotape, they say that it is young adults ranging in age from seventeen to forty.

Although the discourse is only about five minutes in duration, its structure is typical of American expectations of a lecture. As argued in this chapter, the talk is structured and organized as a lecture by two criteria: (1) the display of an ordered development of subtopics and (2) the occurrence of linguistic features that mark the transitions into those subtopics.

# ANALYSIS OF THE LECTURE

The content of a lecture must be structured so as to develop the topic of the talk through subtopics and guide the listener through the relevance of each topic as it is discussed. The organizational structure of the present discourse segment reflects a naturally occurring, sequentially developed chain of related subtopics. It is generally agreed that most lectures open with an introduction and some explanation of why the speaker is talking. The introduction is then followed by the main body of the lecture and an obligatory closing. Cook (1975) calls these naturally formed segments "episodes." Episodic types include an obligatory *focal* (or introductory) episode with optional focal episodes, an obligatory *developmental* episode along with a number of optional developmental episodes, and an obligatory *closing* episode followed by optional closing episodes. These different kinds of episodes combine to form the unified piece that constitutes a lecture.

The focal episode is made up of introductory statements in which the speaker introduces the subject and generally includes his reason for talking about this subject. Developmental episodes form the body of the talk. In a talk about a fish and its mating ritual, we can expect this main body to be a sequenced account of the mating process. The obligatory closing episode reminds the listener of why the topic is being talked about, and of specific ideas that the speaker wants the listener to remember. Although the discourse about the stickleback fish is brief, when analyzed within this framework of episodes, it is a typical lecture, as American society conventionally recognizes a lecture.

There are eight episodes in the stickleback fish talk. The first two episodes form the obligatory focal episode and an optional focal episode, which together introduce the speaker and explain why he is talking. In the first episode, the speaker gives his name, the subject of his talk, and introduces the sign that he will use to refer to a particular species of fish throughout the rest of his talk. The second episode narrows the focus to the uniqueness of the mating ritual of this particular species, the stickleback fish.

The next five episodes form the obligatory developmental episode and four optional developmental episodes. These five episodes are chronologically developed and explain and describe the mating process of this fish. Each succeeding episode develops the topic of the mating process, but the focus of each of these episodes is slightly different. For example, in the first of the five episodes, the speaker explains the normal behavior of the fish and then describes the conditions under which the behavior changes and the mating ritual begins. The second episode contrasts how the males separate from the females and undergo a color change signaling the onset of the mating process. The third episode describes the nest-building activities of the male; the fourth episode explains how the male guards the nest and lures the female to the nest; the fifth and final episode relates the egg-laying process.

The final, closing episode is separate from the preceding five episodes because it is here that the speaker reminds the listeners of the purpose of the talk, that is, that this fish is the focus of scientific study because of its unusual characteristics during mating. He then describes the two characteristics that make this fish and this ritual unusual, which are that the underside of the male changes to red, and that the female swims vertically toward the male rather than horizontally. This last episode is not dependent upon real-time or chronological development. Rather, it provides the specific points the speaker wants to make in closing his talk. The following outline of the lecture reflects the sequencing of the episodes and the larger chunks of talk that they form:

Topic: The Mating Ritual of the Stickleback Fish

Episode 1  
Episode 2  } Focal (or introductory) episodes

Episode 3 ⎤
Episode 4 ⎥
Episode 5 ⎬ Developmental (or main body) episodes
Episode 6 ⎥
Episode 7 ⎦

Episode 8    Closing episode

The analysis thus far shows that the organization of the content can be seen as a lecture format with topic development. But this is not the only assessment we can make to determine what constitutes a lecture. Lecture content is structured not only through the content of its propositions but also through textual features that reflect transition boundaries between episodes and link the episodes together. The suggestion is thus that lecturing is not static in form but is also a process whereby the speaker makes available to listeners features that show the continuity and relationship between subtopics or episodes.

## *Markers That Divide the Text into Episodes*

Serial episodes in texts are linked together by features that can be single or phrasal lexical elements. These discrete grammatical elements serve to segment the message content into idea or informational units by marking the transition into an episode. Speakers use these markers, albeit unconsciously, to show the progression of a cumulative series of subordinate and related subtopics. The term "discourse marker" is used, following Schiffrin (1986), to talk about these elements that serve to highlight the boundaries of contiguous ideas so that hearers can appropriately interpret the continuous flow of information in discourse. In the fish lecture, episodes are closed off with markers that are identifiable on the basis of such factors as the markers' lack of message content and the intuitions of native speakers. The category of discourse markers includes head nods and the signs OK and ANYWAY. These particular markers are not examined here. Instead, the focus is on two markers that are used to begin episodes and shift the listeners' attention to a different, yet related, subtopic: (1) the lexical sign NOW, produced simultaneously by both hands (see Fig. 1) and (2) NOW-THAT, which consists of the lexical sign THAT produced on the left hand the lexical sign NOW produced on the right hand (see Fig. 2).

### NOW as a Discourse Marker

The sign NOW, which is consistently signed with both hands, appears eleven times in the text. This sign is generally understood as an indicator of present time in ongoing discourse, and on some occurrences in the text, the sign functions in this way. On other occasions, however, the sign func-

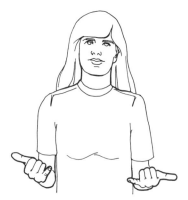

**Fig. 1**   ASL NOW.

tions as a discourse marker, marking a shift into a new subtopic as well as calling attention to what is coming up next in the text. To be sure, it is not always easy to discern in which of the two ways a particular token of NOW is functioning. There are, however, some distributional and formal criteria that distinguish the two uses. The discourse-marker form of NOW is a sign that occurs in an utterance-initial position and can co-occur with topic marking. This discourse-marker form of NOW occurs five times in the data corpus. Three of those occurrences exhibit no final hold in sign articulation, and the other two show only a final hold on the weak hand; the strong hand has no final hold and continues toward the next sign. Also, with some occurrences of this form, there are long pauses before the sign is articu-

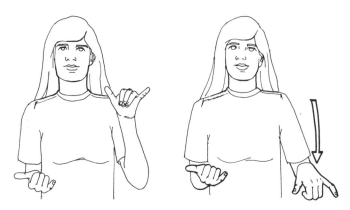

**Fig. 2**   ASL NOW-THAT.

lated, and, in one instance, there is a body shift to the right.[1] The following are some examples of the discourse-marker form and function of NOW that occur in the text:[2]

$$\overline{\qquad\qquad}^{\,t}$$
NOW CL: fish FISH  PRO3 TRUE STRANGE PRO3
'Now, as for the fish, it is truely unique, it is'

$$\underline{\qquad\quad\text{body shift}}$$
NOW  MALE WILL (point to chest) RED BEGIN LOOK-FOR ON
'Now when the male changes (point to chest) to red, (he) begins to search on'

$$\overline{\qquad\qquad}^{\,t}$$
NOW MALE FISH SELF VERY JEALOUS
'Now, as for the male fish, (he) is very jealous'

The temporal form of NOW is also a simultaneous two-hand sign that can occur in utterance-initial position but does not occur with topic marking. This form consistently displays a final hold on both hands and is not accompanied by prior pauses or body shifts:

FISH DECIDE BEGIN NOW BREED
'The fish decide to begin breeding now'

---

[1]I have closely observed two other speakers using NOW. One is a native Deaf speaker and one is a nonnative Deaf speaker. Both speakers use NOW as a discourse marker but formally articulate the sign in ways that are different from the one used by the speaker in this research. This observation calls for the study of such discourse markers across many speakers.

[2]Because ASL has no written system, labels in English are used to represent signed units. The reader should be aware that these gloss-labels are problematic in that they do not allow for all the visual information that might be present to be represented nor has ASL been fully described. For example, the label PRO3 represents a 3rd person pronoun. But this sign has not been fully explored. Thus, at times, it represents a 3rd person pronoun but at other times seems to be working as a determiner.

The translations or full English glosses that are provided are modified literal translations. That is, they are translated as close to literal as possible, yet understandable to a speaker of English, in an attempt to represent, in English, all of the information in the ASL utterance and to show the order in which that information appears in the ASL utterance.

In addition, I translate the sign NOW in ASL as 'now' in English because it is traditionally translated this way, although others could be used. The reader should keep in mind that *now* in English is spoken differently depending on its use as a temporal or discourse marker.

In the sample discourse segments presented in this chapter, the following transcription conventions are used: ASL signs are indicated by upper-case gloss-labels, followed by a fuller English gloss of each segment within single quotation marks. Hyphenated single letter sequences in upper-case indicate fingerspelling. Each + indicates one repetition of the sign immediately preceding it. Parenthetical notations provide additional description of ongoing linguistic events, for example, the occurrence of gestural deictics. Overscoring of the line of signs indicates the co-occurrence of either topic marking (t), body shift, or head nod (hd nd).

NOW FISH LOOK-FOR WOOD THIN NARROW PIECES GREEN PLANT DIFFERENT
'Now the fish search for sticks, thin narrow pieces, green plants, many different things'

NOW ME READY FOR LOOK-FOR PRO3 FISH PRO3 FEMALE
'Now I'm ready to look for it, it's a fish, it's a female'

As these examples reflect, there is variety in the formal articulation of NOW when used as a discourse marker and sameness in the formal articulation when used as a temporal marker, but this sample of language behavior is not sufficient to argue that form alone accounts for the difference in meaning or function.

How, then, can the discourse marker and the temporal marker be differentiated? Another possibility for identifying NOW as either a temporal marker or a discourse marker is to examine its meaning when influenced by discourse context (Schiffrin, 1987). That is, by examining contextual factors, such as the lecture in progress and the surrounding utterances, we can decide if the meaning is temporal or related to the discourse. Indeed, the distinction can even be contextually neutralized: if NOW occurs at a point of topic development that allows a temporal reading, it is not always possible on formal or distributional grounds to assign it an interpretation as either temporal or discourse-related. This particular discourse has five episodes describing biological events that must be related in chronological order. In this discourse, the real-time events of the main body episodes are matched by the speaking time relationship between the utterances themselves. Thus, the distinction between NOW meaning 'present time' and NOW marking discourse can be difficult to discern.

We can examine the meaning of NOW in discourse context by substituting its occurrence with a paraphrase. If we substitute occurrences of NOW in an utterance that contains a time meaning and in an utterance that contains a discourse meaning, we can see which meaning fits the context. That is not to say that there will not be moments when NOW is ambiguous in its meaning. Consider the following examples:

——————————————— t

1. NOW   CL:fish   FISH   PRO3 TRUE STRANGE PRO3
   'Now, as for the fish, it is truly unique, it is'

——————————————— t

   *a.* *TODAY CL:fish FISH PRO3 TRUE STRANGE PRO3[3]
   'Today, as for the fish, it is truly unique, it is'

————————————————————— t

   *b.* ON-TO-THE-NEXT-PART CL:fish FISH PRO3 TRUE STRANGE PRO3
   'On to the next part, as for the fish, it is truly unique, it is'

---

[3]The articulated form of NOW in this utterance entails Movement-Hold. The articulated form of TODAY entails Movement-Movement-Movement-Hold. Thus, these are two different lexical items.

2. FISH DECIDE BEGIN NOW BREED
   'The fish decide to begin breeding now'

   *a.* FISH DECIDE BEGIN GO-AHEAD BREED
   'The fish decide to begin breeding, start ahead'

   *b.* *FISH DECIDE BEGIN ON-TO-THE-NEXT-PART BREED
   'The fish decide to begin breeding on to the next part'

In utterance 1*a,* the sign TODAY is substituted for the discourse marker NOW, and the result is an ungrammatical utterance. But in utterance 1*b,* ON-TO-THE-NEXT-PART is substituted for NOW, and the result is acceptable. Similarly, in sentence 2*a,* when the sign GO-AHEAD is substituted for the temporal marker NOW, the result is an acceptable utterance. But in sentence 2*b,* ON-TO-THE-NEXT-PART is substituted for NOW, and the result is unacceptable. These paraphrases are a way of confirming (or possibly rejecting) intuitions about the meaning attributed to the same lexical item, NOW.

A third and final confirmation of the existence of a temporal use of NOW and a discourse use of NOW came about by asking native speakers to view the videotape. The first step was to view the lecture in its entirety. Then the tape was viewed a second time. During this second viewing, each informant was asked to stop the tape whenever they sensed that the speaker changed or shifted to new focus. All three informants consistently stopped the tape at the junctures where the discourse form of NOW appears and indicated that the speaker was getting ready to talk about something different. Sometimes they identified NOW as signaling the shift; sometimes they identified a closing marker; and sometimes they sensed a shift that they explained by referring to the content of the text itself. Once consistent judgments were obtained about episode shifts marked by NOW, the form was further examined to ascertain the range of its distribution and function.

### The Function of NOW as a Discourse Marker

The textual distribution of NOW provides a basis for ascertaining its discourse function by building on observations about its form and use. As noted earlier, the speaker's introduction consists of two episodes. In the first episode, the speaker says his name, the name of the fish, and how he will refer to the fish. The second episode explains that this fish is unusual and that scientists have been studying its mating habits for a long time. These two episodes are both introductory in nature and thus can be grouped together. NOW appears at the beginning of the first utterance of the second episode and signals a shift from the first episode to the second episode, that is, a shift to continuing and related introductory talk. It is significant that the first token of NOW co-occurs with the marking for topic:

<pre>
                       t
_____
NOW  CL: fish FISH PRO3 TRUE STRANGE PRO3
</pre>
'Now, as for the fish, it is truly unique, it is'

Not only does NOW introduce the second episode, but if its meaning were that of present time (TODAY), it would be nonsense. Also, the temporal marker does not co-occur with topic marking anywhere in the text.

The following segments are the first three episodes of the text, transcribed in their entirety so that NOW as a discourse marker, and as a temporal marker, can be clearly seen in its actual contexts of use:

Episode 1

HELLO ME NAME B-O-B A-L-C-O-R-N
'Hello my name is Bob Alcorn'

ME HERE TALK-ABOUT CL-fish
'And I'm here to talk about a fish'

PRO3 NAME S-T-I-C-K-L-E-B-A-C-K FISH
'It's called the stickleback fish'

CALL ABBREVIATE (discourse marker) OK
'Referring to it in this shortened form, so, Ok"


Episode 2

$$\overline{\hspace{4.5cm}}^{\,t}$$

NOW CL:fish FISH  PRO3 TRUE STRANGE PRO3
'Now, as for the fish, it is truly unique, it is'

SCIENCE-AGENT UP-TIL-NOW STUDY MANY YEARS
'Scientists have been studying it for many years'

POSS BEHAVE TRUE STRANGE HOW BREED HOW
'Its behavior is truly unique as to how it breeds'

STUDY MANY YEAR ANYWAY
'It's been studied for many years, anyway'


Episode 3

$$\underline{\hspace{2cm}}^{\,t\ \ \text{hd}\ \text{nd}}$$

NOW-THAT   PRO3 FISH TRUE STRANGE
'Now, the one I'm talking about, (it's a fish) is truly unique'

PRO3 ALWAYS GROUP-TRAVEL-FORWARD
'It always travels in groups'

WITH  MANY  LARGE-GROUP-COME-TOGETHER  GROUP-TRAVELING-FORWARD
'With many fish, (they) come together as a large group and swim forward'

BUT TIME FEEL SPRING CHANGE WARM FEEL
'But there comes a time and a feeling, it's spring, there's a change and a warmness, and the fish feel it'

FISH DECIDE BEGIN NOW BREED
'The fish decide to begin breeding now'
NOW WILL BEGIN LINES-OF-FISH-MOVING-FORWARD SEPARATE
'Now they will begin, from the lines of fish swimming forward, to separate'

NOW is not used to open the first episode nor is it used to open the third episode. NOW initially occurs at the beginning of the second part of the introduction. This is the only instance of use as a discourse marker in the first three episodes of the text. It is only in the developmental episodes that the form is again used in this capacity.

The next five episodes, as the developmental episodes, constitute the main body of the talk. This group of episodes contains the most content, has an orderly progression of events, and constitutes a straightforward exposition of the details. NOW does not occur at the shift between the introductory episodes and the developmental episodes but does occur at each utterance initial position in the four succeeding episodes within the main body. This repetitive pattern suggests that one function of NOW is to make explicit the ideational progress through these episodes by focusing attention on what the speaker is about to say in relation to what he has just said. Thus, the distribution of NOW in this particular text is a property of its function of marking shifts. That is, its repeated use between related sub-topics emphasizes the forward progression of related episodes in the emerging discourse. With these markers, the speaker maintains the listener's attention to the text and the forward progress through this group of episodes.[4] The following diagram presents a recasting of the earlier-presented outline of text episodes to illustrate the distributional pattern of NOW as a discourse marker.

$$\left.\begin{array}{l}\text{Episode 1}\\\text{NOW Episode 2}\end{array}\right\}\text{ Focal (or introductory) episodes}$$

$$\left.\begin{array}{l}\text{Episode 3}\\\text{NOW Episode 4}\\\text{NOW Episode 5}\\\text{NOW Episode 6}\\\text{NOW Episode 7}\end{array}\right\downarrow\text{ Developmental (or main body) episodes}$$

Episode 8    Closing episode

One way in which the relationship between language and context is reflected in the structure of languages is through deixis. This term indicates a pointing or indexical property of a lexical item and is exemplified

---

[4]I am not suggesting that NOW works alone at these shifts; undoubtedly there are a number of cues, manual and nonmanual, working together (see, for example, Baker, 1976).

through the use of pronouns, tense, and time and place adverbs. Deixis is a way languages grammaticalize features that indicate the context of an utterance. For example, the pronoun *this* in English does not name or refer to any particular entity in all of its uses; rather, it is a place-holder for some particular entity given by the context, as in "bring me a stick about *this* big." Levinson (1983, p. 88) explains discourse deictics as forms serving to indicate "often in very complex ways, just how the utterance that contains them is a response to, or a continuation of, some portion of the prior discourse."

The two uses of NOW discussed here are related to its deitic meaning. Schiffrin (1987) has shown that, in English conversational data, markers which have a deictic meaning make use of such meaning. She found that in discourse use the temporal meaning is internal to the utterances in the discourse itself. In ASL the discourse marker NOW also makes use of this deictic meaning by providing a temporal index to the group of utterances of an episode within the emerging lecture. This adds to the complexity in the use of NOW. When discourse time mirrors event time, i.e., the male fish makes the nest before he protects it, then NOW not only reflects the speaker's focus on the next episode (or discourse time), but also on a new event within the description of the mating process. As Schiffrin observes, this neutralizes the distinction between a temporal use and the discourse use through the structure of the discourse. The temporal only use of NOW establishes a reference time for a content-filled utterance in relation to the real-world event sequence, such as the biological process of mating. In its use as a discourse marker, NOW makes use of the temporal sense to indicate the progression of discourse time while also indicating that the information of the next episode is one more step forward in the real-world mating process.

It remains to be seen if these observations will retain validity across longer texts with different topics. Lectures and workshop talks by native and nonnative Deaf speakers alike have been observed by the researcher, and the use of NOW as a discourse marker seems a fairly common occurrence. For example, one native speaker signed NOW as she discussed a list of qualities defining a professional, using NOW to separate the items on the list. Overall, further study is needed to substantiate the claims made here. The present analysis shows that NOW occurs and functions as a discourse marker by shifting the listener's attention to a new section of the discourse and by maintaining the progression through an episode group.

## NOW-THAT as a Discourse Marker

The sign NOW-THAT occurs at the initial utterance of the episode that begins episode groups. Each time a shift is made into a group of episodes, the marker is not NOW but NOW-THAT. As explained earlier, NOW-THAT is formed by NOW on the right hand and THAT on the left hand. It is used to separate the introductory episode group from the developmental (or main body) episode group, and the developmental episode group from the closing episode. The following diagram will illustrate the distribution of NOW and NOW-THAT:

NOW
Episode 1
Episode 2 } Focal (or introductory) episodes

NOW-THAT Episode 3
NOW          Episode 4
NOW          Episode 5      Developmental (or main body) episodes
NOW          Episode 6
NOW          Episode 7

NOW-THAT Episode 8      Closing episode

As explained earlier, internal episodes in a group are linked by NOW. The third episode (the beginning episode of the developmental group) begins with NOW-THAT. When the speaker finishes with the final episode of the main body, the beginning of the first utterance of the closing episode is NOW-THAT.

### The Form and Function of NOW-THAT

This marker occurs at the utterance-initial position. Liddell (1980) describes the forms of three tokens of THAT that had all previously been considered the same sign. One form of THAT—Liddell's (1980, p. 150) THATc—begins with a backward motion and ends with a hold that separates it from the other forms and means 'that's the one I'm talking about'. In the fish text, it is the form THATc which occurs. Both tokens of NOW-THAT co-occur with topic marking, with the articulation of NOW slightly preceding the articulation of THAT.

The first NOW-THAT occurs at the beginning of the third episode and the second NOW-THAT occurs at the beginning the eighth episode. That is, NOW-THAT occurs at the beginning of the main body episode group, and at the beginning of the third group, the closing. The discourse context reveals an even more interesting feature: the content of the utterances at the beginning of both the third and eighth episodes corefers with the first utterance of the second episode; that is, all three utterances are remarkably similar in form and content. These three utterances are the following:

Beginning of episode 2 (introductory group)

                    t
NOW CL:Fish FISH   PRO3 TRUE STRANGE PRO3
'Now, as for the fish, it is truly unique, it is'

Beginning of the main body episodes

_____t  hd  nd_____
NOW-THAT PRO3 FISH TRUE STRANGE
'Now, the one I'm talking about, it (it's a fish) is truly unique'

Beginning of the closing episode group

_____t_____
NOW-THAT SCIENCE-AGENT STUDY TRUE STRANGE
'Now, the one I'm talking about, as for the scientists, (they) have been studying it, it is truly unique'

If THAT means 'that's the one I'm talking about', then there must be a segment of previous discourse that identifies 'one'. Antecedents do not occur only in the immediately prior discourse, nor do antecedents have to be single lexical items. They can occur further back in the discourse and constitute portions of the discourse (Halliday & Hasan, 1976). In the prior three examples, the use of THAT at the beginning of the main body episodes looks back to episode 1 but also gathers in portions of episode 2. The use of THAT at the beginning of the closing episode looks back not only to the beginning of the main body episodes but also to episode 2, thus requiring the listener to keep in mind all that they have heard so far. The utterance that begins the main body episodes simultaneously looks forward with the use of NOW and looks backward at the prior episode with the use of THAT. The utterance that begins the closing episode simultaneously looks forward and backward, not only to the five episodes before but also even further back to the introduction, to remind the listener of why the speaker is talking about the fish. The repetition embedded in these NOW-THAT utterances provides evidence that this marker is pointing to prior discourse and establishing relevance to the upcoming discussion. This repetition is also typical of how lectures continually remind their audience of their main focus.

In its discourse use, THAT retains the meaning of 'that's the one I'm talking about' because it refers to the fish but also makes use of its deictic property, to look backward to prior discourse. Thus, two forms, NOW-THAT, function together to mark a shift to a slightly different focus but also to remind listeners of what has gone before in the discourse.

## DISCOURSE MARKERS

This analysis follows Schiffrin (1986), who has analyzed several discourse markers in English, including *now*. Her data is a large corpus of conversational interaction from Philadelphia neighborhoods in the 1970s. She points out that, on occasions, the difference between the discourse marker *now* and the adverb *now* is difficult to determine. Three ways to assess the status of *now* in English are through finding co-occurrence violations (e.g., *now then*), which is allowable for one category (discourse marker) and not the other (adverb), through discourse context, or through prosodic features. For example, the utterances "now then, what's next on the schedule?" and "now now" (as an expression of comfort) constitute co-occurrence violations for the adverbial use of *now*. Discourse context, on the other hand, can either distinguish between the categories or be ambiguous if the topic itself has a temporal sequence. For example, if a comparison is being made between "back then" and "now," *now* can be ambiguous as to whether a new topic is being introduced or *now* means something like 'nowdays'. Finally, Schiffrin discovered that *now* as a discourse marker receives no stress but receives intonational marking that signals 'more to come'.

For the discourse functions of *now,* Schiffrin explains how *now* functions on different discourse planes in conversational English. First, in comparisons and opinions, *now* shows "the speaker's progression through a discourse which contains an ordered sequence of subordinate parts" (Schiffrin, 1986, p. 240). On another level of discourse organization, *now* marks when the speaker is shifting orientation, that is, makes explicit the stance that the speaker is taking toward what is being said. In addition, she discusses the impact of deictic meaning on the uses and functions of *now.*

In the fish text, other discourse markers are at work, such as OK, ANYWAY, and KNOW. It is obvious that a rich system of discourse markers exists in ASL and that further study will reveal some similarities to the functions of discourse markers found in spoken languages. It is also obvious that this is not the same system that exists in English, in that English has no marker known as NOW-THAT or ON-TO-THE-NEXT-PART.

## CONSTRUCTED DIALOGUE IN AN ASL LECTURE

Talks that are descriptions of knowledge and that impart information are generally expected to provide a presentation of known facts, to be organized in a predictable way, and thus to be more content-oriented. The content and the structure of organization, however, do not provide a sufficient explanation as to why a speech is "good" or "interesting," since well-organized, content-filled lectures can be quite dull. There is a third criterion that makes a lecture vivid and interesting.

It is a sociolinguistic assumption that strategies and devices typical of ordinary conversation and elements of good storytelling are used to create impressions of vividness and interpersonal involvement (Chafe, 1982; Labov, 1972; Schiffrin, 1981; Tannen, 1982). One such device is reported speech. Reported speech is one of a range of features that makes a lecture vivid and involving. The use of reported speech in a lecture is a strategy that creates interest in the content and seeks to involve the audience in making sense of information.

Tannen (1986) introduces the term "constructed dialogue" to replace "reported speech," a term used when speech is represented as first-person dialogue. She argues that lines of dialogue in conversation, owing to characteristics of human memory, are probably not exactly the same as those that were actually spoken. Thus, the lines of speech are not actually reported verbatim but rather are constructed by speakers based on real people and events. Further evidence for the notion that dialogue is constructed is based on the fact that some lines of dialogue in stories are the thoughts of the participants in the stories, or are interjected by listeners.

Further support for Tannen's notion that reported speech is more appropriately termed "constructed dialogue" is found in ASL discourse. Constructed dialogue can occur between hypothetical persons or animals. It can also occur as anthropomorphically attributed speech, instances of which occur in the fish text examined here.[5] To term this hypothetical dialogue "reported speech" or "direct address" is odd, to say the least.

Lines of dialogue can also appear in lectures, as a type of discourse event. Pufahl (1984, p. 3) shows that constructed dialogue in a technical lecture in English about chemical compounds is "by and large different from the one found in narratives." Most of the dialogue that she examined is used to verbalize possible hearer questions or responses to information, such as "and you say, 'this looks like a mess.' " She suggests that these dialogue lines are strategies used by speakers to create interesting lectures. They serve the function of making lectures interesting or vivid.

Constructed dialogue in the present ASL lecture appears both as utterances that a fish (purportedly) is saying to other fish and as thoughts that a fish (purportedly) is thinking. One occurrence of dialogue is introduced by the speech-framing device SAY and one another occurrence is introduced by WARN. But eight instances of dialogue have no such lexical introducer. The following are examples of constructed dialogue in the fish lecture:

THAT RED FISH WARN NOW ME READY FOR LOOK-FOR PRO3 FISH FEMALE
'That redness is the fish warning "Now I'm ready to look for it, it's a fish, it's a female" '

BEGIN FLIRT KNOW FISH (manual wiggle in water) FEMALE (shift to right, eye-gaze to left) FINE (with fingers wiggling)
'(He) begins to flirt, you know, the fish "dances" and the female (says) "How fine!" '

---

[5]There is anecdotal evidence that this dialogue also occurs between objects and concepts.

FISH (in holding position in front of nest) CHERISH MINE MINE PROTECT
'The fish is guarding the nest "I cherish this, it is mine, it is mine, and I'll protect it"'

HOME PROTECT GET-AWAY GET-AWAY
'It protects its home "get-away, get-away"'

FOLLOW SAY COME-HERE
'(The female) will follow, (the male) says "come here"'

The constructed dialogue in this ASL lecture is different from the dialogue found in ASL narratives. In ASL narratives, there is an exchange of dialogue between speakers, the content of the utterances is longer with more repetition than that in lectures, and there is simply more dialogue.[6] As might be expected in a scientific, content-filled talk, the dialogue in the fish lecture is brief and generally consists of only one or two manual signs accompanied by nonmanual signals. The one exception is a complete utterance spoken by the male fish. There is no actual exchange of talk between the fish. In this lecture, with or without co-occurring, signed introducers such as SAY, the dialogue is marked by ordinary ASL nonmanual markers of constructed dialogue: a difference in head orientation, whereby the head is turned and sometimes also tilted, and a change in eye-gaze.[7]

All of the dialogue in the lecture is attributed to the fish, and all of the utterances are human-like expressions of thoughts or feelings. Evidence that the dialogue can be attributed to the fish is found in (1) the use of the imperative GET-AWAY, which implies an underlying *you,* clearly directed toward the other fish and not the speaker or the audience and (2) the use of the possessive MINE, which is said by the male fish and not the speaker himself.[8]

Clearly there is more work to be done in describing constructed dialogue, but the purpose of this chapter is to discuss the function of dialogue in making the lecture vivid and interesting. The following example demonstrates this point: the male fish is focused on a particular female, the female notices and says FINE (with fingers wiggling). Accompanying this sign is a facial expression reminiscent of a Mae West impression, that is, repeated raising of the eyebrows. A good literal translation might be, 'ooh, I like this', or 'this feels good'. Note that this segment of talk is not informative nor is it content-oriented. Therefore, it must be there to serve another function. Indeed, the segment appears to serve a dual purpose. One purpose is to make the talk vivid and interesting; another purpose is to create an analogous scene through which the information can be under-

---

[6]These features of ASL narratives are suggested by Liddell (1980) and Baker (1983) and also based on observations of the researcher.

[7]Scott Liddell directed my attention to such markers based on his work (1980).

[8]I thank Ceil Lucas for pointing out this evidence to me.

stood more completely. In effect, these are one and the same function, an interactive, communicative function.

To confirm this interpretation, deaf people ranging in age from eighteen to forty were asked to evaluate this speaker. It was a unanimous judgment that the ASL speaker was "good," and many of these speakers said that the talk itself was "clear, fascinating, and interesting."

This use of constructed dialogue, which, in turn, creates visual scenes or pictures, seems to be representative of a style of information noticed by the researcher in lectures by other deaf speakers and in classrooms with deaf teachers. A discourse style that makes the attempt to associate the world that is being talked about with another world, by having listeners make a lateral jump from the topic at hand to a set of terms in which the information can be seen differently, is analogical in nature. In presentations of analogies, the relationship between the two concepts is not always made explicit and is not always a "logical" one, in the Western sense of the word. That is, the fish in the talk are not really similar to a boy and a girl flirting. Rather, the listener is invited to imagine the idea of flirtatious behavior so as to understand the mating ritual of fish.

This creation of scenes through dialogue is a powerful way to present facts and involve the audience in making sense of a phenomenon. Johnstone (1986), in studying persuasive arguments in Arabic, terms these arguments, which are rich with stories and analogies, "analogic persuasion." One persuades another not through logical arguments built from facts but through the beauty and vividness of stories and analogies. Thus the use of a constructed dialogue strategy in this ASL lecture (and others) represents a type of presentation of information in ASL that might be termed an "analogic style." Since people understand and internalize information through the vividness of familiar and shared experiences, the analogic style suggests that listening to and understanding users of ASL is an exercise in cross-cultural communication, and that speakers of a visual language understand and learn about the world differently.

It must be noted, however, that analogic styles are certainly available to speakers of many languages, including English. Consequently, one cannot explain the use of these styles simply by reference to cultural determinism. Rather, the use of this style, or any other, is the result of a particular interaction, a particular context, and a particular audience, in conjunction with cultural predispositions (Johnstone, 1986). That is, users of ASL might choose to use this strategy within particular interactions, whereas speakers of English, for example, might choose to use the same strategy in a different context. Thus, both might find their expectations for a particular interaction in conflict.

## A FINAL POINT ABOUT NOW

Having discussed the phenomenon of constructed dialogue, the occurrence of NOW in dialogue warrants some attention. Some tokens of NOW can easily be assigned to a particular functional category on the basis of their appearance in discourse strategies. In the following ASL segments from episodes 4 and 5, NOW appears first as a discourse marker under a topic marking with FEMALE. Within the episode, it appears again in utterance-initial position, but in this instance is part of an utterance that is actually the dialogue of the fish.

Episode 4

$$\overline{\hspace{2cm}}^{\,t}$$

NOW FEMALE WILL LINES-OF-FISH-MOVING FORWARD GROUP-SWIM-TOGETHER
'Now, as for the female, (they) will, from swimming as a school, form their own group and continue swimming'

      ⋮ (intervening discourse segments)

THAT RED FISH WARN NOW ME READY FOR LOOK-FOR PRO3 FISH PRO3 FEMALE
'That redness is the fish warning, "Now I'm ready to look for it, it's a fish, it's a female"'

Episode 5

$$\overline{\hspace{1.2cm}}^{\,\text{bodyshift}}$$
NOW  MALE WILL (point to chest) RED BEGIN LOOK-FOR ON
'Now when the male changes (indicating the chest) to red, (he) begins to search on'
WATER-MOVING (movement) WATER (point down) GROUND LOOK-FOR GOOD
ROCK (classifer) SCADS-OF FINE++
'Make movements in the water and go down to the floor looking for good rocks, small, round rocks, lots of them and (say) "fine"'

The missing utterances between the two segments of episode 4 are about the male fish separating from the group and swimming alone while his chest area begins to turn red. After it turns red, the male fish is ready to seek a female. Thus, NOW in the second segment of episode 4 has a temporal meaning as seeking a female is the next temporal sequence in the process of mating. NOW occurs as part of the constructed dialogue of the fish.

In the next episode, there occurs a brief repetition of information from the prior episode (the male's chest turns red as a warning that he is ready to look for a mate), and the speaker uses the repetition to introduce the topic of the fish looking for the right place to build a nest. The underside of the male fish cannot turn red twice; it has already been established that the chest turns red. This kind of repetition often occurs in utterances that open new episodes. There is an expectation of a marker to introduce a new focus while reminding the listener of what he already knows. Thus, NOW in the first utterance of episode 5 marks a shift to a new point even though known information is said next. Finally, it is noteworthy that NOW as a discourse marker never appears in constructed dialogue in this text.

## *SUMMARY*

This chapter examines a lecture produced by a user of ASL who is considered to be a good lecturer. The episodic development of the text is illustrated, and two discourse markers that contribute to the structural flow or organization of the lecture are described. The combination of episode development and discourse markers are only two of the factors that constitute this text as a lecture. In addition, constructed dialogue is discussed as a feature of lecture style in ASL that contributes to the impression of vividness in this lecture.

These findings barely scratch the surface of the complex nature of discourse in ASL. They do, however, provide ample evidence that discourse structure in ASL is a rich, undiscovered system. It is hoped that these preliminary findings stimulate further studies of discourse structure in ASL.

Schiffrin (1986) demonstrates that the analysis of discourse markers in English led to the construction of a theory of discourse coherence. As she points out, such work in other languages determines what linguistic resources are drawn upon for use as markers and how such determinations clarify discourse components and their interaction. Studying devices such as constructed dialogue and other stylistic strategies at work in all genres of discourse also builds an understanding of coherence, not only in discourse, but in the lives of the people who use a visual language. Understanding the basis of coherence in talk is understanding the intricacies of human interaction.

In addition, knowledge about how content-oriented discourse is structured in ASL will lead to questions such as how and when children learn to incorporate markers, how and when second language learners should learn these markers, and how interpreters incorporate them into the discourse flow. The answers to such questions have clear implications for communication in deaf education, second language instruction of ASL, and interpreter education. That is, in addition to being of theoretical interest, such answers have practical applications as well.

## *ACKNOWLEDGMENTS*

I would like to thank Robert E. Johnson for originally encouraging this research, for hours spent discussing it, and for reading this chapter. I would also like to thank Scott Liddell for his insightful comments and questions, and Elizabeth Nowell for endless discussions of the data and ideas presented here. I also want to thank Bob Alcorn for a few brief minutes in time doing something that has become very important.

# 12

## Toward a Description of Register Variation in American Sign Language

June Zimmer

## INTRODUCTION

In this chapter, register variation in American Sign Language (ASL) is examined. Register variation, sometimes referred to as style variation, involves differential language use that is sensitive to situational factors. It is generally accepted that speakers use language differently in different situations, and several models have been put forward that attempt to describe the situational dynamics that control register variation. Other than several seminal studies by Ferguson, which describe features found in specific registers such as baby talk (Ferguson, 1978), foreigner talk (Ferguson, 1982), and sports announcer talk (Ferguson, 1983), there are few empirical studies of register variation in particular languages.

Much of the discussion of register variation among deaf Americans centers on the notion of diglossia. In these models, signed English is seen as the "high" variety (used in formal situations, such as an academic conference) and ASL is seen as the "low" variety (used in more informal situations, such as casual talk among friends). Some scholars have noted special features within ASL that are sensitive to situational changes, but no truly empirical study of these differences has yet been made.

What follows is a study of register variation in ASL. The data for this study come from videotaped recordings of a native user of ASL. He was taped in three different situations: a formal lecture in an academic setting, an informal talk, and a television interview. Portions of these tapes were

THE SOCIOLINGUISTICS OF THE DEAF COMMUNITY
Copyright © 1989 by Academic Press Inc.
All rights of reproduction in any form reserved.

transcribed and compared to discover differential language use. While the findings are only preliminary, they do support the notion that language users in general, and users of ASL in particular, vary their language according to the situation of use.

## *SITUATIONAL VARIATION IN LANGUAGE*

Halliday (1968) distinguishes register variation, which he describes as "variation according to use," from dialect variation, described as "variation according to user." Whereas dialect is seen as a function of who the speaker is in terms of social identity, which determines what dialect the speaker habitually speaks, register is seen as a function of what the speaker is doing in terms of social activity, which determines how the speaker will speak in a particular situation. Some clear cases of special registers can be found in "restricted languages" (e.g., pilot radio talk or the sign language used by skin divers).

The models of language variation advanced thus far discuss register in terms of socially constituted and recognized conventions of language use. These conventions are determined by the social structures that obtain in a "speech community." Gumperz (1972, p. 220) describes a speech community as "any aggregate characterized by regular and frequent interaction by means of a shared body of verbal signs and set off from similar aggregates by significant differences in language use." This definition does not preclude the possibility that any individual can be a member of several different speech communities and applies readily in multilingual communities where an individual can control several different languages. It is also possible for separate speech communities to share the same "language," as illustrated by the different national varieties of English existing in many places in the world (Kachru, 1983). Within one national variety, speech communities can be divided according to dialect. Speakers of a "nonstandard" dialect can control both their native dialect and the national standard. An individual speaker controls a range of language variation that can be thought of as his or her "linguistic repertoire" (J. Fishman, 1972). The repertoire of a speaker can include separate languages and dialects, different subgroup and occupational varieties, and, within each of these, a range of variation according to register.

Culture is an important factor in determining the characteristics of a speaker's repertoire. Each culture and subculture defines the speech styles that are relevant to it (Hymes, 1974). Any competent member of the community has access to the conventions operative in certain speech situations. Each speaker is also involved in a range of speech networks, and those with a more extensive system of networks control a more varied linguistic range (J. Fishman, 1972).

# MODELS OF REGISTER VARIATION

Register variation involves the relative level of formality or informality called for, and used by, a speaker in a particular situation. Joos (1968) posits a "finite" number of "styles" and proposes five in particular. The least formal level, called "intimate," is described as the level used among people who know each other very well and who interact on a regular basis. It is characterized by heavy use of ellipsis (especially of phonological segments and certain lexical items such as articles, subject pronouns, etc.) and private language, the meaning of which is known only to the interactants. The next level is dubbed "casual." This style shares many of the features of intimate style, without such a heavy reliance on private language. The third level, "consultative," is the style used in everyday conversation between speakers who are strangers or do not know each other well. It is still characterized by some ellipsis and a use of colloquial speech. But in consultative style, there is an emphasis on making speech as clear and unambiguous as possible. The fourth level Joos calls "formal." He says that the most important function of speech at this level is to impart information, and that the talk does not have a great deal of "social importance" (Joos here seems to equate "social" with interactive). The fifth level Joos calls "frozen," and he says it is characterized by language that is formulaic. This is exemplified by much of the language used in religious services and in the courtroom.

Other writers avoid talking about registers as discrete varieties. Instead, they posit the existence of contextual factors that help to determine a range of language use that will be appropriate or acceptable in any given situation. Crystal and Davey (1969) mention three categories of features that in part determine the type of utterance conventionally prescribed in a particular situation. "Province" features relate an utterance to extra-linguistic factors (e.g., an occupational or professional setting in which speech takes place). "Status" features take into account the participants and their social standing vis à vis one another. "Modality" features concern the purpose(s) served by an utterance. The authors believe that these features act in combination or separately to cause speakers to follow expected conventions for the particular type of discourse in which they are involved.

The most sophisticated model for a description of register variation is proposed by Halliday (1968, 1978) and expanded upon by Gregory and Carroll (1978). Halliday also uses a three-way division to describe the characteristics of a speech situation. He calls his categories the field, the mode, and the tenor of discourse. The field includes the physical setting and the social activity that surrounds and defines a speech event. A major determining factor of field is the degree of emphasis placed on the language itself. At one extreme of this dimension are situations in which language plays a very minor role and is subordinate to the nonverbal interaction. These situations are best exemplified by work or play that involves the collaboration of participants. At the other extreme are situations in which the language itself dominates the interaction, exemplified by gossip, public lectures, and so forth. Halliday also includes subject matter in the field of discourse.

For Halliday, the mode of discourse includes the channel used (i.e., written, spoken, or signed) and involves factors such as whether speech is memorized or spontaneous and monologic or dialogic. The speech "genre" (e.g., conversation, lecture, interview) is also part of the mode. The mode can in part determine the types of cohesion used in a text. Gregory and Carroll (1978) state that certain types of texts exhibit more phonological, grammatical, and lexical cohesion than others, and that texts can also be distinguished by whether deictic processes are intra- or extralinguistic (i.e., whether the referents for pronouns and demonstratives are discourse-internal or are situationally copresent). They state that texts that rely less on shared experience tend to be more "complete" linguistically.

The tenor of discourse in Halliday's model concerns the participants and the interpersonal dynamics involved in their relationship. Halliday mentions two different types of social roles that participants can hold vis à vis one another. First-order roles are defined extralinguistically (e.g., friend, teacher, mother, etc). Second-order roles are defined in relation to the linguistic system (e.g., questioner, informer, responder, lecturer, etc.). These factors constitute the "personal tenor" of the discourse. A discourse also has "functional tenor" (Gregory and Carroll, 1978). This involves the purposes to which language is being applied. Language can be used to inform, discipline, persuade, and so forth. The functional tenor of a discourse can be more or less explicit (e.g., a salesman's choice of "hard" or "soft" sell (Gregory and Carroll, 1978)). Unlike Crystal and Davey (1969), Halliday (1978) and Gregory and Carroll (1978) do not believe that individual factors can act alone. Rather, clusters of features act on a text in aggregate fashion, although different features can have more or less importance in any particular speech situation.

All of these contextual factors serve to determine a range of language use that will be appropriate or acceptable in any given situation. Unlike Joos, Halliday and Gregory and Carroll do not believe that registers constitute totally discrete varieties (except possibly in the special registers mentioned earlier). Rather, features that are often associated with a particular register can also be found in other registers of speech. We can say that in a certain situation, a particular linguistic variable $X$ is likely to occur, but this does not preclude the possibility that $Y$ will occur instead. For example, in a context in which a more "formal" feature is usually found, a more "informal" feature will be used. Hudson (1980, p. 50) discusses the possibility that even within a sentence, individual items can be selected according to different sets of criteria. He gives as an example the sentence, "We obtained some sodium chloride." Depending on context, it may be more appropriate to say either "We got some sodium chloride" or "We obtained some salt." The word "obtained" may be selected for its level of formality, and the term "sodium chloride" may be selected because of its technical description (in scientific jargon, "salt" has a different meaning).

Register, then, is an abstract notion that is not easily definable, and any given speech event may be difficult to categorize as a variant. The concept of the appropriateness or inappropriateness of certain types of language use in particular situational contexts does, however, seem to have psychological reality for groups of speakers. This is illustrated by the ability of people to recognize certain speech styles out of context. Speakers would most likely be able to recognize differences between audiotapes of a radio announcer, a lawyer in court, and a sermon conducted in their native language (Crystal and Davey, 1969). They would also probably have similar opinions about whether a particular type of speech event is appropriate or inappropriate for a particular social situation. Hymes (1974) mentions that people are often seen to use a "significant speech style" outside of the context in which it normally occurs (e.g., in reported speech, in stereotype, and in alluding to particular persons and situations). Use of certain speech styles outside of their normal contexts can involve the phenomenon of linguistic taboo, the flaunting of which can arouse strong feelings in a listener (e.g., in American society, use of "four letter words" is strongly discouraged in most situations.) Furthermore, inappropriate use of register is often used in humor (Halliday, 1968). Enkvist (1987) says that we spend a great deal of time observing speech of different styles and comparing these texts with each other, gaining insight into the "subvarieties" of language that we can expect in any speech situation.

## MODELS OF REGISTER VARIATION IN ASL

As mentioned earlier, there has been no systematic study of the notion of register in ASL, and, until recently, most discussions of situationally conditioned sign variation assumed the existence of a "diglossic" situation. The idea of diglossia was first put forth by Ferguson (1959), after he noticed that several of the communities he was studying have separate language varieties specified for function. One variety, which he termed H (high), is used in more formal situations, whereas the other, termed L (low), is used in more colloquial situations. J. Fishman (1972) later expanded Ferguson's definition of diglossia to include bilingual situations, in which one language plays the H role (e.g., used for school, government) and the other plays the

L role (e.g., used at home and when interacting with peers). Stokoe (1969) posits the existence of diglossia in the Deaf community. He claims that there are two very different types of signing going on in formal and colloquial interactions. Woodward and Markowicz (1975) state that Fishman's description of bilingual diglossia is more explanatory of the situation in the Deaf community, in that signed English seems to be used as the H variety and ASL as the L variety. Lee (1982), however, points out that none of these explanations adequately describes the dynamics involved. She states that both signed English and ASL show up in all of the situations differentiated by Ferguson on the basis of H and L usage. For Lee, alternate use of ASL and English is not tied to register but rather to other factors mostly determined by the characteristics of the participants involved in the interaction (most importantly, level of signing skill and attitudes about English and ASL).

Although no systematic study of register variation in ASL has been done, several authors mention speech situations that call for signing that is more or less "formal" (Baker and Cokely, 1980; Kettrick, 1983; Lee, 1982). They state that more formal signing probably occurs at academic lectures, business meetings, banquets, and church services and that more informal signing occurs with family and friends, or at a party. Authors also list features with which these two different styles are marked. Formal ASL is said to be slower paced and to use a much larger signing space (Baker and Cokely, 1980; Kettrick, 1983). Formal signing is said to be more clear and more fully executed (Kettrick, 1983). In casual signing, the nondominant hand can be deleted (Lee, 1982). That is, formal signing tends to use two-handed variants of signs, whereas informal signing tends to use one-handed variants (Baker and Cokely, 1980; Kettrick, 1983). Signs that contact the forehead in formal singing can contact the cheek or be made in neutral space in casual signing (Baker and Cokely, 1980; Lee, 1982; Kettrick, 1983; Liddell and Johnson, 1985). Certain grammatical markers apparently become "more distinct" in casual signing (Kettrick, 1983). These include discourse and sentence boundary markers and body shifting to indicate reported speech (as opposed to shoulder, head, or eye-gaze shifts). Nonmanual signals appear without a manual component in informal signing, but not in formal signing. These include pronominal indexing that uses eye-gaze, nonmanual adverbs (e.g., "pursed lips" that mean 'very thin') (Kettrick, 1983), and lexical items that have an obligatory nonmanual component, such as NOT#YET (Lee, 1982). Phonological processes such as "assimilation" operate more often in casual than in formal signing (Liddell and Johnson, 1985). In casual signing, a sign such as THINK, which is normally made with a 1-handshape, is made with a *Y*-handshape with extended index finger, in anticipation of the following sign PLAY (Baker and Cokely, 1980). With a sign that has a different handshape on each hand in formal signing, the nondominant hand assimilates to the dominant handshape in casual signing (Liddell and Johnson, 1985).

## THE PRESENT STUDY

The observations discussed here thus far are noteworthy and intuitively appealing. They are, however, based on casual observation rather than on systematic analysis of data. Until such a systematic study is conducted, no empirical conclusions can be drawn as to what register variation looks like in ASL, and what situational factors trigger the use of different linguistic forms.

The project discussed here is a very preliminary attempt at a systematic study of situational variation in ASL. The data for the analysis come from three videotapes of one Deaf native ASL signer. Tape number one consists of a lecture on the subject of linguistic attitudes among Deaf high school students. It is referred to here as "the lecture." Tape number two is a talk addressed to a small audience on the subject of being a "househusband." It is called "the informal talk." The third tape is from a television interview in which this speaker is interviewing a deaf guest. It is called "the interview."

None of these situations falls at the "casual" end on a continuum of formal to informal language, since they are all relatively planned, as opposed to spontaneous, and are each performed for an audience. The level of formality called for in each situation, however, is quite different. The most formal (and the most thoroughly planned) of the three situations is the lecture. As is the tradition at academic conferences, the speaker is presenting a paper that would later be published. Academic lectures constitute, in a way, a special genre. According to Goffman (1981), this genre is characterized by a "serious and impersonal" style.

The informal talk, although not "colloquial," is much less formal than the lecture. In this situation, the main discourse topic is an important factor to consider, along with the size of the audience being addressed. We can expect that a talk given to a small audience, about the things the speaker has experienced while taking care of his son, lends itself to a casual, conversational style, whereas a lecture at an academic conference does not. Also, while the informal talk is still somewhat planned (the speaker is using notes to remind himself of subtopics and anecdotes he wishes to relate), it is much less so than the lecture.

The interview, since it is interactive, is in some sense conversational. But because it was taped for broadcast on television, we can expect it to be much more formal than an everyday conversation among friends. The interactants are together not as friends but as performers for the television audience.

## *Analysis*

Portions of each of these three tapes were transcribed. The transcribed portions were then analyzed to discover similarities and differences that might be linked to similarities and differences in register. Many features were found to distinguish the language used in these three speech situations. The lecture in particular is quite different from the other two tapes. Three areas that differentiate these tapes from each other are discussed here: phonological differences, morphological and lexical differences, and differences in syntax and discourse organization. A close inspection of the lecture also reveals that parts of the text are very different from each other. Therefore, intratextual register variation within the lecture is also discussed here, and three areas in which striking differences exist are described.

### Phonological Differences

The lecture is most noticeably different from the other two tapes in the area of phonology. Especially obvious is a distinct difference in the use of space. The signing space used in the lecture is much larger than that used in the other two tapes. In both the informal talk and the interview, signs made in neutral space (i.e., signs in which the hand(s) does not contact the body) are usually executed within a range extending from the top of the head to the middle of the chest, and usually not beyond shoulder width. In the lecture, however, the signing space often extends considerably beyond these boundaries. In addition to being larger, signs in the lecture are also executed more slowly. Individual signs are of longer duration, and final holds are longer.

Body movements are also much more pronounced in the lecture than in the other two situations. Shifts to indicate reported speech (which usually takes the form of a dialogue between the speaker and one of his students) involve directional shifting of the entire torso. This can be contrasted with the same phenomenon in the informal talk, in which shifting to mark different speakers is done only with movements of the head. In the lecture, the signer often takes a step or two when setting up oppositions or comparisons between two or more categories of items. In the informal talk, this is once again accomplished with head movements, subtle body shifts, or hand-switching, as discussed later.

A technique used extensively in the lecture and rarely in the other two tapes is that of hand-switching. Signed languages differ from spoken languages in that a signer has the use of two articulators. Thus, it is logically possible for a signer to execute two one-handed signs simultaneously, or to switch back and forth between signs made with the left hand and signs made with the right hand. The usual case is for one hand to be "dominant" and for all or most one-handed signs to be made with this hand. At times, though, a speaker will switch dominance for the length of one or more signs. Frishberg (1985) has studied hand-switching in ASL narratives and has discovered that a switch into the nondominant hand can be used for particular pragmatic or semantic purposes. She (ibid., p. 83) says that "the signer can manipulate the [dominance reversals] throughout [a narrative text] for the purpose of creating semantic connections or contrasts between elements within the narrative."

Hand-switching is infrequent in the interview and occurs only with pronouns and determiners. It occurs somewhat more often in the informal talk, and most of the switches also occur with pronouns and determiners. All other cases are like those described by Frishberg, that is, the switch has semantic or pragmatic significance. Consider the following examples of hand-switching from the informal talk.[1] In segment A, the speaker is relating how his son's name was created by combining his own name with that of his wife (also see Figure 1a–h).

Segment A

<pre>
R_____ L_____
PRO.1 P-E-R-R-Y POSS. 1 WIFE A-N-N
'My (name) is Perry, my wife's is Ann'
L/R_____ L/R_____ R_____
ONE-HALF  MATCH  P-E-R-A-N
'Per" and "an," make Peran'
</pre>

In this example, the signer is describing a process that involves a combination of two elements. When indicating his own name and the portion of it ("Per") that occurs in the name of his son, he maintains right-hand dominance. He then switches to left-hand dominance to indicate his wife's name and the portion of it ("an") that also occurs in his son's name. It is significant that he uses both hands for the sign ONE-HALF. This sign is normally one-handed. The use of a two-handed version here helps to reinforce the idea that two elements are being combined (or "connected" in Frishberg's terms).

Hand-switching in the lecture, in contrast, is used more frequently. The following example (B) is a segment of the lecture in which hand-switching is especially pervasive. The speaker is discussing the issue of native versus

---

[1]The samples of ASL discourse presented in this chapter are transcribed in accord with the following conventions: ASL signs are indicated by English gloss-labels in upper-case. Each signed segment is followed by a fuller English gloss, enclosed in single quotation marks. Hyphenated letters, also in upper-case, indicate fingerspelling. In the examples of hand-switching, overscoring of the line of ASL signs indicates the duration and choice of hand(s): *L* for left-hand dominant signs, *R* for right-hand dominant signs, and *L/R* for two-handed signs. + indicates that a sign is duplicated. The number of +'s indicates the number of duplications.

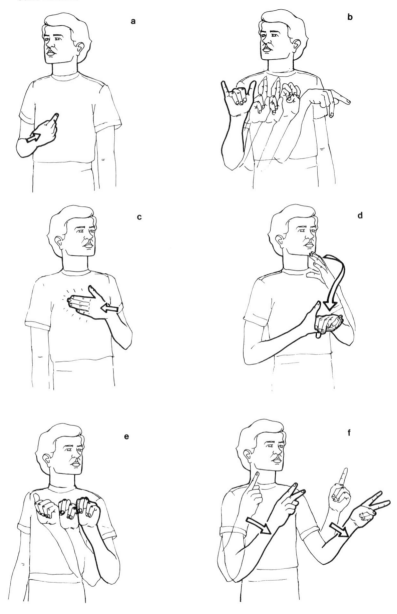

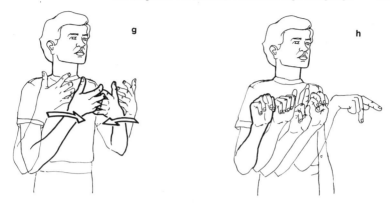

**Fig. 1** (a–h) Hand-switching sequence in segment A. (a) PRO. 1; (b) P-E-R-R-Y; (c) POSS. 1; (d) WIFE, (e) A-N-N; (f) ONE-HALF; (g) MATCH; (h) P-E-R-A-N.

nonnative signers of ASL and indicating that signers who have received the language from their parents are native ASL signers.

Segment B

```
R_____ L____
ALL-OVER DEAF COMMUNITY POSS. 3
'Throughout the deaf community'
L___R_____ L___R___L_____
DET/ PRO.1 TALK A-S-L NATIVE N-A-T-I-V-E DET
'There are those who are native users of ASL'
L_____R___L_____
THERE MEAN THERE
'Those speakers'
R___L_____R_____
MEAN POSS.3 PARENT
'the ones whose parents are deaf'
R_____ L___
A-S-L HAND-DOWN ACCEPT NATIVE A-S-L
'have received the language from them and are native users of ASL'
```

In this example, there appears to be no semantic or pragmatic significance to the switching. Thus, it can only be seen as a stylistic variation occurring in this particular register of signing.

The lecture is also distinguished from the other two tapes by the relative frequency of occurrence of certain phonological processes. Liddell and Johnson (1985) describe several processes that occur in casual signing but not in formal varieties. Assimilation is a process whereby some feature of a sign (e.g., facing, orientation or handshape) assimilates to the same feature of the sign immediately preceding or following it. Handshape assimilation occurs especially often in indexical signs, for example, pointing gestures used as pronouns, locatives, and determiners (Patschke, 1986). The present data were examined for handshape assimilation occurring with indexical signs. In the formal lecture, no overt evidence of assimilation was found. It should be noted, however, that this phenomenon is especially pervasive with first person pronouns, which are often hard to see clearly on a videotape. Nevertheless, some assimilation of this type occurs in the informal talk. In these instances, the *L*-handshape of the first person pronoun assimilates to a following sign with a *B*-handshape. In the lecture, no such assimilation was found.

Other phonological processes discussed by Liddell and Johnson (1985) are perseveration and anticipation. In each of these processes, the base handshape in a two-handed sign is in place for the length of two or more signs. With perseveration, a nondominant base handshape stays in place after the dominant hand has changed to a new sign. With anticipation, the base handshape is in place before the dominant hand begins to make the sign. In connected discourse, this means that a base handshape for one sign is in place while the dominant hand executes two or more signs. No anticipation was found in the section of the lecture analyzed, whereas it occurs fairly regularly in both the informal talk and the interview, in instances such as the following segment (C) from the informal talk. The signer is relating a discussion that he and his wife were having on a particular subject. (The overscore here indicates that the base hand for DISCUSS is in place.)

Segment C

```
L   _____
R   PRO.3   PRO.1   SAY   DISCUSS
    'She and I discussed it'
```

Perseveration does occur in the lecture, but it is infrequent and of short duration (usually continuing over only one extra sign or a part of a sign). In the informal talk and in the interview, it is seen much more often and it lasts longer, as in segment D, extracted from the interview (see segment D and Figure 2a–e). In this example, perseveration occurs twice within one clause. The interviewer is asking whether the interviewee's experience has been the same or different as that of others. He signs the two-handed version of SAME. The nondominant handshape for SAME perseverates through the next two signs of the dominant hand, EXPERIENCE and the fingerspelled word O-R, and then changes to the handshape for the two-handed sign DIFFERENT. This handshape then perseverates through the next one-handed sign, EXPERIENCE.

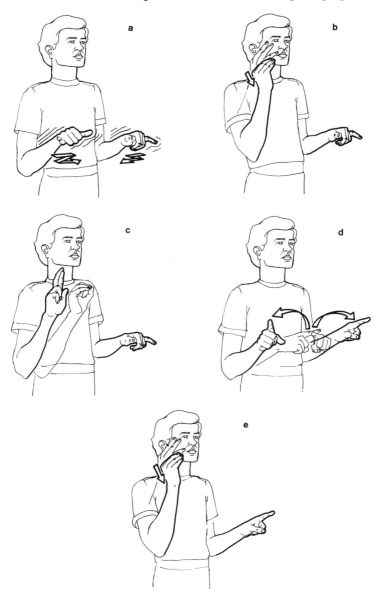

**Fig. 2**    (a–e) Perseveration in segment D. (a) SAME; (b) EXPERIENCE; (c) O-R; (d) DIFFERENT; (e) EXPERIENCE.

Segment D

<u>L</u>                   <u>L</u>
R SAME EXPERIENCE O-R DIFFERENT EXPERIENCE?
'Has it been the same experience or a different experience?'

## Lexical and Morphological Differences

There are also striking differences at the lexical level among the three tapes, and between portions of the lecture. Certain "colloquial" lexical items appear in the informal talk and in the portions of direct speech in the lecture but do not occur in either the interview or the body of the lecture. These include: WHAT-FOR, WHAT'S-UP, EXPERT (F handshape at the chin), FINE (the version that wiggles), PEA-BRAIN, ADORE (kissing the back of the hand), BRAINY, KNOW#THAT, THAT#DET, and the sign usually glossed as SHIT. In some cases, it is not clear whether this is a matter of lexical choice or of semantics, since it is often difficult to find contexts in the lecture where these signs could be appropriately used. In some instances, however, these contexts can be found. An example is the sign EXPERT, which is never used in the lecture. SKILL is used in all contexts where EXPERT would be semantically appropriate.

Some signs occur only in the body of the lecture, never in the informal talk or the interview. These are: AND and THEN. AND is used much like the English word *and* to conjoin two equal elements (lexical items, clauses, etc.). In the other tapes, conjunction of elements is achieved nonlexically. THEN is used to segment ideas. In the informal talk, segmentation is usually achieved syntactically with topicalization.

A certain type of morphological inflection that often occurs in the lecture, but does not occur in either of the other tapes, is articulated by the exaggerated movement of a sign, indicating a process that is difficult or of long duration. One such example occurs with the production of the sign EQUAL (see Figure 3). The lecturer is discussing the difficulty encountered in his attempts to communicate with students on an equal basis. The sign is executed as a series of extremely large circles of the dominant hand, which eventually contacts the nondominant hand, bounces back, and contacts again. The bounce is accompanied by a jerk of the entire body. Several utterances later, the sign HEAD-TOWARD is executed in much the same manner. This same type of inflection is seen with other verbs such as AVOID and NAME.

This type of exaggerated movement may be used in the lecture in place of nonmanual signals. In the informal talk, a long and difficult process is indicated by a nonmanual signal that involves squinted eyes and spread lips. Differential use of nonmanual signals involving facial expression are discussed more fully later.

**Fig. 3**  Exaggerated movement of EQUAL.

## Differences in Syntax and Discourse Organization

Differences among the three tapes are also seen at the syntactic and discourse levels. The most obvious of these is the extensive use of rhetorical questions in the lecture and their infrequent use in the other two tapes. On the other hand, the informal talk uses much more topicalization than is used in the lecture. These observations tie into formal contrasts that function at the discourse level. In the informal talk, topic marking seems to be used as a device to segment the discourse, whereas in the lecture such boundary marking is typically achieved with the lexical item NOW. Another discourse-level feature used in the lecture but not in the informal talk is the use of metaphor. This is discussed more fully in the next section.

A syntactic phenomenon that only occurs in the lecture is the use of a pointing sign with a fingerspelled word. This technique occurs with the words D-E-A-F and A-T-T-I-T-U-D-E, where each word is spelled with the dominant hand (see Figure 4). The last letter of the word is then held while

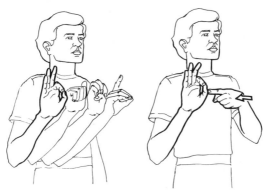

**Fig. 4**  Pointing sign on final hold of D-E-A-F and A-T-T-I-T-U-D-E.

the index finger of the nondominant hand points to the held letter. This occurs several times in the lecture with both of these words.

## Intratextual Register Variation In an Academic Lecture

There are differences between portions of the lecture that are very striking. The intratextual register shifts between three particular portions of the text are of interest: (1) the body of the lecture, consisting of the portions that exhibit all of the features delineated earlier and in which the lecturer is giving factual information or making a point to his audience; (2) direct or so-called reported speech, consisting of the portions that exhibit features associated with a more colloquial register and in which the speaker uses a technique involving the role playing of conversations between two participants (in this case, himself and various of his high school students); and (3) metaphoric/poetic speech, consisting of the portions that exhibit features probably associated with a performance register and typically found in theater and poetry. This type of language is used during the introduction and the closing of the lecture and at various midpoints.

The sections in which direct speech is used are most clearly differentiated from the body of the lecture in the area of lexicon. Extensive use is made of colloquial lexical items (listed earlier), as in the following segment E. The speaker is reporting the speech of one of his students. The student is asking why he needs to study ASL, since he is already fluent in it.

Segment E

HEY WHAT'S-UP TAKE-UP SIGN WHAT-FOR
'Hey, why should I take sign?'
PRO.1 BRAINY EXPERT SIGN-ASL
'I'm already a great signer'
PRO.1 TAKE-UP SIGN WHAT-FOR
'Why should I take it?'


The sections of direct speech also differ somewhat from the body of the lecture at the phonological level. The shortening of the final hold makes the signs appear to flow together rather than appear separated. Signs such as PEA-BRAIN and WHAT-FOR are executed in neutral space rather than at the forehead. The signing space used in the portions of direct speech is often much smaller than that used in the body of the lecture. Phonological processes such as assimilation and perseveration still occur infrequently, but more often than in the body of the lecture.

Nongrammatical facial expression is also used differently in the main-body versus direct-speech portions of the lecture. Facial expression is minimally used in the body of the text, whereas it is used at a level that is often quite exaggerated in the portions of direct speech. A clear exemplification of meaningful nonoccurrence of facial expression in the lecture involves the use of the sign IMPORTANT. There is a nonmanual marker that is often used as an intensifier with this sign. It consists of a movement of the lips in which the signer appears to be saying "po." This nonmanual marker is not used in the body of the lecture, even when the meaning is clearly 'very important'. The intensified meaning is indicated, instead, by exaggeration and intensification of the movement of the sign. This absence of facial gestures in the body of the lecture happens even when the gestures have lexical significance. The only way to distinguish between the lexical items NOT-YET and LATE is by a position of the mouth and tongue. In the body of the lecture, even this facial gesture is frequently omitted.

The portions of text labeled metaphoric/poetic show less contrast with the body of the lecture than do the portions of direct speech, but they are different in some noticeable ways. Phonologically, they are very similar to the lecture. Signs in these portions are also executed in a large signing space and are fully articulated with long final holds. On the whole, phonological processes are rarely at work, the result being that the signs appear clearly signed and separated from each other. The distinctive characteristics are instead found mostly at the morphological, syntactic, and discourse levels. The portions are most clearly marked by a type of poetic line structure, in which a repetition of lexical items and syntactic patterns occurs, as in the following segment F. The signer is discussing the attitudes of deaf students about English and ASL and indicates that he has noticed changes in students' attitudes. Whereas the students originally felt positive toward MCE (manually coded English) and negative toward ASL, they now feel negative toward MCE and positive toward ASL.

Segment F

DEAF CULTURE
'The culture of the deaf'

DEAF LANGUAGE
'The language of the deaf'

POSS.3 ENGLISH
'Some use English'

POSS.3 SIGN LANGUAGE
'Some use sign language'

PRO.1 OBSERVE START CHANGE POSS.3 OPINION
'I've seen opinions begin to change'

BEFORE SAY NEGATIVE+++ CHANGE POSITIVE+++
'Attitudes that were negative, have become positive'

SOME MCE POSITIVE+++ CHANGE NEGATIVE+++
'Attitudes about MCE that were positive have become negative'
SOME ASL NEGATIVE+++ SOME STAY NEGATIVE+++
'Some attitudes about ASL that were negative have stayed negative'

These portions are also marked by creative use of ASL morphological systems. In the beginning of the lecture, the speaker discusses ASL metaphorically as an iceberg, which is resisting attempts to analyze it. Hearing researchers are metaphorically portrayed as a large ship, and deaf researchers as a small boat. The classifier predicate used for a moving vehicle is signed with the nondominant hand. The dominant hand executes the handshape and movements of the sign HEARING. The normal place of articulation for HEARING is at the mouth. But the sign is articulated just above the vehicle classifier. The pattern is then repeated with the signs BOAT and SIGN-ASL (see Figure 5a–c). This type of creative morphology is used only in portions of the tape that show other features of a metaphoric/poetic register.

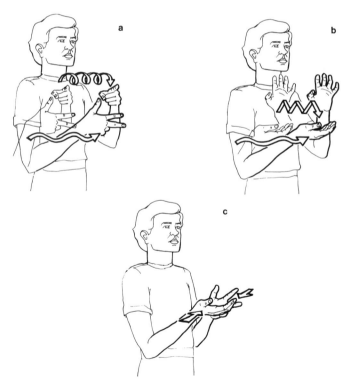

**Fig. 5** Creative morphology of signed metaphors. (a) CL: VEHICLE/HEARING; (b) BOAT/SIGN-ASL; (c) CL: BOAT-VEHICLE-MOVE-TOGETHER.

# SUMMARY

In the prior analysis, some variable features in ASL that are sensitive to changes in register have been described. These findings indicate that the notion of five discrete "styles" as posited by Joos (1968) is too simplistic. Each of the three pieces of data examined here would be classified as "formal" in his system, nevertheless they exhibit marked differences. A system such as that put forward by Halliday (1968, 1978) is much more adequate, since it posits ranges of variation that are sensitive to the interaction of many different factors present in a speech situation. However, even this view fails to capture the kinds of intratextual variation that occur within the lecture examined in this chapter. Even though the field, mode, and tenor of the discourse remain constant, the types of language used in various portions of the text differ greatly.

The present analysis is obviously only a beginning. Most of the features discussed occur at the phonological or lexical levels. A more in-depth analysis will undoubtedly uncover other variable features at the morphological, syntactic, and discourse levels.

Findings of this type have implications for several fields of study. The phenomenon of register variation is of interest to subdisciplines of linguistics, most notably those dealing with language variation and linguistic change. Features at all levels (phonological, morphological, lexical, syntactic, and discourse) seem to show marked differences owing to register variation. Therefore, any comparison of texts leading to statements about variable features that are sensitive to other sociolinguistic factors must be held suspect if register is not held constant. This is also true for studies of historical change. If an older tape of an academic lecture is compared with a newer tape in a much less formal register, there is no way to know whether the differences noted are due to change over time or to register variation.

In the area of interpretation and interpreter training, knowledge of and skill in using register variation is of the utmost importance. An interpreter's goal is to produce a target language message that is equivalent, at all levels, to the original source language message. An interpretation can be quite accurate at the level of content but still be inadequate if expressed in an inappropriate register.

In the area of second-language acquisition and the teaching of ASL, it is equally important to consider differences in register. In order to be truly fluent, a student must not only learn the correct forms and structures of the target language but also must become knowledgeable about when and where particular forms are appropriately used.

Studies of register variation provide us with a great deal of insight into the question of linguistic competence. The present findings indicate that a native speaker of ASL does truly control a range of language variation, a "repertoire" in J. Fishman's (1972) terms, that bears a direct and systematic relationship to a range of social situations and purposes.

Obviously, more work is needed in this area. The present study is focused on but one user of one particular language. It would be of interest to study these differences across a range of speakers and for a much broader range of situations. It would also be of interest to discover the spoken language equivalents of the manual-gestural features described here.

# 13

## Conversational Features and Gender in ASL

Elizabeth Nowell

## INTRODUCTION

Since the publication of Lakoff's (1975) *Language and Women's Place,* the evidence has continued to mount that gender is a salient sociolinguistic variable. Gender differences have been investigated on a range of levels, including but not limited to phonetic variation, word choice and naming, syntactic constructions, and conversational interaction. Several broad trends in analytic approach to gender differences in language are discernible. One trend examines linguistic correlates of gender differences and the role of women in language change.

A second trend considers issues of dominance and power (or the converse) as evidenced by differing language use between men and women (O'Barr & Atkins, 1980; Spender, 1980). Studies within this trend hypothesize that women's lack of power in society is reflected in and reinforced by their use of "powerless" language. This view looks at gender differences as a sociolinguistic manifestation of a sociopolitical problem.

A third trend focuses on gender differences in relation to different socialization and interactive patterns characteristic of each gender. Maltz and Borker (1982) present an analysis of gender differences that suggests men and women comprise different linguistic subcultures. Coates (1986)

THE SOCIOLINGUISTICS OF THE DEAF COMMUNITY
Copyright © 1989 by Academic Press Inc.
All rights of reproduction in any form reserved.

and Aires (1987) both support the view that men and women have different interactive styles that are learned as part of each gender's socialization. Aires (1987, p. 17) describes the talk of men as more "task-oriented, dominant, directive, hierarchical" and that of women as more "social-emotional, expressive, supportive, facilitative, cooperative, personal and egalitarian." When these two subcultural conversational styles come into contact, there are instances of miscommunication, where men and women have different ideas of what is being communicated through talk and how that talk is to be organized. Maltz and Borker also present evidence of similarities within genders across different subcultures in North America.

The latter two trends are significant in relation to the concerns of this chapter, since both approaches to gender differences in language use are situated within a larger sociocultural framework. The studies that Maltz and Borker use to argue for the existence of different subcultures between genders are largely ethnographic. An example of an ethnographic approach is the work of Goodwin (1988), in which differences are described in how boys and girls use language to structure group organization. In light of the developing focus on gender differences as a sociolinguistic concern, an initial question about ASL is what role, if any, gender plays as a sociolinguistic variable in ASL and the deaf community. In general, there is a sparsity of ethnographic studies on Deaf communities (Carmel, 1987, is an exception). Specifically, while some conversational analysis has been done for ASL (see Roy, this volume, for a review of the literature), there are no comparable studies within Deaf communities that investigate whether members of the Deaf community have interactive patterns comparable to those found within various hearing populations. For all practical purposes, a review of the literature on gender differences in language use is a review of spoken language research. Male-female differences in conversational interaction have not been studied in signed interaction.

This chapter presents the results of a preliminary investigation that examines three conversational features for variation between male and female members of the Deaf community. Six interviews with male-female dyads are analyzed for evidence of gender differences in participation according to: the total amount of talk, the use of questions, and the feedback between the subjects, specifically, back-channel production. These three features are not viewed as the only pertinent measures of participation in the interviews. They were selected because multiple reviews of the tapes, over a period of time, established the salience of these three features as indicators of some of the interactive dynamics between the participants in the interviews. Furthermore, these three features are prominent in investigations of spoken language conversations in the hearing population and so allow for a comparison between spoken and signed interaction.

# METHODOLOGY

Six interviews consisting of male-female dyads with either a deaf male interviewer or a hearing female interviewer were videotaped. The subjects all have deaf parents who sign, with one exception (the woman in dyad 3 has hearing parents but also has a deaf sister), and all but two attended deaf residential schools (the women in dyads 1 and 5 attended mainstream programs). All of the subjects in dyads 1–4 are white college students. The subjects in dyads 5 and 6 are also white and college educated but are older, from their mid-twenties to early thirties. Each interview involves participants who were previously unacquainted.

The interview format is question-answer. The subjects were asked to describe their experiences and provide opinions on several topics. The questions were designed to be gender neutral so that neither subject could be considered dominant in expertise.

Two interviews were conducted with a deaf male interviewer (dyads 1 and 2) and two with a female hearing interviewer (dyads 3 and 4). Within the interviews with the female hearing interviewer, there are sections where the interviewer is not present. These sections have been separated from the main body of the interview for analysis. Two additional tapes (dyads 5 and 6) were analyzed for the same three features. Each of these two tapes consists of a male-female dyad interviewed in turn by the deaf male and the hearing female. There are also sections of these two tapes where the interviewers are absent. These sections are also analyzed separately.

The interviewers differ in relation to two major variables, hearing status and gender. It is thus not possible to isolate the individual effect(s) of each in this study, although there is evidence that these two variables operate independently of each other. The present study is mainly concerned with the influence of gender on communication, and so clearly this variable must be controlled across all participants in the study. Within the context of deaf and hearing interaction, the status of deafness can also influence language choice and use. In a comprehensive study, all variables for the interviewer should be isolated to control for possible influence on the subjects' participation.

In the present study, the two interviewer variables of hearing status and gender were seen to exert only minimal influence on the linguistic features targeted for analysis; the subjects' signing time, use of questions and answers, and back-channel production. In comparison to either gender or hearing status, the presence or absence of the interviewer showed greater influence on the subjects' linguistic behavior. This is not to say that the hearing status and gender of the interviewers did not have an effect. For example, in the interviews, there is a difference in the variety of signing used with the hearing female interviewer compared with the deaf male interviewer. The subjects use a more English-like signing variety with the hearing female interviewer and a more ASL-like signing variety with the deaf male interviewer.[1] But no relationship between this variation in language choice and the features under examination in the present study was found.

## DIMENSIONS OF THE SETTING

The three features of speaking time, frequency of questions, and back-channel productions indicate participation along two dimensions of the interview situation. The first dimension is that of the subjects in relation to the context of the interview. In Bateson's (1972) terms, this is the frame of the event, the activity engaged in. The subjects were expected to fulfill certain requirements, in this case, answering a series of questions. Verbal production is a direct result of their role in this interview frame. The first feature, total length of talk, reflects the extent of participation along this dimension.

In addition to the frame of the discourse, there is an interactional dimension between the subjects both within and outside of the formal interview. As coparticipants, they negotiate the alignments between themselves, what Goffman (1981) refers to as their footing. The second two features examined, questions and back-channels between subjects, illuminate the interactional dimension of the relationships between the two subjects in each dyad.

The significance of the frame of this interaction cannot be overstated. The influence of the interview context on the subjects' linguistic behavior necessarily restricts the findings of this study to discussions of the dynamics at work in the particular frame called an interview. Although this research examines only one type of event frame for gender-related differences, other research focuses on conversational interaction, such as Mather (1988), where gender-marked differences are identified in TTY phone calls. Since the present study is limited in scope to specific features of one setting, the findings cannot be extended to a general characteriza-

---

[1]This characterization of language choice represents an intuitive judgment and not an empirical evaluation. In support of the claim, however, are the subjects' increased use of English prepositions and articles, the addition of certain morphological endings, and the literal translation of English idioms or phrases into sign during the conversations with the hearing female interviewer, compared to the more ASL-like signing with the deaf male interviewer.

tion of male-female interaction among Deaf people. Such extrapolation must wait until further research is conducted in a variety of settings.

## Total Length of Talk

One of the most extensively studied areas of differences in the interaction between men and women is relative verbosity. These studies measure the amount of speech in different ways, such as total number or average length of speaking turns. The results generally support the conclusion that men tend to be more verbose than women (Aires, 1987; Argyle, Lalljee and Cook, 1968; Bernard, 1972; Swacker, 1975; Thorne, Kramarae, and Henley, 1983). But studies such as Hirschman (1973) and Aires (1982) also show that, at least among white college students, women may have equal or greater amounts of verbal production compared to men.

The number of turns is also used as an indication of overall participation in studies that look at relatively large groups of individuals interacting freely (Aires, 1982). Because a question-answer format of data gathering was used in the present study, the number of turns was not viewed as a true indication of participation. An interview situation constrains the distribution of turns. Answers alternate between the two subjects, so their turns generally remain proportional to each other. Only if the interviewer directs a question or series of questions to a specific subject do numerical differences between the informants' turns appear. Differences in number of turns can thus be influenced by the interviewer's behavior and such influence must be avoided. Consequently, the total length of speaking time is used in the present study as one measure of each subject's participation.

Once a subject gains the floor, the actual amount of speaking time can be partially self-determined. As such, the total extent of speaking time is defined as the total amount of time spent speaking. The length of talk was determined by timing the total amount of talk, including both speaking-turn time and verbal back-channels. Nonverbal back-channels are not included in the total amount of talk, although they constitute another kind of participation.

Table I presents the total amount of speaking time used by each participant in the six dyads according to the variable of the interviewer (deaf male, hearing female, interviewer absent). The length of talk for each participant was timed at least twice and averaged. The resulting figure is given in minutes:seconds. These findings are similar to those of Aires's (1982) in a comparable white college population where the women participate as much, or more, than their male counterparts.

From the total amount of talk compiled for each gender, it might appear that both genders participate fairly equally. It is thus significant that, in

**Table I**
Total Amount of Speaking Time Across Dyads

| Dyad | Deaf Male | | Hearing Female | | Interviewer Absent | | Totals | |
|------|-----------|------|----------------|------|--------------------|------|---------|-------|
|      | Female | Male | Female | Male | Female | Male | Females | Males |
| 1 | 12:46 | 6:20 | | | | | 12:46 | 6:20 |
| 2 | 7:21 | 14:46 | | | | | 7:21 | 14:46 |
| 3 | | | 10:47 | 11:02 | 2:50 | 1:02 | 13:37 | 12:04 |
| 4 | | | 6:33 | 11:26 | 1:03 | :42 | 7:36 | 12:08 |
| 5 | 4:04 | 3:21 | 4:55 | 2:44 | 6:03 | 3:30 | 15:02 | 9:35 |
| 6 | 6:41 | 3:35 | 4:57 | 3:26 | 2:01 | 2:25 | 13:39 | 9:26 |
| Total | 30:52 | 28:02 | 27:12 | 28:38 | 11:57 | 7:39 | 70:01 | 64:19 |

most of the interviews, there are marked differences in the amount of verbal participation between the subjects. In dyads 1, 5, and 6, the most verbal participant, in total time talking, is a woman. In dyads 2 and 4, the men are most verbal. Only in dyad 3 is participation roughly equivalent.

The gender and hearing status of the interviewer does not appear to significantly affect the length of talk. No correlation between the interviews and the participants' speaking time is evident. Variation in total speaking time for both genders occurs with both the deaf male and the hearing female interviewers. The only significant trend occurs not between the deaf male and hearing female-led interviews, but between the sections of the interviews when the interviewer is present and the sections when the interviewer is absent. During the periods of dyads 3, 4, and 5 when the subjects are alone, the topics of conversation switch from the interview questions to private discussions between the subjects. In dyads 3 and 4, the periods in which the hearing female interviewer is absent are accompanied by a shift in language choice, namely, away from English-like to more ASL-like signing. During these periods of interviewer absence, the women speak more than the men. Prior to the interviewer's departure, the subjects of dyad 6 were instructed to continue discussion of the interview question while they were alone and did so. In that section, the man speaks slightly more than the woman.

In order to look for gender differences, the data of dyads 3, 4, and 5 were separated into two sections, called "on-task" and "off-task," according to whether the subjects are engaging in the formal interview with the interviewer present or are talking between themselves when the interviewer is absent. Table II presents the data in this format and shows the difference between female and male participants.

**Table II**
Total Amount of Speaking Time Across Dyads, by Interview Section

| Dyad | On-Task | | Off-Task | |
|---|---|---|---|---|
| | Female | Male | Female | Male |
| 3 | 10:47 | 11:02 | 2:50 | 1:02 |
| 4 | 6:33 | 11:26 | 1:03 | :42 |
| 5 | 8:59 | 6:05 | 6:03 | 3:30 |
| Total | 26:19 | 28:33 | 9:56 | 5:14 |

*Note*: Dyads 1, 2, and 6 are not included since, in 1 and 2, the interviewer is always present and, in 6, the participants were instructed to remain on-task while alone and did so.

While there is still a range of speaking times among individuals, the total amount of talk for male versus female participants when on-task is as close to equivalence as the all-dyad totals presented in Table I when the interviewer is present. In contrast, the gender totals for off-task talk show a great divergence, the women's amount of talk being almost double the amount of the men's talk.

On-task and off-task are descriptive terms for the particular type of interview situation used in the present study. The talk is not separated into "interview" and "private" because, for the first four dyads, the interviews involve discussion of private topics, namely, the participants' backgrounds and experiences while growing up. Conversational topic per se is thus not the influential factor. What is salient, or seems to be correlated to the amount of participant speaking time, is the frame in which the topic is discussed, namely, the frame of the formal interview or the frame of informal conversation. On the basis of this variable, gender differences are discernible: the female participants speak much more than the male participants during the sections of informal conversation.

These findings are presented as tentative indications of trends, derived from a small data base and restricted to one context, the interview setting. The data indicate, however, that consideration of frames of interaction is important to any analysis of participation.

## SECOND DIMENSION

Moving from the initial focus on total amount of talk as an indicator of participation, it is equally important to recognize that sparsity of talk does not necessarily indicate disinterest. For example, while the male participant in dyad 5 produces markedly less talk than the female participant, he is nonetheless actively engaged in the conversation as evidenced by his nonverbal behavior (head nodding, body position), questions directed to his conversational partner, and manual back-channel production. The point is that participation is not solely defined by how much a person talks. Interaction with a conversational partner also involves listening. Attentive listenership can be signaled in a variety of ways, both verbal and nonverbal. This section explores features that relate to this second dimension of the interview situation, interaction between the subjects. Focusing on the verbal productions of the subjects, two discourse features are examined: questions and back-channels. These two features are separated for purposes of analysis and discussion, but they must be seen as interrelated phenomena. Both are examples of cooperative linguistic actions inasmuch as they serve as feedback that indicates involved and attentive listenership.

## *Questions*

The participants' use of questions has not been as extensively examined as amount or length of talk in linguistic studies of male-female interaction, but here again the view of gender differences as evidence of subcultures or of a power differential emerges. For example, P. M. Fishman (1980, 1983) includes questioning as an element in the interactional strategies of participants in her analysis of the conversations of three heterosexual couples. She describes questioning as part of the labor of conversation, the work done primarily by women to keep the flow of talk going. In her data, women ask two and one-half times as many questions as men, and this imbalance is interpreted as partial evidence of a power differential between men and women that is worked out in verbal interaction.

If men and women represent different subcultures and have different notions of how interaction is "supposed" to proceed (for example, whether it has a socially stratified or equalized basis among the participants), then this gender difference should be apparent in either different interactional styles or variations within one style between men and women. For example, Maltz and Borker (1982, p. 213) hypothesize that questions are used for different purposes: "There are two interpretations of the meaning of questions. Women seem to see questions as part of conversational maintenance, while men seem to view them primarily as requests for information." This is not to present a mutually exclusive dichotomy in the use of questions, but rather a broad guideline of how questions might function differently. Maltz and Borker do not provide evidence to support a functional difference but simply raise this possibility for future consideration.

A third treatment of questions is characterized by Tannen's (1984) approach, which views questions as one of the elements of conversational style. "Machine gun" questions, quick successive questions, are used by both men and women in a high-involvement style to indicate interest and attentiveness. When a person with a high-involvement style interacts with someone with a high-considerateness style, the quick, overlapping questions can be interpreted not as a signal of interest but as one of pushiness, or even disinterest. Tannen analyzes just such an interaction, showing how the speaker with a high-considerateness style backs off, which in turn prompts the speaker with the high-involvement style to ask even more questions in an effort to encourage the coparticipant who now appears recalcitrant. A conversation with a disproportionate number of questions asked by one speaker may not indicate that one participant is laboriously maintaining the conversation but rather that different conversational styles are being employed to cross purposes.

In the present study, the questions exchanged between the subjects are examined. In the question-answer format of the interview frame, questions between the interviewer and the subjects are, of course, required and expected elements of the interaction. Questions are directed to the subjects as part of the formal interview and questions are returned from the subjects as requests for clarification. But there is no basis inherent to the structure of the interview for one subject to ask another subject a question. It is thus individual initiative, and not the interview frame, that motivates subject-to-subject questions.

Table III presents the frequency data of female-initiated versus male-initiated questions across the six dyads. There are no significant differences between the women and men in terms of the number of questions asked. Indeed, the total number for each gender and the individual numbers for dyads 2, 3, and 6 are nearly equivalent. In dyads 1 and 4, the women ask discernibly more questions than the men, and, conversely in dyad 5, the man asks a third more questions than the woman. On the whole, however, the absolute numbers for each dyad are relatively small.

In dyads 3 and 4 with the hearing female interviewer, all but one of the questions occur during the time that the subjects are alone. For example, in dyad 3, there are no questions between the subjects during thirty minutes of the formal interview. But during the seven minutes that they are alone, there are seven questions. The frame of the formal interview seems to restrict interaction between the subjects in this dyad. In dyads 1 and 2 with the deaf male interviewer, there are significantly more questions between participants than in dyads 3 and 4, but it is important to note that the tone and general interaction between the subjects and interviewers of dyads 1 and 2 are different from the other dyads. The subjects in dyads 3, 4, 5, and 6 direct most of their talk to the interviewer, but the subjects in dyads 1 and 2 direct their talk to the interviewer as well as each other.

**Table III**
Distributional Frequency of Subject-to-Subject Questions

| Dyad | Deaf Male | | Hearing Female | | Interviewer Absent | | Total | |
|---|---|---|---|---|---|---|---|---|
| | Female | Male | Female | Male | Female | Male | Female | Male |
| 1 | 6 | 3 | | | | | 6 | 3 |
| 2 | 8 | 8 | | | | | 8 | 8 |
| 3 | | | 0 | 0 | 4 | 3 | 4 | 3 |
| 4 | | | 1 | 0 | 2 | 0 | 3 | 0 |
| 5 | 0 | 2 | 0 | 0 | 15 | 19 | 15 | 21 |
| 6 | 1 | 0 | 2 | 2 | 0 | 0 | 3 | 2 |
| Total | 15 | 13 | 3 | 2 | 21 | 22 | 39 | 37 |

Since there is little gender difference in the overall frequency of questions between subjects, the type of questions asked was also considered. It seems possible that if, in comparison to men, the concerns of women are expressed as much on the metamessage level of interaction as on the level of the actual message and the information exchanged, then women may ask more open-ended questions that encourage extended responses whereas men may ask more specific questions that are intended to elicit brief or succinct responses. This possibility was explored by dividing the questions into two general categories: specific and open. Open questions are those viewed as obvious invitations for extended responses. The following are examples:[2]

WHY CHOSE ACCOUNTING?
'Why did you choose accounting?'

WHY DISCONNECT?
'Why did you feel separate from them?'

This kind of question typically requires a long answer and is a well-known sociolinguistic technique for obtaining extended conversation (Wolfram & Fasold, 1974).

Specific questions are of the yes-no variety or are requests for very particular information. The following are examples:

YOU GROW-UP NEW YORK?
'Did you grow up in New York?'

WHAT YEAR GRADUATE?
'What year did you graduate?'

THAT NAMED RED-GREEN?
'Is that called "red-green"?'

Although this kind of question asks for specific information, this does not imply that all specific questions receive a brief response. The point is that the structure of these questions does not require more than a brief response.

While there are obvious difficulties in categorizing questions with such broad and loose characterizations, the two categories appeared to delineate at least a potential source of contrast in the kinds of questions asked by each gender in the data corpus. As Table IV indicates, however, this particular typology of questions does not bring any gender differences to light. Again, there is a range both within and across each of the dyads. For example, in dyad 2, the man asks the greater number of specific questions

[2]Examples from the data corpus are transcribed in accord with the following conventions: ASL signs are indicated by English gloss-labels in upper case. Each signed segment is followed by a fuller English gloss framed by single quotation marks.

**Table IV**
Distributional Frequency of Subject-to-Subject
Questions, by Type

| Dyad | Specific | | Open | |
|------|----------|------|--------|------|
|      | Female | Male | Female | Male |
| 1 | 4 | 2 | 1 | 1 |
| 2 | 2 | 8 | 5 | 0 |
| 3 | 3 | 1 | 2 | 1 |
| 4 | 2 | 0 | 1 | 0 |
| 5 | 12 | 16 | 2 | 5 |
| 6 | 3 | 2 | 0 | 0 |
| Total | 26 | 29 | 11 | 7 |

and the woman asks the greater number of open-ended questions, as hypothesized. But, in dyad 1, the woman asks the greater number of specific questions and, in dyad 5, the man asks the greater number of open-ended questions. Although there is individual variation, the overall distribution of the two question types is relatively balanced.

The uptake of the questions also does not show any specific pattern. That is, specific questions sometimes receive elaborate answers and open-ended questions sometimes receive brief answers. Moreover, there are no discernible gender differences in how questions are answered.

It is also noteworthy that question asking is not necessarily done by the less talkative member of each pair of subjects. An example is dyad 1, where the woman speaks twice as much as the man but also asks almost twice as many questions. Overall, no relationship between question asking and total time talking is discernible in the data.

## Back-Channel Production

The final feature of participation examined is the manual back-channels exchanged between the subjects. As a working definition, a manual back-channel is defined as any brief manual production that is not an effort to seize the speaking turn. Until now, only linguistic utterances have been included in the discussion. For the category of back-channels, however, both linguistic and nonlinguistic productions are included, that is, all ASL signs and manually articulated gestures that serve as feedback. Linguistic back-channels include ASL signs as *RIGHT* and *TRUE* and repetition by the listener of phrases or single lexical items of a speaker's utterance. Nonlinguistic utterances chiefly include a turning of the hand to a position with the palm open and up and isolated indexing by the listener. This analysis focuses only on back-channels between the subjects and does not include back-channels produced either in response to or by the interviewer.

This definition of manual back-channels is similar to what P. M. Fishman (1978, 1983) refers to as minimal responses. She reports a greater tendency among women than among men to use these devices and suggests that they are used differently by each gender. Maltz and Borker (1982) hypothesize that, for women, minimal responses simply indicate active listenership. For men, minimal responses imply agreement or, in a stronger fashion, some kind of collusion between participants. As they (1982, p. 202) conclude, "The fact that women use these responses more often than men is in part simply that women are listening more often than men are agreeing."

As Table V reflects, the present data do not support the hypothesis that women produce more back-channels than men. The most salient pattern in the distribution of back-channels pertains not to the gender of the subjects in the dyads but rather to the variable of the interviewer. The two discourse situations with the highest frequencies of back-channels are, first, when subjects are with the deaf male interviewer and, second, when subjects are alone. In dyads 3 and 4, the subjects direct their responses to the hearing female interviewer, not to each other, and this may account for the comparatively low amount of subject-to-subject feedback.

Although there is not a significant gender difference in the total number of manual back-channels produced by the subjects, this particular feature of participation is similar to the amount of speech and the use of questions in that there is great variation among the subjects, across the dyads. If anything, the men produce slightly more manual back-channels than the women, but there are not any significant gender differences in the kinds of utterances produced by either gender. Both men and women use the open-palm gesture, indexing, lexical agreement (RIGHT, TRUE), and repetition.

The instances of head nods and other nonmanual forms used as feedback were not targeted for analysis in the present study, but even a cursory examination of the data reveals that they are a vital part of the interaction between the participants in each dyad. For example, while the woman in dyad 6 produces relatively few manual back-channels compared to her male coparticipant, she does exhibit a great amount of head nodding. Although a significant gender difference in the occurrences of head nodding and other nonmanual back-channels (facial expressions) is not discernible in the present data, such phenomena would be primary targets of analysis in a more comprehensive study of subject-to-subject feedback.

It is noteworthy that even when a speaker's eye contact is with the interviewer, manual back-channels by the other subject in the dyad are still produced. On these occasions, the speaker cannot see the back-channels, which are produced in the lap area or when the speaker's head is turned away. With spoken conversations, verbalized utterances by the listener are

**Table V**
Distributional Frequency of Manual Back-Channels

| Dyad | Deaf Male | | Hearing Female | | Interviewer Absent | | Total | |
|---|---|---|---|---|---|---|---|---|
| | Female | Male | Female | Male | Female | Male | Female | Male |
| 1 | 8 | 10 | | | | | 8 | 10 |
| 2 | 28 | 12 | | | | | 28 | 12 |
| 3 | | | 0 | 0 | 2 | 9 | 2 | 9 |
| 4 | | | 0 | 1 | 4 | 4 | 4 | 5 |
| 5 | 2 | 1 | 0 | 5 | 7 | 12 | 9 | 18 |
| 6 | 0 | 13 | 1 | 2 | 9 | 11 | 10 | 26 |
| Total | 38 | 36 | 1 | 8 | 22 | 36 | 61 | 80 |

assumed to be directed to the speaker and hence are referred to as back-channels or feedback. In the signed conversations of the present study, not only nonverbal back-channels (head nodding, nonlinguistic hand gestures) but also linguistic back-channels (*RIGHT*) occur. Insofar as linguistic utterances that serve as back-channels are usually considered in relation to the perlocutionary effect(s) on the speaker, it is thus significant that, in signed interaction, listeners produce manual and nonmanual back-channels that speakers cannot and do not see.

## *CONCLUSION*

For the six dyads in the present study, there are no significant gender differences among the subjects in relation to the three major features examined: total amount of talk, number or kind of questions, and manual back-channels. The only gender difference discernible in the data corpus involves the amount of talk in on-task versus off-task sections. In the on-task interview frame, the participation is equivalent and, in the off-task noninterview frame, the women speak more than the men.

Compared to findings with hearing subjects, this study unveils some interesting differences. For total length of talk in spoken language conversations, the trend of a range of findings is one toward men speaking more than women. In settings similar to that studied here with white college-age subjects (e.g., Aires, 1982), the findings were comparable with those of the present study of signed interaction, with women speaking as much as or more than the men. The gender difference here in the off-task frames, where the women speak so much more than men, has no counterpart in findings with hearing subjects. But again the present data base is relatively small.

In relation to questions, the present findings do not seem to support those with hearing subjects. There is neither a disproprotionate use of questions by women nor a qualitative difference in the kind of question asked, at least as analyzed here. Likewise, the differences reported in the use of back-channels between the genders in the hearing population are not found among the deaf subjects here.

A variety of factors may account for the differences in findings between deaf and hearing subjects. For example, if questions and back-channels were the analytic focus in conversations among unacquainted, hearing, white college-age students, the occurrences of each might be similar to what is reported here with deaf subjects of otherwise identical social status and hence parallel the similarities found in total length of talk between these two groups of subjects. This would not account for the differences among the deaf subjects in the off-task amount of talk. That finding, together with the gender differences found in TTY calls between deaf male and female dyads by Mather (1988), indicates that a broader scope of analysis in a variety of frames may bring out differences not found in the present study.

The need for ethnographic investigations of the Deaf population in general is obvious. Studies could address such fundamental questions as how deaf people organize their talk or whether there is a unified Deaf conversational style or a range of variation based on such factors as gender, location, and age of participants. It is important to emphasize that the subjects in this study represent only a small percentage of the Deaf community. Variation in the Deaf population may involve all features characteristic of the hearing population at large, including age, ethnicity, and socioeconomic background. The system of residential schools for the deaf also makes location a probable source of variation. So too, a central ethnographic task is to determine what features are common across the Deaf community and serve to uniquely distinguish it from the hearing community (broadly defined). If communication has a different role or is given a different value in the Deaf community than in the hearing community, certain of the contrasts should be identifiable.

Finally, ethnographies of how children organize talk and play provide important background for understanding adult differences between the genders in the Deaf community. These differences may be most clear when single-gender interaction is compared with interaction between males and females. Further, such studies could be compared with gender differences that are thought to cut across different subcultures in the hearing population.

# Bibliography

Agar, M. (1973). *Ripping and running: A formal ethnography of urban heroine addicts.* New York: Seminar Press.

Aires, E. (1982). Verbal and nonverbal behavior in single-sex and mixed-sex groups: Are traditional sex roles changing? *Psychological Reports, 51,* 127–134.

Aires, E. (1987). Gender and communication. In P. Shaver and C. Hendrix (Eds.), *Sex and gender* (pp. 149–177). Beverly Hills, CA: Sage Publications.

Alcocer, A. M. (1974). *Proceedings of the Working Conference on Minority Deaf.* Center on Deafness, California State University at Northridge.

Alleyne, M. C. (1971). Acculturation and the cultural matrix of creolization. In D. Hymes (Ed.), *Pidginization and creolization of languages* (pp. 169–186). London & New York: Cambridge University Press.

Anderson, G. B. (1972). Vocational rehabilitation services and the black deaf. *Journal of Rehabilitation of the Deaf, 6*(2), 126–128.

Anisfeld, M., and Lambert, W. E. (1964). Evaluational reactions of bilingual and monolingual children to spoken languages. *Journal of Abnormal and Social Psychology, 69,* 89–97.

Anthony, D. (1971). *Seeing essential English* (Vols. 1 and 2). Anaheim, Ca: Educational Services Division, Anaheim Union School District.

Argyle, M., Lalljee, M., and Cook, M. (1968). The effects of visibility on interaction in a dyad. *Human Relations, 21,* 3–17.

Attinasi, J. J. (1983). Language attitudes and working class ideology in a Puerto Rican barrio of New York. *Ethnic Groups, 5*(1–2), 55–78.

Baker, C. (1976). *Eye-openers in ASL* (pp. 1–13). California Linguistics Association Conference Proceedings, San Diego State University.

Baker, C. (1977). Regulators and turn-taking in American Sign Language discourse. In L. A. Friedman (Ed.), *On the other hand: New perspectives on American Sign Language* (pp. 215–236). New York: Academic Press.

Baker, C. (1978). How does 'Sim-Com' fit into a bilingual approach to education? In F. Caccamise & D. Hicks (Eds.), *Proceedings of the Second National Symposium on Sign Language Research and Teaching* (pp. 13–26). Silver Spring, MD: National Association of the Deaf.

Baker, C. (1983). Implications of linguistic research. In M. McIntire (Ed.), *Proceedings of the Fourth National Conference of Interpreter Trainers* (pp. 169–183). Silver Spring, MD: Registry of Interpreters for the Deaf Publications.

Baker, C., and Battison, R. (Eds.). (1980). *Sign language and the deaf community.* Silver Spring, MD: National Association of the Deaf.

Baker, C., and Cokely, D. (1980). *ASL: A teacher's resource text on grammar and culture.* Silver Spring, MD: T. J. Publishers.

Baker, C., and Padden, C. (1978). Focusing on the nonmanual components of American Sign Language. In P. Siple (Ed.), *Understanding language through sign language research* (pp. 27–57). New York: Academic Press.

Barbag-Stoll, A. (1983). *Social and linguistic history of Nigerian Pidgin English.* Tubingen: Stauffenberg-Verlag.

Barth, F. (1969). *Ethnic groups and boundaries.* Boston, MA: Little, Brown.

Bateson, G. (1972). *Steps to an ecology of mind.* New York: Ballantine.

Battison, R. (1978). *Lexical borrowing in American Sign Language.* Silver Spring, MD: Linstok Press.

Battison, R., Markowicz, H., and Woodward, J. (1975). A good rule of thumb: Variable phonology in American Sign Language. In R. Shuy and F. Fasold (Eds.), *New ways of analyzing variation in English* (pp. 291–302). Washington, DC: Georgetown University Press.

Becker, G. (1980). *Growing old in silence.* Berkeley: University of California Press.

Bellugi, U., and Klima, E. (1980). *The signs of language.* Cambridge, MA: Harvard University Press.

Benderly, B. L. (1980). *Dancing without music. Deafness in America.* Garden City, NY: Anchor Press.

Berger, P., and Luckmann, T. (1966). *The social construction of reality: A treatise on the sociology of knowledge.* Middlesex, England: Penguin Books.

Bergman, E. (1976). Deaf students speak up: How they feel about the teaching and teachers of English. *Teaching English to the Deaf,* **3**(1), 4–14.

Berke, L. (1978). Attitudes of deaf high school students toward American Sign Language. In F. Caccamise & D. Hicks (Eds.), *Proceedings of the Second National Symposium on Sign Language Research and Teaching* (pp. 173–182). Silver Spring, MD: National Association of the Deaf.

Bernard, J. (1972). *The sex game.* New York: Athenaeum.

Bickerton, D. (1975). *The dynamics of creole system.* London: Oxford University Press.

Bickerton, D. (1977). Pidginization and creolization. Language acquisition and language universals. In A. Valdman (Ed.), *Pidgin and creole linguistics* (pp. 49–69). Bloomington: Indiana University Press.

Bickerton, D. (1981). *Roots of language.* Ann Arbor, MI: Karoma Publishers.

Bickerton, D. (1984). *The role of demographics in the origin of creoles.* Paper presented at New Ways of Analyzing Variation Conference XIII, Philadelphia, PA.

Bienvenu, M. J. (1987). *The third culture. Working together.* Address delivered at Convention of Sign Language Interpreters of California.

Biggs, B. G. (1972). Implications of linguistic subgrouping with special reference to Polynesia. In R. C. Green & M. Kelly (Eds.), *Studies in oceanic culture history, Vol. 3. Pacific anthropological records* (13). Honolulu: Bernice P. Bishop Museum.

Bochner, J. H., and Albertini, J. A. (1988). Language varieties in the deaf population and their acquisition by children and adults. In M. Strong (Ed.), *Language learning and deafness* (pp. 3–48). Oxford: Blackwell.

Bokamba, E. G. (1985). *Code-mixing, language variation and linguistic theory: Evidence from*

*Bantu languages.* Paper presented at the 16th Conference on African Linguistics, Yale University, New Haven, CT.

Bornstein, H. (1973). A description of some current sign systems designed to represent English. *American Annals of the Deaf,* **118,** 454–463.

Bornstein, H. (1975). *The Signed English dictionary for preschool and elementary levels.* Washington, DC: Gallaudet College Press.

Boros, A., and Stuckless, R. (1982). The dynamics of social lag among deaf people. In A. Boros & R. Stuckless (Eds.), *Social aspects of deafness: Vol. 6. Deaf people and social changes* (pp. 15–45). Washington, DC: Gallaudet University, Department of Sociology.

Bouchard Ryan, E. (1973). Subjective reactions toward accented speech. In R. Shuy & R. Fasold (Eds.), *Language attitudes: Current trends and prospects* (pp. 60–73). Washington, DC: Georgetown University Press.

Bourhis, R., and Giles, H. (1976). The language of cooperation in Wales: A field study. *Language Sciences,* **42,** 13–16.

Bourhis, R., Giles, H., and Tajfel, H. (1973). Language as a determinant of Welsh identity. *European Journal of Social Psychology,* **3,** 447–460.

Brannon, C., and Livingston, S. (1986). An alternative view of deaf education. Part II. *American Annals of the Deaf,* **131,** 229–231.

Caccamise, F., Dirst, R., DeVries, R. D., Heil, J., Kirchner, C., Kirchner, S., Rinaldi, A. M., and Stangarone, J. (1980). *Introduction for interpreters/transliterators, hearing impaired consumers, hearing consumers.* Silver Spring, MD: Registry of Interpreters for the Deaf Publishers.

Carmel, S. (1976). *Ethnic identity and solidarity in the deaf community in the United States.* Unpublished manuscript.

Carmel, S. (1987). *A study of deaf culture in an American urban deaf community.* Ph.D. dissertation, American University, Washington, D.C.

Casagrande, J. B. (1954). The ends of translation. *International Journal of American Linguistics,* **20**(4), 335–340.

Chafe, W. (1962). Integration and involvement in speaking, writing, and oral literature. In D. Tannen (Ed.), *Spoken and written language: Exploring orality and literacy* (pp. 35–53). Norwood, NJ: Ablex.

Chafe, W., and Danielwicz, J. (1987). *Properties of spoken and written language* (Tech. Rep. No. 5). Berkeley, CA: Center for the Study of Writing.

Chesterfield, R., Barrows Chesterfield, K., Hayes-Latimer, K., and Chavez, R. (1983). The influence of teachers and peers on second language acquisition in bilingual preschool programs. *TESOL Quarterly,* **17**(3), 401–420.

Christiansen, J. B., and Barnartt, S. N. (1987). The silent minority: The socioeconomic status of deaf people. In P. C. Higgins & J. E. Nash (Eds.), *Understanding deafness socially* (pp. 171–196). Springfield, IL: Thomas.

Clyne, M. (1967). *Transference and triggering.* The Hague: Nijhoff.

Clyne, M. (1972). *Perspectives on language contact.* Melbourne: Hawthorne Press.

Coates, J. (1986). *Women, men and language.* New York: Longman.

Cohen, A. D. (1974). Introduction: The lesson of ethnicity. In A. Cohen (Ed.), *Urban ethnicity* (pp. ix–xxiv). London: Tavistock Publications.

Cohen, A. D. (1975). *A sociolinguistic approach to bilingual education experiments in the American Southwest.* Rowley, MA: Newbury House.

Cokely, D. (1978). Program considerations in a bilingual "ASL-English" approach to education. In F. Caccamise & D. Hicks (Eds.), *Proceedings of the Second National Symposium on Sign Language Research and Teaching* (pp. 211–218). Silver Spring, MD: National Association of the Deaf.

Cokely, D. (1983). When is a pidgin not a pidgin? An alternative analysis of the ASL-English contact situation. *Sign Language Studies,* **38,** 1–24.

Cokely, D. (1984a). Foreigner talk and learner's grammar. *Reflector, 8,* 23–30.

Cokely, D. (1984b). *Towards a sociolinguistic model of the interpreting process: Focus on ASL and English.* Doctoral dissertation, Georgetown University, Washington, DC.

Commission on the Education of the Deaf. (1987). *Second Set of Draft Recommendations.* Notice Federal Register, Oct. 14.

Commission on the Education of the Deaf. (1988). *Toward Equality: Education of the deaf.* A Report to the President and the Congress of the United States.

Conference of Interpreter Trainers (CIT). (1986). Task analysis of transliteration and response. In M. McIntire, (Ed.), *New dimensions in interpreter education: Task analysis: Theory and application* (pp. 70–102). Silver Spring, MD: Registry of Interpreters for the Deaf Publications.

Cook, R. (1975). *A communicative approach to the analysis of extended monologue discourse and its relevance to the development of teaching materials for ESP.* M. Litt. thesis, University of Edinburgh, Scotland.

Cooper, R. (1975). Introduction to Language attitudes. II. *International Journal of the Sociology of Language, 6,* 5–9.

Corbett, E., and Jensema, C. (1981). *Teachers of the hearing impaired: Descriptive profiles.* Washington, DC: Gallaudet College Press.

Crandall, K. (1974). *A study of the production of chers and related sign language aspects by deaf children between the ages of three and seven years.* Unpublished doctoral dissertation, Northwestern University, Evanston, IL.

Crandall, K. (1978). Inflectional morphemes in the manual English of young hearing impaired children and their mothers. *Journal of Speech and Hearing Research, 21,* 372–386.

Croneberg, C. (1976). The linguistic community. In W. C. Stokoe, D. Casterline, & C. Croneberg (Eds.), *A dictionary of American Sign Language on linguistic principles* (new ed., pp. 297–311). Silver Spring, MD: Linstok Press.

Crowl, T. K., and MacGinitie, W. H. (1974). The influence of students' speech characteristics on teachers evaluations of oral answers. *Journal of Educational Psychology, 66*(3), 304–308.

Crystal, D., and Davey, D. (1969). *Investigating English style.* Bloomington: Indiana University Press.

Curry, J., and Curry, R. (1978). Deaf students can use their fluency in American Sign Language to develop English competency. In F. Caccamise & D. Hicks (Eds.), *Proceedings of the National Symposium on Sign Language Research and Teaching* (pp. 233–246). Silver Spring, MD: National Association of the Deaf.

Davis, J. E. (1987). *The nature and structure of sign language variation in the United States deaf community.* Doctoral comprehensive paper, University of New Mexico, Departments of Educational Foundations and Linguistics.

Davis, J. E. (in press). Reanalyzing the sign language continuum: Implications for practitioners, trainers, and students of interpretation. In *Proceedings from the RID 1987 National Convention. Interpreting: The art of cross-cultural mediation.* Rockville, MD: Registry of Interpreters for the Deaf Press.

DeCamp, D. (1971). The study of pidgin and creole languages. In D. Hymes (Ed.), *Pidginization and creolization of languages* (pp. 13–39). London & New York: Cambridge University Press.

de Courtenay, J. B. (1972). *A Baudouin de Courtenay Anthology* (E. Standiewicz, Ed. and Trans.). Bloomington: Indiana University Press.

De Santis, S. (1977). *Elbow to hand shift in French and American sign languages.* A paper presented at the annual NWAVE Conference, Georgetown University, Washington, DC.

Di Pietro, R. J. (1978). Code-switching as a verbal strategy among bilinguals. In M. Paradis (Ed.), *Aspects of bilingualism* (pp. 275–282). Columbia, SC: Hornbeam Press.

Dyson, A. H. (1986). *Symbol weaving: Interrelationships between the drawing, talking, and dictating of young children.* Paper presented at the meeting of the American Educational Research Association, San Francisco, CA.

Edwards, J. R. (1977). Students' reactions to Irish regional accents. *Language and Speech,* **20,** 280–285.

Edwards, V. (1978). Language attitudes and underperformance in West Indian children. *Educational Review,* **30**(1), 51–58.

Edwards, V. (1986). *Language in a black community.* San Diego, CA: College Hill Press.

El-Dash, L., and Tucker, G. R. (1975). Subjective reactions to various speech styles in Egypt. *Interactional Journal of the Sociology of Language,* **6,** 33–54.

Enkvist, N. E. (1987). What has discourse linguistics done to stylistics? In S. P. X. Battestini (Ed.), *Developments in linguistics and semiotics: Language teaching and learning communication across cultures. Georgetown University Round Table on Languages and Linguistics, 1986.* Washington, DC: Georgetown University Press.

Erting, C. (1978). Language policy and deaf ethnicity in the United States. *Sign Language Studies,* **19,** 139–152.

Erting, C. (1980). Sign language and communication between adults and children. In C. Baker & R. Battison (Eds.), *Sign language and the deaf community* (pp. 159–176). Silver Spring, MD: National Association of the Deaf.

Erting, C. (1982). *Deafness, communication and social identity: An anthropological analysis of interaction among parents, teachers, and deaf children in a preschool.* Unpublished doctoral dissertation, American University, Washington DC.

Erting, C. (1985). Cultural conflict in a deaf classroom. *Anthropology and Education Quarterly,* **16,** 225–243.

Erting, C., Prezioso, C., and O'Grady Hynes, M. (1987). *Mother signs babytalk.* Paper presented to the Fourth International Conference on Sign Language Research, Lappeenranta, Finland.

Erting, C., and Woodward, J. C. (1974). *Sign language and the deaf community: A sociolinguistic profile.* Paper presented at the annual meeting of the American Anthropological Association, Mexico City. (Revised version published in *Discourse Processes,* **2,** 183–300)

Ewoldt, C. (1985). A descriptive study of the developing literacy of young hearing-impaired children. *Volta Review,* **87,** 109–126.

Fasold, R. (1984). *The sociolinguistics of society.* Oxford: Blackwell.

Ferguson, C. (1959). Diglossia. *Word,* **15,** 325–340.

Ferguson, C. (1978). Talking to children: A search for universals. In J. H. Greenberg *et al.* (Eds.), *Universals of human language* (Vol. 1, pp. 203–224). Stanford, CA: Stanford University Press.

Ferguson, C. (1983). Sports announcer talk: Syntactic aspects of register variation. *Language in Society,* **12,** 152–172.

Ferguson, C. (1982). Simplified registers and linguistic theory. In L. Obler and L. Menn (Eds.), *Exceptional language and linguistics* (pp. 49–66). New York: Academic Press.

Ferguson, C., and DeBose, C. (1977). Simplified registers, broken language and pidginization. In A. Valdman (Ed.), *Pidgin and creole linguistics* (pp. 99–125). Bloomington: Indiana University Press.

Fillmore, C. (1977). Foreword. In L. A. Friedman (Ed.), *On the other hand: New perspectives on American Sign Language* (pp. vii–ix). New York: Academic Press.

Fischer, S. (1978). Sign language and Creoles. In P. Siple (Ed.), *Understanding language through sign language research* (pp. 309–331). New York: Academic Press.

Fischer, S., and Gough, B. (1978). Verbs in American Sign Language. *Sign Language Studies,* **18,** 17–48.

Fishman, J. (1972). *The sociology of language.* Rowley, MA: Newbury House.

Fishman, J. (1974). Language planning and language planning research: The state of the art. In J. Fishman (Ed.), *Advances in language planning* (pp. 15–33). The Hague: Mouton.

Fishman, J. (1977). Language and ethnicity. In H. Giles (Ed.), *Language, ethnicity, and intergroup relations* (pp. 15–57). New York: Academic Press.

Fishman, P. M. (1978). Interaction: The work women do. *Social Problems,* **25,** 397–406.

Fishman, P. M. (1980). Conversational insecurity. In H. Giles, W. P. Robinson, & P. M. Smith (Eds.), *Language: Social psychological perspectives* (pp. 127–132). New York: Pergamon.

Fishman, P. M. (1983). Interaction: The work women do. In B. Thorne, C. Kramarae, & N. Henley (Eds.), *Language, gender and society* (pp. 89–101). Cambridge, MA: Newbury House.

Flournoy, J. A. (1856). A deaf mute commonwealth. *American Annals of the Deaf,* **8,** 120–125.

Frishberg, N. (1985). Dominance reversals and discourse. In W. Stokoe & V. Volterra (Eds.), *Sign Language and Research '83. Proceedings of the Third International Symposium on Sign Language Research* (pp. 79–90). Silver Spring, MD: Linstok Press/CNR.

Frishberg, N. (1986). *Interpreting: An introduction.* Silver Spring, MD: Registry of Interpreters for the Deaf Publications.

Gannon, J. (1981). *Deaf heritage: A narrative history of deaf America.* Silver Spring, MD: National Association of the Deaf.

Gearing, F., and Epstein, P. (1982). Learning to wait: An ethnographic probe into the operations of an item of hidden curriculum. In G. Spindler (Ed.), *Doing the ethnography of schooling* (pp. 243–267). New York: Holt, Rinehart & Winston.

Gee, J., and Kegl, J. (1983). Narrative/story structure, pausing, and American Sign Language. *Discourse Processes,* **6,** 243–254.

Gibbons, J. P. (1983). Attitudes towards languages and code-mixing in Hong Kong. *Journal of Multilingual and Multicultural Development,* 4(2&3) 129–147.

Gilbert, L. (1982). Breaking the language barrier. *Gallaudet Today,* **12**(3), 1–7.

Giles, H. (1977). *Language, ethnicity and intergroup relations.* London: Academic Press.

Giles, H., and Bourhis, R. Y. (1976). Methodological issues in dialect perception: Some social psychological perspectives. *Anthropological Linguistics* 18(7), 294–304.

Glenn, E. S., and Glenn, C. G. (1981). *Man and mankind: Conflict and communication between cultures.* Norwood, NJ: Ablex.

Glickman, N. (1984). The war of the languages: Comparisons between language wars of Jewish and deaf communities. *Deaf American,* **36**(6), 25–33.

Goffman, E. (1981). *Forms of talk,* Philadelphia: University of Pennsylvania Press.

Goodenough, W. (1971). *Culture, language, and society.* Reading, MA: Addison-Wesley.

Goodwin, M. H. (1988). Cooperation and competition across girls' play activities. In A. D. Todd & S. Fisher (Eds.), *Gender and discourse: The power of talk* (pp. 55–94). Norwood, NJ: Ablex.

Gregory, M., and Carroll, S. (1978). *Language and situation: language varieties and their social contexts.* London: Routledge & Kegan Paul.

Griffin, P., and Humphrey, F. (1978). Task and talk at lesson time. In R. Shuy & P. Griffin (Eds.), *Children's functional language and education in the early years.* (pp. 1–189). Arlington, VA: Center for Applied Linguistics.

Grosjean, F. (1982). *Life with two languages.* Cambridge, MA: Harvard University Press.

Gumperz, J. J. (1972). The speech community. In P. P. Giglioli (Ed.), *Language and social context* (pp. 219–231). Harmondsworth: Penguin.

Gumperz, J. J. (1976). The sociolinguistic significance of conversational code switching. In *Papers on language and context* (Working papers of the Language Behavior Research Laboratory, No. 46). Berkeley: University of California.

Gumperz, J. J., and Cook-Gumperz, J. (1981). Ethnic differences in communicative style. In C. A. Ferguson & S. Brice-Heath (Eds.), *Language in the USA* (pp. 430–445). London & New York: Cambridge University Press.

Gumperz, J. J., and Hernandez-Chavez, E. (1971). Bilingualism, bidialectalism and classroom interaction. *In* A. S. Anwar (Ed.), *Language in Social Groups: Essays by John J. Gumperz* (pp. 311–339). Stanford, CA: Stanford University Press.

Gumperz, J. J., and Wilson, R. (1971). Convergence and creolization: A case from the Indo-Aryan-Dravidian border. In D. Hymes (Ed.), *Pidginization and creolization of languages* (pp. 151–167). London & New York: Cambridge University Press.

Gustason, G. (1974–1975). Signing Exact English. *Gallaudet Today* **5,** 11–12.

Gustason, G. (1980). The languages of communication. In G. Gustason & E. Zawolkow (Eds.), *Using Signing Exact English in total communication* (pp. 15–21). Los Alamitos, CA: Modern Signs Press.

Gustason, G. (1983). *Teaching and learning Signing Exact English: An idea book.* Los Alamitos, CA: Modern Signs Press.

Gustason, G., Pfetzing, D., and Zawolkow, E. (Eds.). (1972). *Signing Exact English.* Los Alamitos, CA: Modern Signs Press.

Gustason, G., and Zawolkow, E. (Eds.), (1980). *Using Signing Exact English in total communication.* Los Alamitos, CA: Modern Signs Press.

Hairston, E., and Smith, L. (1983). *Black and deaf in America.* Silver Spring, MD: T.J. Publishers.

Hall, R. A. (1962). The life-cycle of pidgin languages. *Festschrift De Groot* (Lingua Vol. 11), pp. 151–156.

Hall, R. A. (1966). *Pidgin and creole languages.* Ithaca, NY: Cornell University Press.

Halliday, M. A. K. (1968). The users and uses of language. In J. Fishman (Ed.), *Readings in the sociology of language* (pp. 139–169). The Hague: Mouton.

Halliday, M. A. K. (1978). *Language as a social semiotic.* Baltimore, MD: University Park Press.

Halliday, M. A. K. (1980). Three aspects of children's language development: Learning language, learning through language, learning about language. In Y. Goodman, M. Haussler, & D. Stricklant (Eds.), *Oral and written language development research: Impact on the schools* (pp. 7–19). Urbana, IL: National Council of Teachers of English.

Halliday, M. A. K. and Hasan, R. (1976). *Cohesion in English.* London: Longman.

Haugen, E. (1956). *Bilingualism in the Americas: A bibliography and research guide.* Birmingham: University of Alabama Press.

Haugen, E. (1966). *Language conflict and language planning: The case of modern Norwegian.* Cambridge, MA: Harvard University Press.

Haugen, E. (1969). *The Norwegian language in America: A study in bilingual behavior* (pp. 287–298). Bloomington: Indiana University Press.

Haugen, E. (1972). Language planning theory and practice. In A. Dil (Ed.), *The ecology of language: Essays by Einar Haugen.* Stanford, CA: Stanford University Press.

Heath, S. (1978). *Teacher talk: Language in the classroom.* Washington, DC: Center for Applied Linguistics.

Heath, S. (1981). English in our language heritage. In C. Ferguson and S. Brice Heath (Eds.), *Language in the USA* (pp. 6–20). London & New York: Cambridge University Press.

Heath, S. (1983). *Ways with words.* New York: Cambridge University Press.

Heath, S. (1984). *Being literate in America: A sociohistorical perspective.* Keynote address for the annual meeting of the National Reading Conference. St. Petersburg, Florida.

Hewett, N. (1971). Reactions of prospective English teachers toward speakers of a non-standard dialect. *Language Learning, 21*(2), pp. 205–212.

Higgins, P. C. (1980). *Outsiders in a hearing world. A sociology of deafness.* Beverly Hills, CA: Sage Publications.

Higgins, P. C. (1987a). Introduction. In P. C. Higgins & J. E. Nash (Eds.), *Understanding deafness socially* (pp. vii–xviii). Springfield, IL: Thomas.

Higgins, P. C. (1987b). The deaf community. In P. C. Higgins & J. E. Nash (Eds.), *Understanding deafness socially* (pp. 151–170). Springfield, IL: Thomas.

Higgins, P. C., and Nash, J. E. (1987). Editor's introduction (for cultural conflict in a school for deaf children. In P. C. Higgins & J. W. Nash (Eds.), *Understanding deafness socially* (pp. 123–127). Springfield, IL: Thomas.

Hillery, G. (1974). *Communal organizations.* Chicago, IL: Chicago University Press.

Hirschman, L. (1973). *Male-female differences in conversational interaction.* Paper presented at the annual meeting of The Linguistic Society of America, San Diego, CA.

Hodge, V. D. (1978). *Personality and second language learning. Language in education* 12. Arlington, VA: Center for Applied Linguistics.

Horowitz, D. L. (1985). *Ethnic groups in conflict.* Berkeley: University of California Press.

Hudson, R. (1980). *Sociolinguistics.* London & New York: Cambridge University Press.

Hymes, D. (Ed.). (1971). *Pidginization and creolization of languages.* London & New York: Cambridge University Press.

Hymes, D. (1974). Ways of speaking. In R. Bauman & J. Sherzer (Eds.), *Explorations in the ethnography of speaking* (pp. 433–451). London & New York: Cambridge University Press.

Isajiw, W. (1974). Definitions of ethnicity. *Ethnicity,* **1,** 111–124.

Jacobs, L. (1974). *A deaf adult speaks out.* Washington, DC: Gallaudet College Press.

Johnson, R. E. (1983). *Sign language use and evaluation.* Report to the collegiate faculty, Gallaudet University, Department of Linguistics, Washington, DC.

Johnson, R. E., and Erting, C. (1982). Linguistic socialization in the context of emergent deaf ethnicity. In C. Erting & R. Meisegeier (Eds.), *Working papers No. 1: Deaf children and the socialization process.* Washington, DC: Gallaudet College, Sociology Department.

Johnson, R. E., and Liddell, S. K. (1984). Structural diversity in the American Sign Language lexicon. In D. Tosten, V. Mishra, & J. Drogo (Eds.), *Papers from the parasession on lexical semantics* (pp. 173–186). Chicago, IL: Chicago Linguistic Society.

Johnstone, B. (1986). Arguments with Khomeini: Rhetorical situation and persuasive style in cross-cultural perspective. *Text,* **6**(2), 171–187.

Joos, M. (1968). The isolation of styles. In J. Fishman (Ed.), *Readings in the sociology of language* (pp. 185–191). The Hague: Mouton.

Jordan, I. K., Gustason, G., and Rosen, R. (1980). Current communication trends at programs for the deaf. In G. Gustason & E. Zawolkow (Eds.), *Using Signing Exact English in total communication* (pp. 32–37). Los Alamitos, CA: Modern Signs Press.

Jordan, I. K., and Karchmer, M. (1986). Patterns of sign use among hearing impaired students. In A. N. Schildroth & M. A. Karchmer (Eds.), *Deaf children in America* (pp. 125–138). San Diego, CA: College Hill Press.

Kachru, B. (1983). *The other tongue: English across cultures.* Elmsford, NY: Pergamon.

Kachru, B. (1978a). Code-mixing as a communicative strategy in India. In J. Alatis (Ed.), *International dimensions of bilingual education* (pp. 107–124). Washington, DC: Georgetown University Press.

Kachru, B. (1978b). Toward structuring code-mixing: An Indian perspective. In B. Kachru & S. Sridhar (Eds.), *Aspects of scoiolinguistics in South Asia* (Spec. Issue, *International Journal of the Sociology of Language, Vol. 16*).

Kannapell, B. (1974). Bilingualism: A new direction in the education of the deaf. *Deaf American,* June, pp. 9–15.

Kannapell, B. (1978). Linguistic and sociolinguistic perspectives on sign systems for educating deaf children: Toward a true bilingual approach. In F. Caccamise & D. Hicks (Eds.), *Proceedings of the Second National Symposium on Sign Language Research and Teaching* (pp. 219–231). Silver Spring, MD: National Association of the Deaf.

Kannapell, B. (1985). *Language choice reflects identity choice: A sociolinguistic study of deaf college students.* Doctoral dissertation, Georgetown University, Washington, DC.

Karchmer, M., Trybus, R., and Paquin, M. (1978). *Early manual communication, parental hearing status, and the academic achievement of deaf students.* Unpublished manuscript.

Kay, P., and Sankoff, G. (1974). A language-universals approach to pidgins and creoles. In D. DeCamp & I. Hancock (Eds.), *Pidgins and creoles: Current trends and prospects* (pp. 61–72). Washington, DC: Georgetown University Press.

Kettrick, C. (1983). *Fast, formal and casual signing in American Sign Language.* Unpublished manuscript. Masters of Arts thesis, University of Washington, Seattle.

Klima, E., and Bellugi, U. (1979). *The signs of language.* Cambridge, MA: Harvard University Press.

Kluwin, T. (1981a). The grammaticality of manual representations of English in classroom settings. *American Annals of the Deaf,* **126**(4), 417–421.

Kluwin, T. (1981b). A preliminary description of the control of interaction in classrooms using manual communication. *American Annals of the Deaf,* **126**(5), 510–514.

Kluwin, T. (1981c). A rationale for modifying classroom signing systems. *Sign Language Studies,* **31**, 179–187.

Krashen, S. D., and Scarcella, R. C. (1978). *Research in second language acquisition: Selected papers of the Los Angeles Second Language Acquisition Research Forum.* Rowley, MA: Newbury House.

La Forge, P. G. (1983). *Counseling and culture in second language acquisition.* Oxford: Pergamon.

Labov, W. (1972). *Language in the inner city.* Philadelphia: University of Pennsylvania Press.

Lakoff, R. (1975). *Language and woman's place.* New York: Harper & Row.

Lambert, W. E., Hodgson, R. C., Gardner, R. C., and Fillenbaum, S. (1960). Evaluational reactions to spoken languages. *Journal of Abnormal and Social Psychology,* **60**, 44–51.

Lambert, W. E., and Yeni-Komshian, G. (1965). Evaluational reactions of Jewish and Arab adolescents to dialect and language variations. *Journal of Personality and Social Psychology* **2**(1), 84–90.

Lane, H. (1980). A chronology of the oppression of sign language in France and the United States. In H. Lane & F. Grosjean (Eds.), *Recent perspectives on American Sign Language* (pp. 119–161). Hillsdale, NJ: Erlbaum.

Lane, H. (1968). *Bilingual education and the ASL-using minority of the U.S.* Address, California School for the Deaf.

Large, A. (1985). *The artificial language movement.* Oxford: Blackwell.

Lebauer, R. (1984). Using lecture transcripts in EAP lecture comprehension courses. *TESOL,* **18**(1), 41–54.

Lee, D. M. (1982). Are there really signs of diglossia? Reexamining the situation. *Sign Language Studies,* **35**, 127–152.

Lee, D. M. (1983). *Sources and aspects of code-switching in the signing of deaf adult and her interlocutors.* Dissertation, University of Texas, Austin.

Lentz, E. (1977). Informing deaf people about the structure of ASL. In W. C. Stokoe (Ed.), *Proceedings of the First National Symposium Sign Language Research and Teaching at Chicago* (pp. 239–245). Silver Spring, MD: National Association of the Deaf.

Levinson, S. (1983). *Pragmatics.* London & New York: Cambridge University Press.

Liddell, S. K. (1980). *American Sign Language syntax.* The Hague: Mouton.

Liddell, S. K. (1984). THINK and BELIEVE. Sequentiality in American Sign Language. *Language,* **60**, 327–399.

Liddell, S. K., and Johnson, R. E. (1985). *American Sign Language: The phonological base.* Unpublished manuscript, Dept. of Linguistics Interpreting.

Liddell, S. K., and Johnson, R. E. (1986). American Sign Language compound formation processes, lexicalization, and phonological remnants. *Natural Language and Linguistic Theory,* **4**, 445–514.

Light, R. Y., Richard, D. P., and Bell, P. (1978). Development of children's attitudes toward speakers of standard and nonstandard English. *Child Study Journal,* **8**, 253–265.

Lillo-Martin, D. (1986). Two kinds of null arguments in American Sign Language. *Natural Language and Linguistic Theory,* **4**, 415–444.

Livingston, S. (1986). An alternative view of education for the deaf children. Part I. *American Annals of the Deaf,* **131**, 21–25.

Loomis, O. H. (1983). *Cultural conversation: The protection of cultural heritage in the United States.* Washington, DC: U. S. Government Printing Office.

Lou, M. (1988). The history of language use in the education of the deaf in the United States. In M. Strong (Ed.), *Language learning and deafness* (pp. 75–98). London & New York: Cambridge University Press.

Lucas, C., and Borders, D. (1987). Language diversity and classroom discourse. *American Educational Research Journal,* **24**(1), 119–141.

Lucas, C., and Valli, C. (1987). *Language contact in the deaf community.* Paper presented to the New Ways of Analyzing Variation XVI Conference, Austin, TX.

Luetke-Stahlman, B. (1983). Using hearing bilingual instructional models in classrooms. *American Annals of the Deaf,* **128**, 873–877.

Luetke-Stahlman, B. (1986). Building a language base in hearing-impaired students. *American Annals of the Deaf,* **131**, 220–228.

Lunde, A. (1956). *The sociology of the deaf.* Paper presented at the annual meeting of the American Sociological Society, Detroit, MI (cited by Stokoe, 1960).

Maltz, D., and Borker, R. (1982). A cultural approach to male-female miscommunication. In J. J. Gumperz (Ed.), *Language and social identity* (pp. 196–216). London & New York: Cambridge University Press.

Markowicz, H. (1980). Introductory: Myths about American Sign Language. In H. Lane & F. Grosjean (Eds.), *Recent perspectives on American Sign Language* (pp. 1–6). Hillsdale, NJ: Erlbaum.

Markowicz, H., and Woodward, J. (1978). Language and the maintenance of ethnic boundaries in the deaf community. *Communication and Cognition,* **11**, 29–38.

Marmor, G., and Pettito, L. (1979). Simultaneous communication in the classroom: How well is English grammar represented? *Sign Language Studies,* **23**, 99–136.

Mather, S. (1987). Eye gaze and communication in a deaf classroom. *Sign Language Studies,* **54**, 11–30.

Mather, S. (1988). *Gender differences in interruptions and holdings during typed telephone conversations.* Unpublished manuscript.

Matluck, J. H. (1978). *Cultural norms and classroom discourse: Communication problems in the multiethnic school setting.* Unpublished manuscript, University of Texas at Austin.

McDermott, R. P., and Gospodinoff, K. (1981). Social contexts for ethnic borders and school failure. In H. Trueba, G. Pung-Guthrie, & K. Hu-Pei Au (Eds.), *Culture and the bilingual classroom: Studies in classroom ethnography* (pp. 212–230). Rowley, MA: Newbury House.

McGuire, W. (1969). The nature of attitude and attitude change. In G. Lindsey & E. Aronson (Eds.), *Handbook of social psychology* (Vol. 3, pp. 136–314). Reading, MA: Addison-Wesley.

McIntire, M., and Groode, J. (1982). Hello, goodbye and what happens in between. In C. Erting & R. Meisegeier (Eds.), *Social aspects of deafness* (Vol. 1, pp. 299–347). Washington, DC: Gallaudet College.

Meadow, K. P. (1972). Sociolinguistics, sign language and the deaf sub-culture. In T. J. O'Rourke (Ed.), *Psycholinguistics and total communication: The state of the art* (pp. 19–33). Washington, DC: American Annals of the Deaf.

Meadow, K. P. (1980). *Deafness and child development.* Berkeley: University of California Press.

Meadow-Orlans, K. P. (1987). Understanding deafness: Socialization of children and youth. In P. C. Higgins & J. E. Nash (Eds.), *Understanding deafness socially* (pp. 29–58). Springfield, IL: Thomas.

Meath-Lang, B. (1978). A comparative study of experienced and nonexperienced groups of deaf college students: Their attitude toward language learning. *Teaching English to the Deaf,* **5**(2), 9–13.

Meath-Lang, B., Caccamise, F., and Albertini, J. (1982). Deaf persons' views on English language learning: Educational and Sociolinguistic Implications. In H. Hoeman & R. Wilbur (Eds.), *Social aspects of deafness: Vol. 5. Interpersonal communication and deaf people* (pp. 1–31). Washington, DC: Gallaudet University, Dept. of Sociology.

Mehan, H. (1980). The competent student. *Anthropology and Education Quarterly,* **11**, 131–152.

Mehan, H., and Griffin, P. (1979). *Socialization and education: Multiple sources and false dichotomies.* Paper presented at the annual meeting of the American Anthropological Association, Cincinnati, OH.

Michaels, S., and Cazden, C. (1986). Teacher-child collaboration as oral preparation for literacy. In B. Schieffelin and P. Gilmore (Ed.), *Acquisition of literacy: Ethnographic perspectives* (pp. 131–154). Norwood, NJ: Ablex.

Miller, J. (1970). Oralism. *Volta Review,* **27**, 211–217.

Moores, D. (1987). *Educating the deaf: Psychology, principles, and practices* (3rd ed.). Boston, MA: Houghton, Mifflin.

Mougeon, R., Beniak, E., and Valois, D. (1985). *Issues in the study of language contact: Evidence from Ontarian French.* Toronto: Centre for Franco-Ontarian Studies.

Mow, S. (1970). How do you dance without music? In J. A. Little (ed.), *Answers.* Sante Fe: New Mexico School for the Deaf.

Muench, E. (1971). *Preliminary report: Scaling of accentedness by magnitude estimation.* Unpublished manuscript, University of Notre Dame, Notre Dame, IN.

Mühlhäusler, P. (1986). *Pidgin and creole linguistics.* Oxford: Blackwell.

Muysken, P. (1984). The state of the art in interlinguistics. *Revue Québecoise de linguistique,* **14**(1), 49–76.

Nash, A., and Nash, J. E. (1987). Deafness and family life in modern society. In P. C. Higgins & J. E. Nash (Eds.), *Understanding deafness socially* (pp. 101–122). Springfield, IL: Thomas.

Nash, J. E. (1987). Who signs to whom? The American Sign Language community. In P. C. Higgins & J. E. Nash (Eds.), *Understanding deafness socially* (pp. 81–100). Springfield, IL: Thomas.

Nash, J. W., and Nash, A. (1981). *Deafness in society.* Lexington, MA: Lexington Books.

National Center for Law and the Deaf. (1977). Formal request to the Department of Health, Education & Welfare, the Office of Education and Welfare, to the Office of Education, and to the Office of General Counsel for Elementary and Secondary School, that sign language be considered a language for use in bilingual study projects under the Bilingual Education Act. Title VII of the Elementary and Secondary Education Act of 1965 (20 USC 8806), April 22, 1977.

Neisser, A. (1983). *The other side of silence. Sign language and the deaf community in America.* New York: Knopf.

Newport, E. L., and Supalla, T. (1987). *A critical period effect in the acquisition of a primary language.* Unpublished manuscript.

Nida, E. A. (1976). A framework for the analysis and evaluation of theories of translation and response. In R. W. Brislin (Ed.), *Translation applications and research* (pp. 47–91). New York: Gardner Press.

Northcott, W. (1981). Freedom through speech: Every child's right. *Volta Review,* **83**, 162–181.

O'Barr, W., and Atkins, B. (1980). 'Woman's language' or 'powerless language'? In S. McConnell-Gionet, R. Borker, & N. Furman (Eds.), *Women and language in literature and society* (pp. 93–110). New York: Praeger.

Ochs, E., and Schieffelin, B. (1984). Language acquisition and socialization. In R. Shewder & R. Levine (Eds.), *Culture theory: Essays on mind, self and emotion* (pp. 276–320). New York: Cambridge University Press.

O'Grady, L., van Hoek, K., and Bellugi, U. (1987). *The intersection of signing, spelling and script.* Paper presented at the Fourth International Symposium on Sign Language Research, Lappeenranta, Finland.

Osgood, C. E., Succi, G. J., and Tannebaum, H. (1957). *The measurement of meaning.* Urbana: University of Illinois Press.

Padden, C. (1980). The deaf community and the culture of deaf people. In C. Baker & R.

Battison (Eds.), *Sign language and the deaf community* (pp. 89–103). Silver Spring, MD: National Association of the Deaf.

Padden, C. (in press). The acquisition of fingerspelling in deaf children. In P. Siple and S. Fischer (Ed.), *Theoretical issues in sign language research: Psychology.*

Padden, C., and Humphries, T. (1988). *Deaf in America: Voices from a culture.* Cambridge, MA: Harvard University Press.

Padden, C., and Le Master, B. (1985). An alphabet on hand: The acquisition of fingerspelling in Deaf children. *Sign Language Studies, 47,* 161–172.

Padden, C., and Markowicz, H. (1975). Culture conflicts between hearing and deaf communities. In F. B. Crammatte and A. B. Crammatte (Eds.), *Proceedings of the Seventh World Congress of the World Federation of the Deaf* (pp. 407–411). Silver Spring, MD: National Association of the Deaf.

Padden, C., and Perlmutter, D. (1987). American sign language and the architecture of phonological theory. *Natural Language and Linguistic Theory, 5*(3), 335–376.

Patschke, C. (1986). *An examination of three pointing gestures.* Unpublished manuscript, Gallaudet University, Washington, DC.

Patterson, O. (1983). The nature, causes, and implications of ethnic identification. In C. Fried (Ed.), *Minorities: Community and identity. Report of the Dahlem Workshop on Minorities: Community and identity* (pp. 25–50). New York: Springer-Verlag.

Paul, M. E. (1972). American Sign Language and deaf persons: A statement of the problem. *Deafpride Papers: Perspectives and Options,* pp. 14–23.

Peet, I. L. (1871). Institution report. *American Annals of the Deaf, 16,* 239–243.

Pellegreno, D., and Williams, W. (1973). Teacher perception and classroom verbal interaction. *Elementary School Guidance and Counseling, 7*(4), 270–275.

Petronio, K., and DeKorte, N. (1984). *Using a modification of the matched-guise technique to determine attitudes toward sign language use.* Unpublished manuscript.

Pilcher, W. W. (1972). *The Portland longshoremen: A dispersed urban community.* New York: Holt, Rinehart, & Winston.

Poplack, S. (1980). "Sometimes I'll start a sentence in Spanish *y termino en español*": Toward a typology of code-switching, *Linguistics 18,* 581–618.

Poplack, S., Wheeler, S., and Westwood, A. (1987). Distinguishing language contact phenomena: Evidence from Finnish-English bilingualism. In P. Lilius & M. Saari (Eds.), *The Nordic language and modern linguistics* (pp. 33–56). Helsinki: University of Helsinki Press.

Preston, M. S. (1963). *Evaluational reactions to English, Canadian French, and European French voices.* Unpublished master's thesis, McGill University.

Price, S., Fluck, M., and Giles, H. (1983). The effects of language of testing on bilingual preadolescents' attitudes towards Welsh and varieties of English. *Journal of Multilingual and multicultural development, 4*(2&3), 149–161.

Prinz, P., and Prinz, E. (1985). If only you could hear what I see: Discourse development in sign language. *Discourse Processes, 8,* 1–19.

Pufahl, I. (1984). *Show and tell: How a speaker creates involvement in a lecture.* Unpublished paper, Georgetown University, Washington, DC.

Quigley, S., and Kretschmer, R. (1982). *The education of deaf children.* Baltimore, MD: University Park Press.

Ramsey, C. (1984). *American values in a deaf American life.* Unpublished manuscript, Gallaudet University, Department of Linguistics, Washington, DC.

Rawlings, B. (1973). *Characteristics of hearing impaired students by hearing status: US 1970–71* (Series D., No. 10) Washington DC: Gallaudet College, Office of Demographic Studies.

Reilly, J., and McIntire, M. (1980). American Sign Language and Pidgin Sign English: What's the difference? *Sign Language Studies, 27,* 151–192.

Rey, A. (1978). Accent and education: Black American, White American, and Cuban teachers' attitudes toward adult Spanish accented English. *Acta Symbolica, 7–9*(1), 57–71.

Richards, J., and Rodgers, T. (1986). *Approaches and methods in language teaching.* New York: Cambridge University Press.

Rickford, J. R. (1981). A variable rule for a Creole continuum. In D. Sankoff & H. Cedergren (Eds.), *Variation omnibus* (pp. 201–208). Edmonton, Alberta: Linguistic Research, Inc.

Rickford, J. R. (1984). *In defense of the Creole continuum.* Paper presented at New Ways of Analyzing Variation XIII, Philadelphia, PA.

Royce, A. P. (1982). *Ethnic identity: Strategies of diversity.* Bloomington: Indiana University Press.

Rubin, J. (1968). *National bilingualism in Paraguay.* The Hague: Mouton.

Rubin, J. (1984). Bilingual education and language planning. In C. Kennedy (Ed.), *Language planning and language education,* pp. 4–16. London: Allen & Unwin.

Sacks, O. (1988). The revolution of the deaf. *New York Review of Books,* **35**(9), 23–28.

Samarin, M. (1971). Salient and substantive pidginization. In D. Hymes, Ed.), *Pidginization and creolization of languages* (pp. 117–140). London & New York: Cambridge University Press.

Sankoff, G. (1984). *Creoles and universal grammar: The unmarked case.* Colloquium presented at the annual meeting of the Linguistic Society of America, Baltimore, MD.

Sankoff, D., and Miller, C. (1987). *The social correlates and linguistic consequences of lexical borrowing and assimilation.* Social Sciences and Humanities Research Council of Canada, March 1987 Report.

Sankoff, D., and Poplack, S. (1981). A formal grammar for code-switching. *Papers in Linguistics,* **14**(1), 3–46.

Sankoff, D., Poplack, S., and Vanniarajan, S. (1986). *The case of the nonce loan in Tamil* (Tech. Rep. 1348). University of Montreal, Centre de recherches mathématiques.

Saville-Troike, M. (1973). *Bilingual children: A resource document.* Arlington, VA: Center for Applied Linguistics.

Schein, J. D. (1968). *The deaf community.* Washington, DC: Gallaudet College Press.

Schein, J. D. (1987). The demography of deafness. In P. C. Higgins & J. E. Nash (Eds.), *Understanding deafness socially* (pp. 3–28). Springfield, IL: Thomas.

Schein, J. D., and Delk, M. (1974). *The deaf population of the United States.* Silver Spring, MD: National Association of the Deaf.

Schiffrin, D. (1981). Tense variation in narrative. *Language,* **57**(1), 45–62.

Schiffrin, D. (1986). *Discourse markers.* London & New York: Cambridge University Press.

Schowe, B. M. (1979). *Deaf workers on the home front.* Silver Spring, MD: National Association of the Deaf.

Schreiber, F. (1974–1975). And the cons. *Gallaudet Today,* **5,** 5–6.

Schultz, J. (1976). *It's not whether you win or lose, but how you play the game* (Working Papers 1. Newton Classroom Interaction Project). Cambridge, MA: Harvard University School of Education.

Schumann, J. H. (1978). *The pidginization process: A model for second language acquisition.* Rowley, MA: Newbury House.

Seleskovitch, D. (1978). *Interpreting for international conferences.* Washington, DC: Penn & Booth.

Shuy, R. (1979). *The unexpected by-products of fieldwork in discourse.* Unpublished manuscript, Georgetown University and the Center for Applied Linguistics, Washington, DC.

Shuy, R., and Fasold, R. (Eds.). (1973). *Language attitudes: Current trends and prospects.* Washington, DC: Georgetown University Press.

Shuy, R., and Williams, F. (1973). Stereotyped attitudes of selected English dialect communities. In R. Shuy & R. Fasold (Eds.), *Language attitudes: Current trends and prospects* (pp. 85–96). Washington, DC: Georgetown University Press.

Sign Media Inc. (SMI). (1985). *Interpreter models of English to ASL* (Lectures). Videotape.

Smith, D. M. (1972). Some implications for the social status of pidgin languages. In D. M. Smith

& R. W. Shuy (Eds.), *Sociolinguistics in cross-cultural analysis* (pp. 47–56). Washington, DC: Georgetown University Press.

Snow, C. E. (1986). Conversations with children. In P. Fletcher & M. Garman (Eds.), *Language acquisition: Studies in first language development* (2nd ed., pp. 69–89). London & New York: Cambridge University Press.

Spender, D. (1980). *Man made language.* London: Routledge & Kegan Paul.

Spradley, J., and Mann, B. (1975). *The cocktail waitress: Women's work in a male world.* New York: Wiley.

Spradley, T., and Spradley, L. (1980). Preface. In G. Gustason & E. Zawolkow (Eds.), *Using Signing Exact English in Total Communication* (p. 1). Los Alamitos, CA: Modern Signs Press.

Sridhar, S. (1978). On the functions of code-mixing in Kannada. In B. Kachru & S. Sridhar (Eds.), *Aspects of sociolinguistics in South Asia* (Spec. Issue, International Journal of the Sociology of Language, Vol. 16, pp. 109–117).

Sridhar, S., and Sridhar, K. (1980). The syntax and psycholinguistics of bilingual code-mixing. *Canadian Journal of Psychology, 34*(4), 407–416.

Staton, J. (1985). Using dialogue journals for developing thinking, reading, and writing with hearing-impaired students. *Volta Review, 5,* 127–154.

Stevens, R. (1980). Education in schools for deaf children. In C. Baker & R. Battison (Eds.), *Sign language and the deaf community* (pp. 177–191). Silver Spring, MD: National Association of the Deaf.

Stewart, L. G. (1969). *Fostering independence in deaf people.* Paper presented at the Forum of the Council of Organizations Serving the Deaf, New Orleans, LA.

Stewart, L. G., Woodward, J. C., and Erting, C. (1975). Synchronic variation and historical change in American Sign Language. *Language Science, 37,* 9–12.

Stokoe, W. C. (1960). *Sign language structure: An outline of the visual communication system of the American deaf* (Studies in Linguistics, Occasional Papers, Vol. 8). Buffalo, NY: University of Buffalo.

Stokoe, W. C. (1969). Sign language diglossia. *Studies in Linguistics, 21,* 27–41.

Stokoe, W. C. (1978). *Sign language structure* (rev. ed.). Silver Spring, MD: Linstok Press.

Stokoe, W. C. (1985). Comment. *Sign Language Studies, 47,* 181–187.

Stokoe, W. C., Bernard, H. R., and Padden, C. (1976). An elite group in deaf society. *Sign Language Studies, 12,* 189–210.

Strong, M. (1988). *Language learning and deafness.* London & New York: Cambridge University Press.

Stubbs, M. (1980). *Language and literacy: The sociolinguistics of reading and writing.* London: Routledge & Kegan Paul.

Supalla, S. (1986). *Manually Coded English: The modality question in signed language development.* Unpublished master's thesis, University of Illinois at Champaign-Urbana, Urbana.

Supalla, T. (1982). *Structure and acquisition of verbs of motion and location in American Sign Language.* Unpublished doctoral dissertation, University of California at San Diego.

Supalla, T., and Newport, E. (1978). How many seats in a chair? The derivation of nouns and verbs in American Sign Language. In P. Siple (Ed.), *Understanding language through sign language research* (pp. 91–132). New York: Academic Press.

Sussman, A. E. (1973). *An investigation in the relationship between self concepts of deaf adults and their perceived attitudes toward deafness.* Doctoral dissertation, New York University.

Sussman, M. (1965). Sociological theory and deafness: Problems and prospects. In E. R. Stuckless (Ed.) *Research of behavioral aspects of deafness: Proceedings of a National Research Conference of Behavioral Aspects of Deafness* (pp. 51–73). Washington, DC: U.S. Department of Health, Education, and Welfare.

Swacker, M. (1975). The sex of the speaker as a sociolinguistic variable. In B. Thorne and N. Henley (Eds.), *Language and sex: Difference and dominance* (pp. 76–83). Rowley, MA: Newbury House.

Swisher, M. V., and Thompson, M. (1985). Mothers learning simultaneous communication: The dimensions of the task. *American Annals of the Deaf,* **130,** 212–217.

Tannen, D. (1982). Oral and literate strategies in spoken and written narratives. *Language,* **58** (1), 1–21.

Tannen, D. (1984). *Conversational style: Analyzing talk among friends.* Norwood, NJ: Ablex.

Tannen, D. (1986). Introducing constructed dialogue in Greek and American conversational and literacy narratives. In F. Coulmas (Ed.), *Reported speech across languages* (pp. 311–332). The Hague: Mouton.

Taylor, J. B. (1983). Influence of speech variety on teachers' evaluation of reading comprehension. *Journal of Educational Psychology,* **75**(5), 662–667.

Taylor, O. (1973). Teachers' attitudes toward black and nonstandard English as measured by the language attitude scale. In R. Shuy & R. Fasold (Eds.), *Language attitudes: Current trends and prospects* (pp. 175–200). Washington, DC: Georgetown University Press.

Thelander, S. (1976). Code-switching or code-mixing? *Linguistics,* **183,** 103–123.

Thomason, S. (1987). *Language mixture: Social causes and linguistic effects.* Paper presented at the Conference on the Social Context of Language Change, Stanford University, Stanford, CA.

Thorne, B. Kramarae, C., and Henley, N. (Eds.). (1983). *Language, gender and society.* Cambridge, MA: Newbury House.

Todd, L. (1974). *Pidgins and creoles.* London: Routledge & Kegan Paul.

Trybus, R., and Jensema, C. (1978). *Communication patterns and education achievement of hearing impaired students* (Series T, No. 2). Washington, DC: Gallaudet College, Office of Demographic Studies.

Tucker, G. R., and Lambert, W. E. (1969). *Bilingual education of children: The St. Lambert experiment.* Rowley, MA: Newbury House.

Valdes-Fallis, G. (1976). Social interaction and code-switching patterns: A case study of Spanish/English alteration. In G. Keller, R. Taeschner, & S. Viera (Eds.), *Bilingualism in the bicentennial and beyond* (pp. 53–85). New York: Bilingual Press/Editorial Bilingue.

Valdman, A. (1977). *Pidgin and creole linguistics.* Bloomington: Indiana University Press.

Valli, C. (1988). *Language choice: Convergence and divergence.* Unpublished manuscript, Gallaudet University, Washington, DC.

Van Uden, A. (1968). *A world of language for deaf children: Part 1. Basic principles.* St. Michielsgestel, The Netherlands: Institute for the Deaf.

Veditz, G. W. (1913). *The preservation of the sign language* (film). Silver Spring, MD: National Association of the Deaf.

Vernon, M. (1968). The failure of the education of the deaf. *West Virginia Tablet,* May, pp. 1–6.

Vernon, M., and Makowsky, K. (1969). Deafness and minority group dynamics. *Deaf American,* **21,** 3–6.

Wampler, D. (1972). *Linguistics of Visual English.* Santa Rosa, CA: Santa Rosa City Schools.

Weinreich, U. (1953). *Languages in contact.* The Hague: Mouton.

Wells, C. G. (1981). *Learning through interaction: The study of language development.* London & New York: Cambridge University Press.

Whinnom, K. (1971). Linguistic hybridization and the 'special case' of pidgins and creoles. In D. Hymes (Ed.), *Pidginization and creolization of languages* (pp. 91–115). London & New York: Cambridge University Press.

Wilbur, R. B. (1987). *American Sign Language: Linguistic and applied dimensions* (2nd ed.). Boston, MA: Little, Brown.

Wilbur, R. B., and Pettito, L. (1983). Discourse structure in American Sign Language conversations (or, how to know a conversation when you see one). *Discourse Processes,* **6**(3), 225–241.

Williams, F. (1970). Psychological correlates of speech characteristics: On sounding "disadvantaged." *Journal of Speech & Hearing Research,* **13**(3), 472–488.

Williams, F. (1973). Some research notes on dialect attitudes and stereotypes. In R. Shuy & R. Fasold (Eds.), *Language attitudes: Current trends and prospects* (pp. 113–128). Washington, DC: Georgetown University Press.

Williams, F., Hewett, N., Hopper, R., Miller, L. M., Naremore, R. C., Whitehead, J. L. (1976). *Explorations of the linguistic attitudes of teachers.* Rowley, MA: Newbury House.

Williams, F., Whitehead, J., and Miller, L. (1971). Ethnic stereotyping and judgments of children's speech. *Speech monographs,* **38**(3), 166–170.

Williams, F., Whitehead, J., and Traupmann, J. (1971). Teachers' evaluations of children's speech. *Speech Teacher,* **20**(4), 247–254.

Wolfram, W., and Fasold, R. W. (1974). *The study of social dialects in American English.* Englewood Cliffs, NJ: Prentice-Hall.

Woodward, J. C. (1972). Implications for sociolinguistic research among the deaf. *Sign Language Studies,* **1,** 1–7.

Woodward, J. C. (1973a). *Implicational effects of the deaf diglossic continuum.* Unpublished doctoral dissertation, Georgetown University, Washington, DC.

Woodward, J. C. (1973b). Some characteristics of Pidgin Sign English. *Sign Language Studies,* **3,** 39–46.

Woodward, J. C. (1973c). Some observations on sociolinguistic variation and American Sign Language. *Kansas Journal of Sociology,* **9,** 191–200.

Woodward, J. C. (1976). Black southern signing. *Language in Society,* **5,** 211–218.

Woodward, J. C. (1980). Sociolinguistic research on American Sign Language: An historical perspective. In C. Baker & R. Battison (Eds.), *Sign language and the deaf community* (pp. 117–134). Silver Spring, MD: National Association of the Deaf.

Woodward, J. C. (1982). *How you gonna get to heaven if you can't talk with Jesus: On depathologizing deafness.* Silver Spring, MD: TJ Publishers.

Woodward, J. C. (1985). *Sociolinguistic variation involving American Sign Language.* Unpublished manuscript, Gallaudet University, Washington, DC.

Woodward, J. C., and De Santis, S. (1977). Two to one it happens: Dynamic phonology in two sign languages. *Sign Language Studies,* **17,** 329–346.

Woodward, J. C., and Erting, C. (1975). Synchronic variation and historical change in American Sign Language. *Language Science,* **37,** 9–12.

Woodward, J. C., and Markowicz, H. (1975). *Some handy new ideas on pidgins and creoles: Pidgin sign languages.* Paper presented at the Conference on Pidgin and Creole Languages, Hawaii, Honolulu.

# Index

Accommodation theory, 28
American Sign Language, 1, 3, 4, 5, 6, 8, 11,
    41, 43–44, 56–59, 68–69, 82–83, 86–
    102, 105–106, 111, 114–118, 123, 127,
    131, 139, 143, 145, 147, 149, 151
  as a second language, 250, 271
  classifier predicates, 68, 73–74, 131, 165
  comprehension, 221
  eye gaze, 169
  facial expression, 159–160, 163, 269
  head and body shift, 152, 163
  inflected verbs, 68, 74–75, 131–132
  lexicon, 32–36, 131, 143, 152
  miniature signs, 165, 182–184
  morphology, 266–270
  negation, 158
  nonmanual adverbs, 92–96, 101, 158–159
  phonology, 131, 260–266, 269
  role playing, 165, 180–182
  skills assessment, 192–196, 199–201
  syntax, 266–268
  teaching, 70, 141
  use of space, 152, 159, 163

Bidialectalism, 6
Bilingualism, 2, 5, 6, 12, 14, 45, 85–91, 102,
    194–195
  in spoken language communities, 12
  societal, 87
Black signing, 7, 103–119
  code switching, 103, 114–118
  lexical variation, 115–119
  variation, 103
  vs. white signing, 107
British Black English, 6, 20–21

Classroom language use, 6, 7, 141, 145, 165–
    187, 217

vs. home language use, 168–169
Code-mixing, 6, 32–36, 42, 53, 85–96
Code-switching, 5, 12, 14, 27, 33, 36, 42, 53,
    85–92, 114–118
Commission on Education of the Deaf, 4
  draft recommendations, 4
Continuum, 17–19, 86
Convergence, 35

Deaf clubs
  black vs. white, 105, 111
Deaf community, 2, 3, 5, 6, 8, 41–55, 57–58,
    86–91, 126, 129–130, 258, 274
Deaf culture, 51–52, 195, 207–210
  Black deaf, 103–119
Deaf education, 7, 123–146, 206–210
  bilingualism, 166, 204–210, 194–195
  deaf teachers, 166
  hearing teachers, 166
  teachers of the deaf, 52, 211–228
  training programs, 7, 217–219, 227–228
Deafness
  medical perspective on, 141
  cultural perspective on, 141
Diglossia, 5, 17–19, 27, 41–42, 53, 86, 253,
    257–258
Discrimination, 103, 107, 110–111
Discourse analysis, 2, 5, 7, 8, 231–251, 253–
    272, 273–288
  constructed dialogue, 7, 245–248
  conversational style, 7, 8
  discourse markers, 7, 235–245
  gender differences, 273–288
  narrative structure, 232
  register variation, 7, 253–272
  topic, 231
  turn-taking, 68, 231

Education of the Deaf Act (1986), 4
English
  in deaf education, 106, 166, 191–192
  morphology, 131–132, 135, 147, 160
  mouthing, 29–36, 87, 92–96, 150–152, 157,
    161–163
  orthography, 96–97, 102
  skills assessment, 192–196, 199–201
  spoken, 12, 14, 15, 50–57, 87, 92–96, 101–
    102, 111, 127–128, 131–132, 135, 142,
    147, 149, 152, 163
  syntax, 160
  use of, 76–78, 85–102, 166
  word order, 152, 153
English contact signing, 11–39, 41, 52–53,
  56, 59, 75, 77, 81–83, 86–91, 114–118,
  148, 276
Ethnicity, 41–83, 126, 142–143
  definitions of, 44–46
  patrimony, 45–48, 53–56, 58, 70, 82
  paternity, 45–48, 58
  vs. culture, 46

Fingerspelling, 29–36, 74, 87, 92–102
Foreigner talk, 15, 31–32, 36, 147

Gallaudet, Edward Miner, 1
Gallaudet University, 1

Hearing loss, 14, 43, 46–51, 80
Hybridization, 32, 38

Interpreter training, 250, 271
Interpreting, 2, 150–157, 250, 271
  in educational settings, 7, 141
  English to ASL, 6, 8, 85–102, 147–148
  vs. spoken language interpreting, 90
Interpreters, 52, 86, 250

Language acquisition, 12, 14, 17, 48, 54, 74,
  86, 133–134, 168–169, 250
Language attitudes, 2, 8, 27, 191–210, 211–
  228, 269
  matched guise, 213–216
  spoken languages, 211, 213–216
  teachers, 216–217
Language choice, 3, 24, 27, 54, 76
Language contact, 2, 5, 6, 8, 11–39, 53, 85–
  102
Language functions
  in the deaf community, 124, 144

spoken language, 136–139
written language, 136–139
Language planning, 2, 5, 7, 8, 123–146, 206
  instrumental vs. sociolinguistic, 125, 133,
    144
Language policy, 2, 5, 7, 8, 123–146
Language socialization, 8, 86, 126–127, 129,
  273–274
  in elementary school classrooms, 6, 41–
    83, 106
Lexical borrowing, 85, 88–92, 96–102
  established loanwords, 90, 97–99
  nonce borrowing, 90, 97–99
Lexicalization, 96–102
Linguistic interference, 90
Linguistic transference, 90, 92
Linguistic repertoire, 3
Literacy, 134, 136–142

Mainstreaming, 12, 30
Manually Coded English (MCE), 12, 14, 29,
  38, 78, 123–146, 147–148, 166, 170
  Signing Exact English (SEE1), 123
  Signing Exact English (SEE2), 56, 79, 123–
    146
  Signed English, 7, 12, 22, 24, 36, 147, 149,
    166
Metalinguistic awareness, 136–137
Methodology, 6, 8, 17–21, 22

Native signers, 6, 14, 18, 91

Oralism, 127–128, 133, 145, 206–207

Pidgin Sign English (PSE), 6, 15–19, 24, 28,
  38, 52, 86, 147, 207–208
Pidgins and creoles, 4, 5, 11–39, 86

Residential schools, 12, 30, 145

Sign-supported speech (SSS), 56, 57, 80, 83,
  131, 138–140, 143
Socialization, 54–55
Sociolinguistic identity, 7, 206–210
Style shifting, 27

Translation, 88, 151
Transliterating, 6, 7, 88, 147–164

conceptual accuracy, 155
in educational settings, 7
strategies, 152, 154–163
Total Communication, 127–128, 145, 206

Variation, 2, 5, 6, 41, 86, 114–119, 254, 271, 288
Vocational rehabilitation, 52
counselors, 52